Pentaho 3.2 Data Integration

Beginner's Guide

Explore, transform, validate, and integrate your data with ease

María Carina Roldán

BIRMINGHAM - MUMBAI

Pentaho 3.2 Data Integration
Beginner's Guide

First published: April 2010

Production Reference: 1050410

Published by Packt Publishing Ltd.
32 Lincoln Road
Olton
Birmingham, B27 6PA, UK.

ISBN 978-1-847199-54-6

www.packtpub.com

Cover Image by Parag Kadam (paragvkadam@gmail.com)

Credits

Author
María Carina Roldán

Reviewers
Jens Bleuel
Roland Bouman
Matt Casters
James Dixon
Will Gorman
Gretchen Moran

Acquisition Editor
Usha Iyer

Development Editor
Reshma Sundaresan

Technical Editors
Gaurav Datar
Rukhsana Khambatta

Copy Editor
Sanchari Mukherjee

Editorial Team Leader
Gagandeep Singh

Project Team Leader
Lata Basantani

Project Coordinator
Poorvi Nair

Proofreader
Sandra Hopper

Indexer
Rekha Nair

Graphics
Geetanjali Sawant

Production Coordinator
Shantanu Zagade

Cover Work
Shantanu Zagade

Foreword

If we look back at what has happened in the data integration market over the last 10 years we can see a lot of change. In the first half of that decade there was an explosion in the number of data integration tools and in the second half there was a big wave of consolidations. This consolidation wave put an ever growing amount of data integration power in the hands of only a few large billion dollar companies. For any person, company or project in need of data integration, this meant either paying large amounts of money or doing hand-coding of their solution.

During that exact same period, we saw web servers, programming languages, operating systems, and even relational databases turn into a commodity in the ICT market place. This was driven among other things by the availability of open source software such as Apache, GNU, Linux, MySQL, and many others. For the ICT market, this meant that more services could be deployed at a lower cost. If you look closely at what has been going on in those last 10 years, you will notice that most companies increasingly deployed more ICT services to end-users. These services get more and more connected over an ever growing network. Pretty much anything ranging from tiny mobile devices to huge cloud-based infrastructure is being deployed and all those can contain data that is valuable to an organization.

The job of any person that needs to integrate all this data is not easy. Complexity of information services technology usually increases exponentially with the number of systems involved. Because of this, integrating all these systems can be a daunting and scary task that is never complete. Any piece of code lives in what can be described as a software ecosystem that is always in a state of flux. Like in nature, certain ecosystems evolve extremely fast where others change very slowly over time. However, like in nature all ICT systems change. What is needed is another wave of commodification in the area of data integration and business intelligence in general. This is where Pentaho comes in.

Pentaho tries to provide answers to these problems by making the integration software available as open source, accessible, easy to use, and easy to maintain for users and developers alike. Every release of our software we try to make things easier, better, and faster. However, even if things can be done with nice user interfaces, there are still a huge amount of possibilities and options to choose from.

As the founder of the project I've always liked the fact that Kettle users had a lot of choice. Choice translates into creativity, and creativity often delivers good solutions that are comfortable to the person implementing them. However, this choice can be daunting to any beginning Kettle developer. With thousands of options to choose from, it can be very hard to get started.

This is above all others the reason why I'm very happy to see this book come to life. It will be a great and indispensable help for everyone that is taking steps into the wonderful world of data integration with Kettle. As such, I hope you see this book as an open invitation to get started with Kettle in the wonderful world of data integration.

Matt Casters
Chief Data Integration at Pentaho
Kettle founder

The Kettle Project

Whether there is a migration to do, an ETL process to run, or a need for massively loading data into a database, you have several software tools, ranging from expensive and sophisticated to free open source and friendly ones, which help you accomplish the task.

Ten years ago, the scenario was clearly different. By 2000, Matt Casters, a Belgian business intelligent consultant, had been working for a while as a datawarehouse architect and administrator. As such, he was one of quite a number of people who, no matter if the company they worked for was big or small, had to deal with the difficulties that involve bridging the gap between information technology and business needs. What made it even worse at that time was that ETL tools were prohibitively expensive and everything had to be crafted done. The last employer he worked for, didn't think that writing a new ETL tool would be a good idea. This was one of the motivations for Matt to become an independent contractor and to start his own company. That was in June 2001.

At the end of that year, he told his wife that he was going to write a new piece of software for himself to do ETL tasks. It was going to take up some time left and right in the evenings and weekends. Surprised, she asked how long it would take you to get it done. He replied that it would probably take five years and that he perhaps would have something working in three.

Working on that started in early 2003. Matt's main goals for writing the software included learning about databases, ETL processes, and data warehousing. This would in turn improve his chances on a job market that was pretty volatile. Ultimately, it would allow him to work full time on the software.

Another important goal was to understand what the tool had to do. Matt wanted a scalable and parallel tool, and wanted to isolate rows of data as much as possible.

The last but not least goal was to pick the right technology that would support the tool. The first idea was to build it on top of KDE, the popular Unix desktop environment. Trolltech, the people behind Qt, the core UI library of KDE, had released database plans to create drivers for popular databases. However, the lack of decent drivers for those databases drove Matt to change plans and use Java. He picked Java because he had some prior experience as he had written a Japanese Chess (Shogi) database program when Java 1.0 was released. To Sun's credit, this software still runs and is available at `http://ibridge.be/shogi/`.

After a year of development, the tool was capable of reading text files, reading from databases, writing to databases and it was very flexible. The experience with Java was not 100% positive though. The code had grown unstructured, crashes occurred all too often, and it was hard to get something going with the Java graphic library used at that moment, the **Abstract Window Toolkit (AWT)**; it looked bad and it was slow.

As for the library, Matt decided to start using the newly released **Standard Widget Toolkit (SWT)**, which helped solve part of the problem. As for the rest, Kettle was a complete mess. It was time to ask for help. The help came in hands of Wim De Clercq, a senior enterprise Java architect, co-owner of Ixor (`www.ixor.be`) and also friend of Matt. At various intervals over the next few years, Wim involved himself in the project, giving advices to Matt about good practices in Java programming. Listening to that advice meant performing massive amounts of code changes. As a consequence, it was not unusual to spend weekends doing nothing but refactoring code and fixing thousands of errors because of that. But, bit by bit, things kept going in the right direction.

At that same time, Matt also showed the results to his peers, colleagues, and other senior BI consultants to hear what they thought of Kettle. That was how he got in touch with the Flemish Traffic Centre (`www.verkeerscentrum.be/verkeersinfo/kaart`) where billions of rows of data had to be integrated from thousands of data sources all over Belgium. All of a sudden, he was being paid to deploy and improve Kettle to handle that job. The diversity of test cases at the traffic center helped to improve Kettle dramatically. That was somewhere in 2004 and Kettle was by its version 1.2.

While working at Flemish, Matt also posted messages on Javaforge (`www.javaforge.com`) to let people know they could download a free copy of Kettle for their own use. He got a few reactions. Despite some of them being remarkably negative, most were positive. The most interesting response came from a nice guy called Jens Bleuel in Germany who asked if it was possible to integrate third-party software into Kettle. In his specific case, he needed a connector to link Kettle with the German SAP software (`www.sap.com`). Kettle didn't have a plugin architecture, so Jens' question made Matt think about a plugin system, and that was the main motivation for developing version 2.0.

For various reasons including the birth of Matt's son Sam and a lot of consultancy work, it took around a year to release Kettle version 2.0. It was a fairly complete release with advanced support for slowly changing dimensions and junk dimensions (Chapter 9 explains those concepts), ability to connect to thirteen different databases, and the most important fact being support for plugins. Matt contacted Jens to let him know the news and Jens was really interested. It was a very memorable moment for Matt and Jens as it took them only a few hours to get a new plugin going that read data from an SAP/R3 server. There was a lot of excitement, and they agreed to start promoting the sales of Kettle from the `Kettle.be` website and from Proratio (`www.proratio.de`), the company Jens worked for.

Those were days of improvements, requests, people interested in the project. However, it became too much to handle. Doing development and sales all by themselves was no fun after a while. As such, Matt thought about open sourcing Kettle early in 2005 and by late summer he made his decision. Jens and Proratio didn't mind and the decision was final.

When they finally open sourced Kettle on December 2005, the response was massive. The downloadable package put up on Javaforge got downloaded around 35000 times during first week only. The news got spread all over the world pretty quickly.

What followed was a flood of messages, both private and on the forum. At its peak in March 2006, Matt got over 300 messages a day concerning Kettle.

In no time, he was answering questions like crazy, allowing people to join the development team and working as a consultant at the same time. Added to this, the birth of his daughter Hannelore in February 2006 was too much to deal with.

Fortunately, good times came. While Matt was trying to handle all that, a discussion was taking place at the Pentaho forum (http://forums.pentaho.org/) concerning the ETL tool that Pentaho should support. They had selected Enhydra Octopus, a Java-based ETL software, but they didn't have a strong reliance on a specific tool.

While Jens was evaluating all sorts of open source BI packages, he came across that thread. Matt replied immediately persuading people at Pentaho to consider including Kettle. And he must be convincing because the answer came quickly and was positive. James Dixon, Pentaho founder and CTO, opened Kettle the possibility to be the premier and only ETL tool supported by Pentaho. Later on, Matt came in touch with one of the other Pentaho founders, Richard Daley, who offered him a job. That allowed Matt to focus full-time on Kettle. Four years later, he's still happily working for Pentaho as chief architect for data integration, doing the best effort to deliver Kettle 4.0. Jens Bleuel, who collaborated with Matt since the early versions, is now also part of the Pentaho team.

About the Author

María Carina was born in a small town in the Patagonia region in Argentina. She earned her Bachelor degree in Computer Science at UNLP in La Plata and then moved to Buenos Aires where she has lived since 1994 working in IT.

She has been working as a BI consultant for the last 10 years. At the beginning she worked with Cognos suite. However, over the last three years, she has been dedicated, full time, to developing Pentaho BI solutions both for local and several Latin-American companies, as well as for a French automotive company in the last months.

She is also an active contributor to the Pentaho community.

At present, she lives in Buenos Aires, Argentina, with her husband Adrián and children Camila and Nicolás.

Writing my first book in a foreign language and working on a full time job at the same time, not to mention the upbringing of two small kids, was definitely a big challenge. Now I can tell that it's not impossible.

I dedicate this book to my husband and kids; I'd like to thank them for all their support and tolerance over the last year. I'd also like to thank my colleagues and friends who gave me encouraging words throughout the writing process.

Special thanks to the people at Packt; working with them has been really pleasant.

I'd also like to thank the Pentaho community and developers for making Kettle the incredible tool it is. Thanks to the technical reviewers who, with their very critical eye, contributed to make this a book suited to the audience.

Finally, I'd like to thank Matt Casters who, despite his busy schedule, was willing to help me from the first moment he knew about this book.

About the Reviewers

Jens Bleuel is a Senior Consultant and Engineer at Pentaho. He is also working as a project leader, trainer, and product specialist in the services and support department. Before he joined Pentaho in mid 2007, he was software developer and project leader, and his main business was Data Warehousing and the architecture along with designing and developing of user friendly tools. He studied business economics, was on a grammar school for electronics, and has been programming in a wide area of environments such as Assembler, C, Visual Basic, Delphi, .NET, and these days mainly in Java. His customer focus is on the wholesale market and consumer goods industries. Jens is 40 years old and lives with his wife and two boys in Mainz, Germany (near the nice Rhine river). In his spare time, he practices Tai-Chi, Qigong, and photography.

Roland Bouman has been working in the IT industry since 1998, mostly as a database and web application developer. He has also worked for MySQL AB (later Sun Microsystems) as certification developer and as curriculum developer.

Roland mainly focuses on open source web technology, databases, and Business Intelligence. He's an active member of the MySQL and Pentaho communities and can often be found speaking at worldwide conferences and events such as the MySQL user conference, the **O'Reilly Open Source conference (OSCON)**, and at Pentaho community events.

Roland is co-author of the *MySQL 5.1 Cluster DBA Certification Study Guide* (Vervante, ISBN: 595352502) and *Pentaho Solutions: Business Intelligence and Data Warehousing with Pentaho and MySQL* (Wiley, ISBN: 978-0-470-48432-6). He also writes on a regular basis for the **Dutch Database Magazine (DBM)**.

Roland is @rolandbouman on Twitter and maintains a blog at
`http://rpbouman.blogspot.com/`.

Matt Casters has been an independent senior BI consultant for almost two decades. In that period he led, designed, and implemented numerous data warehouses and BI solutions for large and small companies. In that capacity, he always had the need for ETL in some form or another. Almost out of pure necessity, he has been busy writing the ETL tool called Kettle (a.k.a. Pentaho Data Integration) for the past eight years. First, he developed the tool mostly on his own. Since the end of 2005 when Kettle was declared an open source technology, development took place with the help of a large community.

Since the Kettle project was acquired by Pentaho in early 2006, he has been Chief of Data Integration at Pentaho as the lead architect, head of development, and spokesperson for the Kettle community.

> I would like to personally thank the complete community for their help in making Kettle the success it is today. In particular, I would like to thank Maria for taking the time to write this nice book as well as the many articles on the Pentaho wiki (for example, the Kettle tutorials), and her appreciated participation on the forum. Many thanks also go to my employer Pentaho, for their large investment in open source BI in general and Kettle in particular.

James Dixon is the Chief Geek and one of the co-founders of Pentaho Corporation—the leading commercial open source Business Intelligence company. He has worked in the business intelligence market since graduating in 1992 from Southampton University with a degree in Computer Science. He has served as Software Engineer, Development Manager, Engineering VP, and CTO at multiple business intelligence software companies. He regularly uses Pentaho Data Integration for internal projects and was involved in the architectural design of PDI V3.0.

He lives in Orlando, Florida, with his wife Tami and son Samuel.

> I would like to thank my co-founders, my parents, and my wife Tami for all their support and tolerance of my odd working hours.
>
> I would like to thank my son Samuel for all the opportunities he gives me to prove I'm not as clever as I think I am.

Will Gorman is an Engineering Team Lead at Pentaho. He works on a variety of Pentaho's products, including Reporting, Analysis, Dashboards, Metadata, and the BI Server. Will started his career at GE Research and earned his Masters degree in Computer Science at Rensselaer Polytechnic Institute in Troy, New York. Will is the author of *Pentaho Reporting 3.5 for Java Developers* (ISBN: 3193), published by Packt Publishing.

Gretchen Moran is a graduate of University of Wisconsin – Stevens Point with a Bachelor's degree in Computer Information Systems with a minor in Data Communications. Gretchen began her career as a corporate data warehouse developer in the insurance industry and joined Arbor Software/Hyperion Solutions in 1999 as a commercial developer for the Hyperion Analyzer and Web Analytics team. Gretchen has been a key player with Pentaho Corporation since its inception in 2004. As Community Leader and core developer, Gretchen managed the explosive growth of Pentaho's open source community for her first 2 years with the company. Gretchen has contributed to many of the Pentaho projects, including the Pentaho BI Server, Pentaho Data Integration, Pentaho Metadata Editor, Pentaho Reporting, Pentaho Charting, and others.

Thanks Doug, Anthony, Isabella and Baby Jack for giving me my favorite challenges and crowning achievements—being a wife and mom.

Table of Contents

Preface

Pentaho Data Integration (aka Kettle) is an engine along with a suite of tools responsible for the processes of **E**xtracting, **T**ransforming, and **L**oading—better known as the **ETL** processes. PDI not only serves as an ETL tool, but it's also used for other purposes such as migrating data between applications or databases, exporting data from databases to flat files, data cleansing, and much more. PDI has an intuitive, graphical, drag-and-drop design environment, and its ETL capabilities are powerful. However, getting started with PDI can be difficult or confusing. This book provides the guidance needed to overcome that difficulty, covering the key features of PDI. Each chapter introduces new features, allowing you to gradually get involved with the tool.

By the end of the book, you will have not only experimented with all kinds of examples, but will also have built a basic but complete datamart with the help of PDI.

How to read this book

Although it is recommended that you read all the chapters, you don't need to. The book allows you to tailor the PDI learning process according to your particular needs.

The first four chapters, along with Chapter 7 and Chapter 10, cover the core concepts. If you don't know PDI and want to learn just the basics, reading those chapters would suffice. Besides, if you need to work with databases, you could include Chapter 8 in the roadmap.

If you already know the basics, you can improve your PDI knowledge by reading chapters 5, 6, and 11.

Finally, if you already know PDI and want to learn how to use it to load or maintain a datawarehouse or datamart, you will find all that you need in chapters 9 and 12.

While Chapter 13 is useful for anyone who is willing to take it further, all the appendices are valuable resources for anyone who reads this book.

What this book covers

Chapter 1, Getting started with Pentaho Data Integration serves as the most basic introduction to PDI, presenting the tool. The chapter includes instructions for installing PDI and gives you the opportunity to play with the graphical designer (Spoon). The chapter also includes instructions for installing a MySQL server.

Chapter 2, Getting Started with Transformations introduces one of the basic components of PDI—transformations. Then, it focuses on the explanation of how to work with files. It explains how to get data from simple input sources such as txt, csv, xml, and so on, do a preview of the data, and send the data back to any of these common output formats. The chapter also explains how to read command-line parameters and system information.

Chapter 3, Basic Data Manipulation explains the simplest and most commonly used ways of transforming data, including performing calculations, adding constants, counting, filtering, ordering, and looking for data.

Chapter 4—Controlling the Flow of Data explains different options that PDI offers to combine or split flows of data.

Chapter 5, Transforming Your Data with JavaScript Code and the JavaScript Step explains how JavaScript coding can help in the treatment of data. It shows why you need to code inside PDI, and explains in detail how to do it.

Chapter 6, Transforming the Row Set explains the ability of PDI to deal with some sophisticated problems, such as normalizing data from pivoted tables, in a simple fashion.

Chapter 7, Validating Data and Handling Errors explains the different options that PDI has to validate data, and how to treat the errors that may appear.

Chapter 8, Working with Databases explains how to use PDI to work with databases. The list of topics covered includes connecting to a database, previewing and getting data, and inserting, updating, and deleting data. As database knowledge is not presumed, the chapter also covers fundamental concepts of databases and the SQL language.

Chapter 9, Performing Advanced Operations with Databases explains how to perform advanced operations with databases, including those specially designed to load datawarehouses. A primer on datawarehouse concepts is also given in case you are not familiar with the subject.

Chapter 10, Creating Basic Task Flow serves as an introduction to processes in PDI. Through the creation of simple jobs, you will learn what jobs are and what they are used for.

Chapter 11, Creating Advanced Transformations and Jobs deals with advanced concepts that will allow you to build complex PDI projects. The list of covered topics includes nesting jobs, iterating on jobs and transformations, and creating subtransformations.

Chapter 12, Developing and implementing a simple datamart presents a simple datamart project, and guides you to build the datamart by using all the concepts learned throughout the book.

Chapter 13, Taking it Further gives a list of best PDI practices and recommendations for going beyond.

Appendix A, Working with repositories guides you step by step in the creation of a PDI database repository and then gives instructions to work with it.

Appendix B, Pan and Kitchen: Launching Transformations and Jobs from the Command Line is a quick reference for running transformations and jobs from the command line.

Appendix C, Quick Reference: Steps and Job Entries serves as a quick reference to steps and job entries used throughout the book.

Appendix D, Spoon Shortcuts is an extensive list of Spoon shortcuts useful for saving time when designing and running PDI jobs and transformations.

Appendix E, Introducing PDI 4 features quickly introduces you to the architectural and functional features included in Kettle 4—the version that was under development while writing this book.

Appendix F, Pop Quiz Answers, contains answers to pop quiz questions.

What you need for this book

PDI is a multiplatform tool. This means no matter what your operating system is, you will be able to work with the tool. The only prerequisite is to have JVM 1.5 or a higher version installed. It is also useful to have Excel or Calc along with a nice text editor.

Having an Internet connection while reading is extremely useful as well. Several links are provided throughout the book that complement what is explained. Besides, there is the PDI forum where you may search or post doubts if you are stuck with something.

Who this book is for

This book is for software developers, database administrators, IT students, and everyone involved or interested in developing ETL solutions or, more generally, doing any kind of data manipulation. If you have never used PDI before, this will be a perfect book to start with.

You will find this book to be a good starting point if you are a database administrator, a data warehouse designer, an architect, or any person who is responsible for data warehouse projects and need to load data into them.

You don't need to have any prior data warehouse or database experience to read this book. Fundamental database and data warehouse technical terms and concepts are explained in an easy-to-understand language.

Conventions

In this book, you will find a number of styles of text that distinguish between different kinds of information. Here are some examples of these styles, and an explanation of their meaning.

Code words in text are shown as follows: "You read the `examination.txt` file, and did some calculations to see how the students did."

New terms and **important words** are shown in bold. Words that you see on the screen, in menus or dialog boxes for example, appear in our text like this: "Edit the **Sort rows** step by double-clicking it, click the **Get Fields** button, and adjust the grid."

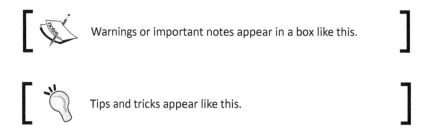

Warnings or important notes appear in a box like this.

Tips and tricks appear like this.

Reader feedback

Feedback from our readers is always welcome. Let us know what you think about this book—what you liked or may have disliked. Reader feedback is important for us to develop titles that you really get the most out of.

To send us general feedback, simply drop an email to `feedback@packtpub.com`, and mention the book title in the subject of your message.

If there is a book that you need and would like to see us publish, please send us a note in the **SUGGEST A TITLE** form on `www.packtpub.com` or email `suggest@packtpub.com`.

If there is a topic that you have expertise in and you are interested in either writing or contributing to a book, see our author guide on `www.packtpub.com/authors`.

Customer support

Now that you are the proud owner of a Packt book, we have a number of things to help you to get the most from your purchase.

> **Downloading the example code for the book**
>
> Visit `http://www.packtpub.com/files/code/9546_Code.zip` to directly download the example code.
>
> The downloadable files contain instructions on how to use them.

Errata

Although we have taken every care to ensure the accuracy of our contents, mistakes do happen. If you find a mistake in one of our books—maybe a mistake in text or code—we would be grateful if you would report this to us. By doing so, you can save other readers from frustration, and help us to improve subsequent versions of this book. If you find any errata, please report them by visiting `http://www.packtpub.com/support`, selecting your book, clicking on the **let us know** link, and entering the details of your errata. Once your errata are verified, your submission will be accepted and the errata added to any list of existing errata. Any existing errata can be viewed by selecting your title from `http://www.packtpub.com/support`.

Piracy

Piracy of copyright material on the Internet is an ongoing problem across all media. At Packt, we take the protection of our copyright and licenses very seriously. If you come across any illegal copies of our works in any form on the Internet, please provide us with the location address or website name immediately so that we can pursue a remedy.

Please contact us at copyright@packtpub.com with a link to the suspected pirated material.

We appreciate your help in protecting our authors, and our ability to bring you valuable content.

Questions

You can contact us at `questions@packtpub.com` if you are having a problem with any aspect of the book, and we will do our best to address it.

1
Getting Started with Pentaho Data Integration

Pentaho Data Integration is an engine along with a suite of tools responsible for the processes of extracting, transforming, and loading—best known as the ETL processes. This book is meant to teach you how to use PDI.

In this chapter you will:

◆ Learn what Pentaho Data Integration is

◆ Install the software and start working with the PDI graphical designer

◆ Install MySQL, a database engine that you will use when you start working with databases

Pentaho Data Integration and Pentaho BI Suite

Before introducing PDI, let's talk about Pentaho BI Suite. The **Pentaho Business Intelligence Suite** is a collection of software applications intended to create and deliver solutions for decision making. The main functional areas covered by the suite are:

◆ **Analysis**: The analysis engine serves multidimensional analysis. It's provided by the **Mondrian** OLAP server and the **JPivot** library for navigation and exploring.

◆ **Reporting**: The reporting engine allows designing, creating, and distributing reports in various known formats (HTML, PDF, and so on) from different kinds of sources. The reports created in Pentaho are based mainly in the **JFreeReport** library, but it's possible to integrate reports created with external reporting libraries such as **Jasper Reports** or **BIRT**.

◆ **Data Mining**: Data mining is running data through algorithms in order to understand the business and do predictive analysis. Data mining is possible thanks to the **Weka Project**.

◆ **Dashboards**: Dashboards are used to monitor and analyze **Key Performance Indicators** (**KPI**s). A set of tools incorporated to the BI Suite in the latest version allows users to create interesting dashboards, including graphs, reports, analysis views, and other Pentaho content, without much effort.

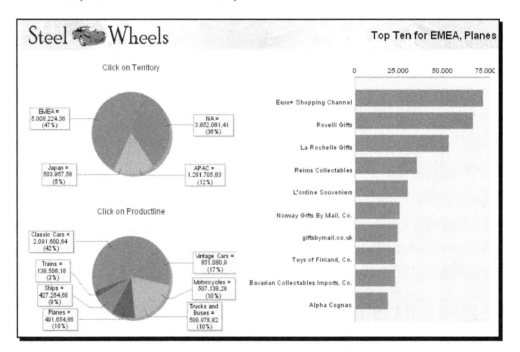

◆ **Data integration**: Data integration is used to integrate scattered information from different sources (applications, databases, files) and make the integrated information available to the final user. Pentaho Data Integration—our main concern—is the engine that provides this functionality.

All this functionality can be used standalone as well as integrated. In order to run analysis, reports, and so on integrated as a suite, you have to use the **Pentaho BI Platform**. The platform has a solution engine, and offers critical services such as authentication, scheduling, security, and web services.

This set of software and services forms a complete BI Platform, which makes Pentaho Suite the world's leading open source Business Intelligence Suite.

Exploring the Pentaho Demo

Despite being out of the scope of this book, it's worth to briefly introduce the Pentaho Demo. The **Pentaho BI Platform Demo** is a preconfigured installation that lets you explore several capabilities of the Pentaho platform. It includes sample reports, cubes, and dashboards for Steel Wheels. Steel Wheels is a fictional store that sells all kind of scale replicas of vehicles.

The demo can be downloaded from `http://sourceforge.net/projects/pentaho/files/`. Under the `Business Intelligence Server` folder, look for the latest stable version. The file you have to download is named `biserver-ce-3.5.2.stable.zip` for Windows and `biserver-ce-3.5.2.stable.tar.gz` for other systems.

In the same folder you will find a file named `biserver-getting_started-ce-3.5.0.pdf`. The file is a guide that introduces you the platform and gives you some guidance on how to install and run it. The guide even includes a mini tutorial on building a simple PDI input-output transformation.

 You can find more about Pentaho BI Suite at `www.pentaho.org`.

Pentaho Data Integration

Most of the Pentaho engines, including the engines mentioned earlier, were created as community projects and later adopted by Pentaho. The PDI engine is no exception—Pentaho Data Integration is the new denomination for the business intelligence tool born as **Kettle**.

 The name Kettle didn't come from the recursive acronym **K**ettle **E**xtraction, **T**ransportation, **T**ransformation, and **L**oading **E**nvironment it has now, but from **KDE** **E**xtraction, **T**ransportation, **T**ransformation and **L**oading **E**nvironment, as the tool was planned to be written on top of KDE, as mentioned in the introduction of the book.

In April 2006 the Kettle project was acquired by the Pentaho Corporation and Matt Casters, Kettle's founder, also joined the Pentaho team as a Data Integration Architect.

When Pentaho announced the acquisition, James Dixon, the Chief Technology Officer, said:

> *We reviewed many alternatives for open source data integration, and Kettle clearly had the best architecture, richest functionality, and most mature user interface. The open architecture and superior technology of the Pentaho BI Platform and Kettle allowed us to deliver integration in only a few days, and make that integration available to the community.*

By joining forces with Pentaho, Kettle benefited from a huge developer community, as well as from a company that would support the future of the project.

From that moment the tool has grown constantly. Every few months a new release is available, bringing to the users, improvements in performance and existing functionality, new functionality, ease of use, and great changes in look and feel. The following is a timeline of the major events related to PDI since its acquisition by Pentaho:

- **June 2006**: PDI 2.3 is released. Numerous developers had joined the project and there were bug fixes provided by people in various regions of the world. Among other changes, the version included enhancements for large scale environments and multilingual capabilities.

- **February 2007**: Almost seven months after the last major revision, PDI 2.4 is released including remote execution and clustering support (more on this in Chapter 13), enhanced database support, and a single designer for the two main elements you design in Kettle—jobs and transformations.

- **May 2007**: PDI 2.5 is released including many new features, the main feature being the advanced error handling.

- **November 2007**: PDI 3.0 emerges totally redesigned. Its major library changed to gain massive performance. The look and feel also changed completely.

- **October 2008**: PDI 3.1 comes with an easier-to-use tool, along with a lot of new functionalities as well.

- **April 2009**: PDI 3.2 is released with a really large number of changes for a minor version—new functionality, visualization improvements, performance improvements, and a huge pile of bug fixes. The main change in this version was the incorporation of dynamic clustering (see Chapter 13 for details).

- In **2010** PDI 4.0 will be released, delivering mostly improvements with regard to enterprise features such as version control.

 Most users still refer to PDI as Kettle, its further name. Therefore, the names PDI, Pentaho Data Integration, and Kettle will be used interchangeably throughout the book.

Using PDI in real world scenarios

Paying attention to its name, Pentaho Data Integration, you could think of PDI as a tool to integrate data.

In you look at its original name, K.E.T.T.L.E., then you must conclude that it is a tool used for ETL processes which, as you may know, are most frequently seen in data warehouse environments.

In fact, PDI not only serves as a data integrator or an ETL tool, but is such a powerful tool that it is common to see it used for those and for many other purposes. Here you have some examples.

Loading datawarehouses or datamarts

The loading of a datawarehouse or a datamart involves many steps, and there are many variants depending on business area or business rules. However, in every case, the process involves the following steps:

Extracting information from one or different databases, text files, and other sources. The extraction process may include the task of validating and discarding data that doesn't match expected patterns or rules.

Transforming the obtained data to meet the business and technical needs required on the target. Transformation implies tasks such as converting data types, doing some calculations, filtering irrelevant data, and summarizing.

Loading the transformed data into the target database. Depending on the requirements, the loading may overwrite the existing information, or may add new information each time it is executed.

Kettle comes ready to do every stage of this loading process. The following sample screenshot shows a simple ETL designed with Kettle:

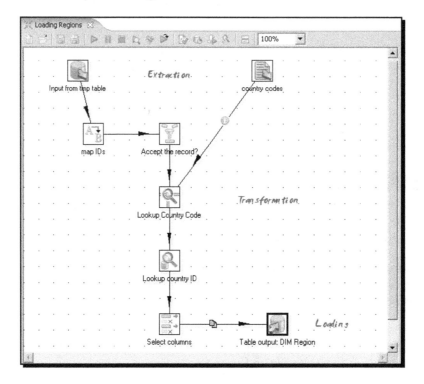

Integrating data

Imagine two similar companies that need to merge their databases in order to have a unified view of the data, or a single company that has to combine information from a main ERP application and a CRM application, though they're not connected. These are just two of hundreds of examples where data integration is needed. **Integrating data** is not just a matter of gathering and mixing data; some conversions, validation, and transport of data has to be done. Kettle is meant to do all those tasks.

Data cleansing

Why do we need that data be correct and accurate? There are many reasons—for the efficiency of business, to generate trusted conclusions in data mining or statistical studies, to succeed when integrating data, and so on. **Data cleansing** is about ensuring that the data is correct and precise. This can be ensured by verifying if the data meets certain rules, discarding or correcting those that don't follow the expected pattern, setting default values for missing data, eliminating information that is duplicated, normalizing data to conform minimum and maximum values, and so on—tasks that Kettle makes possible, thanks to its vast set of transformation and validation capabilities.

Migrating information

Think of a company of any size that uses a commercial ERP application. One day the owners realize that the licences are consuming an important share of its budget and so they decide to migrate to an open source ERP. The company will no longer have to pay licences, but if they want to do the change, they will have to migrate the information. Obviously it is not an option to start from scratch, or type the information by hand. Kettle makes the migration possible, thanks to its ability to interact with most kinds of sources and destinations such as plain files, and commercial and free databases and spreadsheets.

Exporting data

Sometimes you are forced by government regulations to export certain data to be processed by legacy systems. You can't just print and deliver some reports containing the required data. The data has to have a rigid format, with columns that have to obey some rules (size, format, content), different records for heading and tail, just to name some common demands. Kettle has the power to take crude data from the source and generate these kinds of ad hoc reports.

Integrating PDI using Pentaho BI

The previous examples show typical uses of PDI as a standalone application. However, Kettle may be used as part of a process inside the Pentaho BI Platform. There are many things embedded in the Pentaho application that Kettle can do—preprocessing data for an on-line report, sending mails in a schedule fashion, or generating spreadsheet reports.

 You'll find more on this in Chapter 13. However, the use of PDI integrated with the BI Suite is beyond the scope of this book.

Pop quiz – PDI data sources

Which of the following aren't valid sources in Kettle:

1. Spreadsheets
2. Free database engines
3. Commercial database engines
4. Flat files
5. None of the above

Installing PDI

In order to work with PDI you need to install the software. It's a simple task; let's do it.

Time for action – installing PDI

These are the instructions to install Kettle, whatever your operating system.

The only prerequisite to install PDI is to have JRE 5.0 or higher installed. If you don't have it, please download it from `http://www.javasoft.com/` and install it before proceeding. Once you have checked the prerequisite, follow these steps:

1. From `http://community.pentaho.com/sourceforge/` follow the link to **Pentaho Data Integration (Kettle)**. Alternatively, go directly to the download page `http://sourceforge.net/projects/pentaho/files/Data Integration`.

2. Choose the newest stable release. At this time, it is 3.2.0.

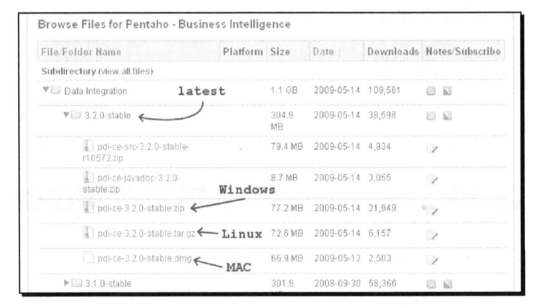

3. Download the file that matches your platform. The preceding screenshot should help you.

4. Unzip the downloaded file in a folder of your choice
    —`C:/Kettle` or `/home/your_dir/kettle`.

5. If your system is Windows, you're done. Under UNIX-like environments, it's recommended that you make the scripts executable. Assuming that you chose Kettle as the installation folder, execute the following command:

```
cd Kettle
chmod +x *.sh
```

What just happened?

You have installed the tool in just a few minutes. Now you have all you need to start working.

Pop quiz – PDI prerequisites

Which of the following are mandatory to run PDI? You may choose more than one option.

1. Kettle
2. Pentaho BI platform
3. JRE
4. A database engine

Launching the PDI graphical designer: Spoon

Now that you've installed PDI, you must be eager to do some stuff with data. That will be possible only inside a graphical environment. PDI has a desktop designer tool named Spoon. Let's see how it feels to work with it.

Time for action – starting and customizing Spoon

In this tutorial you're going to launch the PDI graphical designer and get familiarized with its main features.

1. Start Spoon.

❑ If your system is Windows, type the following command:

```
Spoon.bat
```

❑ In other platforms such as Unix, Linux, and so on, type:

```
Spoon.sh
```

❑ If you didn't make spoon.sh executable, you may type:

```
sh Spoon.sh
```

2. As soon as Spoon starts, a dialog window appears asking for the repository connection data. Click the **No Repository** button. The main window appears. You will see a small window with the tip of the day. After reading it, close that window.

3. A **welcome!** window appears with some useful links for you to see.

4. Close the welcome window. You can open that window later from the main menu.

5. Click **Options...** from the **Edit** menu. A window appears where you can change various general and visual characteristics. Uncheck the circled checkboxes:

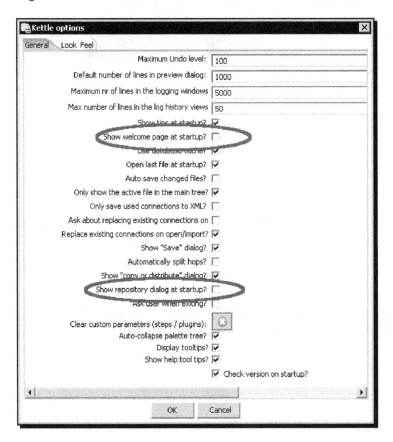

6. Select the tab window **Look Feel**.

7. Change the **Grid size** and **Preferred Language** settings as follows:

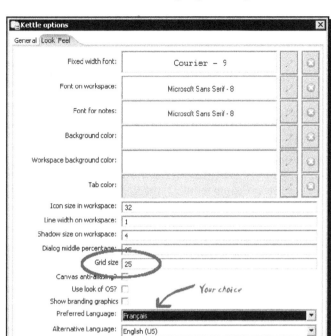

8. Click the **OK** button.

9. Restart Spoon in order to apply the changes. You should neither see the repository dialog, nor the welcome window. You should see the following screen instead:

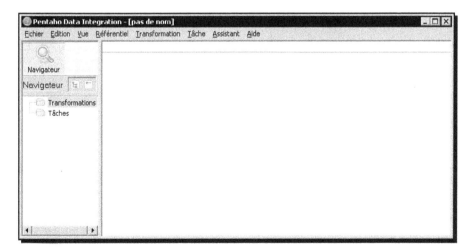

What just happened?

You ran for the first time the graphical designer of PDI Spoon, and applied some custom configuration.

From the **Look Feel** configuration window, you changed the size of the dotted grid that appears in the canvas area while you are working. You also changed the preferred language. In the **Option** tab window, you chose not to show either the repository dialog or the welcome window at startup. These changes were applied as you restarted the tool, not before.

The second time you launched the tool, the repository dialog didn't show up. When the main window appeared, all the visible texts were shown in French, which was the selected language, and instead of the welcome window, there was a blank screen.

Spoon

This tool that you're exploring in this section is the PDI's desktop design tool. With Spoon you design, preview, and test all your work, that is, **transformations** and **jobs**. When you see PDI screenshots, what you are really seeing are Spoon screenshots. The other PDI components that you will meet in the following chapters are executed from terminal windows.

Setting preferences in the Options window

In the tutorial you changed some preferences in the **Options** window. There are several look and feel characteristics you can change beyond those you changed. Feel free to experiment with this setting.

Remember to restart Spoon in order to see the changes applied.

If you choose any language as preferred language other than English, you should select a different language as alternative. If you do so, every name or description not translated to your preferred language will be shown in the alternative language.

Just for the curious people: Italian and French are the overall winners of the list of languages to which the tool has been translated from English. Below them follow Korean, Argentinean Spanish, Japanese, and Chinese.

One of the settings you changed was the appearance of the welcome window at start up. The welcome window has many useful links, all related with the tool: wiki pages, news, forum access, and more. It's worth exploring them.

 You don't have to change the settings again to see the welcome window. You can open it from the menu **Help | Show the Welcome Screen**.

Storing transformations and jobs in a repository

The first time you launched Spoon, you chose **No Repository**. After that, you configured Spoon to stop asking you for the Repository option. You must be curious about what the repository is and why not to use it. Let's explain it.

As said, the results of working with PDI are Transformations and Jobs. In order to save the Transformations and Jobs, PDI offers two methods:

◆ **Repository**: When you use the repository method you save jobs and transformations in a repository. A **repository** is a relational database specially designed for this purpose.

◆ **Files**: The files method consists of saving jobs and transformations as regular XML files in the filesystem, with extension `kjb` and `ktr` respectively.

The following diagram summarizes this:

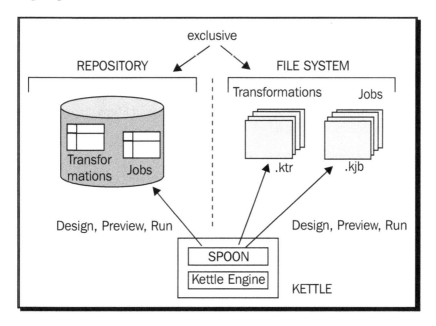

You cannot mix the two methods (files and repository) in the same project. Therefore, you must choose the method when you start the tool.

Why did we choose not to work with repository, or in other words, to work with files? This is mainly for the following two reasons:

◆ Working with files is more natural and practical for most users.

◆ Working with repository requires minimum database knowledge and that you also have access to a database engine from your computer. Having both preconditions would allow you to learn working with both methods. However, it's probable that you haven't.

Throughout this book, we will use the file method. For details of working with repositories, please refer to Appendix A.

Creating your first transformation

Until now, you've seen the very basic elements of Spoon. For sure, you must be waiting to do some interesting task beyond looking around. It's time to create your first transformation.

Time for action – creating a hello world transformation

How about starting by saying Hello to the World? Not original but enough for a very first practical exercise. Here is how you do it:

1. Create a folder named pdi_labs under the folder of your choice.

2. Open Spoon.

3. From the main menu select **File | New Transformation**.

4. At the left-hand side of the screen, you'll see a tree of **Steps**. Expand the **Input** branch by double-clicking it.

5. Left-click the **Generate Rows** icon.

6. Without releasing the button, drag-and-drop the selected icon to the main canvas. The screen will look like this:

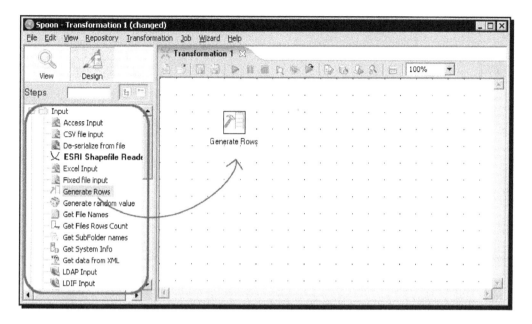

7. Double-click the **Generate Rows** step that you just put in the canvas and fill the text boxes and grid as follows:

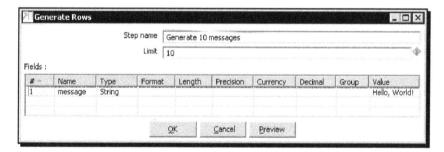

8. From the **Steps** tree, double-click the **Flow** step.

9. Click the **Dummy** icon and drag-and-drop it to the main canvas.

10. Click the **Generate Rows** step and holding the *Shift* key down, drag the cursor towards the **Dummy** step. Release the button. The screen should look like this:

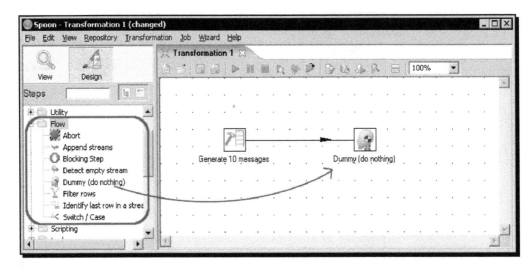

11. Right-click somewhere on the canvas to bring up a contextual menu.

12. Select **New note**. A note editor appears.

13. Type some description such as **Hello World!** and click **OK**.

14. From the main menu, select **Transformation | Configuration**. A window appears to specify transformation properties. Fill the **Transformation name** with a simple name as **hello_world**. Fill the **Description** field with a short description such as **My first transformation**. Finally provide a more clear explanation in the **Extended description** text box and click **OK**.

15. From the main menu, select **File | Save**.

16. Save the transformation in the folder `pdi_labs` with the name `hello_world`.

17. Select the **Dummy** step by left-clicking it.

18. Click on the **Preview** button in the menu above the main canvas.

19. A debug window appears. Click the **Quick Launch** button.

20. The following window appears to preview the data generated by the transformation:

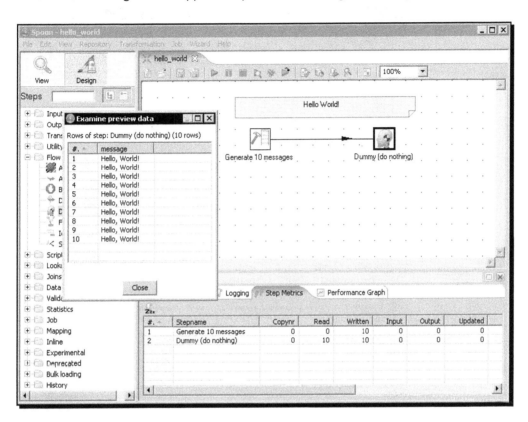

21. Close the preview window and click the **Run** button.

22. A window appears. Click **Launch**.

23. The execution results are shown in the bottom of the screen. The **Logging** tab should look as follows:

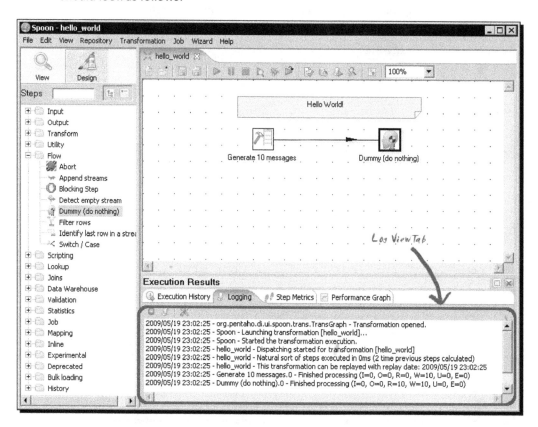

What just happened?

You've just created your first transformation.

First, you created a new transformation. From the tree on the left, you dragged two steps and drop them into the canvas. Finally, you linked them with a hop.

With the **Generate Rows** step, you created 10 rows of data with the message **Hello World!**. The **Dummy** step simply served as a destination of those rows.

After creating the transformation, you did a preview. The preview allowed you to see the content of the created data, this is, the 10 rows with the message **Hello World!**

Finally, you ran the transformation. You could see the results of the execution at the bottom of the windows. There is a tab named **Step Metrics** with information about what happens with each steps in the transformation. There is also a **Logging** tab showing a complete detail of what happened.

Directing the Kettle engine with transformations

As shown in the following diagram, transformation is an entity made of steps linked by hops. These steps and hops build paths through which data flows. The data enters or is created in a step, the step applies some kind of transformation to it, and finally the data leaves that step. Therefore, it's said that a transformation is data-flow oriented.

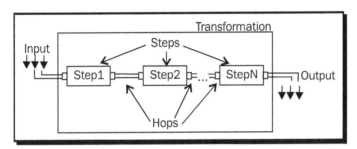

A transformation itself is not a program nor an executable file. It is just plain XML. The transformation contains metadata that tells the Kettle engine what to do.

A **step** is the minimal unit inside a transformation. A big set of steps is available. These steps are grouped in categories such as the input and flow categories that you saw in the example. Each step is conceived to accomplish a specific function, going from reading a parameter to normalizing a dataset. Each step has a configuration window. These windows vary according to the functionality of the steps and the category to which they belong. What all steps have in common are the name and description:

Step property	Description
Name	A representative name inside the transformation.
Description	A brief explanation that allows you to clarify the purpose of the step. It's not mandatory but it is useful.

A **hop** is a graphical representation of data flowing between two steps—an origin and a destination. The data that flows through that hop constitutes the output data of the origin step and the input data of the destination step.

Exploring the Spoon interface

As you just saw, the Spoon is the tool using which you create, preview, and run transformations. The following screenshot shows you the basic work areas:

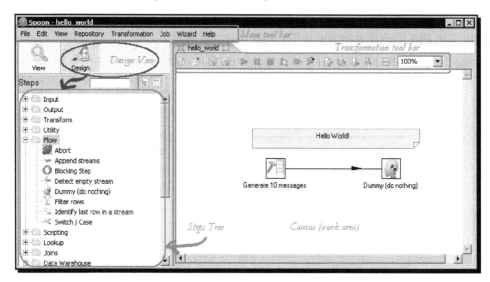

 The words canvas and work area will be used interchangeably throughout the book.

Viewing the transformation structure

If you click the **View** icon in the upper left corner of the screen, the tree will change to show the structure of the transformation currently being edited.

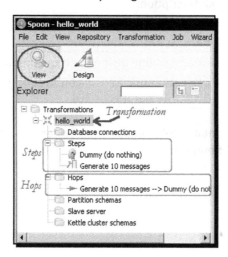

Running and previewing the transformation

The Preview functionality allows you to see a sample of the data produced for selected steps. In the previous example, you previewed the output of the Dummy Step. The **Run** option effectively runs the whole transformation.

Whether you preview or run a transformation, you'll get an execution results window showing what happened. Let's explain it through an example.

Time for action – running and previewing the hello_world transformation

Let's do some testing and explore the results:

1. Open the `hello_world` transformation.

2. Edit the **Generate Rows** step, and change the limit from `10` to `1000` so that it generates 1,000 rows.

3. Select the **Logging** tab window at the bottom of the screen.

4. Click on **Run**.

5. In the **Log level** drop-down list, select **RowLevel** detail.

6. Click on **Launch**.

7. You can see how the logging window shows every task in a very detailed way.

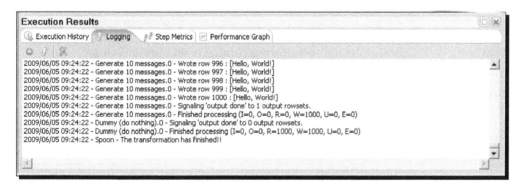

8. Edit the **Generate Rows** step, and change the limit to **10,000** so that it generates 10,000 rows.

9. Select the **Step Metrics**.

10. Run the transformation.

11. You can see how the numbers change as the rows travel through the steps.

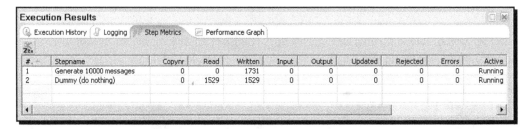

What just happened?

You did some tests with the `hello_world` transformation and saw the results in the **Execution Results** window.

Previewing the results in the Execution Results window

The **Execution Results** window shows you what is happening while you preview or run a transformation.

The **Logging** tab shows the execution of your transformation, step by step. By default, the level of the logging detail is **Basic** but you can change it to see different levels of detail—from a minimal logging (level **Minimal**) to a very detailed one (level **RowLevel**).

The **Step Metrics** tab shows, for each step of the transformation, the executed operations and several status and information columns. You may be interested in the following columns:

Column	Description
Read	Contains the number of rows coming from previous steps
Written	Contains the number of rows leaving from this step toward the next
Input	Number of rows read from a file or table
Output	Number of rows written to a file or table
Errors	Errors in the execution. If there are errors, the whole row becomes red
Active	Tells the current status of the execution

In the example, you can see that the **Generate Rows** step writes rows, which then are read by the **Dummy** step. The **Dummy** step also writes the same rows, but in this case those go nowhere.

Pop quiz – PDI basics

For each of the following, decide if the sentence is true or false:

1. There are several graphical tools in PDI, but Spoon is the most used.

2. You can choose to save Transformations either in files or in a database.

3. To run a Transformation, an executable file has to be generated from Spoon.

4. The grid size option in the Look and Feel windows allows you to resize the work area.

5. To create a transformation, you have to provide external data.

Installing MySQL

Before skipping to the next chapter, let's devote some minutes to the installation of MySQL.

In Chapter 8 you will begin working with databases from PDI. In order to do that, you will need access to some database engine. As MySQL is the world's most popular open source database, it was the database engine chosen for the database-related tutorials in the book.

In this section you will learn to install the MySQL database engine both in Windows and Ubuntu, the most popular distribution of Linux these days. As the procedures for installing the software are different, a separate explanation is given for each system.

Time for action – installing MySQL on Windows

In order to Install MySQL on your Windows system, please follow these instructions:

1. Open an internet browser and type `http://dev.mysql.com/downloads/mysql/`.

2. Select the Microsoft Windows platform and download the mysql-essential package that matches your system: 32-bit or 64-bit.

3. Double-click the downloaded file. A wizard will guide you through the process.

4. When asked about the setup type, select **Typical**.

5. Several screens follow. When the wizard is complete you'll have the option to configure the server. Check **Configure the MySQL Server now** and click **Finish**.

6. A new wizard will be launched that lets you configure the server.

7. When asked about the configuration type, select **Standard Configuration**.

8. When prompted, set the Windows options as shown in the next screenshot:

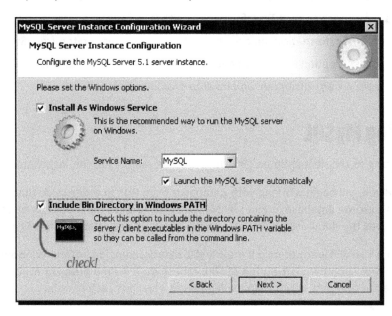

9. When prompted for the security options, provide a password for the root user. You'll have to retype the password.

 Provide a password that you can remember. You'll need it later to connect to the MySQL server.

10. In the next window click on **Execute** to proceed with the configuration. When the configuration is done, you'll see this:

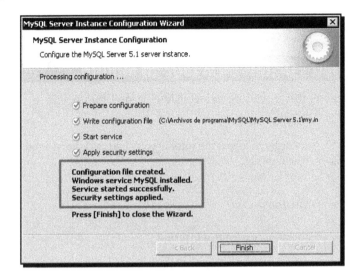

11. Click on **Finish**. After installing MySQL it is recommended that you install the GUI tools for administering and querying the database.

12. Open an Internet browser and type
`http://dev.mysql.com/downloads/gui-tools/`.

13. Look for the **Windows downloads** and download the **Windows (x86)** package.

14. Double-click the downloaded file. A wizard will guide you through the process.

15. When asked about the setup type, select **Complete**.

16. Several screens follow. Just follow the wizard instructions.

17. When the wizard ends, you'll have the GUI tools added to the MySQL menu.

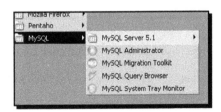

What just happened?

You downloaded and installed MySQL on your Windows system. You also installed MySQL GUI tools, a software package that includes an administrator and a query browser utility and that will make your life easier when working with the database.

Time for action – installing MySQL on Ubuntu

This tutorial shows you the procedure to install MySQL on Ubuntu.

 In order to follow the tutorial you need to be connected to the Internet.

Please follow these instructions:

1. Check that you have access to the Internet.

2. Open the Synaptic package manager from **System | Administration | Synaptic Package Manager**.

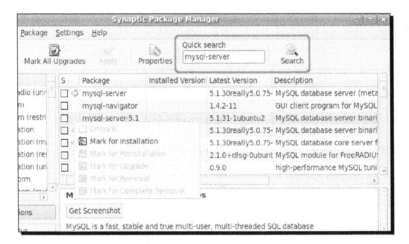

3. Under **Quick search** type `mysql-server` and click on the **Search** button.

4. Among the results, locate `mysql-server-5.1`, click in the tiny square to the left, and select **Mark for Installation**.

5. You'll be prompted for confirmation. Click on **Mark**.

6. Now search for a package named `mysql-admin`.

7. When found, mark it for installation in the same way.

8. Click on **Apply** on the main toolbar.

9. A window shows up asking for confirmation. Click on **Mark** again. What follows is the download process followed by the installation process.

10. At a particular moment a window appears asking you for a password for the root user—the administrator of the database. Enter a password of your choice. You'll have to enter it twice.

 Think of a password that you can remember. You'll need it later to connect to the MySQL server.

11. When the process ends, you will see the changes applied.

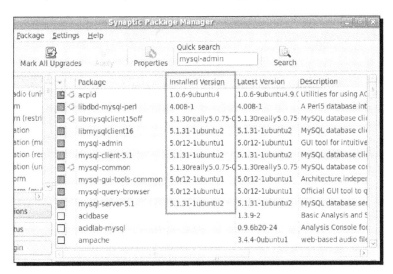

12. Under **Applications** a new menu will also be added to access the GUI tools.

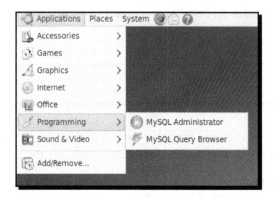

What just happened?

You installed MySQL server and GUI Tools in your Ubuntu system.

The previous directions are for standard installations. For custom installations, instructions related to other operating systems, or for troubleshooting, please check the MySQL documentation at—`http://dev.mysql.com/doc/refman/5.1/en/installing.html`.

Summary

In this first chapter, you were introduced to Pentaho Data Integration. Specifically, you learned what Pentaho Data Integration is and you installed the tool. You were also introduced to Spoon, the graphical designer of PDI, and you created your first transformation.

As an additional exercise, you installed a MySQL server and the MySQL GUI tools. You will need this software when you start working with databases in Chapter 8.

Now that you've learned the basics, you're ready to begin creating your own transformations to explore real data. That is the topic of the next chapter.

2

Getting Started with Transformations

In the previous chapter you used the graphical designer Spoon to create your first transformation: Hello world. Now you will start creating your own transformations to explore data from the real world. Data is everywhere; in particular you will find data in files. Product lists, logs, survey results, and statistical information are just a sample of the different kinds of information usually stored in files. In this chapter you will create transformations to get data from files, and also to send data back to files. This in turn will allow you to learn the basic PDI terminology related to data.

Reading data from files

Despite being the most primitive format used to store data, files are broadly used and they exist in several flavors as fixed width, comma-separated values, spreadsheet, or even free format files. PDI has the ability to read data from all types of files; in this first tutorial let's see how to use PDI to get data from text files.

Time for action – reading results of football matches from files

Suppose you have collected several football statistics in plain files. Your files look like this:

```
Group|Date|Home Team |Results|Away Team|Notes
Group 1|02/June|Italy|2-1|France|
Group 1|02/June|Argentina|2-1|Hungary
Group 1|06/June|Italy|3-1|Hungary
Group 1|06/June|Argentina|2-1|France
Group 1|10/June|France|3-1|Hungary
Group 1|10/June|Italy|1-0|Argentina
--------------------------------------------
World Cup 78
Group 1
```

You don't have one, but many files, all with the same structure. You now want to unify all the information in one single file. Let's begin by reading the files.

1. Create the folder named pdi_files. Inside it, create the input and output subfolders.

2. By using any text editor, type the file shown and save it under the name group1.txt in the folder named input, which you just created. You can also download the file from Packt's official website.

3. Start Spoon.

4. From the main menu select **File | New Transformation**.

5. Expand the **Input** branch of the steps tree.

6. Drag the **Text file input** icon to the canvas.

7. Double-click the text input file icon and give a name to the step.

8. Click the **Browse...** button and search the file group1.txt.

9. Select the file. The textbox **File or directory** will be temporarily populated with the full path of the file—for example, C:\pdi_files\input\group1.txt.

10. Click the **Add** button. The full text will be moved from the **File or directory** textbox to the grid. The configuration window should look as follows:

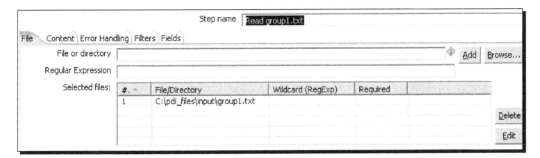

11. Select the **Content** tab and fill it like this:

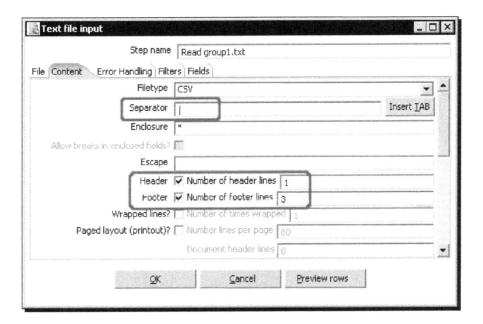

12. Select the **Fields** tab. Click the **Get Fields** button. The screen should look like this:

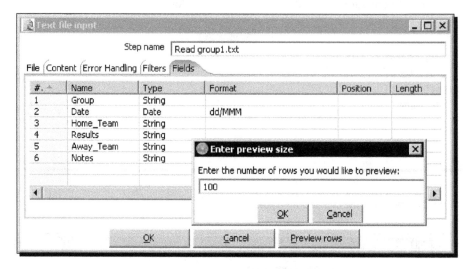

13. In the small window that proposes you a number of sample lines, click **OK**.

14. Close the **scan results** window.

15. Change the second row. Under the **Type** column select **Date**, and under the **Format** column, type dd/MMM.

16. The result value is text, not a number, so change the fourth row too. Under the **Type** column select **String**.

17. Click the **Preview rows** button, and then the **OK** button.

18. The previewed data should look like the following:

19. Expand the **Transform** branch of the steps tree.

20. Drag the **Select values** icon to the canvas.

21. Create a hop from the **Text file input** step to the **Select values** step.

 Remember that you do it by selecting the first step, then dragging toward the second while holding down the *Shift* key.

22. Double-click the **Select values** step icon and give a name to the step.

23. Select the **Remove** tab.

24. Click the **Get fields to remove** button.

25. Delete every row except the first and the last one by left-clicking them and pressing *Delete*.

26. The tab window looks like this:

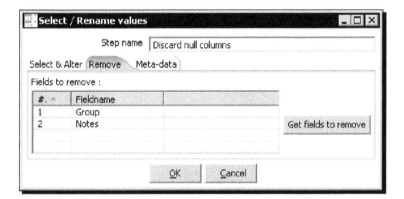

27. Click **OK**.

28. From the **Flow** branch of the steps tree, drag the **Dummy** icon to the canvas.

29. Create a hop from the **Select values** step to the **Dummy** step. Your transformation should look like the following:

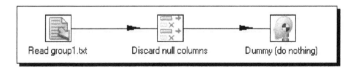

30. Configure the transformation by pressing *Ctrl+T* and giving a name and a description to the transformation.

31. Save the transformation by pressing *Ctrl+S*.

32. Select the **Dummy** step.

33. Click the **Preview** button located on the transformation toolbar:

34. Click the **Quick Launch** button.

35. The following window appears, showing the final data:

What just happened?

You read your plain file with results of football matches into a transformation.

By using a Text file input step, you told Kettle the full path to your file, along with the characteristics of the file so that Kettle was able to read the data correctly—you specified that the file had a header, had three rows at the end that should be ignored, and specified the name and type of the columns.

After reading the file, you used a Select values step to remove columns you didn't need— the first and the last column.

With those two simple steps, you were able to preview the data in your file from inside the transformation.

Another thing you may have noticed is the use of shortcuts instead of the menu options—for example, to save the transformation.

> Many of the menu options can be accessed more quickly by using shortcuts. The available shortcuts for the menu options are mentioned as part of the name of the operation—for example, **Run F9**.
>
> For a full shortcut reference please check Appendix D.

Input files

Files are one of the most used input sources. PDI can take data from several types of files, with very few limitations.

When you have a file to work with, the first thing you have to do is to specify where the file is, how it looks, and what kinds of values it contains. That is exactly what you did in the first tutorial of this chapter.

With the information you provide, Kettle can create the dataset to work within the current transformation.

Input steps

There are several steps that allow you to take a file as the input data. All those steps such as Text file Input, Fixed file input, Excel Input, and so on are under the Input step category.

Despite the obvious differences that exist between these types of files, the ways to configure the steps have much in common. The following are the main properties you have to specify for an input step:

- **Name of the step**: It is mandatory and must be different for every step in the transformation.
- **Name and location of the file**: These must be specified of course. At the moment you create the transformation, it's not mandatory that the file exists. However, if it does, you will find it easier to configure this step.
- **Content type**: This data includes delimiter character, type of encoding, whether a header is present, and so on. The list depends on the kind of file chosen. In every case, Kettle propose default values, so you don't have to enter too much data.

◆ **Fields**: Kettle has the facility to get the definitions automatically by clicking the **Get Fields** button. However, Kettle doesn't always guess the data types, size, or format as expected. So, after getting the fields you may change what you consider more appropriate, as you did in the tutorial.

◆ **Filtering**: Some steps allow you to filter the data—skip blank rows, read only the first *n* rows, and so on.

After configuring an input step, you can preview the data just as you did, by Clicking the **Preview Rows** button. This is useful to discover if there is something wrong in the configuration. In that case, you can make the adjustments and preview again, until your data looks fine.

Reading several files at once

Until now you used an input step to read one file. But you have several files, all with the very same structure. That will not be a problem because with Kettle it is possible to read more than a file at a time.

Time for action – reading all your files at a time using a single Text file input step

To read all your files follow the next steps:

1. Open the transformation, double-click the input step, and add the other files in the same way you added the first.

2. After Clicking the **Preview rows** button, you will see this:

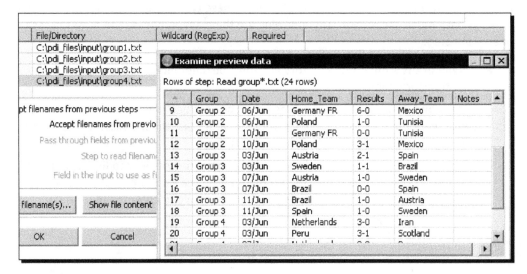

What just happened?

You read several files at once. By putting in the grid the names of all the input files, you could get the content of every specified file one after the other.

Time for action – reading all your files at a time using a single Text file input step and regular expressions

You could do the same thing you did above by using a different notation.
Follow these instructions:

1. Open the transformation and edit the configuration windows of the input step.

2. Delete the lines with the names of the files.

3. In the first row of the grid, type `C:\pdi_files\input\` under the **File/Directory** column, and `group[1-4]\.txt` under the **Wildcard (Reg.Exp.)** column.

4. Click the **Show filename(s)...** button. You'll see the list of files that match the expression.

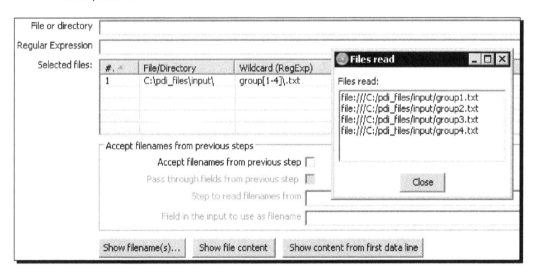

5. Close the tiny window and click **Preview rows** to confirm that the rows shown belong to the four files that match the expression you typed.

What just happened?

In this particular case, all filenames follow a pattern—group1.txt, group2.txt, and so on. In order to specify the names of the files, you used a regular expression. In the column **File/Directory** you put the static part of the names, while in the **Wildcard (Reg.Exp.)** column you put the regular expression with the pattern that a file must follow to be considered: the text group followed by a number between 1 and 4, and then .txt. Then, all files that matched the expression were considered as input files.

Regular expressions

There are many places inside Kettle where you may or have to provide a regular expression. A regular expression is much more than specifying the known wildcards ? and *.

Here you have some examples of regular expressions you may use to specify filenames:

The following regular expression ...	Matches ...	Examples
.*\.txt	Any txt file	thisisaValidExample.txt
test(19|20)\d\d-(0[1-9]|1[012])\.txt	Any txt file beginning with test followed by a date using the format yyyy-mm	test2009-12.txt test2009-01.txt
(?i)test.+\.txt	Any txt file beginning with test, upper or lower case	TeSTcaseinsensitive.tXt

 Please note that the * wildcard doesn't work the same as it does on the command line. If you want to match any character, the * has to be preceded by a dot.

Here are some useful links in case you want to know more about regular expressions:

- Regular Expression Quick Start:
  http://www.regular-expressions.info/quickstart.html

- The Java Regular Expression Tutorial:
  http://java.sun.com/docs/books/tutorial/essential/regex/

- Java Regular Expression Pattern Syntax: http://java.sun.com/javase/6/docs/api/java/util/regex/Pattern.html

Troubleshooting reading files

Despite the simplicity of reading files with PDI, obstacles and errors appear. Many times the solution is simple but difficult to find if you are new to PDI. Here you have a list of common problems and possible solutions for you to take into account while reading and previewing a file:

Problem	Diagnostic	Possible solutions
You get the message **Sorry, no rows found to be previewed.**	This happens when the input file doesn't exist or is empty. It also may happen if you specified the input files with regular expressions and there is no file that matches the expression.	Check the name of the input files. Verify the syntax used, check that you didn't put spaces or any strange character as part of the name. If you used regular expressions, check the syntax. Also verify that you put the filename in the grid. If you just put it in the **File or directory** textbox, Kettle will not read it.
When you preview the data you see a grid with blank lines	The file contains empty lines, or you forgot to get the fields.	Check the content of the file. Also check that you got the fields in the **Fields** tab.
You see the whole line under the first defined field.	You didn't set the proper separator and Kettle couldn't split the different fields.	Check and fix the separator in the **Content** tab.
You see strange characters.	You left the default content but your file has a different format or encoding.	Check and fix the **Format** and **Encoding** in the **Content** tab. If you are not sure of the format, you can specify **mixed**.
You don't see all the lines you have in the file	You are previewing just a sample (100 lines by default). Or you put a limit to the number of rows to get. Another problem may be that you set the wrong number of header or footer lines.	When you preview, you see just a sample. This is not a problem. If you raise the previewed number of rows and still have few lines, check the **Header**, **Footer** and **Limit** options in the **Content** tab.

Problem	Diagnostic	Possible solutions
Instead of rows of data, you get a window headed **ERROR** with an extract of the log	Different errors may happen, but the most common has to do with problems in the definition of the fields.	You could try to understand the log and fix the definition accordingly. For example if you see: **Couldn't parse field [Integer] with value [Italy].** The error is that PDI found the text **Italy** in a field that you defined as `Integer`. If you made a mistake, you could fix it. On the other hand, if the file has errors, you could read all fields as String and you will not get the error again. In chapter 7 you will learn how to overcome these situations.

Grids

Grids are tables used in many Spoon places to enter or display information. You already saw grids in several configuration windows—**Text file input**, **Text file output**, and **Select values**.

Many grids contain field information. Examples of these grids are the **Field** tab window in the **Text Input** and **Output** steps, or the main configuration window of the **Select Values** step. In these cases, the grids are usually accompanied by a **Get Fields** button. The **Get Fields** button is a facility to avoid typing. When you press that button, Kettle fills the grid with all the available fields.

For example, when reading a file, the **Get Fields** button fills the grid with the columns of the incoming file. When using a **Select Values** step or a File output step, the **Get Fields** button fills the grid with all the fields entering from a previous step.

Every time you see a **Get Fields** button, consider it as a shortcut to avoid typing. Kettle will bring the fields available to the grid; you will only have to check the information brought and make minimal changes.

There are many places in Spoon where the grid serves also to edit other kinds of information. One example of that is the grid where you specify the list of files in a **Text File Input** step. No matter what kind of grid you are editing, there is always a contextual menu, which you may access by right-clicking on a row. That menu offers editing options to copy, paste, or move rows of the grid.

When the number of rows in the grid is big, use shortcuts! Most of the editing options of a grid have shortcuts that make the editing work easier and quicker.

You'll find a full list of shortcuts for editing grids in Appendix E.

Have a go hero – explore your own files

Try to read your own text files from Kettle. You must have several files with different kinds of data, different separators, and with or without header or footer. You can also search for files over the Internet; there are plenty of files there to download and play with. After configuring the input step, do a preview. If the data is not shown properly, fix the configuration and preview again until you are sure that the data is read as expected. If you have trouble reading the files, please refer to the *Troubleshooting reading files* section seen earlier for diagnosis and possible ways to solve the problems.

Sending data to files

Now you know how to bring data into Kettle. You didn't bring the data just to preview it; you probably want to do some transformation on the data, to finally send it to a final destination such as another plain file. Let's learn how to do this last task.

Time for action – sending the results of matches to a plain file

In the previous tutorial, you read all your "results of matches" files. Now you want to send the data coming from all files to a single output file.

1. Create a new transformation.

2. Drag a **Text file input** step to the canvas and configure it just as you did in the previous tutorial.

3. Drag a **Select values** step to the canvas and create a hop from the **Text file input** step to the **Select values** step.

4. Double-click the **Select values** step.

5. Click the **Get fields to select** button.

6. Modify the fields as follows:

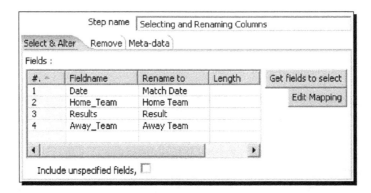

7. Expand the **Output** branch of the steps tree.

8. Drag the **Text file output** icon to the canvas.

9. Create a hop from the **Select values** step to the **Text file output** step.

10. Double-click the **Text file output** step and give it a name.

11. In the file name type: `C:/pdi_files/output/wcup_first_round`.

 Note that the path contains forward slashes. If your system is Windows, you may use back or forward slashes. PDI will recognize both notations.

12. In the **Content** tab, leave the default values.

13. Select the **Fields** tab and configure it as follows:

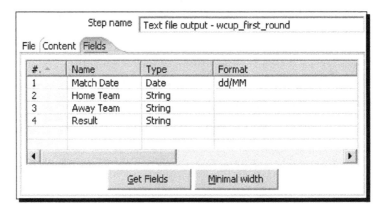

14. Click **OK**.

15. Give a name and description to the transformation.

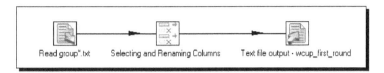

16. Save the transformation.

17. Click **Run** and then **Launch**.

18. Once the transformation is finished, check the file generated. It should have been created as C:/pdi_files/output/wcup_first_round.txt and should look like this:

```
Match Date;Home Team;Away Team;Result
02/06;Italy;France;2-1
02/06;Argentina;Hungary;2-1
06/06;Italy;Hungary;3-1
06/06;Argentina;France;2-1
10/06;France;Hungary;3-1
10/06;Italy;Argentina;1-0
01/06;Germany FR;Poland;0-0
02/06;Tunisia;Mexico;3-1
06/06;Germany FR;Mexico;6-0
...
```

What just happened?

You gathered information from several files and sent all the data to a single file. Before sending the data out, you used a **Select Value** step to select the data you wanted for the file and to rename the fields so that the header of the destination file looks clearer.

Output files

We saw that PDI could take data from several types of files. The same applies to output data. The data you have in a transformation can be sent to different types of files. All you have to do is redirect the flow of data towards an **Output** step.

Output steps

There are several steps that allow you to send the data to a file. All those steps are under the **Output** step category: **Text file output** and **Excel Output** are examples of them.

For an **Output** step, just like you do for an **Input** step, you also have to define:

* **Name of the step**: It is mandatory and must be different for every step in the transformation.
* **Name and location of the file**: These must be specified. If you specify an existing file, the file will be replaced by a new one (unless you check the **Append** checkbox present in some of the output steps).
* **Content type**: This data includes delimiter character, type of encoding, whether to put a header, and so on. The list depends on the kind of file chosen. If you check **Header**, the header will be built with the names of the fields.

 If you don't like the names of the fields as header names in your file, you may use a **Select values** step just to rename those fields.

* **Fields**: Here you specify the list of fields that has to be sent to the file, and provide some format instructions. Just like in the input steps, you may use the **Get Fields** button to fill the grid. In this case, the grid is going to be filled based on the data that arrives from the previous step. You are not forced to send every piece of data coming to the output step, nor to send the fields in the same order.

Some data definitions

From the Kettle's point of view, data can be anything ready to be processed by software (for example files or data in databases). Whichever the subject or origin of the data, whichever its format, Kettle transformations can get the data for further processing and delivering.

Rowset

Transformations deals with datasets, that is, data presented in a tabular form, where:

* Each column represents a **field**. A field has a name and a data type. The data type can be any of the common data types—number (float), string, date, Boolean, integer, or big number.
* Each **row** corresponds to a given member of the dataset. All rows in a dataset have the same structure, that is, all rows have the same fields, in the same order. A field in a row may be null, but it has to be present.

♦ The dataset is called **rowset**. The following is an example of rowset. It is the rowset generated in the World Cup tutorial:

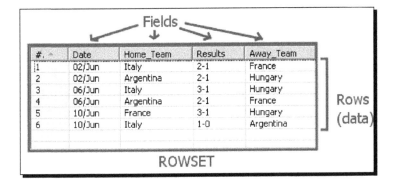

Streams

Once the data is read, it travels from step to step, through the hops that link those steps.

Nothing happens in the hops except data flowing. The real manipulation of data, as well as the modification of a stream by adding or removing columns, occurs in the steps.

Right-click on the **Select values** step of the transformation you created. In the contextual menu select **Show output fields**. You'll see this:

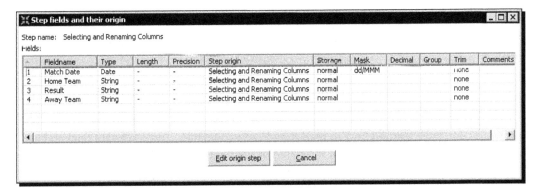

This window shows the metadata of the data that leaves this step, this is, name, type, and other properties of each field leaving this step towards the following step.

In the same way, if you select **Show input fields**, you will see the metadata of the data that left the previous step.

The Select values step

The **Select values** step allows you to select, rename, and delete fields, or change the metadata of a field. The step has three tabs:

- **Select & Alter**: This tab is also used to rename the fields or reorder them. This is how we used it in the last exercise.

- **Remove**: This tab is useful to discard undesirable fields. We used it in the matches exercise to drop the first and last fields. Alternatively, we could use the **Select & Alter** tab, and specify the fields that you want to keep. Both are equivalent for that purpose.

- **Meta-data**: This tab is used when you want to change the definition of a field such as telling Kettle to interpret a string field as a date. We will see examples of this later in this book.

 You may use only one of the **Select Values** step tabs at a time. Kettle will not restrain you from filling more than one tab, but that could lead to unexpected behavior.

Have a go hero – extending your transformations by writing output files

Suppose you read your own files in the previous section, modify your transformations by writing some or all the data back into files, however, changing the format, headers, number or order of fields, and so on this time around. The objective is to get some experience to see what happens. After some tests, you will feel confident with input and output files, and be ready to move forward.

Getting system information

Until now, you have learned how to read data from known files, and send data back to files. What if you don't know beforehand the name of the file to process? There are several ways to handle this with Kettle. Let's learn the simplest.

Time for action – updating a file with news about examinations

Imagine you are responsible to collect the results of an annual examination that is being taken in a language school. The examination evaluates writing, reading, speaking, and listening skills. Every professor gives the exam to the students, the students take the examination, the professors grade the examinations in the scale 0-100 for each skill, and write the results in a text file, like the following:

```
student_code;name;writing;reading;speaking;listening
80711-85;William Miller;81;83;80;90
20362-34;Jennifer Martin;87;76;70;80
75283-17;Margaret Wilson;99;94;90;80
83714-28;Helen Thomas;89;97;80;80
61666-55;Maria Thomas;88;77;70;80
```

All the files follow that pattern.

When a professor has the file ready, he/she sends it to you, and you have to integrate the results in a global list. Let's do it with Kettle.

1. Before starting, be sure to have a file ready to read. Type it or download the sample files from the Packt's official website.

2. Create the file where the news will be appended. Type this:

```
---------------------------------------------------------------
Annual Language Examinations
Testing writing, reading, speaking and listening skills
---------------------         ---------------------------------
student_code;name;writing;reading;speaking;listening;file_
processed;process_date
```

Save the file as `C:/pdi_files/output/examination.txt`.

3. Create a new transformation.

4. Expand the **Input** branch of the steps tree.

5. Drag the **Get System Info** and **Text file input** icons to the canvas.

6. Expand the **Output** branch of the steps tree, and drag a **Text file output** step to the canvas.

7. Link the steps as follows:

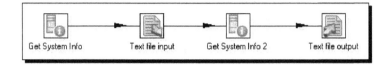

8. Double-click the first **Get System Info** step icon and give it a name.

9. Fill the grid as follows:

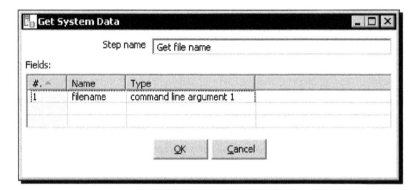

10. Click **OK**.

11. Double-click the **Text file Input** step icon and configure it like here:

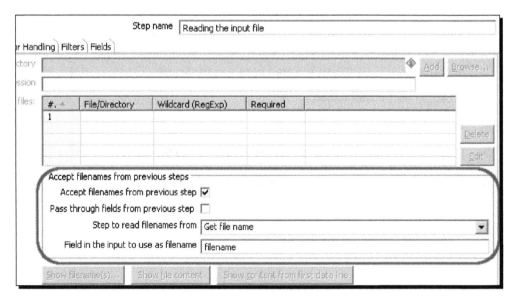

12. Select the **Content** tab.

13. Check the **Include filename in output?** checkbox and type `file_processed` in the **Filename fieldname** textbox.

14. Check the **Add filenames to result** checkbox.

15. Select the **Fields** tab and Click the **Get Fields** button to fill the grid.

16. Click **OK**.

17. Double-click the second **Get System Info** step icon and give it a name.

18. Add a field named `process_date`, and from the list of choices select **system date (fixed)**.

19. Double-click the **Text file output** step icon and give it a name.

20. Type `C:/pdi_files/output/examination` as the filename.

21. In the **Fields** tab, press the **Get Fields** button to fill the grid.

22. Change the format of the **Date** row to **yy/MM/dd**.

23. Give a name and description to the transformation and save it.

24. Press *F9* to run the transformation.

25. Fill in the argument grid, writing the full path of the file created.

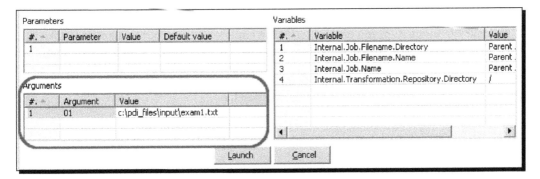

26. Click **Launch**.

27. The output file should look like this:

```
---------------------------------------------------------
Annual Language Examinations
Testing writing, reading, speaking and listening skills
---------------------------------------------------------
student_code;name;writing;reading;speaking;listening;file_
processed;process_date
80711-85;William Miller;81;83;80;90;C:\exams\exam1.txt;28-05-2009
20362-34;Jennifer Martin;87;76;70;80;C:\exams\exam1.txt;28-05-2009
75283-17;Margaret Wilson;99;94;90;80;C:\exams\exam1.txt;28-05-2009
83714-28;Helen Thomas;89;97;80;80;C:\exams\exam1.txt;28-05-2009
61666-55;Maria Thomas;88;77;70;80;C:\exams\exam1.txt;28-05-2009
```

28. Run the transformation again.

29. This time fill the argument grid with the name of a second file.

30. Click **Launch**.

31. Verify that the data from this second file was appended to the previous data in the output file.

What just happened?

You read a file whose name is known at runtime, and fed a destination file by appending the contents of the input file.

The first **Get System Info** step tells Kettle to take the first command line argument, and assume that it is the name of the file to read.

In the **Text File Input** step, you didn't specify the name of the file, but told Kettle to take as the name of the file, the field coming from the previous step, which is the read argument.

With the second Get System Info step you just took from the system, the date, which you used later to enrich the data sent to the destination file.

The destination file is appended with new data every time you run the transformation. Beyond the basic required data (student code and grades), the name of the processed file and the date on which the data is being appended are added as part of the data.

When you don't specify the name and location of a file (like in this example), or when the real file is not available at design time, you won't be able to use the **Get Fields** button, nor preview to see if the step is well configured. The trick is to configure the step by using a real file identical to the expected one. After the step is configured, change the name and location of the file as needed.

Getting information by using Get System Info step

The **Get System Info** step allows you to get different information from the system. In this exercise, you took the system date and an argument. If you look to the available list, you will see more than just these two options.

Here we used the step in two different ways:

- ◆ As a resource to take the name of the file from the command line
- ◆ To add a field to the dataset

The use of this step will be clearer with a picture.

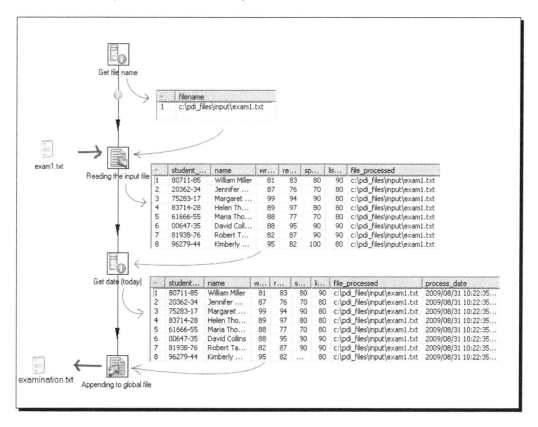

In this example, the **Text File Input** doesn't know the name or the location of the file. It takes it from the previous step, which is a **Get System Info** Step. As the Get System Info serves as a supplier of information, the hop that leaves the step changes its look and feel to show the situation.

The second time the **Get System Info** is used, its function is simply to add a field to the incoming dataset.

Data types

Every field must have a data type. The data type can be any of the common data types—number (float), string, date, Boolean, integer, or big number. Strings are simple, just text for which you may specify a length. Date and numeric fields have more variants, and are worthy of while a separate explanation.

Date fields

Date is one the main data types available in Kettle. In the matches tutorial, you have an example of date field—the match date field. Its values were 2/Jun, 6/Jun, 10/Jun. Take a look at how you defined that field in the Text file input step. You defined the field as a date field with format dd/MMM. What does it mean? To Kettle it means that it has to interpret the field as a date, where the first two positions represent the day, then there is a slash, and finally there is the month in letters (that's the meaning of the three last positions).

Generally speaking, when a date field is created, like the text input field of the example, you have to define the format of the data so that Kettle can recognize in the field the different components of the date. There are several formats that may be defined for a date, all of them combinations of letters that represents date or time components. Here are the most basic ones:

Letters	Meaning
y	Year
M	Month
d	Day
H	Hour (0-23)
m	Minutes
s	Seconds

Now let's see the other end of the same transformation—the output step. Here you set another format for the same field: dd/MM. According the table, this means the date has to have two positions for the day, then a slash, and then two positions for the month. Here, the format specification represents the mask you want to apply when the date is shown. Instead of 2/Jun, 6/Jun, 10/Jun, in the output file, you expect to see 02/06, 06/06, 10/06.

In the examination tutorial, you also have a **Date** field—the process date. When you created it, you didn't specify a format because you took the system date which, by definition, is a date and Kettle knows it. But when writing this date to the output file, again you defined a format, in this case it was yyyy/MM/dd.

In general, when you are writing a date, the format attribute is used of format the data before sending it to the destination. In case you don't specify a format, Kettle sets a default format.

As said earlier, there are more combinations to define the format to a date field. For a complete reference, check the Sun Java API documentation located at `http://java.sun.com/javase/6/docs/api/java/text/SimpleDateFormat.html`.

Numeric fields

Numeric fields are present in almost all Kettle transformations. In the Examination example, you encountered numeric fields for the first time. The input file had four numeric fields. As the numbers were all integer, you didn't set a specific format. When you have more elaborate fields such as numbers with separators, dollar signs, and so on, you should specify a format to tell Kettle how to interpret the number. If you don't, Kettle will do its best to interpret the number, but this could lead to unexpected results.

At the other extreme of the flow, when writing to the output file text, you may specify the format in which you want the number to be shown.

There are several formats you may apply to a numeric field. The format is basically a combination of predefined symbols, each with a special meaning. The following are the most used symbols:

Symbol	Meaning
#	Digit Leading zeros are not shown
0	Digit If the digit is not present, zero is displayed in its place
.	Decimal separator
-	Minus sign
%	Field has to be multiplied by 100 and shown as a percentage

These symbols are not used alone. In order to specify the format of your numbers, you have to combine them. Suppose that you have a numeric field whose value is 99.55; the following table shows you the same value after applying different formats to it:

Format	Result
#	100
0	100
#.#	99.6
#.##	99.55
#.000	99.550
000.000	099.550

If you don't specify a format for your numbers, you may still provide a **Length** and **Precision**. Length is the total number of significant figures, while precision is the number of floating-point digits.

If you neither specify format nor length or precision, Kettle behaves as follow. While reading, it does its best to interpret the incoming number, and when writing, it sends the data as it comes without applying any format.

For a complete reference on number formats, you can check the Sun Java API documentation available at `http://java.sun.com/javase/6/docs/api/java/text/DecimalFormat.html`.

Running transformations from a terminal window

In the examination exercise, you specified that the name of the input file will be taken from the first command-line argument. That means when executing the transformation, the filename has to be supplied as an argument. Until now, you only ran transformations from inside Spoon. In the last exercise, you provided the argument by typing it in a dialog window. Now it is time to learn how to run transformations with or without arguments from a terminal window.

Time for action – running the examination transformation from a terminal window

Before executing the transformation from a terminal window, make sure that you have a new examination file to process, let's say `exam3.txt`. Then follow these instructions:

1. Open a terminal window and go to the directory where Kettle is installed.

   ❑ On Windows systems type:

   ```
   C:\pdi-ce>pan.bat /file:c:\pdi_labs\examinations.ktr c:\
   pdi_files\input\exam3.txt
   ```

   ❑ On Unix, Linux, and other Unix-based systems type:

   ```
   /home/yourself/pdi-ce/pan.sh /file:/home/yourself/pdi_labs/
   examinations.ktr c:/pdi_files/input/exam3.txt
   ```

   ❑ If your transformation is in another folder, modify the command accordingly.

2. You will see how the transformation runs, showing you the log in the terminal.

```
C:\WINDOWS\system32\cmd.exe
C:\pdi-ce>pan.bat /file:c:\pdi_labs\examinations.ktr c:\pdi_files\input\exam3.txt
INFO  04-06 13:13:56,281 - Pan - Start of run.
INFO  04-06 13:13:57,796 - Using "C:\DOCUME~1\ADMIN~1\CONFIG~1\Temp\vfs_cache" as temporary fil
INFO  04-06 13:13:58,609 - Examination results - Dispatching started for transformation [Examina
INFO  04-06 13:13:58,640 - Examination results - This transformation can be replayed with replay
/04 13:13:58
INFO  04-06 13:13:58,656 - Get file name.0 - Finished processing (I=0, O=0, R=1, W=1, U=0, E=0)
INFO  04-06 13:13:59,015 - Reading the input file.0 - Opening file: c:\pdi_files\input\exam3.txt
INFO  04-06 13:13:59,359 - Reading the input file.0 - Finished processing (I=19, O=0, R=1, W=18,
INFO  04-06 13:13:59,390 - Get date (today).0 - Finished processing (I=0, O=0, R=18, W=18, U=0,
INFO  04-06 13:13:59,421 - Appending to global file.0 - Finished processing (I=0, O=18, R=18, W=
INFO  04-06 13:13:59,421 - Pan - Finished!
INFO  04-06 13:13:59,421 - Pan - Start=2009/06/04 13:13:58.406, Stop=2009/06/04 13:13:59.421
INFO  04-06 13:13:59,421 - Pan - Processing ended after 1 seconds.
INFO  04-06 13:13:59,421 - Examination results -
INFO  04-06 13:13:59,421 - Examination results - Step Reading the input file.0 ended successfull
8 lines. ( 18 lines/s)
INFO  04-06 13:13:59,421 - Examination results - Step Get date (today).0 ended successfully, pro
s. ( 18 lines/s)
INFO  04-06 13:13:59,421 - Examination results - Step Appending to global file.0 ended successfu
 18 lines. ( 18 lines/s)
INFO  04-06 13:13:59,421 - Examination results - Step Get file name.0 ended successfully, proces
 1 lines/s)

C:\pdi-ce>
```

3. Check the output file. The contents of `exam3.txt` should be at the end of the file.

What just happened?

You executed a transformation with **Pan**, the program that runs transformations from terminal windows. As part of the command, you specified the name of the transformation file and provided the name of the file to process, which was the only argument expected by the transformation. As a result, you got the same as if you had run the transformation from Spoon—a small file appended to the global file.

When you are designing transformations, you run them with Spoon; you don't use Pan. Pan is mainly used as part of batch processes, for example processes that run every night in a scheduled fashion.

 Appendix B tells you all the details about using Pan.

Have a go hero – using different date formats

Change the main transformation of the last tutorial so that the `process_date` is saved with a full format, that is, including day of week (Monday, Tuesday, and so on), month in letters (January, February, and so on), and time.

Go for a hero – formatting 99.55

Create a transformation to see for yourself the different formats for the number 99.55. Test the formats shown in the *Numeric fields* section and try some other options as well.

 To test this, you will need a dataset with a single row and a single field—the number. You can generate it with a **Generate rows** step.

Pop quiz–formatting data

Suppose that you read a file where the first column is a numeric identifier: 1, 2, 3, and so on. You read the field as a Number. Now you want to send the data back to a file. Despite being a number, this field is regular text to you because it is a code. How do you define the field in the **Text output** step (you may choose more than one option):

a.   As a Number. In the format, you put #.

b.   As a String. In the format, you put #.

c.   As a String. You leave the format blank.

XML files

Even if you're not a system developer, you must have heard about XML files. XML files or documents are not only used to store data, but also to exchange data between heterogeneous systems over the Internet. PDI has many features that enable you to manipulate XML files. In this section you will learn to get data from those files.

Time for action – getting data from an XML file with information about countries

In this tutorial you will build an Excel file with basic information about countries. The source will be an XML file that you can download from the Packt website.

1.   If you work under Windows, open the kettle.properties file located in the C:/Documents and Settings/yourself/.kettle folder and add the following line:

```
LABSOUTPUT=c:/pdi_files/output
```

On the other hand, if you work under Linux (or similar), open the `kettle.properties` file located in the `/home/yourself/.kettle` folder and add the following line:

```
LABSOUTPUT=/home/yourself/pdi_files/output
```

2. Make sure that the directory specified in `kettle.properties` exists.

3. Save the file.

4. Restart Spoon.

5. Create a new transformation.

6. Give a name to the transformation and save it in the same directory you have all the other transformations.

7. From the Packt website, download the resources folder containing a file named `countries.xml`. Save the folder in your working directory. For example, if your transformations are in `pdi_labs`, the file will be in `pdi_labs/resources/`.

 The last two steps are important. Don't skip them! If you do, some of the following steps will fail.

8. Take a look at the file. You can edit it with any text editor, or you can double-click it to see it within an explorer. In any case, you will see information about countries. This is just the extract for a single country:

```xml
<?xml version="1.0" encoding="UTF-8"?>
<world>
...
  <country>
        <name>Argentina</name>
        <capital>Buenos Aires</capital>
        <language isofficial="T">
                <name>Spanish</name>
                <percentage>96.8</percentage>
        </language>
        <language isofficial="F">
                <name>Italian</name>
                <percentage>1.7</percentage>
        </language>
        <language isofficial="F">
```

```
           <name>Indian Languages</name>
           <percentage>0.3</percentage>
        </language>
   </country>
 ...
 </world>
```

9. From the **Input** steps, drag a **Get data from XML** step to the canvas.

10. Open the configuration window for this step by double-clicking it.

11. In the **File or directory** textbox, press *Ctrl+Space*. A drop-down list appears as shown in the next screenshot:

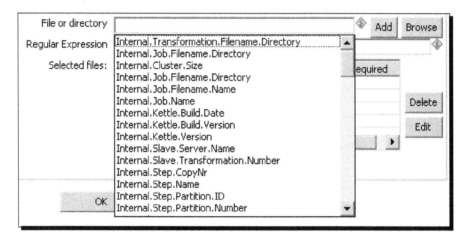

12. Select `Internal.Transformation.Filename.Directory`. The textbox gets filled with this text.

13. Complete the text so that you can read `${Internal.Transformation.Filename.Directory}/resources/countries.xml`.

14. Click on the **Add** button. The full path is moved to the grid.

15. Select the **Content** tab and click **Get XPath nodes**.

16. In the list that appears, select **/world/country/language**.

17. Select the **Fields** tab and fill the grid as follows:

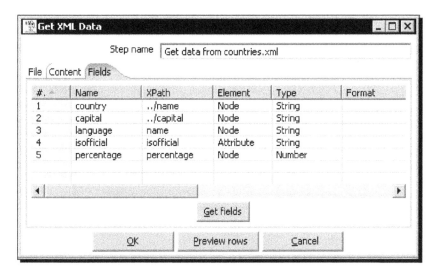

18. Click **Preview rows**, and you should see something like this:

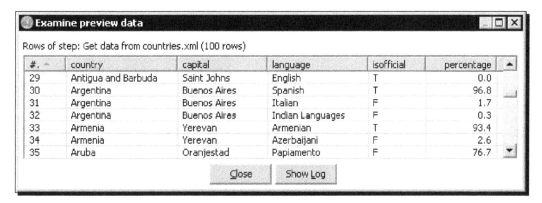

19. Click **OK**.

20. From the **Output** steps, drag an **Excel Output** step to the canvas.

21. Create a hop from the **Get data from XML** step to the **Excel Output** step.

22. Open the configuration window for this step by double-clicking it.

23. In the **Filename** textbox press *Ctrl+Space*.

24. From the drop-down list, select $\{\text{LABSOUTPUT}\}$.

25. By the side of that text type /countries_info. The complete text should be $\{\text{LABSOUTPUT}\}$/countries_info.

26. Select the **Fields** tab and click the **Get Fields** button to fill the grid.

27. Click **OK**. This is your final transformation.

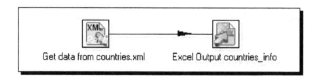

Get data from countries.xml   Excel Output countries_info

28. Save the transformation.

29. Run the transformation.

30. Check that the countries_info.xls file has been created in the output directory and contains the information you previewed in the input step.

What just happened?

You got information about countries from an XML file and saved it in a more readable format—an Excel spreadsheet—for the common people.

To get the information, you used a **Get data from XML** step. As the source file was taken from a folder relative to the folder where you stored the transformation, you set the directory to $\{\text{Internal.Transformation.Filename.Directory}\}$. When the transformation ran, Kettle replaced $\{\text{Internal.Transformation.Filename.Directory}\}$ with the real path of the transformation: c:/pdi_labs/.

In the same way, you didn't put a fixed value for the path of the final Excel file. As directory, you used $\{\text{LABSOUTPUT}\}$. When the transformation ran, Kettle replaced $\{\text{LABSOUTPUT}\}$ with the value you wrote in the kettle.properties file. The output file was then saved in that folder: c:/pdi_files/output.

What is XML

XML stands for **EXtensible Markup Language**. It is basically a language designed to describe data. XML files or documents contain information wrapped in tags. Look at this piece of XML taken from the countries file:

```
<?xml version="1.0" encoding="UTF-8"?>
<world>
...
 <country>
    <name>Argentina</name>
    <capital>Buenos Aires</capital>
    <language isofficial="T">
        <name>Spanish</name>
        <percentage>96.8</percentage>
    </language>
    <language isofficial="F">
        <name>Italian</name>
        <percentage>1.7</percentage>
    </language>
    <language isofficial="F">
        <name>Indian Languages</name>
        <percentage>0.3</percentage>
    </language>
 </country>
...
</world>
```

The first line in the document is the XML declaration. It defines the XML version of the document, and should always be present.

Below the declaration is the body of the document. The body is a set of nested elements. An **element** is a logical piece enclosed by a start-tag and a matching end-tag—for example, `<country> </country>`.

Within the start-tag of an element, you may have attributes. An **attribute** is a markup construct consisting of a name/value pair—for example, `isofficial="F"`.

These are the most basic terminology related to XML files. If you want to know more about XML, you can visit `http://www.w3schools.com/xml/`.

PDI transformation files

Despite the `.ktr` extension, PDI transformations are just XML files. As such, you are able to explore them inside and recognize different XML elements. Look the following sample text:

```
<?xml version="1.0" encoding="UTF-8"?>
<transformation>
  <info>
    <name>hello_world</name>
    <description>My first transformation</description>
    <extended_description>
        This transformation generates 10 rows
        with the message Hello World.
    </extended_description>
  ...
</transformation>
```

This is an extract from the `hello_world.ktr` file. Here you can see the root element named `transformation`, and some inner elements such as `info` and `name`.

Note that if you copy a step by selecting it in the Spoon canvas and pressing *Ctrl+C* , and then pass it to a text editor, you can see its XML definition. If you copy it back to the canvas, a new identical step will be added to your transformation.

Getting data from XML files

In order to get data from an XML file, you have to use the **Get Data From XML** input step. To tell PDI which information to get from the file, it is required that you use a particular notation named XPath.

XPath

XPath is a set of rules used for getting information from an XML document. In XPath, XML documents are treated as trees of **nodes**. There are several types of nodes; elements, attributes, and texts are some of them. As an example, `world`, `country,` and `isofficial` are some of the nodes in the sample file.

Among the nodes there are relationships. A node has a parent, zero or more children, siblings, ancestors, and descendants depending on where the other nodes are in the hierarchy.

In the sample countries file, `country` is the the parent of the elements `name`, `capital`, and `language`. These three elements are children of `country`.

To select a node in an XML document, you have to use a path expression relative to a **current node**.

The following table has some examples of path expressions that you may use to specify fields. The examples assume that the current node is `language`.

Path expression	Description	Sample expression
`node_name`	Selects all child nodes of the node named `node_name`.	`percentage` This expression selects all child nodes of the node percentage. It looks for the node percentage inside the current node language.
`.`	Selects the current node	`language`
`..`	Selects the parent of the current node	`../capital` This expression selects all child nodes of the node `capital`. It doesn't look in the current node (`language`), but inside its parent, which is `country`.
`@`	Selects an attribute	`@isofficial` This expression gets the attribute `isofficial` in the current node `language`.

 Note that the expressions name and `../name` are not the same. The first selects the name of the language, while the second selects the name of the country.

For more information on XPath, follow this link: `http://www.w3schools.com/XPath/`.

Configuring the Get data from XML step

In order to specify the name and location of an XML file, you have to fill the **File** tab just as you do in any file input step. What is different here is how you get the data.

The first thing you have to do is select the path that will identify the current node. You do it by filling the **Loop XPath** textbox in the **Content** tab. You can type it by hand, or you can select it from the list of available paths by Clicking the **Get XPath nodes** button.

Once you have selected a path, PDI will generate one row of data for every found path.

In the tutorial you selected `/world/country/language`. Then PDI generates one row for each `/world/country/language` element in the file.

After selecting the loop XPath, you have to specify the fields to get. In order to do that, you have to fill the grid in the **Fields** tab by using XPath notation as explained in the preceding section.

Note that if you click the **Get fields** button, PDI will fill the grid with the child nodes of the current node. If you want to get some other node, you have to type its XPath by hand.

Also note the notation for the attributes. To get an attribute, you can use the @ notation as explained, or you can simply type the name of the attribute without @ and select **Attribute** under the **Element** column, as you did in the tutorial.

Kettle variables

In the last tutorial, you used the string ${Internal.Transformation.Filename. Directory} to identify the folder where the current transformation was saved. You also used the string ${LABSOUTPUT} to define the destination folder of the output file.

Both strings, ${Internal.Transformation.Filename.Directory} and ${LABSOUTPUT}, are Kettle variables, that is, keywords linked to a value. You use the name of a variable, and when the transformation runs, the name of the variable is replaced by its value.

The first of these two variables is an environment variable, and it is not the only available. Other known environment variables are ${user.home}, ${java.io.tmpdir}, and ${java.home}. All these variables are ready to use any time you need.

The second variable is a variable you defined in the kettle.properties file. In this file you may define as many variables as you want. The only thing you have to keep in mind is that those variables will be available inside Spoon after you restart it.

These two kinds of variables—environment variables and variables defined in the kettle.properties file—are the most primitive kinds of variables found in PDI. All of these variables are string variables and their scope is the Java virtual machine.

How and when you can use variables

Any time you see a red dollar sign by the side of a textbox, you may use a variable. Inside the textbox you can mix variable names with static text, as you did in the tutorial when you put the name of the destination as ${LABSOUTPUT}/countries_info.

To see all the available variables, you have to position the cursor in the textbox, press *Ctrl+Space*, and a full list is displayed for you to select the variable of your choice. If you put the mouse cursor over any of the variables for a second, the actual value of the variable will be shown.

If you know the name of the variable, you don't need to select it from the list. You may type its name, by using either of these notations—${<name>} or %%<name>%%.

Have a go hero – exploring XML files

Now you can explore by yourself. On the Packt website there are some sample XML files. Download them and try this:

- Read the `customer.xml` file and create a list of customers.
- Read the `tomcat-users.xml` file and get the users and their passwords.
- Read the `areachart.xml` and get the color palette, that is, the list of colors used.

 The customer file is included in the Pentaho Report Designer software package. The others come with the Pentaho BI package. This software has many XML files for you to use. If you are interested you can download the software from `http://sourceforge.net/projects/pentaho/files/`.

Have a go hero – enhancing the output countries file

Modify the transformation in the tutorial so that the Excel output uses a template. The template will be an Excel file with the header and format already applied, and will be located in a folder inside the `pdi_labs` folder.

 Templates are configured in the **Content** tab of the Excel configuration window. In order to set the name for the template, use internal variables.

Have a go hero – documenting your work

As explained, transformations are nothing different than XML files. Now you'll create a new transformation that will take as input the transformations you've created so far, and will create a simple Excel spreadsheet with the name and description of all your transformations. If you keep this sheet updated by running the transformation on a regular basis, it will be easier to find a particular transformation you created in the past.

 To get data from the transformations files, use the **Get data from XML** step. As wildcard, use `.*\.ktr`. Doing so, you'll get all the files. On the other hand, as **Loop XPath**, use `/transformation/info`.

Summary

In this chapter you learned how to get data from files and put data back into files. Specifically, you learned how to:

◆ Get data from plain files and also from XML files

◆ Put data into text files and Excel files

◆ Get information from the operating system such as command-line arguments and system date

We also discussed the following:

◆ The main PDI terminology related to data, for example datasets, data types, and streams

◆ The Select values step, a commonly used step for selecting, reordering, removing and changing data

◆ How and when to use Kettle variables

◆ How to run transformations from a terminal with the `Pan` command

Now that you know how to get data into a transformation, you are ready to start manipulating data. This is going to happen in the next chapter.

3
Basic Data Manipulation

In the previous chapter, you learned how to get data into PDI. Now you're ready to begin transforming that data. This chapter explains the simplest and most used ways of transforming data. We will cover the following:

- Executing basic operations
- Filtering and sorting of data
- Looking up data outside the main stream of data

By the end of this chapter, you will be able to do simple but meaningful transformations on different types of data.

Basic calculations

You already know how to create a transformation and read data from an external source. Now, taking that data as a starting point, you will begin to do basic calculations.

Time for action – reviewing examinations by using the Calculator step

Can you recollect the exercise about examinations you did in the previous chapter? You created an incremental file with examination results. The final file looked like the following:

```
----------------------------------------------------------
Annual Language Examinations
Testing writing, reading, speaking and listening skills
----------------------------------------------------------
student_code;name;writing;reading;speaking;listening;file_
processed;process_date
80711-85;William Miller; 81;83;80;90;C:\pdi_files\input\first_turn.
txt;28-05-2009
20362-34;Jennifer Martin; 87;76;70;80;C:\pdi_files\input\first_turn.
txt;28-05-2009
75283-17;Margaret Wilson; 99;94;90;80;C:\pdi_files\input\first_turn.
txt;28-05-2009
83714-28;Helen  Thomas; 89;97;80;80;C:\pdi_files\input\first_turn.
txt;28-05-2009
61666-55;Maria Thomas; 88;77;70;80;C:\pdi_files\input\first_turn.
txt;28-05-2009
...
```

Now you want to convert all grades in the scale 0-100 to a new scale from 0 to 5. Also, you want to take the average grade to see how the students did.

1. Create a new transformation, give it a name and description, and save it.

2. By using a **Text file input** step, read the examination.txt file. Give the name and location of the file, check the **Content** tab to see that everything matches your file, and fill the **Fields** tab as here:

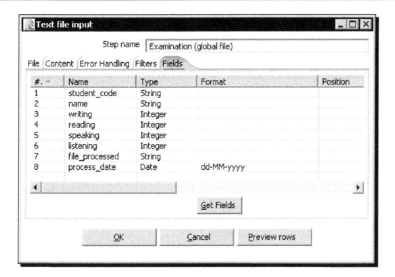

3. Do a preview just to confirm that the step is well configured.

 Notice that you have several lines as header. Because the names of the fields are not in the first row, you won't be able to use the **Get Fields** button successfully. You will have to write the fields manually, or you can avoid it by doing the following: Configure the step with a copy of the file that doesn't have the extra heading, just the heading row with the names of the fields. Then, restore the name of your file in the **File** tab, adjust the number of headings in the **Content** tab, and your step is ready.

4. Use the **Select values** step to remove the fields you will not use—file_processed and process_date.

5. Drag another **Select values** step to the canvas. Select the **Meta-data** tab and change the meta-data of the numeric fields like here:

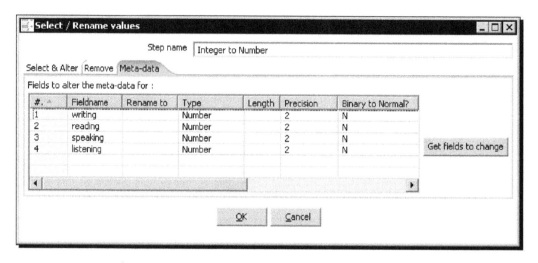

6. Near the upper-left corner of the screen, above the step tree, there is a textbox for searching. Type `calc` in the textbox. While you type, a filter is applied to show you only the steps that contain, in their name or description, the text you typed. You should be seeing this:

7. Among the steps you see, select the **Calculator** step and drag it to the canvas.

8. To remove the filter, clear the typed text.

9. Create a hop from the **Text file input** step to the **Calculator** step.

10. Edit the **Calculator** step and fill the grid as follows:

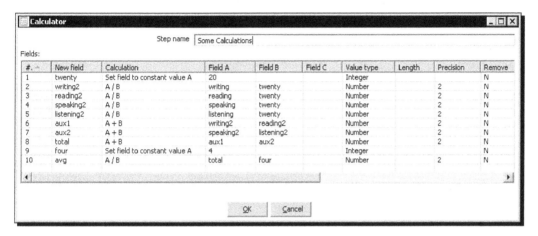

11. To fill the **Calculation** column, simply select the operation from the list provided. Be sure to fill every column in the grid like shown in the screenshot.

 You don't have to feel like you are doing data entry instead of learning PDI. You can avoid typing by copying and pasting similar rows, and then fixing the values properly. Appendix D has a list of shortcuts you can use when editing grids like these.

12. Leave the **Calculator** step selected and click the **Preview this transformation** button followed by the **Quick Launch** button. You should see something similar to the following screenshot:

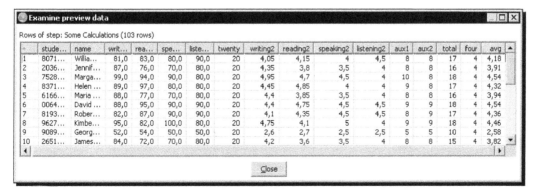

The numbers may vary according to the contents of your file.

13. Edit the calculator again and change the content of the **Remove** column like here:

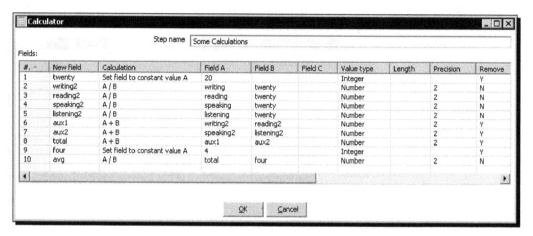

#. ▲	New field	Calculation	Field A	Field B	Field C	Value type	Length	Precision	Remove
1	twenty	Set field to constant value A	20			Integer			Y
2	writing2	A / B	writing	twenty		Number		2	N
3	reading2	A / B	reading	twenty		Number		2	N
4	speaking2	A / B	speaking	twenty		Number		2	N
5	listening2	A / B	listening	twenty		Number		2	N
6	aux1	A + B	writing2	reading2		Number		2	Y
7	aux2	A + B	speaking2	listening2		Number		2	Y
8	total	A + B	aux1	aux2		Number		2	Y
9	four	Set field to constant value A	4			Integer			Y
10	avg	A / B	total	four		Number		2	N

14. From the **Transform** category of steps, add a **Sort rows** step and create a hop from the **Calculator** step to this new step.

15. Edit the **Sort rows** step by double-clicking it, click the **Get Fields** button, and adjust the grid as follows:

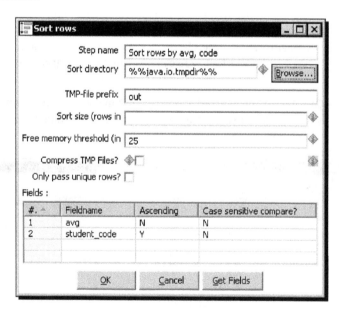

#. ▲	Fieldname	Ascending	Case sensitive compare?
1	avg	N	N
2	student_code	Y	N

16. Click **OK**.

17. Drag a third **Select values** step, create a hop from the **Sort rows** step to this new step, and use it to keep only the fields by which you ordered the data:

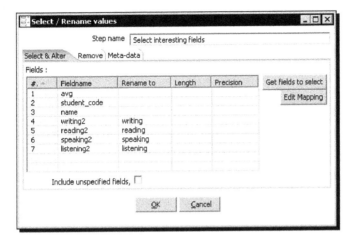

18. From the **Flow** category of steps, add a **Dummy step** and create a hop from the last **Select values** step to this.

19. Select the **Dummy step** and do a preview.

20. The final preview looks like the following screenshot:

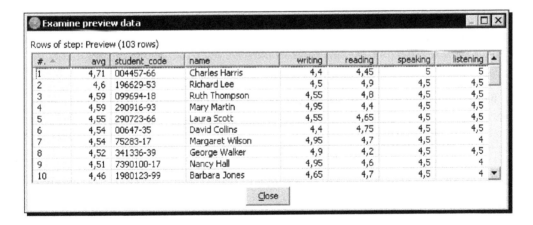

If you get an error or a different result, review the explanation and make sure that you followed the instructions correctly. Do a preview on each step to discover in which one you have the problem. If you realize that the problem is in any of the steps that read the input files, please refer to the *Troubleshooting reading files* section in Chapter 2.

What just happened?

You read the `examination.txt` file, and did some calculations to see how the students did. You did the calculations by using the **Calculator** step.

First of all, you removed the fields you didn't need from the stream of data.

After that, you did the following calculations:

By dividing by 20, you converted all grades from the scale 0-100 to the scale 0-5.

Then, you calculated the average of the grades for the four skills—writing, reading, listening, and speaking. You created two auxiliary fields, `aux1` and `aux2`, to calculate partial sums. After that, you created the field `total` with the sum of `aux1` and `aux2`, another auxiliary field with the number **4**, and finally the `avg` as the division of the total by the field `four`.

In order to obtain the new grades, as well as the average with two decimal positions, you need the result of the operation to be of a numeric type with precision **2**. Therefore, you had to change the metadata, by adding a **Select values** step before the **Calculator**. With the **Select values** you changed the type of the numeric fields from integer to number, that is, float numbers. If you didn't, the quotients would have been rounded to integer numbers. You can try and see for yourself!

The first time you edited the calculator, you set the field **Remove** to N for every row in the calculator grid. By doing this, you could preview every field created in the calculator, even the auxiliary ones such as the fields `twenty`, `aux1`, and `aux2`. You then changed the field to Y so that the auxiliary fields didn't pass to the next step.

After doing the calculations, you sorted the data by using a **Sort rows** step. You specified the order by `avg` descending, then by `student_code` ascending.

Sorting data

For small datasets, the sorting algorithm runs mainly using the JVM memory. When the number of rows exceeds 5,000, it works differently. Every five thousand rows, the process sorts them and writes them to a temporary file. When there are no more rows, it does a merge sort on all those files and gives you back the sorted dataset. You can conclude that for huge datasets a lot of reading and writing operations are done on your disk, which slows down the whole transformation. Fortunately, you can change the number of rows in memory (5,000 by default) by setting a new value in the **Sort size (rows in memory)** textbox. The bigger this number, the faster the sorting process.

Note that a sort size that works in your system may not work in a machine with a different configuration. To avoid that risk, you can use a different approach. In the **Sort rows** configuration window, you can set a **Free memory threshold (in %)** value. The process begins to use temporary files when the percentage of available memory drops below the indicated threshold. The lower the percentage, the faster the process.

As it's not possible to know the exact amount of free memory, it's not recommended to set a very small free memory threshold. You definitely shouldn't use that option in complex transformations or when there is more than one sort going on, as you could still run out of memory.

The two final steps were added to keep only the fields of interest, and to preview the result of the transformation. You can change the **Dummy** step for any of the output steps you already know.

You've used the **Dummy** step several times but still nothing has been said about it. Mainly it was because it does nothing! However, you can use it as a placeholder for testing purposes as in the last exercise.

Note that in this tutorial you used the **Select values** step in three different ways:

- To remove fields by using the **Remove** tab.
- To change the meta-data of some fields by using the **Meta-data** tab.
- To select and rename fields by using the **Select** tab.

Remember that the **Select values** step's tabs are exclusive! You can't use more than one in the same step!

Besides calculation, in this tutorial you did something you hadn't before—searching the step tree.

 When you don't remember where a step is in the steps tree, or when you just want to find if there is a step that does some kind of operation, you could simply type the search criterion in the textbox above the steps tree. PDI does a search and filters all the steps that have that text as part of their name or description.

Adding or modifying fields by using different PDI steps

In this tutorial you used the **Calculator** step to create new fields and add them to your dataset. The **Calculator** is one the many steps that PDI has to create new fields by combining existent ones. Usually you will find these steps under the **Transform** category of the steps tree. The following table describes some of them (the examples refer to the examination file):

Step	Description	Example
Split Fields	Split a single field into two or more. You have to give the character that acts as separator.	Split the name into two fields: Name and Last Name. The separator would be a space character.
Add constants	Add one or more constants to the input rows	Add two constants: four and twenty. Then you could use them in the **Calculator** step without defining the auxiliary fields.
Replace in string	Replace all occurrences of a text in a string field with another text	Replace the – in the student code by a /. For example: 108418-95 would become 108418/95.
Number range	Create a new field based on ranges of values. Applies to a numeric field.	Create a new field called exam_range with two ranges: Range A with the students with average grade below 3.5, and Range B with students with average grade greater or equal to 3.5.
Value Mapper	Creates a correspondence between the values of a field and a new set of values.	Suppose you calculated the average grade as an integer number ranging from 0 to 5. You can map the average to A, B, C, D, like this: Old value: 5; New value: A Old value: 3, 4; New value: B Old value: 1, 2; New value: C Old value: 0; New value: D

Step	Description	Example
User Defined Java Expression	Creates a new field by using a Java expression that involves one or more fields. This step may eventually replace any of the above but it's only recommended for those familiar with Java.	Create a flag (a Boolean field) that tells if a student passed. A student passes if his/her average grade is above `4.5`. The expression to use could be: `(((writing+reading+speaking+ listening)/4)>4.5)?true:false`

Any of these steps when added to your transformation, are executed for every row in the stream. It takes the row, identifies the fields needed to do its tasks, calculates the new field(s), and adds it to the dataset.

For details on a particular step, don't hesitate to visit the Wiki page for steps:
`http://wiki.pentaho.com/display/EAI/Pentaho+Data+Integration+v3.2.+St eps`

The Calculator step

The **Calculator** step you used in the tutorial, allows you to do simple calculations not only on numeric fields, but also on data and text. The **Calculator** step is not the only means to do calculations, but it is the simplest. It allows you to do simple calculations in a quick fashion.

The step has a grid where you can add all the fields you want to. Every row represents an operation that involves from one up to three operands (depending on the selected operation). When you select an operation, the description of the operation itself tells you which argument it needs. For example:

- If you select **Set constant field to value A**, you have to provide a constant value under the column name **A**.
- If you select **A/B**, the operation needs two arguments, and you have to provide them by indicating the fields to use in the columns named **A** and **B** respectively.

The result of every operation becomes a new field in your dataset, unless you set the **Remove** column to `Y`. The name of the new field is the one you type under the **New field** column.

For each and every row of the data set, the operations defined in the **Calculator** are calculated in the order in which they appear. Therefore, you may create auxiliary fields and then use them in rows of the **Calculator** grid that are below them. That is what you did in the tutorial when you defined the auxiliary fields `aux1` and `aux2` and then used them in the field `total`.

Just like every grid in Kettle, you have a contextual menu (and its corresponding shortcuts) that lets you manipulate the rows by deleting, moving, copying and pasting, and so on.

The Formula step

The **Formula** step is another step you can use for doing calculations. Let's give it a try by using it in the examination tutorial.

Time for action – reviewing examinations by using the Formula step

In this tutorial you will redo the previous exercise, but this time you will do the calculations with the **Formula** step.

1. Open the transformation you just finished.

2. Delete from the transformation the **Calculator** step, and put in its place a **Formula** step. You will find it under the **Scripting** category of steps.

3. Add a field named `writing`.

4. When you click the cell under the **Formula** column, a window appears to edit the formula for the new field.

5. In the upper area of the window, type `[writing]/20`. You will notice that the sentence is red if it is incomplete or the syntax is incorrect. In that case, the error is shown below the editing area, like in the following example:

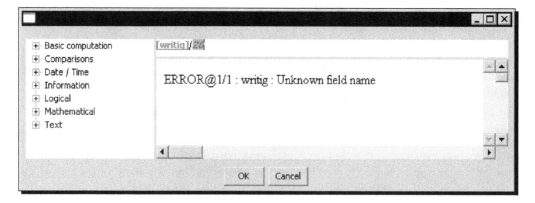

6. As soon as the formula is complete and correct, the red color disappears.

7. Click **OK**.

8. The formula you typed will be displayed in the cell you clicked.

9. Set `Number` as the type for the new field, and type `writing` in the **Replace value** column.

10. Add three more fields to the grid in the same way you added this field so that the grid looks like the following:

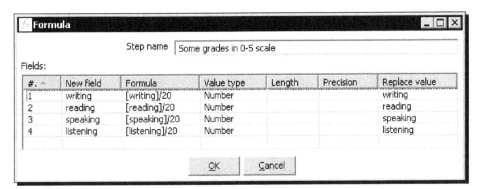

11. Click **OK**.

12. Add a second **Formula** step.

13. Add a field named `avg` and click the **Formula** cell to edit it.

14. Expand the **Mathematical** category of functions to the leftside of the window, and click the **AVERAGE** function.

15. The explanation of the selected function appears to guide you.

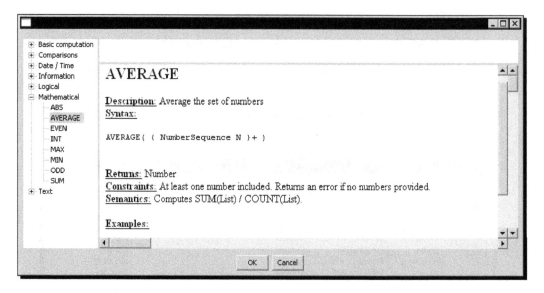

16. In the editing area, type `average([writing];[reading];[speaking]; [listening])`.

17. Click **OK**.

18. Set the **Value type** to `Number`.

19. Click **OK**.

20. Create a hop from this step to the **Sort rows** step.

21. Edit the last **Select values** step.

22. Click **Get fields to select**.

23. A question appears to ask you what to do. Click **Clear and add all**.

24. The grid is reloaded with the modified fields.

25. Click on the **Dummy** step and do a preview.

26. There should be no difference with what you had in the Calculator version of the tutorial:

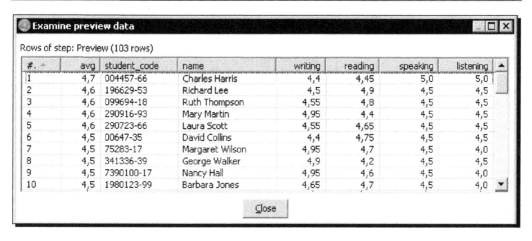

# ▲	avg	student_code	name	writing	reading	speaking	listening
1	4,7	004457-66	Charles Harris	4,4	4,45	5,0	5,0
2	4,6	196629-53	Richard Lee	4,5	4,9	4,5	4,5
3	4,6	099694-18	Ruth Thompson	4,55	4,8	4,5	4,5
4	4,6	290916-93	Mary Martin	4,95	4,4	4,5	4,5
5	4,6	290723-66	Laura Scott	4,55	4,65	4,5	4,5
6	4,5	00647-35	David Collins	4,4	4,75	4,5	4,5
7	4,5	75283-17	Margaret Wilson	4,95	4,7	4,5	4,0
8	4,5	341336-39	George Walker	4,9	4,2	4,5	4,5
9	4,5	7390100-17	Nancy Hall	4,95	4,6	4,5	4,0
10	4,5	1980123-99	Barbara Jones	4,65	4,7	4,5	4,0

What just happened?

You read the `examination.txt` file, and did some calculations using the Formula step to see how the students did.

It may happen that the preview window shows you less decimal positions than expected. This is a preview issue. One of the ways you have to see the numbers with more decimals is to send the numbers to an output file with a proper format and see the numbers in the file.

As you saw, you have quite a lot of functions available for building formulas and expressions. To reference a field you have to use square brackets, like in `[writing]`. You may reference only the current fields of the row. You have no way to access previous rows of the grid as you have in the **Calculator** step and so you needed two **Formula** steps to replace a single **Calculator**. But you saved auxiliary fields because the **Formula** allows you to type complex formulas in a single field without using partial calculations.

When the calculations are not simple, that is, they require resolving a complex formula or involve many operands, then you might prefer the **Formula** step over the **Calculator**.

The **Formula** step uses the library `Libformula`. The syntax used in `LibFormula` is based on the `OpenFormula` standard. For more information on `OpenFormula`, you may visit http://wiki.oasis-open.org/office/About_OpenFormula.

Have a go hero – listing students and their examinations results

Let's play a little with the examination file. Suppose you decide that only those students whose average grade was above 3.9 will pass the examination; the others will not. List the students ordered by average (desc.), last name (asc.), and name (asc.). The output list should have the following fields:

◆ Student code

◆ Name

◆ Last Name

◆ Passed (yes/no)

◆ average grade

Pop quiz – concatenating strings

Suppose that you want to create a new field as the student_code plus the name of the student separated by a space, as for example 867432-94 Linda Rodriguez. Which of the following are possible solutions for your problem:

a. Use a Calculator, using the calculation a+b+c, where a is student_code, b is a space, and c is the name field.

b. Use a Formula, using as formula [student_code]+" "+[name]

c. Use a Formula, using as formula [student_code]&" "&[name]

You may choose more than one option.

Calculations on groups of rows

You just learned to do simple operations for every row of a dataset. Now you are ready to go beyond. Suppose you have a list of daily temperatures of a given country over a year. You may want to know the overall average temperature, the average temperature by region, or the coldest day of the year. When you work with data, these types of calculations are a common requirement. In this section you will learn to address those requirements with PDI.

Time for action – calculating World Cup statistics by grouping data

Let's forget the examinations for a while, and retake the World Cup tutorial from the previous chapter. The file you obtained from that tutorial was a list of results of football matches. These are sample rows of the final file:

```
Match Date;Home Team;Away Team;Result
02/06;Italy;France;2-1
02/06;Argentina;Hungary;2-1
06/06;Italy;Hungary;3-1
06/06;Argentina;France;2-1
10/06;France;Hungary;3-1
10/06;Italy;Argentina;1-0
. . .
```

Now you want to take that information to obtain some statistics such as the maximum number of goals per match in a given day. To do it, follow these instructions:

1. Create a new transformation, give it a name and description, and save it.

2. By using a **Text file input** step, read the `wcup_first_round.txt` file you generated in Chapter 2. Give the name and location of the file, check the **Content** tab to see that everything matches your file, and fill the **Fields** tab.

3. Do a preview just to confirm that the step is well configured.

4. From the **Transform** category of step, select a **Split Fields** step, drag it to the work area, and create a hop from the **Text file input** to this step.

5. Double-click the **Split Fields** steps and fill the grid like done in the following screenshot:

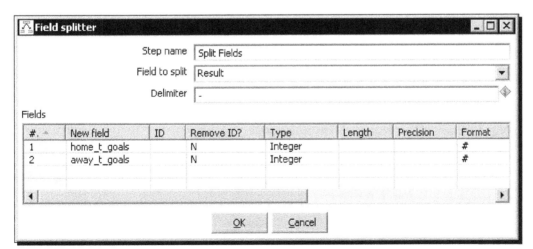

6. Add a **Calculator** step to the transformation and create a hop from the **Split Fields** step to this step and edit the step to create the following new fields:

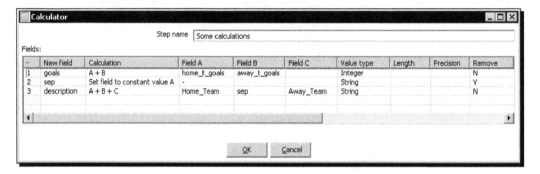

7. Add a **Sort rows** step to the transformation, create a hop from the **Calculator** step to this step, and sort the fields by Match_Date.

8. Expand the **Statistics** category of steps, and drag a **Group by** step to the canvas. Create a hop from the **Sort rows** step to this new step.

9. Edit the **Group by** step and fill the configuration window as shown next:

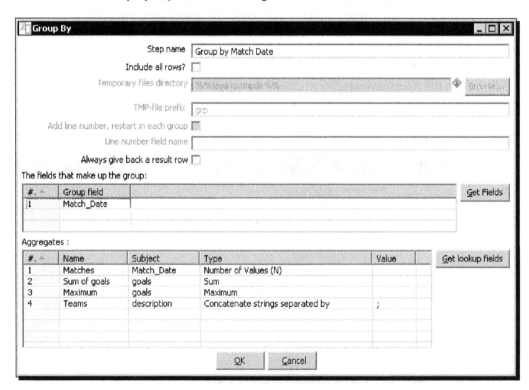

10. When you click the **OK** button, a window appears to warn you that this step needs the input to be sorted on the specified keys—the `Range` field in this case. Click **I understand**, and don't worry because you already sorted the data in the previous step.

11. Add a final **Dummy** step.

12. Select the **Dummy** and the **Group by** steps, left-click one and holding down the *Shift* key, left-click the other.

13. Click the **Preview this transformation** button. You will see the the following:

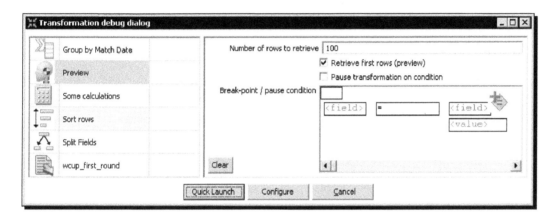

14. Click **Quick Launch**. The following window appears:

15. Double-click the **Sort rows** step. A window appears with the data coming out of the **Sort rows** step.

16. Double-click the **Dummy** step. A window appears with the data coming out of the **Dummy** step.

17. If you rearrange the preview windows, you can see both preview windows at a time, and understand better what happened with the numbers. The following would be the data shown in the windows:

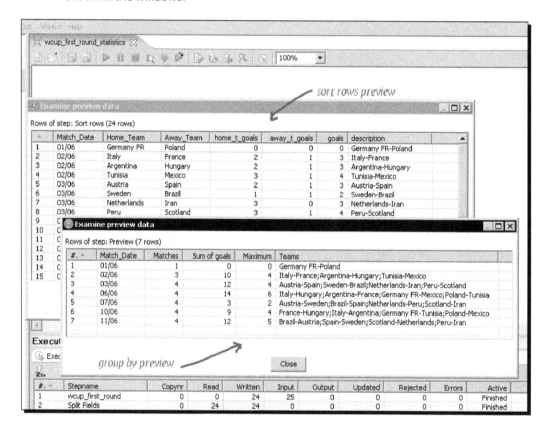

What just happened?

You opened a file with results from several matches and got some statistics from it.

In the file, there was a column with the match result in the format n-m, with n being the goals of the home team and m being the goals of the away team. With the **Split Fields** step, you split this field in two—one with each of these two numbers.

With the **Calculator** you did two things:

♦   You created a new field with the total number of goals for each match.

♦   You created a description for the match.

Note that in order to create a description, you used the + operator to concatenate string rather than add numbers.

After that, you ordered the data by match date with a **Sort rows** step.

In the preview window of the **Sort rows** step, you could see all the calculated fields: home team goals, away team goals, match goals, and description.

Finally, you did some statistical calculations:

◆ First, you grouped the rows by match date. You did this by typing `Match_Date` in the upper grid of the **Group by** step.

◆ Then, for every match date, you calculated some statistics. You did the calculations by adding rows in the lower grid of the step, one for every statistic you needed.

Let's see how it works. Because the **Group by** step was preceded by a **Sort rows** step, the rows came to the step already ordered. When the rows arrive to the **Group by** step, Kettle creates groups based on the field(s) indicated in the upper grid—the **Match_Date** field in this case. The following drawing shows this idea:

#.	Match_Date	Home_Team	Away_Team	home_t_goals	away_t_goals	goals	description
1	01/06	Germany FR	Poland	0	0	0	Germany FR-Poland
2	02/06	Italy	France	2	1	3	Italy-France
3	02/06	Argentina	Hungary	2	1	3	Argentina-Hungary
4	02/06	Tunisia	Mexico	3	1	4	Tunisia-Mexico
5	03/06	Austria	Spain	2	1	3	Austria-Spain
6	03/06	Sweden	Brazil	1	1	2	Sweden-Brazil
7	03/06	Netherlands	Iran	3	0	3	Netherlands-Iran
0	03/06	Peru	Scotland	3	1	4	Peru-Scotland
9	06/06	Italy	Hungary	3	1	4	Italy-Hungary
10	06/06	Argentina	France	2	1	3	Argentina-France
11	06/06	Germany FR	Mexico	6	0	6	Germany FR-Mexico
12	06/06	Poland	Tunisia	1	0	1	Poland-Tunisia
13	07/06	Austria	Sweden	1	0	1	Austria-Sweden
14	07/06	Brazil	Spain	0	0	0	Brazil-Spain
15	07/06	Netherlands	Peru	0	0	0	Netherlands-Peru
16	07/06	Scotland	Iran	1	1	2	Scotland-Iran
17	10/06	France	Hungary	3	1	4	France-Hungary
18	10/06	Italy	Argentina	1	0	1	Italy-Argentina
19	10/06	Germany FR	Tunisia	0	0	0	Germany FR-Tunisia
20	10/06	Poland	Mexico	3	1	4	Poland-Mexico
21	11/06	Brazil	Austria	1	0	1	Brazil-Austria
22	11/06	Spain	Sweden	1	0	1	Spain-Sweden
23	11/06	Scotland	Netherlands	3	2	5	Scotland-Netherlands
24	11/06	Peru	Iran	4	1	5	Peru-Iran

group field

sample group

Then, for every group, the fields that you put in the lower grid are calculated. Let's see, for example, the group for the match date 03/06. For the rows in this group, Kettle calculated the following:

- ◆ Matches: The number of matches played on 03/06. There were 4.

- ◆ Sum of goals: The total number of goals converted on 03/06. There were 3+2+3+4=12.

- ◆ Maximum: The maximum number of goals converted in a single match played on **03/06**. The maximum among 3, 2, 3, and 4 was 4.

- ◆ Teams: The descriptions of the teams which played on **03/06**, separated by ; : **Austria-Spain; Sweden-Brazil; Netherlands-Iran; Peru-Scotland**.

The same calculations were made for every group. You can verify the details by looking in the preview window.

Look at the **Step Metrics** tab in the **Execution Results** area of the screen:

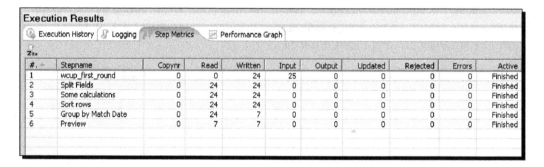

Note that 24 rows entered the **Group by** step and only 7 came out of that step towards the **Dummy** step. That is because after the grouping, you no longer have the detail of matches. The output of the **Group by** step is your new data now—one row for every group created.

Group by step

The **Group by** step allows you to create groups of rows and calculate new fields over those groups.

In order to define the groups, you have to specify which field(s) are the keys. For every combination of values for those fields, Kettle builds a new group.

In the tutorial you grouped by a single field `Match_date`. Then for every value of `Match_date`, Kettle created a different group.

The **Group by** step operates on consecutive rows. Suppose that the rows are already sorted by date, but those with date 10/06 are above the rest. The step traverses the dataset and each time the value for any of the grouping field changes, it creates a new group. If you see it this way, you will notice that the step will work even if the data is not sorted by the grouping field.

 As you probably don't know how the data is ordered, it is safer and recommended that you sort the data by using a **Sort rows** step just before using a **Group by** step.

Once you have defined the groups, you are free to specify new fields to be calculated for every group. Every new field is defined as an aggregate function over some of the existent fields.

Let's review some of the fields you created in the tutorial:

◆ The `Matches` field is the result of applying the `Number of values` function over the field `Match_date`.

◆ The `Sum of goals` field is the result of applying the `Sum` function over the field `goals`.

◆ The `Maximum` field is the result of applying the `Maximum` function over the field `goals`.

Finally, you have the option to calculate aggregate functions over the whole dataset. You do this by leaving the upper grid blank. Following the same example, you could calculate the total number of matches and the average number of goals for all those matches. This is how you do it:

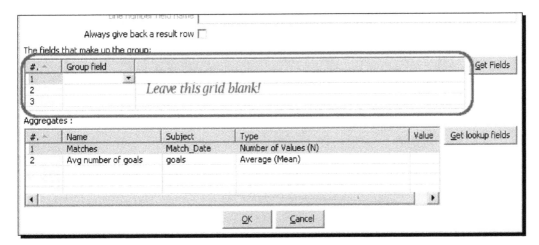

The following is what you get:

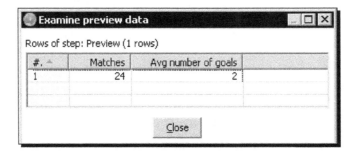

In any case, as a result of the **Group by** step, you will no longer have the detailed rows, unless you check the **Include all rows?** checkbox.

Have a go hero – calculating statistics for the examinations

Here you have one more task related with the examinations file. Create a new transformation, read the file, and calculate:

- The number of students who passed
- The number of students who failed
- The average writing, reading, speaking, and listening grade obtained by students who passed
- The average writing, reading, speaking, and listening grade obtained by students who failed
- The minimum and maximum average grade among students who passed
- The minimum and maximum average grade among students who failed

 Use the **Number range** step to define the range of the average grade; then use a **Group by** step to calculate the statistics.

Have a go hero – listing the languages spoken by country

Read the file with countries' information you used in Chapter 2. Build a file where each row has two columns—the name of a country and the list of spoken languages in that country.

 As aggregate, use the option **Concatenate strings separated by**.

Filtering

Until now you learned how to accomplish several kinds of calculations that enriched the set of data. There is still another kind of operation that is frequently used, and does not have to do with enriching the data but with discarding data. It is filtering unwanted data. Now you will learn how to discard rows under given conditions.

Time for action – counting frequent words by filtering

Let's suppose, you have some plain text files, and you want to know what is said in them. You don't want to read them, so you decide to count the times that words appear in the text, and see the most frequent ones to get an idea of what the files are about.

 Before starting, you'll need at least one text file to play with. The text file used in this tutorial is named `smcng10.txt` and is available for you to download from the Packt website.

Let's work:

1. Create a new transformation.

2. By using a **Text file input** step, read your file. The trick here is to put as a separator a sign you are not expecting in the file, for example |. By doing so, the entire line would be recognized as a single field. Configure the **Fields** tab by defining a single string field named `line`.

3. From the **Transform** category of step, drag to the canvas a **Split field to rows** step, and create a hop from **Text file input** step to this new step.

4. Configure the step like this:

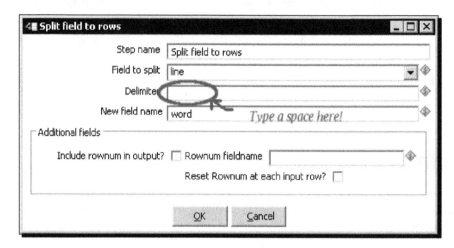

5. With this last step selected, do a preview. Your preview window should look like this:

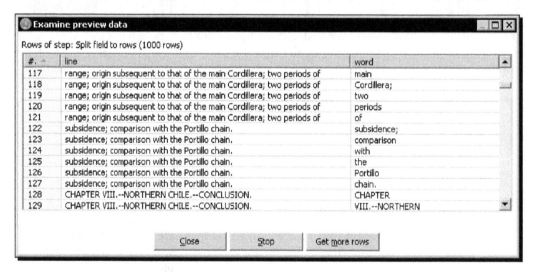

6. Close the preview window.

7. Expand the **Flow** category of steps, and drag a **Filter rows** step to the work area.

8. Create a hop from the last step to the **Filter rows** step.

9. Edit the **Filter rows** step by double-clicking it.

10. Click the `<field>` textbox to the left of the `=` sign. The list of fields appears. Select `word`.

11. Click the `=` sign. A list of operations appears. Select `IS NOT NULL`.

12. The window looks like the following:

13. Click **OK**.

14. From the **Transform** category of steps drag a **Sort rows** step to the canvas, and create a hop from the **Filter rows** step to this new step.

15. Sort the rows by `word`.

16. From the **Statistics** category, drag a **Group by** step, and create a hop from the **Sort rows** step to this step.

17. Configure the grids in the **Group by** configuration window like shown:

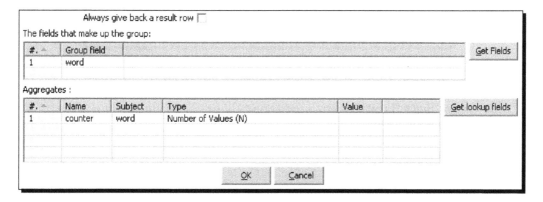

18. Add a **Calculator** step, create a hop from the last step to this, and calculate the new field `len_word` representing the length of the words. For that, use the calculator function `Return the length of a string A` and select `word` from the drop-down menu for **Field A**.

19. Expand the **Flow** category and drag another **Filter rows** step to the canvas.

20. Create a hop from the **Calculator** step to this step and edit it.

21. Click `<field>` and select `counter`.

22. Click the = sign, and select >.

23. Click `<value>`. A small window appears.

24. In the **Value** textbox of the little window, `enter 2`.

25. Click **OK**.

26. Position the mouse cursor over the icon in the upper-right corner of the window. When the text **Add condition** shows up, click on the icon.

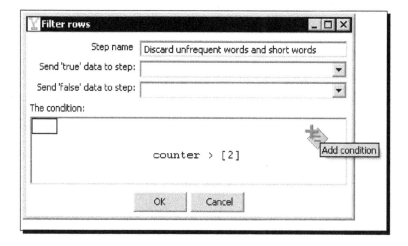

27. A new blank condition is shown below the one you created.

28. Click on **null = []** and create the condition `len_word>3`, in the same way you created the condition `counter>2`.

29. Click **OK**.

30. The final condition looks like this:

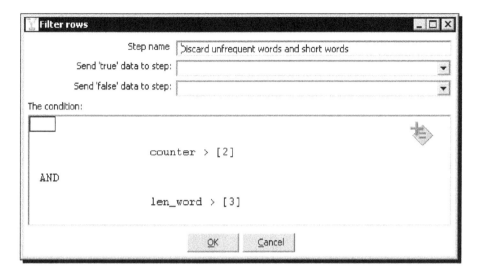

31. Add one more **Filter rows** step to the transformation and create a hop from the last step to this new step.

32. On the left side of the condition, select `word`.

33. As comparator select **IN LIST**.

34. At the end of the condition, inside the textbox **value**, type the following:
`a;an;and;the;that;this;there;these.`

35. Click the upper-left square above the condition and the word **NOT** will appear.

36. The condition looks like the following:

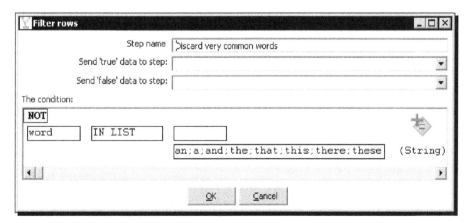

37. Add a **Sort rows** step, create a hop from the previous step to this step, and sort the rows in the descending order of `counter`.

38. Add a **Dummy** step at the end of the transformation, create a hop from the last step to the **Dummy** step.

39. With the **Dummy** step selected, preview the transformation. The following is what you should see now:

What just happened?

You read a regular plain file and arranged the words that appear in the file in some particular fashion.

The first thing you did was to read the plain file and split the lines so that every word became a new row in the dataset. Consider, for example, the following line:

```
subsidence; comparison with the Portillo chain.
```

The splitting of this line resulted in the following rows being generated:

#. ▲	line	word
122	subsidence; comparison with the Portillo chain.	subsidence;
123	subsidence; comparison with the Portillo chain.	comparison
124	subsidence; comparison with the Portillo chain.	with
125	subsidence; comparison with the Portillo chain.	the
126	subsidence; comparison with the Portillo chain.	Portillo
127	subsidence; comparison with the Portillo chain.	chain.

Thus, a new field named word became the basis for your transformation.

First of all, you discarded rows with null words. You did it by using a filter with the condition word IS NOT NULL. Then, you counted the words by using the **Group by** step you learned in the previous tutorial. Once you counted the words, you discarded those rows where the word was too short (length less than 4) or too common (comparing to a list you typed).

Once you applied all those filters, you sorted the rows in the descending order of the number of times the word appeared in the file so that you could see the most frequent words.

Scrolling down a little the preview window to skip some prepositions, pronouns, and other very common words that have nothing to do with a specific subject, you found words such as shells, strata, formation, South, elevation, porphyritic, Valley, tertiary, calcareous, plain, North, rocks, and so on. If you had to guess, you would say that this was a book or article about geology, and you would be right. The text taken for this exercise was Geological Observations on South America by Charles Darwin.

Filtering rows using the Filter rows step

The **Filter rows** step allows you to filter rows based on conditions and comparisons.

The step checks the condition for every row. Then it applies a filter letting pass only the rows for which the condition is true. The other rows are lost.

In the counting words exercise, you used the **Filter rows** step several times so you already have an idea of how it works. Let's review it.

In the **Filter rows** setting window you have to enter a condition. The following table summarizes the different kinds of conditions you may enter:

Condition	Description	Example
A single field followed by `IS NULL` or `IS NOT NULL`	Checks whether the value of a field in the stream is null	`word IS NOT NULL`
A field, a comparator, and a constant	Compares a field in the stream against a constant value.	`counter > 2`
Two fields separated by a comparator	Compares two fields in the stream	`line CONTAINS word`

You can combine conditions as shown here:

```
counter > 2
AND
len_word>3
```

You can also create subconditions such as:

```
    (
    counter > 2
AND
    len_word>3
    )
OR
    (word in list geology; sun)
```

In this last example, the condition lets the word geology pass even if it appears only once. It also lets the word sun pass, despite its length.

When editing conditions, you always have a contextual menu which allows you to add and delete sub-conditions, change the order of existent conditions, and more.

Maybe you wonder what the **Send 'true' data to step:** and **Send 'false' data to step:** textboxes are for. Be patient, you will learn how to use them in Chapter 4.

Have a go hero – playing with filters

Now it is your turn to try filtering rows. Modify the **counting_words** transformation in the following way:

♦ Alter the **Filter rows** steps. By using a **Formula** step create a flag (a Boolean field) that evaluates the different conditions (`counter>2`, and so on). Then use only one **Filter rows** step that filters the rows for which the flag is true. Test it and verify that the results are the same as before the change.

In the **Formula editing** window, use the options under the **Logic** category.

Then in the **Filter rows** step, you can type `true` or `Y` as the value against which you compare the flag.

◆ Add a sub-condition to avoid excluding some words, just like the one in the example: `(word in list geology; sun)`. Change the list of words and test the filter to see that the results are as expected.

Have a go hero – counting words and discarding those that are commonly used

If you take a look at the results in the tutorial, you may notice that some words appear more than once in the final list because of special signs such as `.`, `)` or `"`, or because of lower or upper case letters. For example, look how many times the word rock appears: `rock` (99 occurrences) - `rock,` (51 occurrences) – `rock.` (11 occurrences) – `rock."` (1 occurrence) - `rock:` (6 occurrences) - `rock;` - (2 occurrences). You can fix this and make the word rock appear only once: Before grouping the words, remove all extra signs and convert all words to lower case or upper case, so they are grouped as expected.

Try one or more of the following steps: **Formula**, **Calculator**, **Replace in string**.

Looking up data

Until now, you have been working with a single stream of data. When you did calculations or created conditions to compare fields, you only involved fields of your stream. Usually, this is not enough, and you need data from other sources. In this section you will learn to look up data outside your stream.

Time for action – finding out which language people speak

An International Musical Contest will take place and 24 countries will participate, each presenting a duet. Your task is to hire interpreters so the contestants can communicate in their native language. In order to do that, you need to find out the language they speak:

1. Create a new transformation.

2. By using a **Get Data From XML** step, read the `countries.xml` file that contains information about countries that you used in Chapter 2.

To avoid configuring the step again, you can open the transformation that reads this file, copy the **Get data from XML** step, and paste it here.

3. Drag a **Filter rows** step to the canvas.

4. Create a hop from the **Get data from XML** step to the **Filter rows** step.

5. Edit the **Filter rows** step and create the condition- `isofficial= T`.

6. Click the **Filter rows** step and do a preview. The list of previewed rows will show the countries along with the official languages:

Now let's create the main flow of data:

7. From the book website download the list of contestants. It looks like this:

```
ID;Country;Duet
1;Russia;Mikhail Davydova
;;Anastasia Davydova
2;Spain;Carmen Rodriguez
;;Francisco Delgado
3;Japan;Natsuki Harada
;;Emiko Suzuki
4;China;Lin Jiang
;;Wei Chiu
5;United States;Chelsea Thompson
;;Cassandra Sullivan
6;Canada;Mackenzie Martin
;;Nathan Gauthier
7;Italy;Giovanni Lombardi
;;Federica Lombardi
```

8. In the same transformation, drag a **Text file Input** step to the canvas and read the downloaded file.

 The ID and `country` have values only in the first of the two lines for each country. In order to repeat the values in the second line use the flag **Repeat** in the **Fields** tab. Set it to Y.

9. Expand the **Lookup** category of steps.

10. Drag a **Stream lookup** step to the canvas.

11. Create a hop from the **Text file input** you just created, to the **Stream lookup** step.

12. Create another hop from the **Filter rows** step to the **Stream lookup** step.

13. Edit the **Stream lookup** step by double-clicking it.

14. In the **Lookup step** drop-down list, select **Filter official languages**, the step that brings the list of languages.

15. Fill the grids in the configuration window as follows:

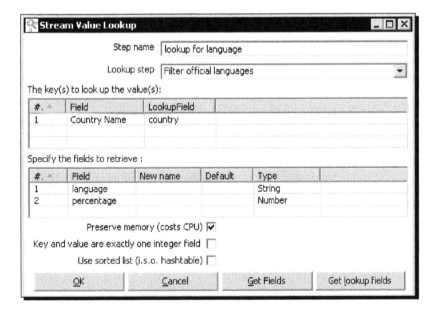

Note that `Country Name` is a field coming from the text file stream, while the country field comes from the countries stream.

16. Click **OK**.

17. The hop that goes from the **Filter rows** step to the **Stream lookup** step changes its look and feel, to show that this is the stream where the **Stream lookup** is going to look:

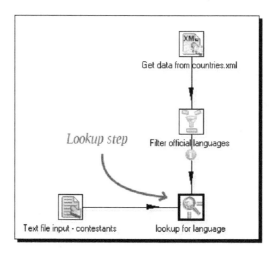

18. After the **Stream lookup**, add a **Filter rows** step.

19. In the **Filter rows** step, type the condition `language-IS NOT NULL`.

20. By using a **Select values** step, rename the fields `Duet, Country Name` and `language` to `Name, Country,` and `Language`.

21. Drag a **Text file output** step to the canvas and create the file `people_and_languages.txt` with the selected fields.

22. Save the transformation.

23. Run the transformation and check the final file, which should look like this:

```
Name|Country|Language
Mikhail Davydova|Russia|
Anastasia Davydova|Russia|
Carmen Rodriguez|Spain|Spanish
Francisco Delgado|Spain|Spanish
Natsuki Harada|Japan|Japanese
Emiko Suzuki|Japan|Japanese
```

```
Lin Jiang|China|Chinese
Wei Chiu|China|Chinese
Chelsea Thompson|United States|English
Cassandra Sullivan|United States|English
Mackenzie Martin|Canada|French
Nathan Gauthier|Canada|French
Giovanni Lombardi|Italy|Italian
Federica Lombardi|Italy|Italian
```

What just happened?

First of all, you read a file with information about countries and the languages spoken in those countries.

Then you read a list of people along with the country they come from. For every row in this list, you told Kettle to look for the country (Country Name field) in the countries stream (country field), and to give you back a language and the percentage of people that speaks that language (language and percentage fields). Let's explain it with a sample row: The row for Francisco Delgado from Spain. When this row gets to the **Stream lookup** step, Kettle looks in the list of countries for a row with the country Spain. It finds it. Then, it returns the value of the columns language and percentage: Spanish and 74.4.

Now take another sample row—the row with the country Russia. When the row gets to the **Stream lookup** step, Kettle looks for it in the list of countries, but it doesn't find it. So what you get as language is a null string.

Whether the country is found or not, two new fields are added to your stream—language and percentage.

After the **Stream lookup** step, you discarded the rows where language is null, that is, those whose country wasn't found in the list of countries.

With the successful rows you generated an output file.

The Stream lookup step

The **Stream lookup** step allows you to look up data in a secondary stream.

You tell Kettle which of the incoming streams is the stream used to look up, by selecting the right choice in the **Lookup** step list.

The upper grid in the configuration window allows you to specify the names of the fields that are used to look up.

In the left column, **Field**, you indicate the field of your main stream. You can fill this column by using the **Get Fields** button, and deleting all the fields you don't want to use for the search.

In the right column, **Lookup Field**, you indicate the field of the secondary stream.

When a row of data comes to the step, a lookup is made to see if there is a row in the secondary stream for which, every pair (Field, LookupField) in the grid has the value of Field equal to the value of LookupField. If there is one, the look up will be successful.

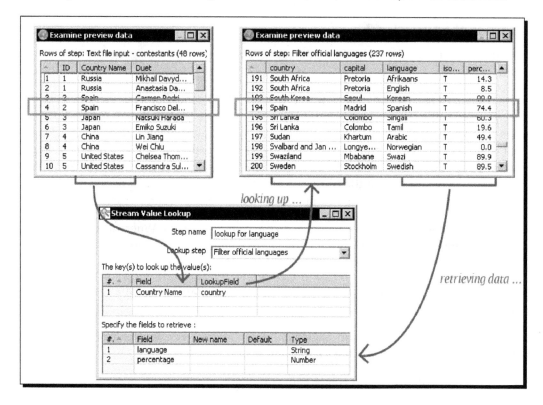

In the lower grid, you specify the names of the secondary stream fields that you want back as a result of the look up. You can fill this column by using the **Get lookup fields** button, and deleting all the fields you don't want to retrieve.

After the lookup, new fields are added to your dataset—one for every row of this grid.

For the rows for which the look up is successful, the values for the new fields will be taken from the lookup stream.

For the others, the fields will remain null, unless you set a default value.

When you use a **Stream lookup**, all lookup data is loaded into memory. Then the stream lookup is made using a **hash table algorithm**. Even if you don't know how this algorithm works, it is important that you know the implications of using this step:

◆ First, if the data where you look is huge, you take the risk of running out of memory.

◆ Second, only one row is returned per key. If the key you are looking for is present more than once in the lookup stream, only one will be returned—for example, in the tutorial where there are more than one official languages spoken in a country, you get just one. Sometimes you don't care, but on some occasions this is not acceptable and you have to try some other methods. You'll learn other ways to do this later in the book.

Have a go hero – counting words more precisely

The tutorial where you counted the words in a file worked pretty well, but you may have noticed that it has some details you can fix or enhance.

You discarded a very small list of words, but there are much more that are quite usual in English—prepositions, pronouns, auxiliary verbs, and many more. So here is the challenge: Get a list of commonly used words and save it in a file. Instead of excluding words from a small list as you did with a **Filter rows** step, exclude the words that are in your common words file.

Use a **Stream lookup** step.
Test the transformation with the same file, and also with other files, and verify that you get better results with all these changes.

Summary

This chapter covered the simplest and most common ways of transforming data. Specifically, it covered how to:

- Use different transformation steps to calculate new fields
- Use the **Calculator** and the **Formula** steps
- Filter and sort data
- Calculate statistics on groups of rows
- Look up data

After learning basic manipulation of data, you may now create more complex transformations, where the streams begin to split and merge. That is the core subject of the next chapter.

4

Controlling the Flow of Data

In the previous chapter, you learned the basics of transforming data. Basically you read data from some file, did some transformation to the data, and sent the data back to a different output. This is the simplest scenario. Think of a different situation. Suppose you collect results from a survey. You receive several files with the data and those files have different formats. You have to merge those files somehow and generate a unified view of the information. You also want to put aside the rows of data whose content is irrelevant. Finally, based on the rows that interest you, you want to create another file with some statistics. This kind of requirement is very common. In this chapter you will learn how to implement it with PDI.

Splitting streams

Until now, you have been working with simple, straight flows of data. When you deal with real problems, those simple flows are not enough. Many times, the rows of your dataset have to take different paths. This situation is handled very easily, and you will learn how to do it in this section.

Time for action – browsing new PDI features by copying a dataset

Before starting, let's introduce the Pentaho BI Platform Tracking site. At the tracking site you can see the current Pentaho roadmap and browse their issue tracking system. The PDI page for that site is `http://jira.pentaho.com/browse/PDI`.

In this exercise, you will export the list of proposed new features for PDI from the site, and generate detailed and summarized files from that information.

1. Access the main Pentaho tracking site page: `http://jira.pentaho.com`.

2. In the main menu, click on **FIND ISSUES**.

3. On the left side, select the following filters:

❑ **Project: Pentaho Data Integration {Kettle}**

❑ **Issue Type: New Feature**

❑ **Status: Open**

4. At the bottom of the filter list, click **View >>**. A list of found issues will appear.

5. Above the list, select **Current field** to export the list to an Excel file.

6. Save the file to the folder of your choice.

 The Excel file exported from the JIRA site is a Microsoft Excel 97-2003 Worksheet. PDI doesn't recognize this version of worksheets. So, before proceeding, open the file with Excel or Calc and convert it to Excel 97/2000/XP.

7. Create a transformation.

8. Read the file by using an **Excel Input** step. After selecting the file, click on the **Sheets** tab, and fill it as shown in the next screenshot so that it skips the header rows and the first column:

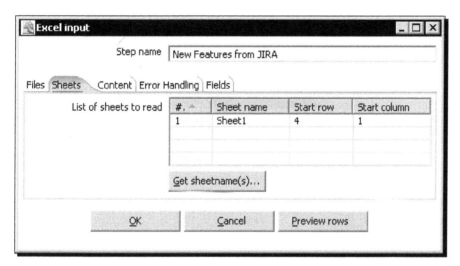

9. Click the **Fields** tab and fill the grid by clicking the **Get fields from header row...** button.

10. Click the **Preview rows** just to be sure that you are reading the file properly. You should see all the contents of the Excel file except the three heading lines.

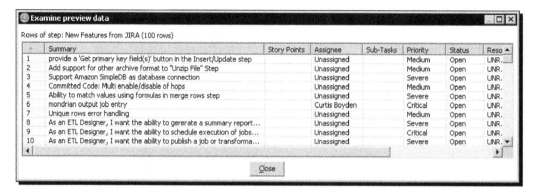

11. Click **OK**.

12. Add a **Filter rows** step to drop the rows where the Summary field is null.

13. After the **Filter rows** step, add a **Value Mapper** step and fill it like here:

14. After the **Value Mapper** step, add a **Sort rows** step and order the rows by priority_order (asc.), Summary (asc.).

15. After that add an **Excel Output** step, and configure it to send the `priority_order` and `Summary` fields to an Excel file named `new_features.xls`.

16. Drag a **Group by** step to the canvas.

17. Create a new hop from the **Sort rows** step to the **Group by** step.

18. A warning window appears asking you to decide whether you wish to **Copy** or **Distribute**.

19. Click **Copy** to send the rows toward both output steps.

20. The hops leaving the **Sort rows** step change to show you the decision you made. So far you have this:

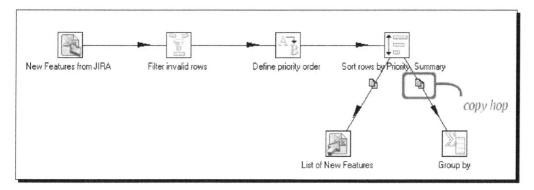

21. Configure the **Group by** steps like shown:

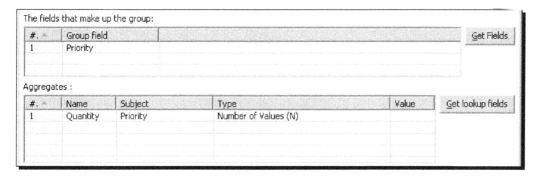

22. Add a new **Excel Output** step to the canvas and create a hop from the **Group by** step to this new step.

23. Configure the **Excel Output** step to send the `Priority` and `Quantity` fields to an Excel file named `new_features_summarized.xls`.

24. Save the transformation and run it.

25. Verify that both files, `new_features.xls` and `new_features_summarized.xls`, have been created.

26. The first file should look like this:

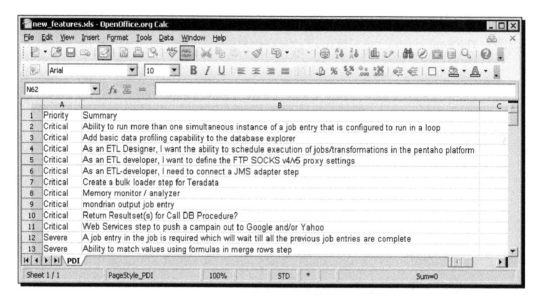

27. And the second file should look like this:

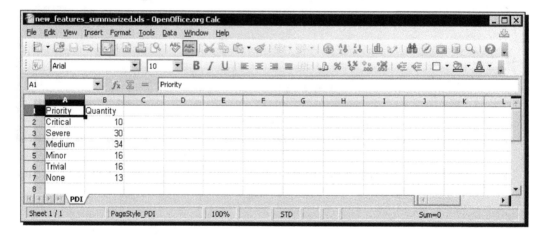

What just happened?

After exporting an Excel file with the PDI new features from the JIRA site, you read the file and created two Excel files—one with a list of the issues and the other with a summary of the list.

The first steps of the transformation are well known—read a file, filter null rows, map a field, and sort.

 Note that the mapping creates a new field to give an order to the `Priority` field so that the more severe issues are first in the list, while the minor priorities remain at the end of the list.

You linked the **Sort rows** step to two different steps. This caused PDI to ask you what to do with the rows leaving the step. By answering **Copy**, you told PDI to create a copy of the dataset. After that, two identical copies left the **Sort rows** step, each to a different destination step.

From the moment you copied the dataset, those copies became independent, each following its way. The first copy was sent to a detailed Excel file. The other copy was used to create a summary of the fields, which then was sent to another Excel file.

Copying rows

At any place in a transformation, you may decide to split the main stream into two or more streams. When you do so, you have to decide what to do with the data that leaves the last step—copy or distribute.

To **copy** means that the whole dataset is copied to each of the destination steps. Once the rows are sent to those steps, each follows its own way.

When you copy, the hops that leave the step from which you are copying change visually to indicate the copy action.

In the tutorial, you created two copies of the main dataset. You could have created more than two, like in this example:

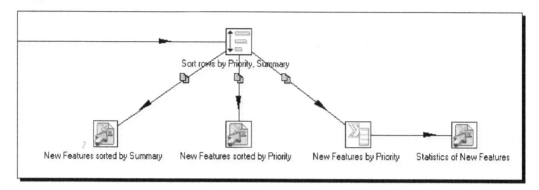

When you split the stream into two or more streams, you can do whatever you want with each one as if they had never been the same. The transformations you apply to any of those output streams will not modify the data in the others.

> You shouldn't assume a particular order in the execution of the output streams of a step. All the output streams receive the rows in synch and you don't have control over the order in which they are executed.

Have a go hero – recalculating statistics

Do you remember the exercise from Chapter 3 where you calculated some statistics? You created two transformations. One was to generate a file with students that failed. The other was to create a file with some statistics such as average grade, number of students who failed, and so.

Now you can do all that work in a single transformation, reading the file once.

Distributing rows

As said, when you split a stream, you can copy or distribute the rows. You already saw that copy is about creating copies of the whole dataset and sending each of them to each output stream. To **distribute** means the rows of the dataset are distributed among the destination steps. Let's see how it works through a modified exercise.

Time for action – assigning tasks by distributing

Let's suppose you want to distribute the issues among three programmers so that each of them implements a subset of the new features.

1. Select **Transformation** | **Copy transformation to clipboard** in the main menu. Close the transformation and select **Transformation** | **Paste transformation from clipboard**. A new transformation is created identical to the one you copied. Change the description and save the transformation under a different name.

2. Now delete all the steps after the **Sort rows** step.

3. Change the filter step to keep only the unassigned issues: `Assignee` field equal to the string `Unassigned`. The condition looks like the next screenshot:

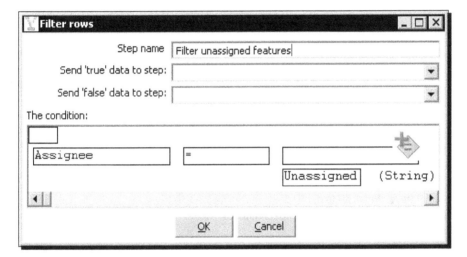

4. From the **Transform** category of steps, drag an **Add sequence** step to the canvas and create a hop from the **Sort rows** step to this new step.

5. Double-click the **Add sequence** step and replace the content of the **Name of value** textbox with `nr`.

6. Drag three **Excel Output** steps to the canvas.

7. Link the **Add sequence** step to one of these steps.

Configure the **Excel Output** step to send the fields nr, Priority, and Summary to an Excel file named f_costa.xls (the name of one of the programmers). The **Fields** tab should look like this:

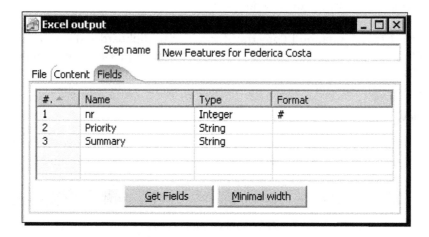

8. Create a hop from the **Add sequence** step to the second **Excel Output** step. When asked to decide between **Copy** and **Distribute**, select **Distribute**.

9. Configure the step like before, but name the file as b_bouchard.xls (the second programmer).

10. Create a hop from the **Add sequence** step to the last **Excel Output** step.

11. Configure this last step like before, but name the file as a_mercier.xls (the last programmer).

12. The transformation should look like the following:

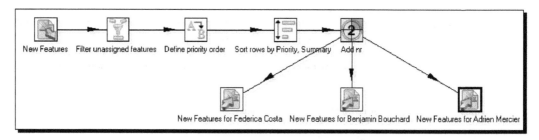

13. Run the transformation and look at the execution tab window to see
what happened:

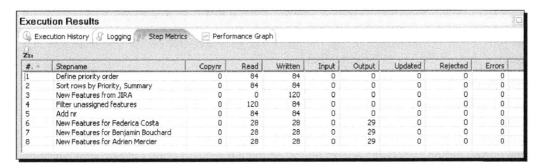

14. To see which rows belong to which of the created files, open any of them. It should
look like this:

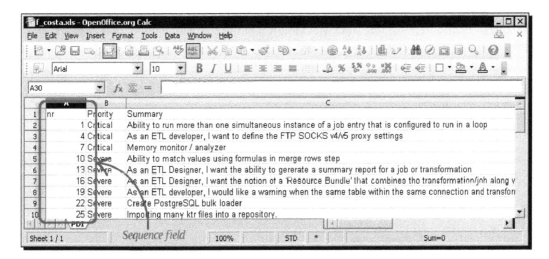

What just happened?

You distributed the issues among three programmers.

In the execution window, you could see that 84 rows leave the **Add sequence** step, and 28
arrive to each of the **Excel Output** steps, that is, a third of the number of rows to each of
them. You verified that when you explored the Excel files.

In the transformation, you added an **Add sequence** step that did nothing more than adding
a sequential number to the rows. This sequence helps you recognize that one out of every
three rows were distributed to every file.

Here you saw a practical example for the distributing option. When you distribute, the destination steps receive the rows in turn. For example, if you have three target steps, the first row goes to the first target step, the second row goes to the second step, the third row goes to the third step, the fourth row now goes to the first step, and so on.

As you could see, when distributing, the hop leaving the step from which you distribute is plain; it doesn't change its look and feel.

Despite this example showing clearly how the **Distribute...** method works, this is not how you will regularly use this option. The **Distribute...** option is mainly used for performance reasons. Throughout this book you will always use the **Copy...** option. To avoid being asked for the action to take every time you create more that one hop leaving a step, you can set the **Copy...** option as default; you do this by opening the PDI options window (**Edit|Options ...** from the main menu) and unchecking the option **Show "copy or distribute" dialog?**. Remember that to see the change applied, you will have to restart Spoon.

Once you have changed this option, the default method is copying rows. If you want to distribute rows, you can change the action by right-clicking the step from which you want to copy or distribute, selecting **Data Movement...** in the contextual menu that appears, and then selecting the desired option.

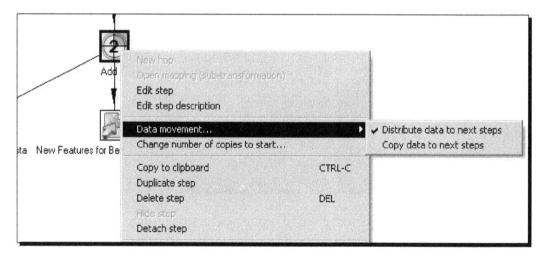

Pop quiz – data movement (copying and distributing)

Look at the following transformations:

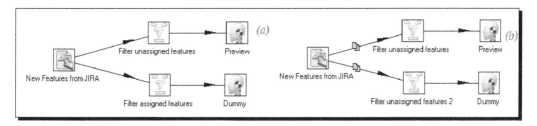

If you do a preview on the Steps named **Preview**, which of the following is true:

a.   The number of rows you see in (a) is greater or equal than the number of rows you see in (b)

b.   The number of rows you see in (b) is greater or equal than the number of rows you see in (a)

c.   The dataset you see in (a) is exactly the same as you see in (b) no matter what data you have in the Excel file.

You can create a transformation and test each option to check the results for yourself. To be sure you understand correctly where and when the rows take one or other way, you can preview every step in the transformation, not just the last one.

Splitting the stream based on conditions

In the previous section you learned to split the main stream of data into two or more streams. The whole dataset was copied or distributed among the destination steps. Now you will learn how to put conditions so that the rows take one way or another depending on the conditions.

Time for action – assigning tasks by filtering priorities with the Filter rows step

Following with the JIRA subject, let's do a more realistic distribution of tasks among programmers. Let's assign the serious task to our most experienced programmer, and the remaining tasks to others.

1. Create a new transformation.

2. Read the JIRA file and filter the unassigned tasks, just as you did in the previous tutorial.

3. Add a **Filter rows** step and two **Excel Output** steps to the canvas, and link them to the other steps as follows:

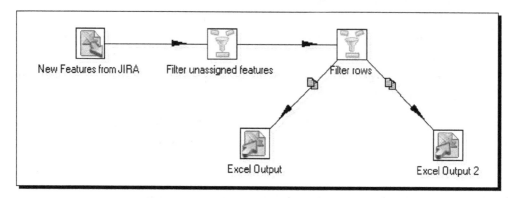

4. Configure one of the **Excel Output** steps to send the fields, Priority and Summary, to an Excel file named b_bouchard.xls (the name of the senior programmer).

5. Configure the other **Excel Output** step to send the fields Priority and Summary to an Excel file named new_features_to_develop.xls.

6. Double-click the **Filter row** step to edit it.

7. Enter the condition Priority = Critical OR Priority = Severe.

8. From the first drop-down list, **Send 'true' data to step**, select the step that creates the b_bouchard.xls Excel file.

9. From the other drop-down list, **Send 'false' data to step**, select the step that creates the Excel new_features_to_develop.xls Excel file.

10. Click **OK**.

11. The hops leaving the **Filter rows** step change to show which way a row will take, depending on the result of the condition.

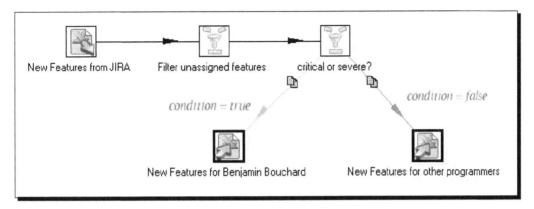

12. Save the transformation.

13. Run the transformation, and verify that the two Excel files were created.

14. The files should look like this:

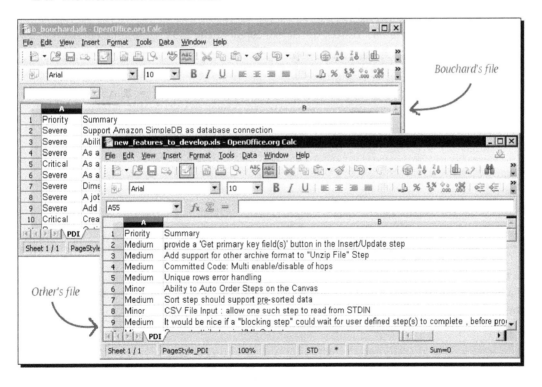

What just happened?

You sent the list of PDI new features to two Excel files—one file with the critical issues and the other file with the rest of the issues.

In the **Filter row** step, you put a condition to evaluate if the priority of a task was severe or critical. For every row coming to the filter, the condition was evaluated. The rows that had a severe or critical priority were sent toward the **Excel Output** step that creates the b_bouchard.xls file. The rows with another priority were sent towards the other **Excel Output** step, the one that creates the new_features_to_develop.xls file.

PDI steps for splitting the stream based on conditions

When you have to make a decision, and upon that decision split the stream in two, you can use the **Filter row** step as you did in this last exercise. In this case, the **Filter rows** step acts as a decision maker. It has a condition and two possible destinations. For every row coming to the filter, the step evaluates the condition. Then if the result of the condition is true, it decides to send the row toward the step selected in the first drop-down list of the configuration window—**Send 'true' data to step**.

If the result of the condition is false, it sends the row toward the step selected in the second drop-down list of the configuration window: **Send 'false' data to step**.

Sometimes you have to make nested decisions; consider the next figure for example:

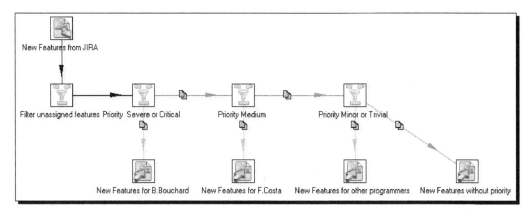

In the transformation shown in the preceding diagram, the conditions are as simple as testing if a field is equal to a value. In situations like this you have a simpler way for accomplishing the same..

Time for action – assigning tasks by filtering priorities with the Switch/ Case step

Let's use a Switch/Case step to replace the nested Filter Rows steps shown in the preceding diagram

1. Create a transformation like the following:

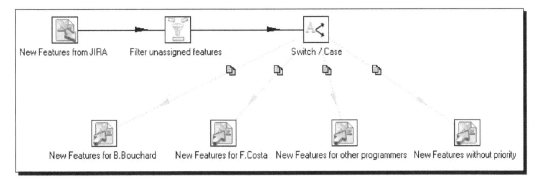

2. You will find the **Switch/Case** step in the **Flow** category of steps.

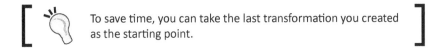

To save time, you can take the last transformation you created as the starting point.

3. Note that the hops arriving to the **Excel Output** steps look strange. They are dotted orange lines. This look and feel shows you that the target steps are unreachable. In this case, it means that you still have to configure the **Switch/Case** step. Double-click it and fill it like here:

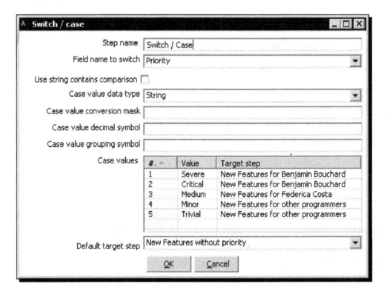

4. Save the transformation and run it

5. Open the Excel files generated to see that the transformation distributed the task among the files based on the given conditions.

What just happened?

In this tutorial you learned to use the **Switch/Case** step. This step routes rows of data to one or more target steps based on the value encountered in a given field.

In the **Switch/Case** step configuration window, you told Kettle where to send the row depending on a condition. The condition to evaluate was the equality of the field set in **Field name to switch** and the value indicated in the grid. In this case, the field name to switch is **Priority**, and the values against which it will be compared are the different values for priorities: **Severe**, **Critical**, and so on. Depending on the values of the **Priority** field, the rows will be sent to any of the target steps. For example, the rows where **Priority=Medium**, will be sent toward the target step **New Features for Federica Costa**.

Note that it is possible to specify the same target step more than once.

The **Default target step** represents the step where the rows that don't match any of the case values are sent. In this example, the rows with a priority not present in the list will be sent to the step **New Features without priority**.

Have a go hero – listing languages and countries

Open the transformation you created in the *Finding out which language people speak* tutorial in Chapter 3. If you run the transformation and check the content of the output file, you'll notice that there are missing languages. Modify the transformation so that it generates two files—one with the rows where there is a language, that is, the rows for which the lookup didn't fail, and another file with the list of countries not found in the `countries.xml` file.

Pop quiz – splitting a stream

Continuing with the contestant exercise, suppose that the number of interpreters you will hire depends on the number of people that speak each language:

Number of people that speaks the language	Number of interpreters
Less than 3	1
Between 3 and 6	2
More that 6	3

You want to create a file with the languages with a single interpreter, another file with the languages with two interpreters, and a final file with the languages with three interpreters. Which of the following would solve your situation when it comes to splitting the languages into three output streams:

a. A **Number range** step followed by a **Switch/Case** step.

b. A **Switch/Case** step.

c. Both

 In order to figure out the answer, create a transformation and count the number of people that speak each language. You'll have to use a **Sort rows** step followed by a **Group by** step. After that, try to develop each alternative solution and see what happens.

Merging streams

You've just seen how the rows of a dataset can take different paths. Here you will learn the opposite—how data coming from different places is merged into a single stream.

Time for action – gathering progress and merging all together

Suppose that you delivered the Excel files you generated in the *Assigning tasks by filtering priorities* tutorial earlier in the chapter. You gave the `b_bouchard.xls` to Benjamin Bouchard, the senior programmer. You also gave the other Excel file to a project leader who is going to assign the tasks to different programmers. Now they are giving you back the worksheets, with a new column indicating the progress of the development. In the case of the shared file, there is also a column with the name of the programmer who is working on every issue. Your task is now to unify those sheets.

Here is what the Excel files look like:

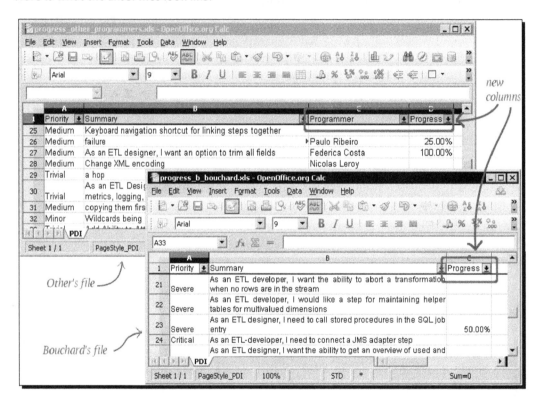

1. Create a new transformation.

2. Drag an **Excel Input** step to the canvas and read one of the files.

3. Add a **Filter row** step to keep only the rows where the progress is not null, that is, the rows belonging to tasks whose development has been started.

4. After the filter, add a **Sort rows** step, and configure it to order the fields by `Progress`, in descending order.

5. Add another **Excel Input** step, read the other file, and filter and sort the rows just like you did before. Your transformation should look like this:

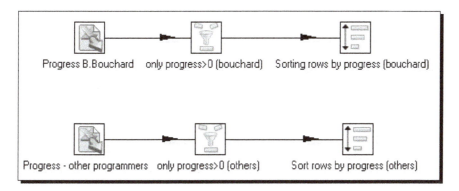

6. From the **Transform** category of steps, select the **Add Constants** step and drag it onto the canvas.

7. Link the step to the stream that reads the B. Bouchard's file; edit the step and add a new field named `Programmer`, with type `string` and value **Benjamin Bouchard**.

8. After this step, add a **Select values** step and reorder the fields so that they remain in a specific order `Priority`, `Summary`, `Programmer`, `Progress`—to resemble the other stream.

9. Now, from the **Transform** category add an **Add sequence** step, name the new field `ID`, and link the step with the **Select values** step.

10. Create a hop from the **Sort rows** step of the other stream to the **Add sequence** step. Your transformation should look like the one shown next:

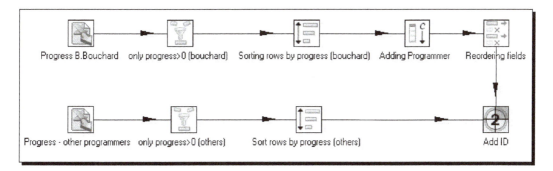

11. Select the **Add sequence** step and do a preview. You will see this:

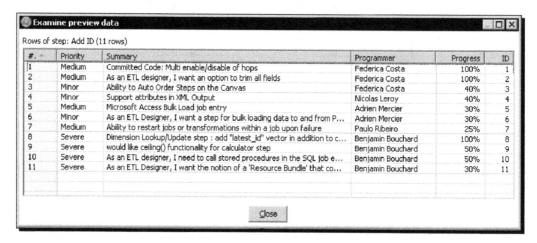

What just happened?

You read two similar Excel files and merged them into one single dataset.

First of all, you read, filtered, and sorted the files as usual. Then you altered the stream belonging to B. Bouchard, so it looked similar to the other. You added the field `Programmer`, and reordered the fields.

After that, you used an **Add sequence** step to create a single dataset containing the rows of both streams, with the rows numbered.

PDI options for merging streams

You can create a union of two or more streams anywhere in your transformation. To create a union of two or more data streams, you can use any step. The step unifies the data, takes the incoming streams in any order, and then it completes its task in the same way as if the data came from a single stream.

In the example, you used an **Add sequence** step as the step to join two streams. The step gathered the rows from the two streams, and then proceeded to numerate the rows with the sequence name `ID`.

This is only one example of how you can mix streams together. As said, any step can be used to unify two streams. Whichever the step, the most important thing you have to have in mind is that you cannot mix rows that have a different layout. The rows have to have the same lengths, the same data types, and the same fields in the same order.

Fortunately, there is a **trap detector** that provides warnings at design time if a step is receiving mixed layouts.

You can try this out. Delete the **Select values** step. Create a hop from the **Add constants** step to the **Add sequence** step. A warning message appears as shown next:

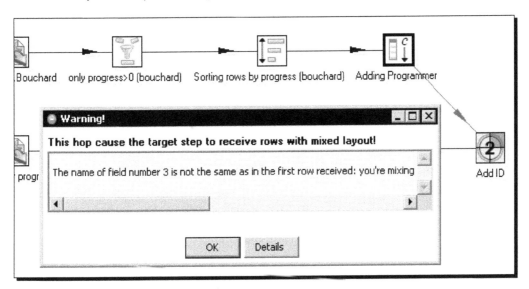

In this case, the third field of the first stream, Programmer (String), does not have the same name or the same type as the third field of the second stream, Progress (Number).

Note that PDI warns you but it doesn't prevent you from mixing row layouts when creating the transformation.

If you want Kettle to prevent you from running transformations with mixed row layouts, you can check the option **Enable safe mode** in the window that shows up when you dispatch the transformation. Have in mind that doing this will cause a performance drop.

When you use an arbitrary step to unify, the rows remain in the same order as they were in their original stream, but the streams are joined in any order. Take a look at the example's preview. The rows of the Bouchard's stream as well as the rows of the other stream remained sorted within its original group. However, whether the Bouchard's stream appeared before or after the rows of the other stream was just a matter of chance. You didn't decide the order of the streams; PDI decided it for you. If you care about the order in which the union is made, there are some steps that can help you. Here are the options you have:

If you want to ...	You can do this ...
Append two or more streams, and don't care about the order	Use any step. The selected step will take all the incoming streams in any order, and then will proceed with its specific task.
Append two streams in a given order	Use the **Append streams** step from the **Flow** category. It helps to decide which stream goes first.
Merge two streams ordered by one or more fields	Use a **Sorted Merge** step from the **Joins** category. This step allows you to decide on which field(s) to order the incoming rows before sending them to the destination step(s). The input streams must be sorted on that field(s).
Merge two streams keeping the newest when there are duplicates	Use a **Merge Rows (diff)** step from the **Joins** category.
	You tell PDI the key fields, that is, the fields that say that a row is the same in both streams. You also give PDI the fields to compare when the row is found in both streams.
	PDI tries to match rows of both streams, based on the key fields. Then it creates a field that will act as a flag, and fills it as follows: ◆ If a row was only found in the first stream, the flag is set to `deleted`. ◆ If a row was only found in the second stream, the flag is set to `new`. ◆ If the row was found in both streams, and the fields to compare are the same, the flag is set to `identical`. ◆ If the row was found in both streams, and at least one of the fields to compare is different, the flag is set to `changed`.

Let's try one of these options.

Time for action – giving priority to Bouchard by using Append Stream

Suppose you want the Bouchard's row before the other rows. You can modify the transformation as follows:

1. From the **Flow** category of steps, drag an **Append Streams** step to the canvas. Rearrange the steps and hops so the transformation looks like this:

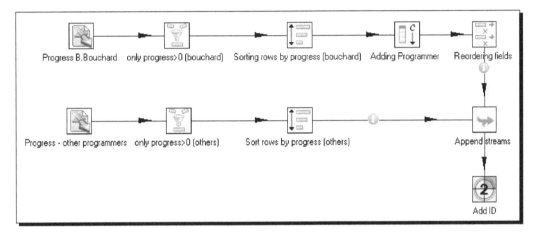

2. Edit the **Append streams** step and select as the **Head hop** the one belonging to the Bouchard's rows, and as the **Tail hop** the other. Doing this, you indicate toPDI how it has to order the streams.

3. Do a preview on the **Add sequence** step. You should see this:

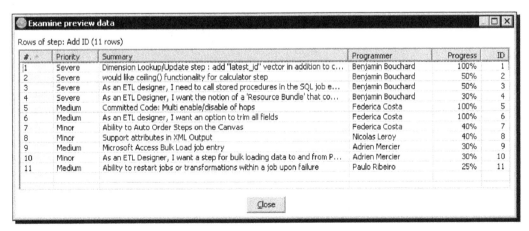

What just happened?

You changed the transformation to give priority to Bouchard's issues.

You made it by using the **Append Streams** step. By telling that the head hop was the one coming from the Bouchard's file, you got the expected order—first the rows with the tasks assigned to Bouchard, sorted by progress descending, and then the rows with the tasks assigned to other programmers, also sorted by progress descending.

 Whether you use arbitrary steps or some of the special steps mentioned here to merge streams, don't forget to verify the layouts of the streams you are merging. Pay attention to the warnings of the trap detector and avoid mixing row layouts.

Have a go hero – sorting and merging all tasks

Modify the previous exercise so that the final output is sorted by priority. Try two possible solutions:

- Sort the input streams on their own and then use a **Sorted Merge** step.
- Merge the stream with a **Dummy** step and then sort.

Which one do you think would give the best performance?

 Refer to the **Sort rows** step issues in Chapter 3.

In which circumstances would you use the other option?

Have a go hero – trying to find missing countries

As you saw in the countries exercises, there are missing countries in the countries.xml file. In fact, the countries are there, but with different names. For example, Russia in the contestant file is Russian Federation in the XML file. Modify the transformation that looks for the language. Split the stream in two—one for the rows where a language was found and the other for the rows where no language was found. For this last stream, use a **Value Mapper** step to rename the countries you identified as wrong, that is, rename Russia as Russian Federation. Then look again for a language now with the new name. Finally, merge the two streams and create the output file with the result.

Summary

In this chapter, you learned different options that PDI offers to combine or split flows of data. The chapter covered the following:

- Copying and distributing rows
- Splitting streams based on conditions
- Merging independent streams in different ways

With the concepts you learned in the initial chapters, the range of tasks you are able to perform is already broad. In the next chapter, you will learn how to insert JavaScript code in your transformations not only as an alternative to perform some of those tasks, but also as a way to accomplish other tasks that are complicated or even unthinkable to carry out with regular PDI steps.

5

Transforming Your Data with JavaScript Code and the JavaScript Step

Whichever transformation you need to do on your data, you have a big chance of finding that PDI steps are able to do the job. Despite that, it may happen that there are not proper steps that serve your requirements, or that an apparently minor transformation consumes a lot of steps linked in a very confusing arrangement difficult to test or understand. Putting colorful icons here and there is funny and practical, but there are some situations like the ones described above where you inevitably will have to code. This chapter explains how to do it with JavaScript and the special JavaScript step.

In this chapter you will learn how to:

♦ Insert and test JavaScript code in your transformations

♦ Distinguish situations where coding is the best option, from those where there are better alternatives

Doing simple tasks with the JavaScript step

One of the traditional steps inside PDI is the JavaScript step that allows you to code inside PDI. In this section you will learn how to use it for doing simple tasks.

Time for action – calculating scores with JavaScript

The International Musical Contest mentioned in Chapter 4 has already taken place. Each duet performed twice. The first time technical skills were evaluated, while in the second, the focus was on artistic performance.

Each performance was assessed by a panel of five judges who awarded a mark out of a possible 10.

The following is the detailed list of scores:

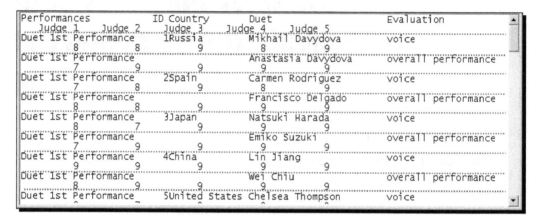

Note that the fields don't fit in the screen, so the lines are wrapped and dotted lines are added for you to distinguish each line.

Now you have to calculate, for each evaluated skill, the overall score as well as an average score.

1. Download the sample file from the Packt website.

2. Create a transformation and drag a **Fixed file input** step to the canvas to read the file.

3. Fill the configuration window as follows:

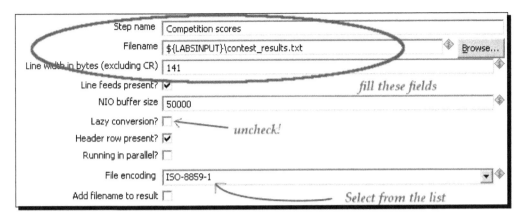

4. Press the **Get Fields** button. A window appears to help you define the columns.

5. Click between the fields to add markers that define the limits. The window will look like this:

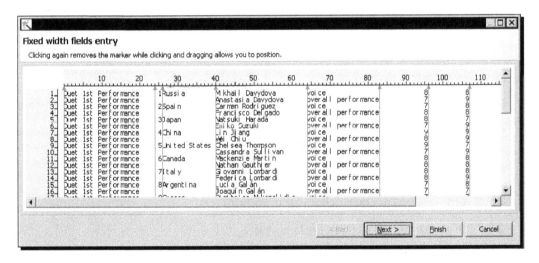

6. Click on **Next >**. A new window appears for you to configure the fields.

7. Click on the first field at the left of the window and change the name to Performance. Verify that the type is set to String.

8. To the right, you will see a preview of the data for the field.

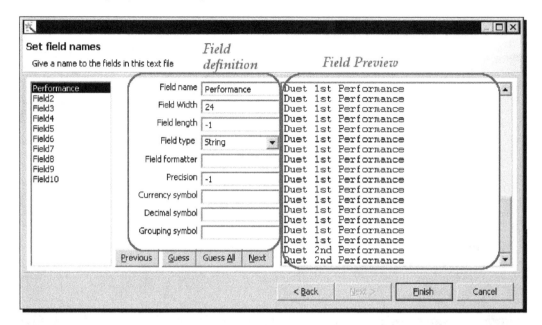

9. Select each field to the left of the window, change the names, and adjust the types. Set `ID`, `Country`, `Duet`, and `Skill` fields as `String`, and fields from `Judge 1` to `Judge 5` as `Integer`.

10. Go back and forth between these two windows as many times as you need until you are done with the definitions of the fields.

11. Click on **Finish**.

12. The grid at the bottom is now filled.

13. Set the column **Trim type** to **both** for every field.

14. The window should look like the following:

#	Name	Type	Format	Width	Length	Precision	Currency	Decimal	Group	Trim type
1	Performance	String		24						both
2	ID	String		2						both
3	Country	String		14						both
4	Duet	String		24						both
5	Skill	String		19						both
6	Judge1	Integer	#	13						both
7	Judge2	Integer	#	11						both
8	Judge3	Integer	#	11						both
9	Judge4	Integer	#	11						both
10	Judge5	Integer	#	11						both

15. Click on **Preview the transformation**. You should see this:

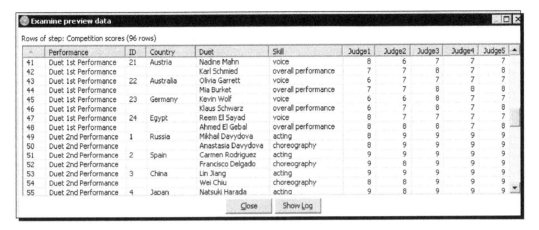

16. From the **Scripting** category of steps, select a **Modified JavaScript Value** step and drag it to the canvas.

17. Link the step to the **Fixed file input** step, and double-click it to configure it.

18. Most of the configuration window is blank, which is the editing area. Type the following text in it:

```
var totalScore;
var wAverage;

totalScore = Judge1 + Judge2 + Judge3 + Judge4 + Judge5;

wAverage = 0.35 * Judge1 + 0.35 * Judge2
           + 0.10 * Judge3 + 0.10 * Judge4 + 0.10 * Judge5;
```

19. Click on the **Get variables** button.

20. The grid under the editing area gets filled with the two variables defined in the code. The window looks like this:

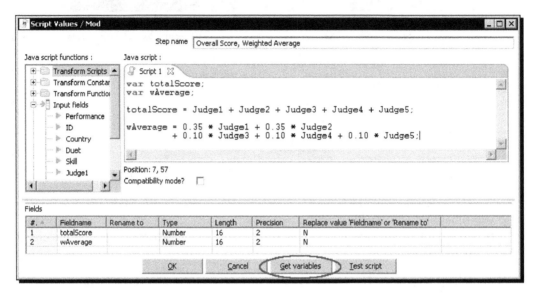

21. Click on **OK**.

22. Keep the **JavaScript** step selected and do a preview.

23. This is how the final data looks like:

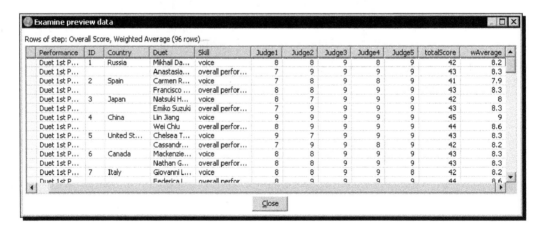

What just happened?

You read the detailed list of scores and added two fields with the overall score and an average score for each evaluated skill.

In order to read the file, you used a step you hadn't used before—the **Fixed file input** step. You configured the step with the help of a wizard. You could have also filled the field grid manually if you wanted to.

After reading the file, you used a **JavaScript** step to create new fields. The code you typed was pure JavaScript code. In this case, you typed a simple code to calculate the total score and a weighted average combining the fields from Judge 1 to Judge 5.

Note that the average was defined by giving more weight, that is, more importance, to the scores coming from Judge 1 and Judge 2.

For example, consider the first line of the file. This is how the new fields were calculated:

```
totalScore = Judge1 + Judge2 + Judge3 + Judge4 + Judge5 = 8+8+9+8+9
             = 42
wAverage = 0.35*Judge1 + 0.35*Judge2+ 0.10*Judge3 + 0.10*Judge4 +
0.10*Judge5 = 0.35*8 + 0.35*8+ 0.10*8 + 0.10*8 + 0.10*8 = 8.2
```

In order to add these new fields to your dataset, you brought them to the grid at the bottom of the window.

Note that this is not the only way to do calculations in PDI. All you did with the **JavaScript** step can also be done with other steps.

Using the JavaScript language in PDI

JavaScript is a scripting language primarily used in website development. However, inside PDI you use just the core language; you neither run a web browser nor do you care about HTML. There are many available JavaScript engines. PDI uses the **Rhino** engine, from **Mozilla**. Rhino is an open source implementation of the core JavaScript language; it doesn't contain objects or methods related to manipulation of web pages. If you are interested in knowing more about Rhino, you can visit `https://developer.mozilla.org/en/Rhino_Overview`.

The core language is not too different from other languages you might know. It has basic statements, block statements (statements enclosed by curly brackets), conditional statements (if..else and switch case), and loop statements (for, do..while, and while). If you are interested in the language itself, you can access a good JavaScript guide following this link: `https://developer.mozilla.org/En/Core_JavaScript_1.5_Guide`.

Besides the basics, an interesting feature included in the PDI implementation is **E4X**, a programming language extension that allows you to manipulate XML objects inside JavaScript. You can find an E4X tutorial as well as a reference manual at `https://developer.mozilla.org/En/E4X/Processing_XML_with_E4X`.

Finally, there is a complete tutorial and reference at `http://www.w3schools.com/js/`. Despite being quite oriented to web development, which is not your concern, it is clear, complete, and has plenty of examples.

Inserting JavaScript code using the Modified Java Script Value step

The **Modified Java Script Value** step (**JavaScript** step in short) allows you to insert JavaScript code inside your transformation. The code you type here is executed once per row coming to the step.

Let's explore its dialog window.

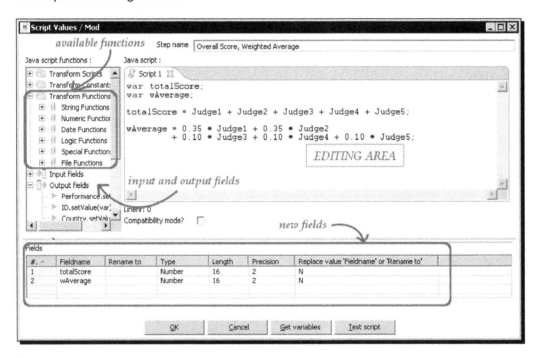

Most of the window is occupied by the editing area. It's there that you write JavaScript code using the standard syntax of the language and the functions and fields from the tree to the left of the window.

The **Transform Functions** branch of the tree contains a rich list of functions, ready to use.

The functions are grouped by category.

♦ **String**, **Numeric**, **Date**, and **Logic** categories contain usual JavaScript functions.

 This is not a full list of JavaScript functions. You are allowed to use JavaScript functions even if they are not in this list.

♦ The **Special** category contains a mix of utility functions. Most of them are not JavaScript functions but Kettle functions. You will use some of them later in this chapter.

♦ Finally, the **File** category, as its name suggests, contains a list of functions that do simple verifications or actions related to files and folders—for example, `fileExist()` or `createFolder()`.

To add a function to your script, simply double-click on it, and drag it to the location in your script where you wish to use it, or just type it.

 If you are not sure about how to use a particular function or what a function does, just right-click on the function and select **Sample**. A new script window appears with a description of the function and sample code showing how to use it.

The **Input fields** branch contains the list of the fields coming from previous steps. To see and use the value of a field for the current row, you need to double-click on it or drag it to the code area. You can also type it by hand as you did in the tutorial.

When you use one of these fields in the code, it is treated as a JavaScript variable. As such, the name of the field has to follow the conventions for a variable name—for example, it cannot contain dots, nor can it start with non-character symbols.

As Kettle is quite permissive with names, you can have fields in your stream whose names are not valid to be used inside JavaScript code.

 If you intend to use a field with a name that doesn't follow the name rules, rename it just before the **JavaScript** step with a **Select values** step. If you use that field without renaming it, you will not be warned when coding, but you'll get an error or unexpected results when you execute the transformation.

The **Output fields** is a list of the fields that will leave the step.

Adding fields

At the bottom of the window, there is a grid where you put the fields you created in the code. This is how you add a new field:

1. Define the field as a variable in the code—for example, `var totalScore`.
2. Fill the grid manually or by clicking the **Get variables** button. A new row will be filled for every variable you defined in the code.

That was exactly what you did for the new fields, `totalScore` and `wAverage`.

In the JavaScript code you can create and use all variables you need without declaring them. However, if you intend to add a variable as a field in your stream, the declaration with the `var` sentence is mandatory.

 The variables you define in the JavaScript code are not Kettle variables. JavaScript variables are local to the step, and have nothing to do with the Kettle variables you know.

Modifying fields

Instead of adding a field, you may want to change the value and eventually the data type of an existent field. You can do that but not directly in the code.

Imagine that you wanted to change the field `Skill`, converting it to uppercase. To accomplish this, double-click the **JavaScript** step and add the following two lines:

```
var uSkill;
uSkill = upper(Skill);
```

Add the new field to the grid at the bottom:

Fields

#. ▲	Fieldname	Rename to	Type	Length	Precision	Replace value 'Fieldname' or 'Rename to'
1	totalScore		Number	16	2	N
2	wAverage		Number	16	2	N
3	uSkill	Skill	String			Y

By renaming `uSkill` to `Skill` and setting the **Replace value 'Fieldname' or 'Rename to'** to `Y`, the `uSkill` field is renamed to `Skill` and replaces the old `Skill` field.

 Don't use the `setValue()` function to change existent fields. It may cause problems and remains just for compatibility reasons.

Turning on the compatibility switch

In the JavaScript window, you might have seen the **Compatibility mode** checkbox. This checkbox, unchecked by default, causes JavaScript to work like it did in version 2.5 of the JavaScript engine. With that version, you could modify the values and their types directly in the code, which allows mixing data types, thus causing many problems.

Old JavaScript programs run in compatibility mode. However, when creating new code, you should make use of the new engine; that is, you should leave the compatibility mode turned off.

 Do not check the compatibility switch. Leaving it unchecked, you will have a cleaner, faster, and safer code.

Have a go hero – adding and modifying fields to the contest data

Take the contest file as source and do the following:

- Add a field named `average`. For the first performance, calculate the average as a weighted average, just like you did in the tutorial. For the second performance, calculate the field as a regular average, that is, the sum of the five scores divided by five.

- Modify the `Performance` field. Replace `Duet 1st Performance` and `Duet 2nd Performance` by `1st` and `2nd`.

There is no single way to code this, but here you have a list of functions or sentences you can use: `if..then...else, indexOf(), substr()`

Testing your code

After you type a script, you may want to test it. You can do it from inside the JavaScript configuration window. Let's try it:

Time for action – testing the calculation of averages

Let's test the code you've just created.

1. Double-click the **JavaScript** step.

2. Click on the **Test script** button.

3. A window appears to create a set of rows for testing. Fill it like here:

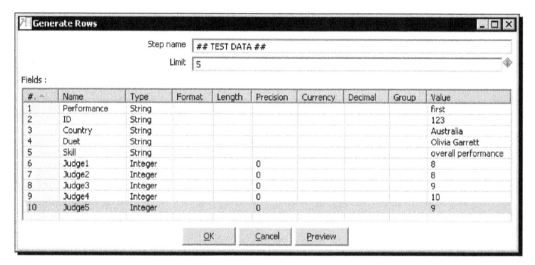

4. Click on **Preview the transformation**. A window appears showing five identical rows with the provided sample values. Close the preview window.

5. Click on **OK** to test the code.

A window appears with the result that will appear when we execute the script with the test data.

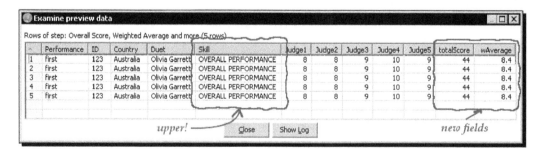

What just happened?

You tested the code of the **JavaScript** step.

You clicked on the **Test script** button, and created a dataset that served as the basis for testing the script. You previewed the test dataset.

After that, you did the test itself. A window appeared showing you how the created dataset looks like after the execution of the script—the `totalScore` and `wAverage` fields were added, and the `skill` field was converted to uppercase.

Testing the script using the Test script button

The **Test script** button allows you to check that the script does what it is intended to do. It actually generates a transformation in the back with two steps—a **Generate Rows** step sending data to a copy of the **JavaScript** step. Just after clicking on the button, you are allowed to fill the **Generates Rows** window with the test dataset.

The first thing that the test function does is to verify that the code is properly written; that is, that there are no syntax errors in the code. Try deleting the last parenthesis in the code and click on the **Test script** button. When you click **OK** to see the result of the execution, instead of a dataset you will see an error window.

If the script is syntactically correct, what follows is the preview of the JavaScript for the transformation in the back, that is, the JavaScript code applied to the test dataset.

If you don't see any error and the previewed data shows the expected results, you are done. If not, you can check the code, fix it, and test it again until you see that the step works properly.

Have a go hero – testing the new calculation of the average

Open the transformation of the previous Hero section, and test:

- The weighted average code
- The regular code

 To test one or the other, simply change the test data. Don't touch your code!

Enriching the code

In the previous section, you learned how to insert code in your transformation by using a **JavaScript** step. In this section, you will see how to use variables from outside to give flexibility to your code. You also will learn how to take control of the rows from inside the **JavaScript** step.

Time for action – calculating flexible scores by using variables

Suppose that by the time you are creating the transformation, the weights for calculating the weighted average are unknown. You can modify the transformation by using parameters. Let's do it:

1. Open the transformation of the previous section and save it with a new name.

2. Press *Ctrl+T* to open the **Transformation properties** dialog window.

3. Select the **Parameters** tab and fill it like here:

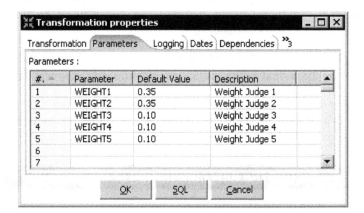

4. Replace the **JavaScript** step by a new one and double-click it.

5. Expand the **Transform Scripts** branch of the tree at the left of the window.

6. Right-click the script named `Script 1`, select **Rename**, and type `main` as the new name.

7. Position the mouse cursor over the editing window and right-click to bring up the following contextual menu:

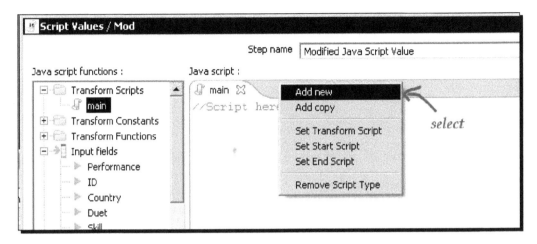

8. Select **Add new** to add the script, which will execute before your main code.

9. A new script window appears. The script is added to the list of scripts under **Transform Scripts**.

10. Bring up the contextual menu again, but this time clicking on the title of the new script. Select **Set Start Script**.

11. Right-click the script in the tree list, and rename the new script as Start.

12. In the editing area of the new script, type the following code to bring the transformation parameters to the JavaScript code:

```
w1 = str2num(getVariable('WEIGHT1',0));
w2 = str2num(getVariable('WEIGHT2',0));
w3 = str2num(getVariable('WEIGHT3',0));
w4 = str2num(getVariable('WEIGHT4',0));
w5 = str2num(getVariable('WEIGHT5',0));

writeToLog('Getting weights...');
```

13. Select the main script by clicking on its title and type the following code:

```
var wAverage;

wAverage = w1 * Judge1 + w2 * Judge2
        + w3 * Judge3 + w4 * Judge4 + w5 * Judge5;

writeToLog('row:' + getProcessCount('r') + ' wAverage:' +
num2str(wAverage));
if (wAverage >=7)
        trans_Status = CONTINUE_TRANSFORMATION;
else
        trans_Status = SKIP_TRANSFORMATION;
```

14. Click **Get variables** to add the `wAverage` variable to the grid.

15. Close the JavaScript window.

16. With the JavaScript step selected, click on the **Preview this transformation** button.

17. When the preview window appears, click on **Configure**.

18. In the window that shows up, modify the parameters as follows:

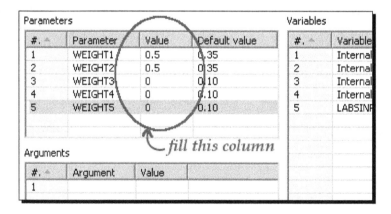

19. Click **Launch**.

20. The preview window shows this data:

21. The log window shows this:

```
. . .
2009/07/23 14:46:54 - wAverage with Param..0 - Getting weights...
2009/07/23 14:46:54 - wAverage with Param..0 - row:1 wAverage:8
2009/07/23 14:46:54 - wAverage with Param..0 - row:2 wAverage:8
2009/07/23 14:46:54 - wAverage with Param..0 - row:3 wAverage:7.5
2009/07/23 14:46:54 - wAverage with Param..0 - row:4 wAverage:8
2009/07/23 14:46:54 - wAverage with Param..0 - row:5 wAverage:7.5
. . .
```

What just happened?

You modified the code of the **JavaScript** step to use parameters.

First, you created four parameters for the transformation, containing the weights for the calculation.

Then in the **JavaScript** step, you created a `Start` script to read the variables. That script executed once, before the main script. Note that you didn't declare the variables. You could have done it, but it's not mandatory unless you intend to add them as output fields.

In the main script, the script that is executed for every row, you typed the code to calculate the average by using those variables instead of fixed numbers.

After the calculation of the average, you kept only the rows for which the average was greater or equal to 7. You did it by setting the value of `trans_Status` to `CONTINUE_TRANSFORMATION` for the rows you wanted to keep, and to `SKIP_TRANSFORMATION` for the rows you wanted to discard.

In the preview window, you could see that the average was calculated as a weighted average of the scores you provided, and that only the rows with an average greater or equal to 7 were kept.

Using named parameters

The parameters that you put in the transformation dialog window are called **named parameters**. They can be used through the transformation as regular variables, as if you had created them before—for example, in the kettle.properties file.

> From the point of view of the transformation, the main difference between variables defined in the kettle.properties file and named parameters is that the named parameters have a default value that can be changed at the time you run the transformation.

In this case, the default values for the variables defined as named parameters WEIGHT1 to WEIGHT5 were 0.35, 0.35, 0.10, 0.10, and 0.10—the same that you had used in previous exercises. But when you executed, you changed the default and used 0.50, 0.50, 0, 0, and 0 instead. This caused the formula for calculating the weighted average to work as an average of the first two scores. Take, for example, the numbers for the first row of the file. Consider the following code line:

```
wAverage = w1 * Judge1 + w2 * Judge2 + w3 * Judge3 + w4 * Judge4 + w5
  * Judge5;
```

It was calculated as:

```
wAverage = 0.50 * 8 + 0.50 * 8 + 0 * 9 + 0 * 8 + 0 * 9;
```

giving a weighted average equal to 8.

Note that the named parameters are ready to use through the transformation as regular variables. You can see and use them at any place where the icon with the dollar sign is present.

If you want to use a named parameter or any other Kettle variable such as LABSINPUT or java.io.tmpdir inside the JavaScript code, you have to use the getVariable() function as you did in the Start script.

When you run the transformation from the command line, you also have the possibility to specify values for named parameters. For details about this, check Appendix B.

Using the special Start, Main, and End scripts

The **JavaScript** step allows you to create multiple scripts. The **Transformation Script** list displays a list with all scripts of the step.

In the tutorial, you added a special script named `Start` and used it to read the variables. The **Start Script** is a script that executes only once, before the execution of the main script you already know.

The **Main script**, the script that is created by default, executes for every row. As this script is executed after the start script, all variables defined in the main script there are accessible here. As an example of this, in the tutorial you used the start script to set values for the variables `w1` through `w5`. Then in the main script you used those variables.

It is also possible to have an **End Script** that executes at the end of the execution of the step, that is, after the main script has been executed for all rows.

 When you create a `Start` or an `End` script, don't forget to give it a name so that you can recognize it. If you don't, you may get confused because nothing in the step shows you the type of the scripts.

Beyond main, start, and end scripts, you can use extra scripts to avoid overloading the main script with code. The code in the extra scripts will be available after the execution of the special function `LoadScriptFromTab()`.

Note that in the exercises, you wrote some text to the log by using the `writeToLog()` function. That had the only purpose of showing you that the start script executed at the beginning and the main script executed for every row. You can see this sequence in the execution log.

Using transformation predefined constants

In the tree to the left-hand side of the JavaScript window, under **Transformation Constants**, you have a list of predefined constants. You can use those constants to change the value of the predefined variable, `trans_Status`, such as:

```
trans_Status = SKIP_TRANSFORMATION
```

Here is how it works:

Value of the `trans_Status` variable	Effect on the current row
`SKIP_TRANSFORMATION`	The current row is removed from the dataset
`CONTINUE_TRANSFORMATION`	The current row is retained
`ERROR_TRANSFORMATION`	The current row causes abortion of the transformation

In other words, you can use that constant to control what will happen to the rows. In the exercise you put:

```
if (wAverage >=7)
    trans_Status = CONTINUE_TRANSFORMATION;
else
    trans_Status = SKIP_TRANSFORMATION;
```

This means a row where the average is greater than or equal to 7 will continue its way to the following steps. On the contrary, a row with a lower average will be discarded.

Pop quiz – finding the 7 errors

Look at the following screenshot:

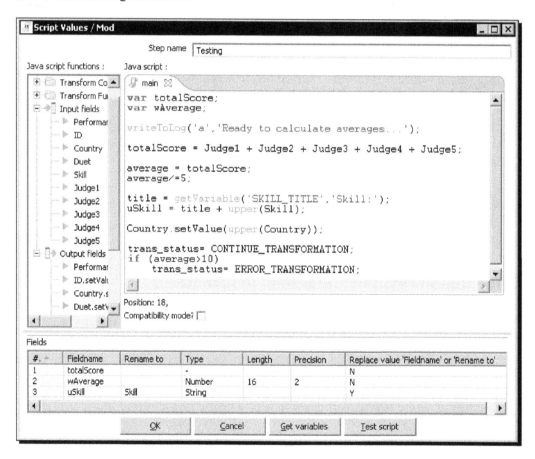

Does it look good? Well, it is not. There are seven errors in it. Can you find them?

Have a go hero – keeping the top 10 performances

Modify the last tutorial. By using a **JavaScript** step, keep the top 10 performances, that is, the 10 performances with the best average.

 Sort the data using a regular **Sort rows** step. Give the `getProcessCount()` function a try.

Have a go hero – calculating scores with Java code

If you are a Java programmer, or just curious, you will like to know that you can access Java libraries from inside the **JavaScript** step. On the book site there is a JAR file named `pdi_chapter_5.jar`. The JAR file contains a class with two methods—`w_average()` and `r_average()`, for calculating a weighted average and a regular average.

Here is what you have to do:

1. Download the file from Packt's site, copy it to the `libext` folder inside the PDI installation folder, and restart Spoon.

2. Replace the JavaScript calculation of the averages by a call to one of these methods. You'll have to specify the complete name of the class. Consider the next line for example:

    ```
    wAverage = Packages.Averages.w_average(Judge1, Judge2, Judge3, Judge4, Judge5);
    ```

3. Preview the transformation and verify that it works properly.

The Java file is available as well. You can change it by adding new methods and trying them from PDI.

Likewise, you can try using any Java objects, as long as they are in PDI's classpath. Don't forget to type the complete name as in the following examples:

```
java.lang.Character.isDigit(c);
var my_date = new java.util.Date();
var val = Math.floor(Math.random()*100);
```

Reading and parsing unstructured files

It is marvelous to have input files where the information is well formed; that is, the number of columns and the type of its data is precise, all rows follow the same pattern, and so on. However, it is common to find input files where the information has little or no structure, or the structure doesn't follow the matrix (n rows by m columns) you expect. In this section you will learn how to deal with such files.

Time for action – changing a list of house descriptions with JavaScript

You won the lottery and decided to invest the money in a new house. You asked a real-estate agency for a list of candidate houses for you and it gave you this:

```
. . .
Property Code: MCX-011
Status: Active
5 bedrooms
5 baths
Style: Contemporary
Basement
Laundry room
Fireplace
2 car garage
Central air conditioning
More Features: Attic, Clothes dryer, Clothes washer, Dishwasher

Property Code: MCX-012
4 bedrooms
3 baths
Fireplace
Attached parking
More Features: Alarm System, Eat in Kitchen, Powder Room

Property Code: MCX-013
3 bedrooms
. . .
```

You want to compare the properties before visiting them, but you're finding it hard to do so because the file doesn't have a precise structure. Fortunately, you have the **JavaScript** step, which will help you to give the file some structure.

1. Create a new transformation.

2. Get the sample file from Packt site and read it with a **Text file input** step. Uncheck the **Header** checkbox and create a single field named `text`.

3. Do a preview. You should see the content of the file under a single column named `text`. Add a JavaScript step after the input step and double-click it to edit it.

4. In the editing area, type the following JavaScript code to create a field with the code of the property:

```
var prop_code;

posCod = indexOf(text,'Property Code:');
if (posCod>=0)
        prop_code = trim(substr(text,posCod+15));
```

5. Click **Get variables** to add the `prop_code` variable to the grid under the code.

6. Click **OK**.

7. With the **JavaScript** step selected, do a preview. You should see this:

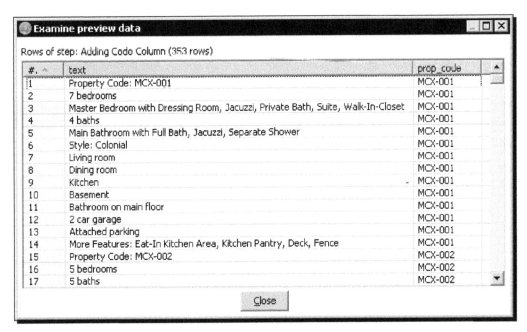

What just happened?

You read a file where each house was described in several rows. You added to every row the code of the house to which that row belonged. In order to obtain the property code, you identified the lines with a code, and then you cut the `Property Code:` text with the `substr` function and discarded the leading spaces with `trim`.

Looking at previous rows

The code you wrote may seem a little strange at the beginning, but it is not. It creates a variable named `prod_code`, which will be used to create a new field to identify the properties. When the JavaScript code detects a property header row such as `Property Code: MCX-002`, it sets the variable `prop_code` to the code it finds in that line—MCX – 002 in this case.

Until a new header row appears, the `prop_code` variable keeps that value. Thus all the rows following a row like the one shown above will have the same value for the variable `prop_code`.

The variable is then used to create a new field, which will contain for every row, the code for the house to which it belongs.

This is an example of when you can keep values from previous rows to be used in the current row.

Note that here you use JavaScript to see and use values from previous rows, but you can't modify them! JavaScript always works on the current row.

Have a go hero – enhancing the houses file

Modify the exercise from the tutorial by doing the following:

1. After keeping the property code, discard the rows that headed each property description.

2. Create two new fields named `feature` and `description`. Fill the `feature` field with the feature described in the row (Exterior construction) and the `description` field with the description of that feature (Brick). If you think that is not worth keeping some features (Living Room), you may discard some rows. Discard also the original field `text`. Here you have a sample house description showing a possible output after the changes:

```
prop_code; Feature; Description
MCX-023;bedrooms;4
MCX-023;baths;4
MCX-023;Style;Colonial
MCX-023;family room;yes
MCX-023;basement;yes
MCX-023;fireplace;yes
MCX-023;Heating features;Hot Water Heater
MCX-023;Central air conditioning present;yes
MCX-023;Exterior construction;Stucco
MCX-023;Waterview;yes
MCX-023;More Features;Attic, Living/Dining Room, Eat-In-Kitchen
```

Have a go hero – fill gaps in the contest file

Take a look at the contest file. Each performance occupies two rows, one showing each evaluated skill. The name of the country appeared only in the first row.

Open the first version of the contest transformation and modify it to fill the column `Country` where it is blank.

Avoiding coding by using purpose-built steps

You saw through the exercises how powerful the **JavaScript** step is for helping you in your transformations. In older versions of PDI, coding JavaScript was the only means you had for doing specific tasks. In the latest releases of PDI, actual steps appeared that eliminate the need for coding in many cases. Here you have some examples of that:

♦ **Formula**: You saw it in Chapter 3. Before the appearance of this step, there were a lot of functions such as the text functions that you could only solve with JavaScript.

♦ **Analytic Query**: This step offers a way to retrieve information from rows before or after the current.

♦ **Split field to rows**: The step is used to create several rows from a single string value. You used this step in Chapter 3 to create a new row for each word found in a file.

Analytic Query and **Split fields to row** are examples of where not only the need for coding was eliminated, they also eliminated the need for accessing internal objects and functions such as `Clone()` or `putRow()` that you probably saw in old sample code or when browsing the PDI forum. The use of those objects and functions can lead to odd behavior and data corruption, and so their use is strongly discouraged.

Despite the appearance of new steps, you still have the choice to do the tasks with code.

In fact, quite a lot of tasks you do with regular PDI steps may also be done with JavaScript, by using the **JavaScript** step. This is a temptation to programmers who end up with transformations having plenty of **JavaScript** steps.

 Whenever there is a step that does what you want to do, you should prefer that step to coding.

Why should you prefer to use a specific step rather than code? Here are some reasons:

- To code takes more time to develop. You don't have to waste your time coding if there are steps that can solve your problem.

- Code is hard to maintain. If you have to modify or fix a transformation, it will be much easier to tackle the change if the transformation is a bunch of colorful steps with meaningful names than if the transformation consists of just a couple of JavaScript icons.

- A bunch of icons is self documented. A **JavaScript** step is like Pandora's box. Until you open it, you don't know exactly what it does, or whether it contains just a line of code or thousands.

- JavaScript is inherently slow. Faster alternatives for simple expressions are the **User Defined Java Expression** and **Calculator** steps. They are typically more than twice as fast. The next PDI release will feature a **User Defined Java Class** step. One of the purposes of this step, intended to be used by Java developers, is to overcome the drawbacks of JavaScript.

On the contrary, there are situations where you may prefer or have to use JavaScript. Let's enumerate some of them:

- To handle unstructured input data
- For accessing Java libraries
- When you need to use a function provided by the JavaScript language that is not provided by any of the regular PDI steps
- When the JavaScript code saves a lot of regular PDI steps (as well as screen space), and you think it is not worth showing the details of what those steps do

In the end, it is up to you to choose one or the other option. The following exercise will help you a little in the recognition of pros and cons.

Have a go hero – creating alternative solutions

Redo the following Hero exercises you did in this chapter:

◆ Adding and modifying fields to the contest data
◆ Keeping the top 10 performances
◆ Enhancing the houses file
◆ Filling gaps in the contest file

Do these exercises without using JavaScript when possible. In each case, compare both versions, having in mind the following:

◆ Time to develop
◆ Maintenance
◆ Documentation
◆ Capability to handle unstructured data
◆ Number of steps required
◆ Performance

Decide which option you would choose if you had to decide.

To keep the 10 first performances, use an **Add Sequence** step.
To fill the gaps, use an **Analytic Query** step.

Summary

In this chapter, you learned to code JavaScript into PDI. Specifically, you learned:

◆ What the JavaScript step is and how to use it
◆ How to modify fields and add new fields to your dataset from inside your JavaScript step
◆ How to deal with unstructured input data

You also considered the pros and cons of coding JavaScript inside your transformations, as well as alternative ways to do things, avoiding writing code when possible.

As a bonus, you learned the concept of named parameters.

If you feel confident with all you've learned until now, you are certainly ready to move on to the next chapter, where you will learn in a simple fashion how to solve some sophisticated problems such as normalizing data from pivot tables.

6
Transforming the Row Set

So far, you have been working with simple datasets, that is, datasets where the each row represented a different entity (for example a student) and each column represented a different attribute for that entity (for example student name). There are occasions when your dataset doesn't resemble such a simple format, and working with it as is, may be complicate or even impossible. In other occasions your data simply does not have the structure you like or the structure you need.

Whichever your situation, you have to transform the dataset in an appropriate format and the solution is not always about changing or adding fields, or about filtering or adding rows. Sometimes it has to do with twisting the whole dataset. In this chapter you will learn how to:

◆ Convert rows to columns

◆ Convert columns to rows

◆ Operate on sets of rows

You will also be introduced to a core subject in data warehousing: Time dimensions.

Converting rows to columns

In most datasets each row belongs to a different element such as a different match or a different student. However, there are datasets where a single row doesn't completely describe one element. Take, for example, the `real-estate` file from Chapter 5. Every house was described through several rows. A single row gave incomplete information about the house. The ideal situation would be one in which all the attributes for the house were in a single row. With PDI you can convert the data into this alternative format. You will learn how to do it in this section.

Time for action – enhancing a films file by converting rows to columns

In this tutorial we will work with a file that contains list of all French movies ever made. Each movie is described through several rows. This is how it looks like:

```
...
Caché
Year: 2005
Director:Michael Haneke
Cast: Daniel Auteuil, Juliette Binoche, Maurice Bénichou
Jean de Florette
Year: 1986
Genre: Historical drama
Director: Claude Berri
Produced by: Pierre Grunstein
Cast: Yves Montand, Gérard Depardieu, Daniel Auteuil
Le Ballon rouge
Year: 1956
Genre: Fantasy | Comedy | Drama
...
```

In order to process the information of the file, it would be better if the rows belonging to each movie were merged into a single row. Let's work on that.

1. Download the file from the Packt website.

2. Create a transformation and read the file with a **Text file input** step.

3. In the **Content** tab of the **Text file input** step put : as separator. Also uncheck the **Header** and the **No empty rows** options.

4. In the **Fields** tab enter two string fields—feature and description. Do a preview of the input file to see if it is well configured. You should see two columns—feature with the texts to the left of the semicolons, and description with the text to the right of the semicolons.

5. Add a JavaScript step and type the following code that will create the film field:

```
var film;

if (getProcessCount('r') == 1) film = '';

if (feature == null)
        film = '';
else if (film == '')
        film = feature;
```

6. Click on the **Get variables** button to add to the dataset the field `film`.

7. Add a **Filter rows** step with the condition `description IS NOT NULL`.

8. With the **Filter rows** step selected, do a preview. This is what you should see:

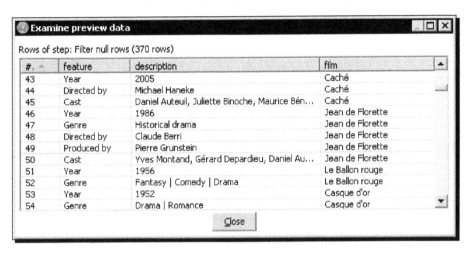

9. After the filter step, add a **Row denormalizer** step. You can find it under the **Transform** category.

10. Double-click the step and fill it like here:

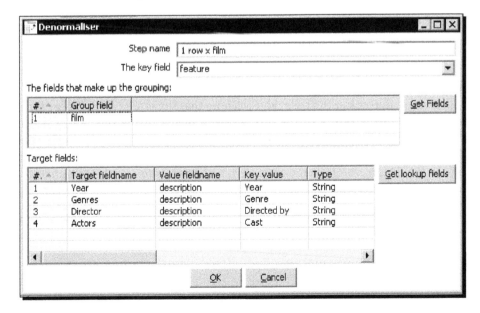

11. From the **Utility** category select an **If field value is null** step.

12. Double-click it , check the **Select fields** option, and fill the **Fields** grid as follows:

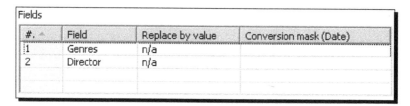

# ▲	Field	Replace by value	Conversion mask (Date)
1	Genres	n/a	
2	Director	n/a	

13. With this last step selected, do a preview. You will see this:

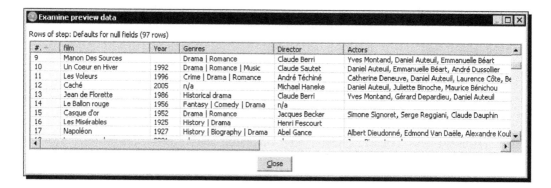

Examine preview data

Rows of step: Defaults for null fields (97 rows)

# ▲	film	Year	Genres	Director	Actors
9	Manon Des Sources		Drama | Romance	Claude Berri	Yves Montand, Daniel Auteuil, Emmanuelle Béart
10	Un Coeur en Hiver	1992	Drama | Romance | Music	Claude Sautet	Daniel Auteuil, Emmanuelle Béart, André Dussollier
11	Les Voleurs	1996	Crime | Drama | Romance	André Téchiné	Catherine Deneuve, Daniel Auteuil, Laurence Côte, Be
12	Caché	2005	n/a	Michael Haneke	Daniel Auteuil, Juliette Binoche, Maurice Bénichou
13	Jean de Florette	1986	Historical drama	Claude Berri	Yves Montand, Gérard Depardieu, Daniel Auteuil
14	Le Ballon rouge	1956	Fantasy | Comedy | Drama	n/a	
15	Casque d'or	1952	Drama | Romance	Jacques Becker	Simone Signoret, Serge Reggiani, Claude Dauphin
16	Les Misérables	1925	History | Drama	Henri Fescourt	
17	Napoléon	1927	History | Biography | Drama	Abel Gance	Albert Dieudonné, Edmond Van Daële, Alexandre Kout

Close

What just happened?

You read a file with a selection of films in which each film was described through several rows.

First of all, you created a new field with the name of the film by using a small piece of JavaScript code. If you look at the code, you will note that the empty rows are key for calculating the new field. They are used in order to distinguish between one film and the next and that is the reason for unchecking the `No empty rows` option. When the code executes for an empty row, it sets the film to an empty value. Then, when it executes for the first line of a film (`film == ''` in the code), it sets the new value for the `film` field. When the code executes for other lines, it does nothing but the film already has the right value.

After that, you used a **Row denormalizer** step to translate the description of films from rows to columns, so the final dataset had a single row by film.

Finally, you used a new step to replace some null fields with the text `n/a`.

Converting row data to column data by using the Row denormalizer step

The **Row denormaliser** step converts the incoming dataset into a new dataset by moving information from rows to columns according to the values of a key field.

To understand how the **Row denormaliser** works, let's do a sketch of the desired final dataset:

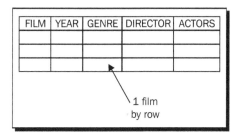

Here, a film is described by using a single row. On the contrary, in your input file the description for every film was spread over several rows.

To tell PDI how to combine a group of rows into a single one, there are three things you have to think about:

◆ Among the input fields there must be a **key field**. Depending on the value of that key field, you decide how the new fields will be filled. In your example, the key field is feature. Depending on the value of the column feature, you will send the value of the field description to some of the new fields: Year, Genres, Director, or Actors.

◆ You have to decide which field or fields make up the groups of rows. In our example, that field is film. All rows with the same value for the field film make up a different group.

◆ Decide the rules that have to be applied in order to fill the new target fields. All rules follow this pattern:

  ❑ If the value for the key field is equal to A, then put the value of the field B into the new field C.

  ❑ A sample rule could be: If the value for the field feature (our key field) is equal to Directed by, put the value of the field description into the new field Director.

Once you are clear about these three things, all you have to do is fill the **Row denormaliser** configuration window to tell PDI how to do this task.

1. Fill the **key field** textbox with the name of the key field. In the example, the field is feature.

2. Fill the upper grid with the fields that make up the grouping. In this case, it is film.

 The dataset must be sorted on the grouping fields. If not, you will get unexpected results.

3. Finally, fill the lower grid. This grid contains the rules for the new fields. Fill it following this example:

To add this rule ...	Fill a row like this ...
If the value for the key field is equal to A, put the value of the field B into the new field C.	**Key value**: A
	Value fieldname: B
	Target fieldname: C

This is how you fill the row for the sample rule:

If the value for the field feature (our key field) is equal to 'Directed by,' put the value of the field description into the new field Director.	**Key value**: Directed by
	Value fieldname: description
	Target fieldname: Director

For every rule you must fill a different row in the target fields' grid.

Let's see how the Row denormalizer works for the following sample rows:

feature	description	film
Directed by	Claude Berri	Manon Des Sources
Produced by	Pierre Grunstein	Manon Des Sources
Genre	Drama | Romance	Manon Des Sources
Cast	Yves Montand, Daniel Auteuil, Emmanuelle Béart	Manon Des Sources

PDI creates an output row for the film Manon Des Sources. Then it processes every row looking for values to fill the new fields.

Let's take the first row. The value for the key field `feature` is `Directed by`. PDI searches in the target fields' grid to see if there is an entry where the **Key value** is `Directed by`; it finds it.

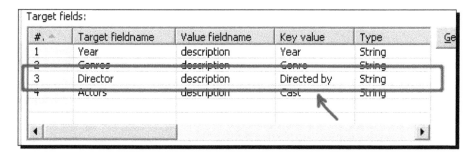

Then it puts the value of the field `description` as the content for the target field `Director`. The output row is now like this:

Film	Year	Genres	Director	Actors
Manon Des Sources			Claude Berri	

Now take the second row. The value for the key field `feature` is 'Produced by.'

PDI searches in the target fields' grid to see if there is an entry where the **Key value** is `Produced by`. It cannot find it, and the information for this row is lost.

The following screenshot shows the rule applied to the third sample row. It also shows how the final output row looks like:

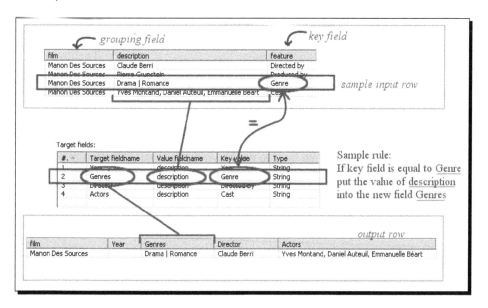

Note that the presence of rows is not mandatory for every key value entered in the target fields' grid. If an entry in the grid is not used, the target field is created anyway but it remains empty.

In this sample film, the year was not present. Then the field `Year` remained empty.

Have a go hero – houses revisited

Take the output file for the Hero exercise to enhance the houses file from the previous chapter. You can also download the sample file from the Packt site. Create a transformation that reads that file and generates the following output:

#.	prop_code	Style of the House	Fireplace	Bathrooms	Bedrooms
1	MCX-001	Colonial	No	4	7
2	MCX-002	Colonial	Yes	5	5
3	MCX-003	Colonial	Yes	5	4
4	MCX-004	unknown	No	3	4
5	MCX-005	unknown	No	4	4
6	MCX-006	Colonial	Yes	6	4
7	MCX-007	Colonial	Yes	5	3
8	MCX-008	Colonial	Yes	4	5
9	MCX-009	Colonial	Yes	5	5
10	MCX-010	unknown	Yes	5	5
11	MCX-011	Contemporary	Yes	5	5
12	MCX-012	unknown	Yes	3	4
13	MCX-013	Contemporary	Yes	4	3
14	MCX-014	unknown	Yes	5	4
15	MCX-015	Tudor	Yes	3	5
16	MCX-016	Colonial	No	4	5
17	MCX-017	Tudor	Yes	3	4
18	MCX-018	Ranch	No	2	3
19	MCX-019	unknown	No	3	4
20	MCX-020	Contemporary	Yes	4	6
21	MCX-021	unknown	No	5	7
22	MCX-022	Colonial	Yes	4	4
23	MCX-023	Colonial	Yes	4	4

Aggregating data with a Row denormalizer step

In the previous section, you learned how to use the **Row denormalizer** step to combine several rows into one. The **Row denormalizer** step can also be used to take as input a dataset and generate as output a new dataset with aggregated or consolidated data. Let's see it with an example.

Time for action – calculating total scores by performances by country

Let's work now with the contest file from Chapter 5. You will need the output file for the Hero exercise. Fill gaps in the contest file from that chapter. If you don't have it, you can download it from the Packt website.

In this tutorial, we will calculate the total score for each performance by country.

1. Create a new transformation.

2. Read the file with a **Text file input** step and do a preview to see that the step is well configured. You should see this:

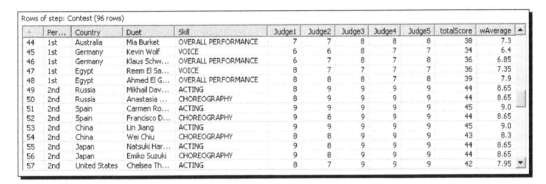

	Per...	Country	Duet	Skill	Judge1	Judge2	Judge3	Judge4	Judge5	totalScore	wAverage
44	1st	Australia	Mia Burket	OVERALL PERFORMANCE	7	7	8	8	8	38	7.3
45	1st	Germany	Kevin Wolf	VOICE	6	6	8	7	7	34	6.4
46	1st	Germany	Klaus Schw...	OVERALL PERFORMANCE	6	7	8	7	8	36	6.85
47	1st	Egypt	Reem El Sa...	VOICE	8	7	7	7	7	36	7.35
48	1st	Egypt	Ahmed El G...	OVERALL PERFORMANCE	8	8	8	7	8	39	7.9
49	2nd	Russia	Mikhail Dav...	ACTING	8	9	9	9	9	44	8.65
50	2nd	Russia	Anastasia ...	CHOREOGRAPHY	8	9	9	9	9	44	8.65
51	2nd	Spain	Carmen Ro...	ACTING	9	9	9	9	9	45	9.0
52	2nd	Spain	Francisco D...	CHOREOGRAPHY	9	8	9	9	9	44	8.65
53	2nd	China	Lin Jiang	ACTING	9	9	9	9	9	45	9.0
54	2nd	China	Wei Chiu	CHOREOGRAPHY	8	8	9	9	9	43	8.3
55	2nd	Japan	Natsuki Har...	ACTING	9	8	9	9	9	44	8.65
56	2nd	Japan	Emiko Suzuki	CHOREOGRAPHY	9	8	9	9	9	44	8.65
57	2nd	United States	Chelsea Th...	ACTING	8	7	9	9	9	42	7.95

Rows of step: Contest (96 rows)

3. With a **Select values** step, keep only the following columns: `Country`, `Performance`, and `totalScore`.

4. With a **Sort Rows** step sort the data by `Country` ascendant.

5. After the **Sort Rows** step, put a **Row denormalizer** step.

6. Double-click this last step to configure it.

7. As the key field put `Performance`, and as group fields put `Country`.

8. Fill the target fields' grid like shown:

Target fields:

	Target fieldname	Value fieldname	Key value	Type	F...	L...	P...	C...	D...	G...	N...	Aggregation
1	score_1st_performance	totalScore	1st	Integer								Sum
2	score_2nd_performance	totalScore	2nd	Integer								Sum

9. Close the window.

10. With the **Row denormalizer** step selected, do a preview. You will see this:

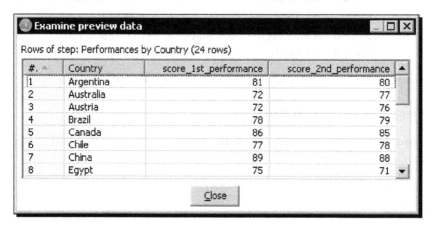

What just happened?

You read the contest file, grouped the data by country, and then created a new column for every performance. As values for those new fields you put the sum of the scores by performance and by country.

Using Row denormalizer for aggregating data

The purpose for which you used the **Row denormaliser** step in this tutorial was different from the purpose in the previous tutorial. In this case, you put the countries in rows, the performances in columns, and in the cells you put sums. The final dataset was kind of a cross tab like those you create with the DataPilot tool in Open Office, or the Pivot in Excel. The big difference is that here the final dataset is not interactive because, in essence, PDI is not. Another difference is that here you have to know the names or elements for the columns in advance.

Let's explain how the **Row denormalizer** step works in these cases. Basically, the way it works is quite the same as before:

The step groups the rows by the grouping fields and creates a new output row for each group.

The novelty here is the **aggregation** of values. When more than one row in the group matches the value for the key field, PDI calculates the new output field as the result of applying an aggregate function to all the values. The aggregate functions available are the same you already saw when you learned the **Group by** step—sum, minimum, first value, and so on. Take a look at the following sample rows:

#. ▲	Country	Performance	totalScore
49	India	1st	38
50	India	1st	39
51	India	2nd	41
52	India	2nd	40

The first two rows had 1st as the value for the key field Performance. According to the rule of the **Row denormaliser** step, the values for the field totalScore of these two rows go to the new target field score_1st_performance. As the rule applies for two rows, the values for those rows have to be added, as Sum was the selected aggregation function.

So, the output data for this sample group is this:

#. ▲	Country	score_1st_performance	score_2nd_performance
13	India	77	81

The value for the new field score_1st_performance is 77 and is the sum of 38 and 39, the values of the field totalScore for the input rows where Performance was "1st."

> Please note the difference between the **Row denormaliser** and the **Group by** step for aggregating. With the **Row denormaliser** step, you generate another new field for each interesting key value. Using the **Group by** step for the tutorial, you couldn't have created the two columns shown in the preceding screenshot—score_1st_performance and score_2nd_performance.

Have a go hero – calculating scores by skill by continent

Create a new transformation. Read the contest file and generate the following output:

Continent	VoiceScore	OverallPScore	ActingScore	ChoreographyScore
Africa	36	39	35	36
America	39	40	39	39
Asia	39	40	41	40
Europe	38	39	39	39
Oceania	34	38	39	38

To get the continent for each country, download the countries.txt file from the Packt website and get the information with a **Stream lookup** step.

Normalizing data

Some datasets are nice to see but complicate to process further. Take a look at the matches file we saw in Chapter 3:

```
Match Date;Home Team;Away Team;Result
02/06;Italy;France;2-1
02/06;Argentina;Hungary;2-1
06/06;Italy;Hungary;3-1
06/06;Argentina;France;2-1
10/06;France;Hungary;3-1
10/06;Italy;Argentina;1-0
...
```

Imagine you want to answer these questions:

1. How many teams played?

2. Which team converted most goals?

3. Which team won all matches it played?

The dataset is not prepared to answer those questions, at least in an easy way. If you want to answer those questions in a simple way, you will first have to normalize the data, that is, convert it to a suitable format before proceeding. Let's work on it.

Time for action – enhancing the matches file by normalizing the dataset

Now you will convert the matches file you generated in Chapter 2 to a format suitable for answering the proposed questions.

1. Search on your disk for the file you created in Chapter 2, or download it from the Packt website.

2. Create a new transformation and read the file by using a **Text file input** step.

3. With a **Split Fields** step, split the `Result` field in two: `home_t_goals` and `away_t_goals`. (Do you remember having done this in chapter 3?)

4. From the **Transform** category of steps, drag a **Row Normalizer** step to the canvas.

5. Create a hop from the last step to this new one.

6. Double-click the **Row Normalizer** step to edit it and fill the window as follows:

7. With the **Row Normalizer** selected, do a preview. You should see this:

What just happened?

You read the matches file and converted the dataset to a new one where both the home team and the away team appeared under a new column named `team`, together with another new column named `goals` holding the goals converted by each team. With this new format, it is really easy now to answer the questions proposed at the beginning of the section.

Modifying the dataset with a Row Normalizer step

The **Row Normalizer** step modifies your dataset, so it becomes more suitable for processing. Usually this involves transforming columns into rows.

To understand how it works, let's take as example the file from the tutorial. Here is a sketch of what we want to have at the end:

What we have now is this:

	Match Date	Home Team	Goals	Away Team	Goals
1st Match →	02/06	Italy	2	France	1
2nd Match →	02/06	Argentina	2	Hungary	1
	...	...	...	...	...

Now it is just a matter of creating a correspondence between the old columns and the new ones.

Just follow these steps and you have the work done:

Step	Example
Identify the new desired fields. Give them a name.	`team`, `goals`.
Look at the old fields and identify which ones you want to translate to the new fields.	`Home_Team`, `home_t_goals`, `Away_Team`, `away_t_goals`.
From that list, identify the columns you want to keep together in the same row, creating a sort of classification of the fields. Give each group a name. Also, give a name to the classification.	You want to keep together the fields `Home_Team` and `home_t_goals`. So, you create a group with those fields, and name it `home`.
	Likewise, you create a group named `away` with the fields `Away_Team` and `away_t_goals`.
	Name the classification as `class`.
Define a correspondence between the fields identified above, and the new fields.	The old field `Home_Team` goes to the new field `team`.
	The old field `home_t_goals` goes to the new field `goals`.
	The old field `Away_Team` goes to the new field `team`.
	The old field `away_t_goals` goes to the new field `goals`.

Transcript all these definitions to the **Row Normalizer** configuration window as shown below:

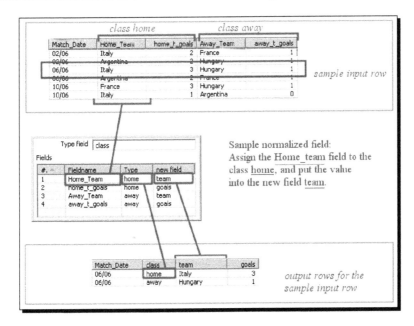

In the fields grid, insert one row for each of the fields you want to normalize.

Once you normalize, you have a new dataset where the fields for the groups you defined were converted to rows.

The number of rows in the new dataset is equal to the number of groups defined by the number of rows in the old dataset. In the tutorial, the final number is 24 rows x 2 groups = 48 rows.

Note that the fields not mentioned in the configuration of the **Row Normalizer** (Match_Date field in the example) are kept without changes. They are simply duplicated for each new row.

In the tutorial, every group was made by two fields: Home_Team and home_t_goals for the first group, and Away_Team and away_t_goals for the second. When you normalize, a group may have just one field, two fields (as in this example), or more than two fields.

Summarizing the PDI steps that operate on sets of rows

The **Row Normaliser** and **Row denormalizer** steps you learned in this chapter are some of the PDI steps which, rather than treating single rows, operate on sets of rows. The following table gives you an overview of the main PDI steps that fall into this particular group of steps:

Step	Purpose
Group by	Builds aggregates such as Sum, Maximum, and so on, on groups of rows.
Univariate Statistics	Computes some simple statistics. It complements the **Group by**. It has less capabilities than that step but provides more aggregate functions such as median and percentiles.
Split Fields	Splits a single field into more than one. Actually it doesn't operate on a set of rows, but it's common to use it combined with some of the steps in this table. For example: You could use a **Group by** step to concatenate a field, followed by a **Split Fields** step that splits that concatenated field into several columns.
Row Normaliser	Transforms columns into rows making the dataset more suitable for processing.
Row denormaliser	Moves information from rows to columns according to the values of a key field.
Row flattener	Flattens consecutive rows. You could achieve the same by using a **Group by** to concatenate the field to flatten, followed by a **Split Field** step.
Sort rows	Sorts rows based on field values. Alternatively, it can keep only unique rows.
Split field to rows	Splits a single string field and creates a new row for each split term.
Unique rows	Removes double consecutive rows and leaves only unique occurrences.

For examples on using these steps or for getting more information about them, please refer to Appendix C, *Quick reference: Steps and Job Entries.*

Have a go hero – verifying the benefits of normalization

Extend the transformation and answer the questions proposed at the beginning of the section:

◆ How many teams played?

◆ Which team converted most goals?

◆ Which team won all matches it played?

> For answering the third question, you'll have to modify the **Row Normalizer** step as well.

If you are not convinced that the normalizer process makes the work easier, you can try to answer the questions without normalizing. That effort will definitively convince you!

Have a go hero – normalizing the Films file

Consider the output of the first *Time for action* section in this chapter. Generate the following output:

#.	feature	description
56	film	Caché
57	year	2005
58	genres	-
59	director	Michael Haneke
60	cast	Daniel Auteuil, Juliette Binoche, Maurice Bénichou
61	film	Jean de Florette
62	year	1986
63	genres	Historical drama
64	director	Claude Berri
65	cast	Yves Montand, Gérard Depardieu, Daniel Auteuil
66	film	Le Ballon rouge
67	year	1956
68	genres	Fantasy | Comedy | Drama
69	director	-
70	cast	
71	film	Casque d'or
72	year	1952

You have two options here:

◆ To modify the tutorial by sending the output to a new file. Then to use that new file to do this exercise.

◆ To extend the stream in the original transformation by adding new steps after the Row Denormalizer step.

After doing the exercise, think about this: Does it make sense to denormalize and then normalize again? What is the difference between the original file and the output of this exercise? Could you have done the same without denormalizing and normalizing?

Have a go hero – calculating scores by judge

Take the contest file and generate the following output, where the columns represent the minimum, maximum, and average score given by every judge:

#.	Judge	min_score	max_score	avg_score
1	Judge 1	6	9	7
2	Judge 2	6	9	7
3	Judge 3	7	9	8
4	Judge 4	7	9	7
5	Judge 5	7	9	8

This exercise may appear difficult at first, but here's a clue: After reading the file, use a **Group by** step to calculate all the values you need for your final output. Leave the group field empty so that the step groups all rows in the dataset.

Generating a custom time dimension dataset by using Kettle variables

Dimensions are sets of attributes useful for describing a business. A list of products along with their shape, color, or size is a typical example of dimension. The **time dimension** is a special dimension used for describing a business in terms of when things happened. Just think of a time dimension as a list of dates along with attributes describing those dates. For example, given the date 05/08/2009, you know that it is a day of August, it belongs to the third quarter and it is Wednesday. These are some of the attributes for that date.

In the following tutorial you will create a transformation that generates the dataset for a time dimension. The dataset for a time dimension has one row for every date in a given range of dates and one column for each attribute of the date.

Time for action – creating the time dimension dataset

In this tutorial we will create a simple dataset for a time dimension.

First we will create a stream with the days of the week:

1. Create a new transformation.

2. Press *Ctrl+T* to access the **Transformation** settings window.

3. Select the **Parameters** tab and fill it like shown in the next screenshot:

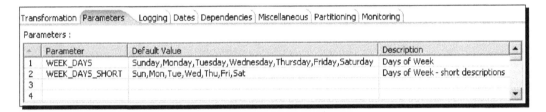

4. Expand the **Job** category of steps.

5. Drag a **Get Variables** step to the canvas, double-click the step, and fill the window like here:

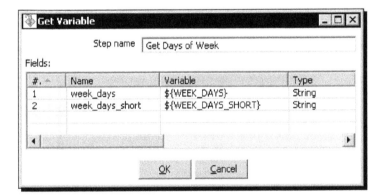

6. After the **Get Variables** step, add a **Split Fields** step and use it to split the field `week_days` into seven `String` fields named `sun, mon, tue, wed, thu, fri,` and `sat`. As **Delimiter**, set a comma (,).

7. Add one more **Split Fields** step and use it to split the field `week_days_short` into seven `String` fields named `sun_sh, mon_sh, tue_sh, wed_sh, thu_sh, fri_sh,` and `sat_sh`. As **Delimiter**, set a comma (,).

8. After this last step, add a **Row Normalizer** step.

9. Double-click the **Row Normalizer** step and fill it as follows:

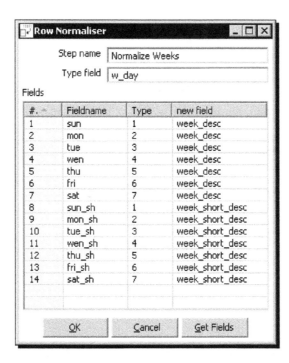

10. Keep the **Row Normalizer** step selected and do a preview. You will see this:

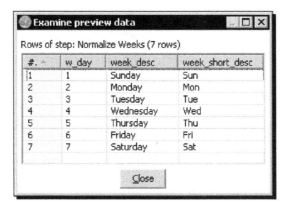

Now let's build the main stream:

1. Drag a **Generate Rows** step, an **Add sequence** step, a **Calculator** step, and a **Filter rows** step to the canvas.

2. Link them so you get this:

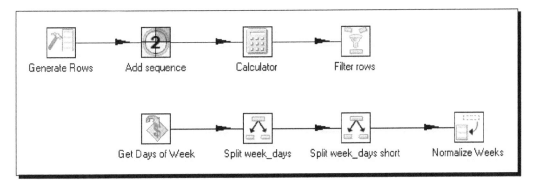

3. Double-click the **Generate Rows** step and use it to generate `45000` lines. Add a single `Date` field named `first_day`. As **Format** select `yyyyMMdd` and as **Value** write `19000101`.

4. Double-click the **Add sequence** step. In the **Name of value** textbox, type `days`.

5. Double-click the **Calculator** step and fill the window as shown next:

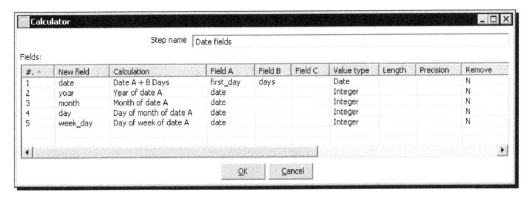

6. Double-click the **Filter rows** step and add the filter `date <= 31/12/2020`. When you enter the date `31/12/2020`, make sure to set the **Type** to `Date` and the **Conversion format** to `dd/MM/yyyy`. After the **Filter rows** step add a **Stream lookup** step.

7. Create two hops—one from the **Filter rows** step to the **Stream lookup** step and the other from the **Row Normalizer** step to the **Stream lookup** step.

8. Double-click the **Stream lookup** step. In the upper grid add a row, setting `week_day` under the **Field** column and `w_day` under the **LookupField** column. Use the lower grid to retrieve the **String** fields `week_desc` and `week_short_desc`. Finally, after the **Stream lookup** step, add a **Select values** step.

9. Use the **Select values** step to remove the unused fields `first_day` and `days`. Create a hop from the **Stream lookup** step to this step.

10. With the **Select values** step selected, click the **preview** button.

11. When the preview window appears click on **Configure**.

12. Fill the column value in the **Parameters** grid of the transformation execution window as follows:

	Parameter	Value	Defa
1	WEEK_DAYS	Domingo,Segunda-feira,Terça-feira,Quarta-feira,Quinta-feira,Sexta-feira,Sábado	Sund
2	WEEK_DAYS_SHORT	Dom.,2da,3a,4ta,5ta,6ta,Sáb.	Sun,

13. Click the **Launch** button. You will see this:

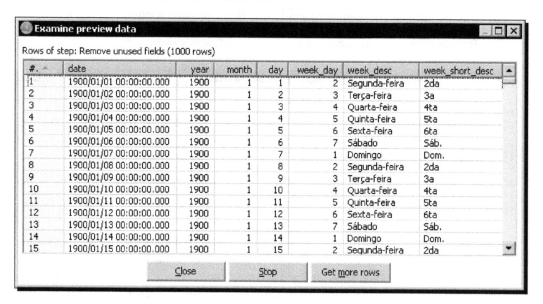

Examine preview data

Rows of step: Remove unused fields (1000 rows)

#.	date	year	month	day	week_day	week_desc	week_short_desc
1	1900/01/01 00:00:00.000	1900	1	1	2	Segunda-feira	2da
2	1900/01/02 00:00:00.000	1900	1	2	3	Terça-feira	3a
3	1900/01/03 00:00:00.000	1900	1	3	4	Quarta-feira	4ta
4	1900/01/04 00:00:00.000	1900	1	4	5	Quinta-feira	5ta
5	1900/01/05 00:00:00.000	1900	1	5	6	Sexta-feira	6ta
6	1900/01/06 00:00:00.000	1900	1	6	7	Sábado	Sáb.
7	1900/01/07 00:00:00.000	1900	1	7	1	Domingo	Dom.
8	1900/01/08 00:00:00.000	1900	1	8	2	Segunda-feira	2da
9	1900/01/09 00:00:00.000	1900	1	9	3	Terça-feira	3a
10	1900/01/10 00:00:00.000	1900	1	10	4	Quarta-feira	4ta
11	1900/01/11 00:00:00.000	1900	1	11	5	Quinta-feira	5ta
12	1900/01/12 00:00:00.000	1900	1	12	6	Sexta-feira	6ta
13	1900/01/13 00:00:00.000	1900	1	13	7	Sábado	Sáb.
14	1900/01/14 00:00:00.000	1900	1	14	1	Domingo	Dom.
15	1900/01/15 00:00:00.000	1900	1	15	2	Segunda-feira	2da

Close   Stop   Get more rows

What just happened?

You generated data for a time dimension with dates ranging from 01/01/1900 through 31/12/2020. Time dimensions are meant to answer questions related with time such as: Do I sell more on Mondays or on Fridays? Am I selling more this quarter than the same quarter last year? The list of attributes you need to include in your time dimension depends on the kind of question you want to answer. Typical fields in a time dimension include: year, month (a number between 1 and 12), description of month, day of month, week day, and quarter.

In the tutorial you created a few attributes, but you could have added much more. Among the attributes included you had the week day. The week descriptions were taken from named parameters, which allowed you to set the language of the week descriptions at the time you ran the transformation. In the tutorial you specified Portuguese descriptions. If you had left the parameters grid empty, the transformation would have used the English descriptions that you put as default.

Let's explain how you build the stream with the number and descriptions for the days of the week. First, you created a dataset by getting the variables with the descriptions for the days of the week. After creating the dataset, you split the descriptions and by using the **Row Normalize** step, you converted that row into a list of rows, one for every day of the week. In other words, you created a single row with all the descriptions for the days of the week. Then you normalized it to create the list of days.

 This method used for creating the list of days of a week is very useful when you have to create a very small dataset. It avoids the creation of external files to hold that data.

The transformation you created was inspired by the sample transformation `General - Populate date dimension.ktr` found in the `samples/transformations` folder inside the PDI installation folder. You can take a look at that transformation. It builds the dataset in a slightly different way, also by using **Row Normalizer** steps.

Getting variables

To create the secondary stream of the tutorial, you used a **Get Variables** step. The **Get Variables** step allows you to get the value of one or more variables. In this tutorial you read two variables that had been defined as named parameters.

When put as the first step of a stream like in this case, this step creates a dataset with one single row and as many fields as read variables.

The following is the dataset created by the **Get Variables** step in the time dimension tutorial:

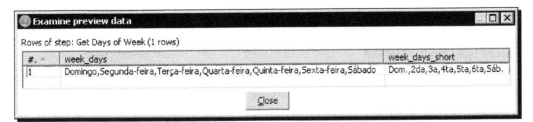

When put in the middle of a stream, this step adds to the incoming dataset, as many fields as the number of variables it reads. Let's see how it works.

Time for action – getting variables for setting the default starting date

Let's modify the transformation so that the starting date depends on a parameter.

1. Press *Ctrl+T* to open the transformation settings window.

2. Add a parameter named START_DATE with default value 01/12/1999.

3. Add a **Get variables** step between the **Calculator** step and the **Filter rows** step .

4. Edit the **Get variables** step and a new field named start_date. Under **Variable** write ${START_DATE}. As **Type** select Date, and under **Format** select or type dd/MM/yyyy.

5. Modify the filter step so the condition is now: date>=start_date and date<=31/12/2020.

6. Modify the **Select values** step to remove the start_date field.

7. With the **Select values** step selected do a preview. You will see this:

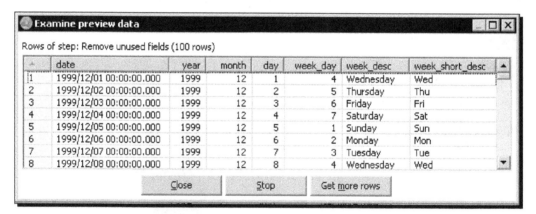

What just happened?

You added a starting date as a named parameter. Then you read that variable into a new field and used it to keep only the dates that are greater or equal to its value.

Using the Get Variables step

As you just saw, the **Get Variables** step allows you to get the value of one or more variables. In the main tutorial you saw how to use the step at the beginning of a stream. Now you saw how to use it in the middle. The following is the dataset after the **Get Variables** step for this last exercise:

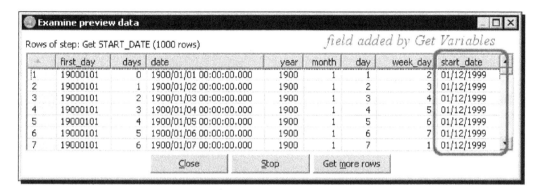

With the **Get Variables** step, you can read any Kettle variable—variables defined in the `kettle.properties` file, internal variables as for example `${user.dir}`, named parameters as in this tutorial, or variables defined in another transformation (you haven't yet learned about these variables but you will soon).

As you know, the type of Kettle variables is `String` by default. However, at the time you get a variable, you can change its metadata. As an example of that, in this last exercise you converted `${START_DATE}` to a `Date` by using the mask `dd/MM/yyyy`.

Note that you specified the variables as `${name of the variable}`. You could have used `%%name of the variable%%` also. The full specification of the name of a variable allows you to mix variables with plain text.

Suppose that instead of a date you create a parameter named `YEAR` with default value `1950`.

In the **Get variables** step you may specify `01/01/${YEAR}` as the value.

When you execute the transformation, this text will be expanded to `01/01/1950` or to `01/01/` plus the year you enter if you overwrite the default value.

> Note that the purpose of using the **Get Variable** step is to have the values of variables as fields in the dataset. Otherwise, you don't need to use this step for using a variable. You just use it wherever you see a dollar sign icon.

Have a go hero – enhancing the time dimension

Modify the time dimension generation by doing the following:

♦   Add the following fields to the dataset, taking as model the generation of weeks: `Name of month`, `Short name of month`, and `Quarter`.

♦   Add two more parameters: `start_year` and `end_year`. Modify the transformation so that it generates dates only between those years. In other words, you have to discard dates out of that range. You may assume that the parameters will be between 1900 and 2020.

Pop quiz – using Kettle variables inside transformations

There are some Kettle predefined variables that hold information about the logged in user: `user.country`, `user.language`, etc. The following tasks involve the use of some of those variables. Which of the tasks can be accomplished without using a **Get Variables** step or a **JavaScript** step (Remember from the previous chapter that you can also get the value for a Kettle variable with a **Javascript** step):

a.   Create a file named `hello_<user>.txt`, where `<user>` is the name of the logged user.

b.   Create a file named `hello.txt` that contains a single line with the text `Hello, <user>!`, `<user>` being is the name of the logged user.

c.   Write to the log (by using the **Write to log** step) a greeting message like `Hello, user!`. The message has to be written in a different language depending on the language of the logged user.

d.   All of the above

e.   None of the above

Summary

In this chapter, you learned to transform your dataset by applying two magical steps: **Row Normalizer** and **Row denormalizer**. These two steps aren't the kind of steps you use every day such as a **Filter Rows** or a **Select values** step. But when you need to do the kind of task they achieve, you are really grateful that these steps exist. They do a complex task in a quite simple way. You also learned what a time dimension is and how to create a dataset for a time dimension.

So far, you've been learning to transform data. In the next chapter, you will set that kind of learning aside for a while. The chapter will be devoted to an essential subject when it comes to working in productive environments and dealing with real data—data validation and error handling.

7
Validating Data and Handling Errors

So far, you have been working alone in front of your own computer. In the "Time for action" exercises, the step-by-step instructions along with the error-free sample data helped you create and run transformations free of errors. During the "Have a go hero" exercises, you likely encountered numerous errors, but tips and troubleshooting notes were there to help you get rid of them.

This is quite different from real scenarios, mainly for two reasons:

◆ Real data has errors—a fact that can't be avoided. If you fail to heed it, the transformations that run with your sample data will probably crash when running with real data.

◆ In most cases, who runs your final work is decided by an automated process and is not user defined. Therefore, if a transformation crashes, there will be nobody to fix the problem.

In this chapter you will learn about the options that PDI offers to treat errors and validate data so that your transformations are well prepared to be run in a productive environment.

Capturing errors

Suppose that you are running or previewing a transformation from Spoon. As you already know, if an error occurs it is shown in the **Logging** window inside the **Execution Results** pane. As a consequence, you can look at the error, try to fix it, and run the transformation again. This is far from what happens in real life. As said, transformations in real scenarios are supposed to be automated. Therefore, it is not acceptable to have a transformation that crashes without someone who notices it and reacts to that situation. On the contrary, it's your duty to do everything you can to trap errors that may happen, avoiding unexpected crashes when possible. In this section you will learn how to do that.

Time for action – capturing errors while calculating the age of a film

In this tutorial you will use the output of the denormalizing process from the previous chapter. You will calculate the age of the films and classify them according to their age.

1. Get the file with the films. You can take the transformation that denormalized the data and generate the file with a **Text file output** step, or you can take a sample file from the Packt website.

2. Create a new transformation and read the file with a **Text file input** step.

3. Do a preview of the data. You will see the following:

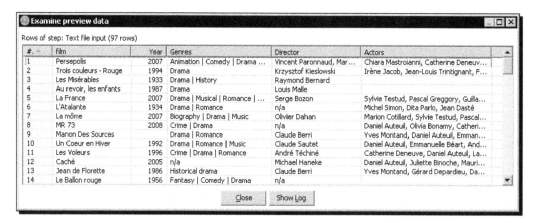

4. After the **Text file input** step, add a **Get System Info** step.

5. Edit the step, add a new field named `today`, and choose `Today 00:00:00` as its value.

6. Add a **JavaScript** step.

7. Edit the step and type the following piece of code:
    ```
    var diff;
    film_date = str2date('01/01/' + Year, 'dd/MM/yyyy');
    diff = dateDiff(film_date,today,"y");
    ```

8. Click on **Get variables** to add `diff` as a new field.

9. Add a **Number range** step, edit it, and fill its window as follows:

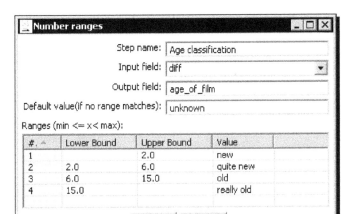

10. With a **Sort rows** step, sort the data by `diff`.

11. Finally, add a **Group by** step and double-click to edit it.

12. As group field put `age_of_film`. In the **Aggregates** grid create a field named `number_of_films` to hold the number of films with that age. Put `film` as the **Subject** and select `Number of values (N)` as the **Type**.

13. Add a **Dummy** step at the end and do a preview. You will be surprised by an error like this:

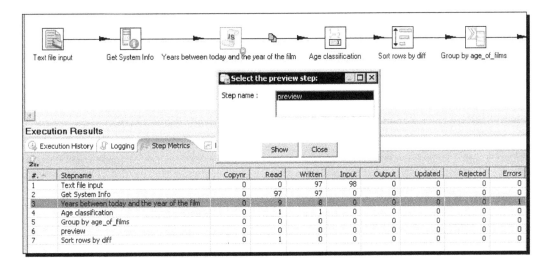

14. Look at the logging window. It looks like this:

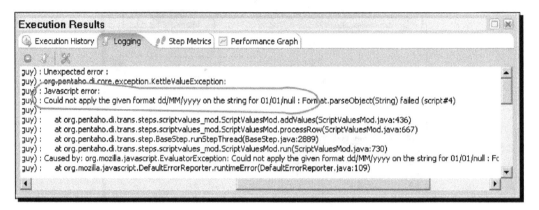

15. Now drag **Write to log** step to the canvas from the **Utility** category.

16. Create a hop from the **JavaScript** step to this new step.

17. Select the **JavaScript** step, right-click it to bring up a contextual menu, and select **Define error handling....**

18. The error handling settings window appears. Fill it like shown:

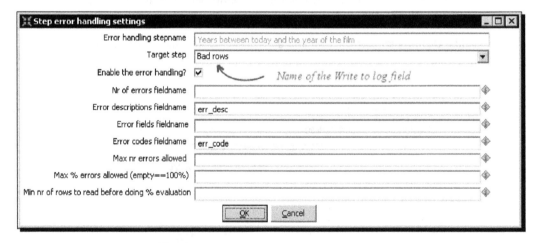

19. Click on **OK**.

20. Save the transformation and do a new preview on the **Dummy** step. You will see this:

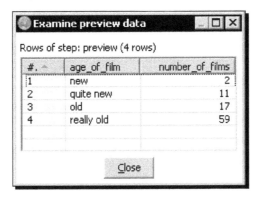

21. The logging window will show you this:

```
... - Bad rows.0 -
... - Bad rows.0 - ------------> Linenr 1------------------------
... - Bad rows.0 - null
... - Bad rows.0 -
... - Bad rows.0 - Javascript error:
... - Bad rows.0 - Could not apply the given format dd/MM/yyyy
on the string for 01/01/null : Format.parseObject(String) failed
(script#4)
... - Bad rows.0 -
... - Bad rows.0 - --> 4:0
... - Bad rows.0 - SCR-001
... - Bad rows.0 -
... - Bad rows.0 - ====================
... - Bad rows.0 -
... - Bad rows.0 - ------------> Linenr 2------------------------
... - Bad rows.0 - null
... - Bad rows.0 -
... - Bad rows.0 - Javascript error:
... - Bad rows.0 - Could not apply the given format dd/MM/yyyy
on the string for 01/01/null : Format.parseObject(String) failed
(script#4)
... - Bad rows.0 -
... - Bad rows.0 - --> 4:0
...
```

The date was cut from the log for clarity of the log messages.

22. Now do a preview on the **Write to log** step. This is what you see:

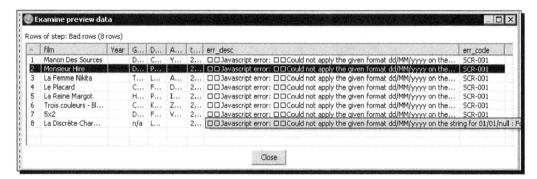

What just happened?

You created a transformation to read a list of films and group them according to their age, that is, how old the movie is. You were surprised by an unexpected error caused by the rows in which the year was undefined. Then you implemented error handling to capture that error and to avoid the abortion of the transformation. With the treatment of the error, you split the stream in two:

♦ The rows that caused the error went to a new stream that wrote to the log information about the error

♦ The rows that passed the **JavaScript** step without problem went through the main path

Using PDI error handling functionality

With the error handling functionality, you can capture errors that otherwise would cause the transformation to halt. Instead of aborting, the rows that cause the errors are sent to a different stream for further treatment.

You don't need to implement error handling in every step, but in those where it's more likely to have errors when running the transformation. A typical situation where you should consider handling errors is in a **JavaScript** step. A code that works perfectly when designing might fail while executing against real data, where the most common errors are related to data type conversions or indexes out of range. Another common use of error handling is when working with databases (you will see more on this later in the book).

To configure the error handling, you have to right-click the step and select **Define Error handling**.

Note that not all steps support error handling. The **Define Error handling** option is available only when clicking on steps that support it.

After opening the settings window, you have to fill it just as you did in the tutorial. You have to specify the target step for the bad rows along with the name of the extra fields being added, as part of the treatment of errors:

Field	Description
Nr of errors fieldname	Name for the field that will have the number of errors
Error fields fieldname	Name for the field that will have the name of the field(s) that caused the errors
Error codes fieldname	Name for the field that will have the error code
Error descriptions fieldname	Name for the field that will have the error description

The first two are trivial. The last two deserve an explanation. The values for the error code and description fields are the same as those you see in the **Logging** tab when you don't trap the error. In the tutorial there was a JavaScript error with code SCR-001 and description JavaScript error: Could not apply the given format.... You saw this code as well as its description in the **Logging** tab when you didn't trap the error and the transformation crashed, and in the preview you made at the end of the error stream. This particular error was a JavaScript one, but the kind of error you get depends always on the kind of step where it occurs.

You are not forced to fill all the textboxes in the error setting window. Only the fields for which you provide a name will be added to the dataset. By doing a preview on the target step, you can see the extra fields that were added.

Aborting a transformation

You can handle the errors by detecting and sending bad rows to an extra stream. But when the errors are too many or when the errors are severe, the best option is to cancel the whole transformation. Let's see how to force the abortion of a transformation in such a situation.

Time for action – aborting when there are too many errors

1. Open the transformation from the previous tutorial and save it under a different name.

2. From the **Flow** category, drag an **Abort** step to the canvas.

3. Create a hop from the **Write to log** step to the **Abort** step.

4. Double-click the **Abort** step. Enter 5 as **Abort threshold**. As **Abort message**, type Too many errors calculating age of film!.

5. Click **OK**.

6. Select the **Dummy** step and do a preview. As a result, a warning window shows up informing you that there were no rows to display. In the **Step Metrics** tab, the **Abort after 5 errors** line becomes red to show you that there was an error:

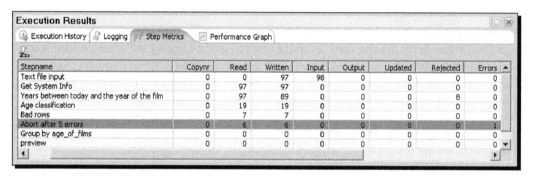

Stepname	Copynr	Read	Written	Input	Output	Updated	Rejected	Errors
Text file input	0	0	97	98	0	0	0	0
Get System Info	0	97	97	0	0	0	0	0
Years between today and the year of the film	0	97	89	0	0	0	8	0
Age classification	0	19	19	0	0	0	0	0
Bad rows	0	7	7	0	0	0	0	0
Abort after 5 errors	0	6	6	0	0	0	0	1
Group by age_of_films	0	0	0	0	0	0	0	0
preview	0	0	0	0	0	0	0	0

7. The log looks like this:

```
...  - Bad rows.0 -
...  - Bad rows.0 - ====================
...  - Abort after 5 errors.0 - Row nr 6 causing abort :
[Trois couleurs - Blanc], [null], [Comedy | Drama],
[Krzysztof Kieslowski], [Zbigniew Zamachowski, Julie Delpy],
[2009/08/18 00:00:00.000], [
...  - Abort after 5 errors.0 - Javascript error:
...  - Abort after 5 errors.0 - Could not apply the given
format dd/MM/yyyy on the string for 01/01/null : Format.
parseObject(String) failed (script#4)
...  - Abort after 5 errors.0 -
...  - Abort after 5 errors.0 - --> 4:0], [SCR-001]
...  - Abort after 5 errors.0 - Too many errors calculating age of
film!
...  - Abort after 5 errors.0 - Finished processing (I=0, O=0, R=6,
W=6, U=0, E=1)
```

```
. . .
. . . - Spoon - The transformation has finished!!
. . . - error_handling_with_abort - ERROR (version 3.2.0-GA, build
10572 from 2009-05-12 08.45.26 by buildguy) : Errors detected!
```

What just happened?

You forced the abortion of a transformation after five erroneous rows.

Aborting a transformation using the Abort step

Through the use of the **Abort** step, you force the abortion of a transformation. Its main use is in error handling.

You can use the **Abort** step to force the abortion as soon as a row arrives to it, or after a certain number of rows as you did in the tutorial. To decide between one and the other option, you use the **Abort threshold** option. If threshold is 0, the **Abort** step will abort after the first row arrives. If threshold is N, the **Abort** step will cause the abortion of the transformation when the row number N+1 arrives at it.

Beyond the error handling situation, you may use the **Abort** step in any unexpected situation. Examples of that could be when you expect parameters and they are not present or when an incoming file is empty when it shouldn't be. In situations like these, you can force an abnormal ending of the execution just by adding an **Abort** step after the step that detects the anomaly.

Fixing captured errors

In the *Time for action—capturing errors while calculating the age of a film* section of this chapter, you sent the bad rows to the log. However, when you capture errors, you can send the bad rows toward any step as long as the step knows how to treat those rows. Let's see an example of that.

Time for action – treating errors that may appear

1. Open the transformation from the tutorial and save it under a different name.

2. From the **Transform** category, drag the **Add constants** step to the canvas.

3. Create a hop from the **Write to log** step to the **Add constants** step.

4. Add an Integer constant named diff with value 999, and a String constant named age_of_film with value unknown.

5. After the **Add constants** step, add a **Select values** step and use it to remove the fields `err_code` and `err_desc`.

6. Create a hop from the **Select values** step to the **Sort rows** step. Your transformation should look like this:

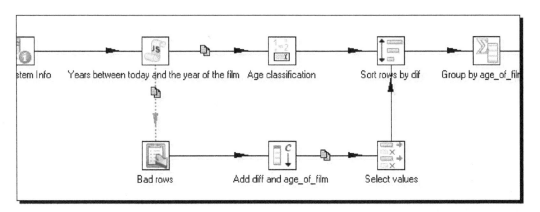

> Note that you are merging two streams. Those streams must have the same metadata. If you get a trap detector warning, please verify that you executed these instructions exactly as explained.

7. Select the **Dummy** step and do a preview. You will see this:

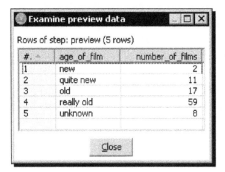

Examine preview data

Rows of step: preview (5 rows)

#. ▲	age_of_film	number_of_films
1	new	2
2	quite new	11
3	old	17
4	really old	59
5	unknown	8

Close

What just happened?

You modified the transformation so that you didn't end up discarding the erroneous rows. In the error stream (the stream after the red dotted line), you fixed the rows by putting default values for the new fields. After that you returned the rows to the main stream.

Treating rows coming to the error stream

If the errors are not severe enough to discard the rows, if you can somehow guess what data was supposed to be there instead of the error, or if you have default values for erroneous data, you can do your best to fix the errors and send the rows back to the main stream.

What you did instead of discarding the rows with no year information was to fix the rows and send them back to the main stream. The **Group by** step grouped them under a separate category named unknown.

There are no rules for what to do with bad rows where you handle errors. You always have the option to discard the bad rows or try to fix them. Sometimes you can fix only a few and discard the rest of them. It always depends on your particular data or business rules.

Pop quiz – PDI error handling

What does the PDI error-handling functionality do:

    a.   Avoids the happening of unexpected errors

    b.   Captures errors that happen and discards erroneous rows so you can continue working with valid data

    c.   Captures errors that happen and sends erroneous rows to a new stream, letting you decide what to do with them

Have a go hero – capturing errors while seeing who wins

On the Packt website you will find a modified football match file named `wcup_modified.txt`. This modified file has some intentional errors.

Download the file and do the following:

1. Create a transformation, read the file with a **Text file input** step. Set all fields as string.

2. Add a **JavaScript** step and type the following code in it:

```
var result_desc;
result_split = Result.split('-');
home_g = str2num(result_split[0]);
away_g = str2num(result_split[1]);
if (home_g > away_g)
        result_desc = Home_Team + ' wins';
else if (home_g < away_g)
        result_desc = Away_Team + ' wins';
else result_desc = 'Nobody wins';
```

3. In the grid below the code, add the string variable `result_desc`.

4. Do a preview on the **JavaScript** step and see what happens.

5. Now try any of the following two solutions:

   ❑ Handle the errors and discard the rows that cause those errors. Abort if there are more than 10 errors.

   ❑ Handle the errors and fix the transformation by setting a default result description for the rows that cause the errors.

Avoiding unexpected errors by validating data

To avoid unexpected errors that happen or just to meet your requirements is a common practice to validate your data before processing it. Let's do some validations.

Time for action – validating genres with a Regex Evaluation step

In this tutorial you will read the modified films file and validate the genres field.

1. Create a new transformation.

2. Read the modified films file just as you did in the previous tutorial.

3. In the **Content** tab, check the **Rownum in output?** option and fill the **Rownum fieldname** with the text `rownum`.

4. Do a preview. You should see this:

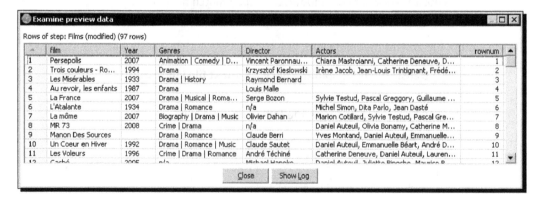

5. After the **Text file input** step, add a **Regex Evaluation** step. You will find it under the **Scripting** category of steps.

6. Under the **Step settings** box, select `Genres` as the **Field to evaluate**, and type `genres_ok` as the **Result Fieldname**.

7. In the **Regular expression** textbox type `[A-Za-z\s\-]*(\|[A-Za-z\s\-]*)*`.

8. Add the **Filter rows** step, an **Add constants** step, and two **Text file output** steps and link them as shown next:

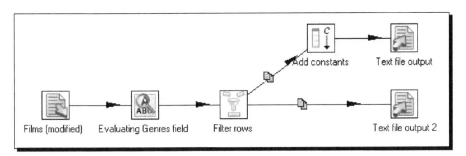

9. Edit the **Add constants** step.

10. Add a `String` constant named `err_code` with value `GEN_INV` and a `String` constant named `err_desc` with value `Invalid list of genres`.

11. Configure the **Text file output** step after the **Add constant** step to create the `${LABSOUTPUT}/films_err.txt` file, with the fields `rownum`, `err_code`, and `err_desc`.

12. Configure the other **Text file output** step to create the `${LABSOUTPUT}/films_ok.txt` file, with the fields `film`, `Year`, `Genres`, `Director`, and `Actors`.

13. Double-click the **Filter rows** step and add the condition **genres_ok = Y**, **Y** being a **Boolean** value. Send true data to the stream that generates the `films_ok.txt` file. Send false data to the other stream.

14. Run the transformation.

15. Check the generated files. The `films_err.txt` file looks like the following:

```
rownum;err_code;err_desc
12;GEN_INV;Invalid list of genres
18;GEN_INV;Invalid list of genres
20;GEN_INV;Invalid list of genres
21;GEN_INV;Invalid list of genres
22;GEN_INV;Invalid list of genres
33;GEN_INV;Invalid list of genres
34;GEN_INV;Invalid list of genres
...
```

The `films_ok.txt` file looks like this:

```
film;Year;Genres;Director;Actors
Persepolis;2007;Animation | Comedy | Drama | History;Vincent
Paronnaud, Marjane Satrapi;Chiara Mastroianni, Catherine Deneuve,
Danielle Darrieux
Trois couleurs - Rouge;1994;Drama;Krzysztof Kieslowski;Irène
Jacob, Jean-Louis Trintignant, Frédérique Feder, Jean-Pierre
Lorit, Samuel Le Bihan
Les Misérables;1933;Drama | History;Raymond Bernard;

...
```

What just happened?

You read the films file and checked that the `Genres` field was a list of strings separated by `|`. You created two files:

◆ One file with the valid rows.

◆ Another file with the rows with an invalid `Genres` field. Note that the `rownum` field you added when you read the file is used here for identifying the wrong lines.

In order to check the validity of the `Genres` field, you used a regular expression. The expression you typed accepts any combination of characters, spaces, or hyphens separated by a pipe. The `*` symbol allows empty genres as well. For a detailed explanation of regular expressions, please refer to Chapter 2.

Validating data

As said, you would validate data mainly for two reasons:

◆ To prevent the transformation from aborting because of unexpected errors

◆ To check that your data meets some pre-existing requirements

For example, consider some of the sample data from previous chapters:

◆ In the match file, the results field had to be a string formed by two numbers separated by a -

◆ In the real estate file, the flag for Fireplace had to be `Yes` or `No`

◆ In the contest file the name of the country had to be a valid country, not a random string

If your data doesn't meet these requirements, it is possible that you don't have errors but you will still be working with invalid data.

In the last tutorial you just validated one of the fields. If you want to validate more than one field, you have a specific step that simplifies that work: The **Data Validator**.

Time for action – checking films file with the Data Validator

Let's validate not only the Genres field, but also the Year field.

1. Open the last transformation and save it under a new name.

2. Delete all steps except the **Text file input** and **Text file output** steps.

3. In the **Fields** tab of the **Text file input** step, change the **Type** of the Year from Integer to String.

4. From the **Validation** category add a **Data Validator** step. Also add a **Select values** step. Link all steps as follows:

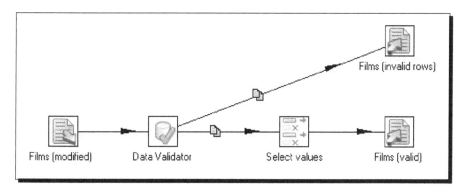

5. Double-click the **Data Validator** step.

6. Check the **Report all errors, not only the first** option found on at the top of the window. This will enable the **Output one row, concatenate errors with separator** option. Check this option too, and fill the textbox to the right with a slash /. Click on **New validation** and type genres as the name of the validation rule.

7. Click on **OK**.

8. Click on **genres**. The right half of the window is filled with checkboxes and textboxes where you will define the rule.

9. Fill the header of the rule definition as follows:

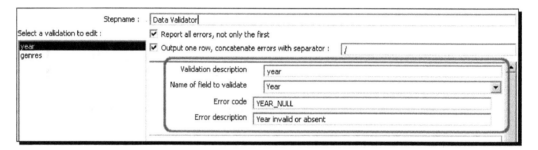

10. In the **Regular expression expected to match** textbox, type
`[A-Za-z\s\-]*(\|[A-Za-z\s\-]*)*`

11. Click on **New validation** and type `year` as the name of the validation rule.

12. Click on **OK**.

13. Click on **year** and fill the header of the rule definition as follows:

14. In the data block, select the **Only numeric data expected** checkbox option.

15. Click on **OK**.

16. Right-click the **Data Validator** step and select **Define error handling....**

17. Fill the error handling settings window as follows: As **Target step**, select the step that generates the file with invalid rows. Check the **Enable the error handling?** checkbox. Type `err_desc` as **Error description** field **name**, `err_field` as **Error fields**, and `err_code` as **Error codes**. Click on **OK**.

18. Use the **Select values** step to change the metadata for the `Year` from `String` to `Integer`.

19. Save the transformation and run it.

20. Check the generated files. The `films_err.txt` file now has more detail, as you validated two fields.

```
rownum;err_code;err_desc
9;YEAR_NULL;Year invalid or absent
        12;GEN_INV;Invalid list of genres
        18;GEN_INV;Invalid list of genres
        20;GEN_INV;Invalid list of genres
        21;GEN_INV;Invalid list of genres
        22;GEN_INV;Invalid list of genres
        33;GEN_INV;Invalid list of genres
        34;GEN_INV;Invalid list of genres
47;YEAR_NULL/GEN_INV;Year invalid or absent/Invalid list of genres
48;YEAR_NULL/GEN_INV;Year invalid or absent/Invalid list of genres
49;YEAR_NULL;Year invalid or absent
. . .
```

21. The `films_ok.txt` file should have less rows instead, as the films with year invalid or absent are no longer sent to this file.

What just happened?

You used the **Data Validator** step to validate both the genres list and the year. You created a file with the good rows, and another file with the information to show you which errors were found.

Defining simple validation rules using the Data Validator

The **Data Validator** step, or **DV** for short, allows you to define simple validation rules to describe the expected characteristics for the incoming fields. The good thing about the DV step is that it concentrates several validations into a single step, and obviously it supports error handling.

For every validation rule, you have to specify these fields:

Field	Description
Name of the field to validate	Name of the incoming field whose value will be validated with this rule
Error code	The error code to pass to error handling. If omitted, a default is set
Error description	The error description to pass to error handling. If omitted, a default is set

The error code and error description are useful to identify which field was erroneous when you have more than one validation rule in a single DV step.

It is possible for more than one field to cause a row pass to error handling. In that case, you can generate one output row per error or a single row with all error descriptions concatenated. In the tutorial you chose this last option.

In the settings window, once you select a validation rule, you have two blocks of settings—the **Data block** where you define the expected data for a field and the **Type block** where you validate if a field matches a given type or not.

In the **Data block** you set the actual validation rule for a field.

The following table summarizes the kinds of validations you may apply in this block:

Validation	Data block options
Allowing (only) null values	**Null allowed? / Only null values allowed?**
Making sure that the length of the selected field is between a range of values	**Max string length / Min string length**. You may use one or both at the same time.
Making sure that the value of the selected field is between a range of values	**Maximum value / Minimum value** You may use one or both at the same time.
Making sure that the selected field matches a pattern	◆ **Only numeric data expected** ◆ **Expected start string** ◆ **Expected end string** ◆ **Regular expression expected to match**
Making sure that the selected field doesn't match a pattern	◆ **Not allowed start string** ◆ **Not allowed end string** ◆ **Regular expression not allowed to match**
Making sure that the selected field is one of the values in a given list	◆ **Allowed values** (when you have a fixed list) ◆ **Read allowed values from another step?** (when the list comes from another stream)

In the tutorial, you used just a couple from this long list of options. For the validation of the genres, you used a regular expression that the field had to match. For the year, you checked that the field wasn't null and that it contained only numeric data.

Let's briefly explain what you did to validate the year. You read the year as a `String`. Then with the DV you checked that it contained only numeric data. If the data was valid, you changed the metadata to `Integer` after the row left the DV step.

Why didn't you simply validate whether the year was an Integer? This is because the type validation just checks that the year is an integer field, rather than checking if it can be converted into an integer. In this case, the year is of type `String` because you read it as a String in the **Text file input** step.

What would happen if you read the year as an Integer? The invalid fields would cause an error in the **Text file input** step, and the row would never arrive to the DV step to be validated.

> The type block allows you to validate the type of an incoming field. This just checks the real data type, rather than checking if the field can be converted into a given data type.

Have a go hero – validating the football matches file

From the Packt website, download the `valid_countries.txt` file. Modify the transformation from the previous "Hero" section doing the following things.

After reading the file, apply the following validation rules:

Field	Validation rule
Match_Date	dd/mm, where dd/mm is a valid date.
Home_Team	Belongs to the list of countries in the `valid_countries.txt` file.
Away_Team	Belongs to the list of countries in the `valid_countries.txt` file.
Result	n-n where n is a number.

Also validate that Home_Team is different from Away_Team.

Use a **Data Validator** step when possible.

Send the bad rows to a file of invalid data and the good rows to the **JavaScript** step.

Test your transformation and check that every validation rule is applied as expected.

Cleansing data

While validation means mainly rejecting data, **data cleansing** detects and tries to fix not only invalid data, but also data considered illegal or inaccurate in a specific domain.

For example, consider a field representing a year. A year containing non-numeric symbols should always be considered invalid and then rejected.

Now look at the films example. In this specific case, the year might not be important to you. If you find a non-numeric value, you could just replace it by a null year meaning unknown and keep the data.

On the contrary, the simple rule that looks for numeric values is not enough. A year equal to 1084 should also be considered invalid as it is impossible to have a film made at that time. However, as it is a common error to type 0 instead of 9, you may assume that there was a human mistake and you could replace the 0 in 1084 by a 9 automatically.

Doing data cleansing actually involves trying to detect and deal with these kinds of situations, knowing in advance the rules that apply.

Data cleansing, also known as **data cleaning** or **data scrubbing**, may be done manually or automatically depending on the complexity of the cleansing. With PDI you can use the automated option. For the validating part of the process, you can use any of the steps or mechanisms explained above. While for the cleaning part you can use any PDI step that suits, there are some steps that are particularly useful.

Step	Purpose
If field value is null	If a field is null, it changes its value to a constant. It can be applied to all fields of the same data type, or to particular fields.
Null if...	Sets a field value to null if it is equal to a constant value.
Number range	Creates ranges based on a numeric field. An example of use is converting floating numbers to a discrete scale such as 0, 0.25, 0.50, and so on.
Value Mapper	Maps values of a field from one value to another. For example, you can use this step to convert yes/no, true/false, or 0/1 values to Y/N.
Stream lookup	Looks up values coming from another stream. In data cleansing, you can use it to set a default value if your field is not in a given list.
Database lookup	Same as **Stream lookup** but looking in a database table.
Unique rows	Removes double consecutive rows and leaves only unique occurrences.

For examples that use these steps or for getting more information about them, please refer to Appendix C, *Job Entries and Steps Reference*.

Have a go hero – cleansing films data

From the Packt's website, download the fix_genres.txt file. The file has the following lines:

```
erroneous;fixed
commedy;comedy
sci-fi; science fiction
science-fiction; science fiction
musical;music
historical;history
```

Create a new transformation and do the following:

Read the modified films file that you have used throughout the chapter. Validate that the genre is a list of strings separated by |. Send the bad rows to a file of bad rows. So far, this is the same as you did in the last two tutorials. Now clean the genres in the lists. For every genre:

1. Check that it is not null. If it is null, discard it.

2. Split composed genres in two. For example, `Historical drama` becomes `historical` and `drama`.

3. Standardize the descriptions:

   ◆ Remove trailing spaces.

   ◆ Change the descriptions to lower case.

4. Check that it is not misspelled. For doing that, use the `miss_genres.txt` file. If the genre is in the list, replace the text by the correct description.

5. After all this cleaning add a **Dummy** step and preview the results.

> To validate each genre, you can split the `Genres` field into rows. After the cleansing, you can recover the original lines by grouping the rows, using as aggregate `Concatenate strings separated by |` to concatenate the validated genres.

Summary

In this chapter, you learned two essential subjects when it comes to the running of transformations by nontechnical users, in productive environments, with real data— validating data and handling errors.

In the next chapter, we go back to the development, this time with a subject that most of you must be waiting for since Chapter 1—working with databases.

8
Working with Databases

Database systems are the main mechanism used by most organizations to store and administer organizational data. Online sales, bank-related operations, customer service history, and credit card transactions are some examples of data stored in databases.

This is the first of two chapters fully dedicated to working with databases. This chapter provides an overview of the main database concepts. It also covers the following topics:

◆ Connecting to databases

◆ Previewing and getting data from a database

◆ Inserting, updating, and deleting data from a database

Introducing the Steel Wheels sample database

As you were told in the first chapter, there is a Pentaho Demo that includes data for a fictional store named Steel Wheels and you can download it from the Internet. This data is stored in a database that is going to be the starting point for you to learn how to work with databases in PDI. Before beginning to work on databases, let's briefly introduce the Steel Wheels database along with some database definitions.

A **relational database** is a collection of items stored in tables. Typically, all items stored in a table belong to a particular type of data. The following table lists some of the tables in the Steel Wheels database:

Table	Content
CUSTOMERS	Steel Wheels' customers
EMPLOYEES	Steel Wheels' employees
PRODUCTS	Products sold by Steel Wheels
OFFICES	Steel Wheels' offices
ORDERS	Information about sales orders
ORDERDETAILS	Details about the sales orders

The items stored in the tables represent an entity or a concept in the real world. As an example, the CUSTOMERS table stores items representing customers. The ORDERS table stores items that represent sales orders in the real world.

In technical terms, a **table** is uniquely identified by a name such as CUSTOMERS, and contains columns and rows of data.

You can think of a table as a PDI dataset. You have fields (the columns of the table) and rows (the records of the table).

The **columns**, just like the fields in a PDI dataset, have a metadata describing their name, type, and length. The **records** hold the data for those columns; each record represents a different instance of the items in the table. As an example, the table CUSTOMERS describes the customers with the columns CUSTOMERNUMBER, CUSTOMERNAME, CONTACTLASTNAME and so forth. Each record of the table CUSTOMERS belongs to a different Steel Wheels' customer.

A table usually has a primary key. A **primary key** or **PK** is a combination of one or more columns that uniquely identify each record of the table. In the sample table, CUSTOMERS, the primary key is made up of a single column—CUSTOMERNUMBER. This means there cannot be two customers with the same customer number.

Tables in a relational database are usually related to one another. For example, the CUSTOMERS and ORDERS tables are related to convey the fact that real-world customers have placed one or more real-world orders. In the database, the ORDERS table has a column named CUSTOMERNUMBER with the number of the customer who placed the order. As said, CUSTOMERNUMBER is the column that uniquely identifies a customer in the CUSTOMERS table. Thus, there is a relationship between both tables. This kind of relationship between columns in two tables is called **foreign key** or **FK**.

Connecting to the Steel Wheels database

The first thing you have to do in order to work with a database is tell PDI how to access the database. Let's learn how to do it.

Time for action – creating a connection with the Steel Wheels database

In this first database tutorial, you will download the sample database and create a connection for accessing it from PDI.

 The Pentaho BI demo includes the sample data. So, if you have already downloaded the demo as explained in Chapter 1, just skip the first three steps. If the Pentaho BI demo is running on your machine, the database server is running as well. In that case, skip the first four steps.

1. Go to the Pentaho Download site: `http://sourceforge.net/projects/pentaho/files/`.

2. Under the **Business Intelligence Server | 1.7.1-stable**, look for the file named `pentaho_sample_data-1.7.1.zip` and download it.

3. Unzip the downloaded file.

4. Run `start_hypersonic.bat` under Windows or `start_hypersonic.sh` under Unix-based operating systems. If you download the sample data, you will find these scripts in the folder named `pentaho-data`. If you download the Pentaho BI server instead, you will find them in the folder named `data`. The following screen is displayed when the database server starts:

```
C:\WINDOWS\system32\cmd.exe                                           _ □ ×

C:\Pentaho-software\pentaho_sample_data-1.7.1\pentaho-data>java -cp lib\hsqldb.jar org.hsq
ldb.Server -database.0 sampledata\sampledata -dbname.0 sampledata -database.1 shark\shark
-dbname.1 shark -database.2 hibernate\hibernate -dbname.2 hibernate -database.3 quartz\qua
rtz -dbname.3 quartz
[Server@e09713]: [Thread[main,5,main]]: checkRunning(false) entered
[Server@e09713]: [Thread[main,5,main]]: checkRunning(false) exited
[Server@e09713]: Startup sequence initiated from main() method
[Server@e09713]: Loaded properties from [C:\Pentaho-software\pentaho_sample_data-1.7.1\pen
taho-data\server.properties]
[Server@e09713]: Initiating startup sequence...
[Server@e09713]: Server socket opened successfully in 16 ms.
[Server@e09713]: Database [index=0, id=0, db=file:sampledata\sampledata, alias=sampledata]
 opened sucessfully in 500 ms.
[Server@e09713]: Database [index=1, id=1, db=file:shark\shark, alias=shark] opened sucessf
ully in 63 ms.
[Server@e09713]: Database [index=2, id=2, db=file:hibernate\hibernate, alias=hibernate] op
ened sucessfully in 1359 ms.
[Server@e09713]: Database [index=3, id=3, db=file:quartz\quartz, alias=quartz] opened suce
ssfully in 62 ms.
[Server@e09713]: Startup sequence completed in 2000 ms.
[Server@e09713]: 2009-09-05 12:10:20.171 HSQLDB server 1.8.0 is online
[Server@e09713]: To close normally, connect and execute SHUTDOWN SQL
[Server@e09713]: From command line, use [Ctrl]+[C] to abort abruptly
```

Don't close this window. It would cause the database server to stop.

5. Open Spoon and create a new transformation.

6. Click on the **View** option that appears in the upper-left corner of the screen.

7. Right-click the **Database connections** option and click on **New**.

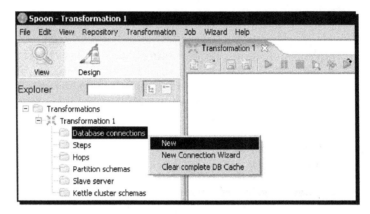

8. Fill the Database Connection dialog window as follows:

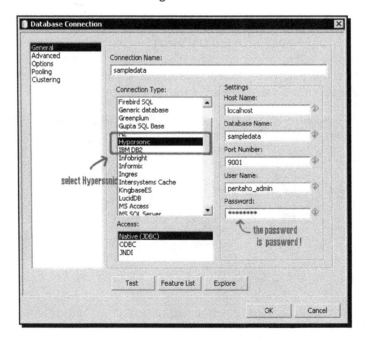

9. Click on the **Test** button. The following window shows up:

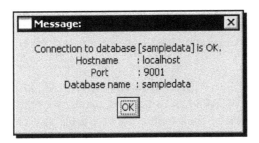

 If you get an error message instead of the **Message** window shown in the previous screenshot, please recheck the data you entered in the connection window. Also verify that the database is running, that is, the terminal window is still opened and doesn't show an error message. If you see an error, or if you don't see the terminal, please start the database server again as explained at the beginning of the tutorial.

10. Click on **OK** to close the test window.

11. Click on **OK** again to close the database definition window. A new database connection is added to the tree.

12. Right-click on the database connection and click on **Share**. The connection is available in all transformations you create from now onwards. The shared connections are shown in bold letters.

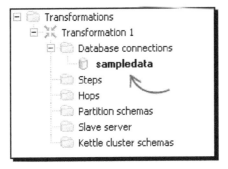

13. Save the transformation.

What just happened?

You created and tested a connection to the Pentaho Sample database. Finally, you shared the connection so that it could be reused in other transformations.

Connecting with Relational Database Management Systems

Even if you've never worked with databases, you must have heard terms such as MySQL, Oracle, DB2, or MS SQL server. These are just some of many **Relational Database Management Systems** (**RDBMS**) on the market. An RDBMS is a software that lets you create and administer relational databases.

In the tutorial you worked with **HyperSQL DataBase (HSQLDB)**, just another RDBMS formerly known as Hypersonic DB. HSQLDB has a small, fast database engine written in Java. HSQLDB is currently being used in many open source software projects such as OpenOffice.org 3.1 as well as in commercial projects and products such as Mathematica. You can get more information about HSQLDB at `http://hsqldb.org/`.

PDI has the ability to connect with both commercial RDBMSes such as Oracle or MS SQL server and free RDBMSes such as MySQL. In order to get connected to a particular database, you have to define a connection to it.

A database connection describes all parameters needed to connect PDI to a database.

To create a connection, you must give the connection a name and fill at least the general settings:

Setting	Description	Steel Wheels sample
Connection type	Type of database system: HSQLDB, Oracle, MySQL, Firebird, and so on.	`HSQLDB`
Method of access	Native (JDBC), ODBC, JNDI, or OCI. The available options depend on the type of DB.	`Native (JDBC)`
Host name	Name or IP address for the host where the database is.	`localhost`
Database name	Identifies the database to which you want to connect.	`sampledata`
Port number	PDI sets as default the most usual port number for the selected type of database. You can change it of course.	`9001`
User Name / Password	Name of the user and password to connect to the database.	`pentaho_admin/` `password`

 If you don't find your database engine in the list, you will still be able to connect to it by specifying as connection type, the **Generic database** option. In that case, you have to provide a connection URL and the driver class name.

After creating a connection, you can click the **Test** button to check that the connection has been defined correctly and that you can reach them from PDI.

The database connections will be available just in the transformation where you defined them, unless you share it for reuse as you did in the tutorial. Normally, you share connections because you know that you will use them later in many transformations.

The information about shared connections is stored in a file named `shared.xml`, located in the same folder as the `kettle.properties` file.

When you have shared connections and you save the transformation, the connection information is saved in the transformation itself.

If there is more than one shared connection, all of them will be saved along with the transformation, even if the transformation doesn't use them all. To avoid this, go to the editing options and check the **Only save used connections to XML?** option. This option limits the XML content of a transformation to just the used connections.

Pop quiz – defining database connections

Which options do you have to connect to the same database in several transformations:

    a.   Define the connection in each transformation that needs it

    b.   Define a connection once and share it

    c.   Either of the above options

    d.   Neither of the above options

Have a go hero – connecting to your own databases

You must have access to a database, whether local or in the network to which you are logged in. Get the connection information for the database. From PDI create a connection to the database and test it to verify that you can access it from PDI.

Exploring the Steel Wheels database

In the previous section, you learned about what RDBMSs are and how to connect to an RDBMS from PDI. Before beginning to work with the data in a database, it would be useful to get familiarized with that database. In this section, you will learn to explore databases with the PDI Database explorer.

Time for action – exploring the sample database

Let's explore the sample database:

1. Open the transformation you just created.

2. Right-click the connection in the **Database connections** list and select **Explore** in the contextual menu. The **Database explorer on connection** window opens.

3. Expand the `Tables` node of the tree and select `CUSTOMERS`. This is how the explorer looks:

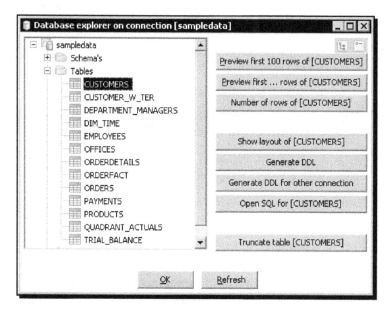

4. Click on the **Open SQL for [CUSTOMERS]** option.

5. The following SQL editor window appears:

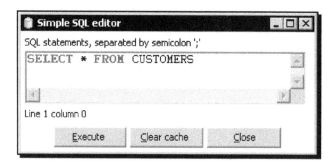

6. Modify the text in the window so that you have the following:

```
SELECT
   CUSTOMERNUMBER
, CUSTOMERNAME
, CITY
, COUNTRY
 FROM CUSTOMERS
```

7. Click on **Execute**. You will see the following result:

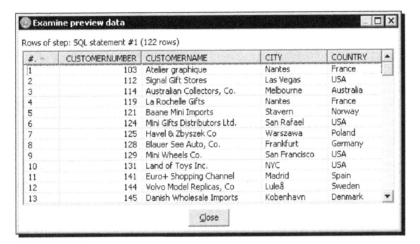

8. Close the preview window (the window that tells the result of the execution) and the SQL editor window.

9. Click on **OK** to close the database explorer window.

What just happened?

You explored the Pentaho sample database with the PDI Database explorer.

A brief word about SQL

Before explaining the details of the database explorer, it's worth giving an introduction to SQL—a central topic in relational database terminology.

SQL, that is, **Structured Query Language** is the language that lets you access and manipulate databases in a RDBMS.

SQL can be divided into two parts—DDL and DML.

The **DDL**, that is, **Data Definition Language** is the branch of the language that basically allows creating or deleting databases and tables.

The following is an example of DDL. It is the DDL statement that creates the CUSTOMERS table.

```
CREATE TABLE CUSTOMERS
(
  CUSTOMERNUMBER INTEGER
, CUSTOMERNAME VARCHAR(50)
, CONTACTLASTNAME VARCHAR(50)
, CONTACTFIRSTNAME VARCHAR(50)
, PHONE VARCHAR(50)
, ADDRESSLINE1 VARCHAR(50)
, ADDRESSLINE2 VARCHAR(50)
, CITY VARCHAR(50)
, STATE VARCHAR(50)
, POSTALCODE VARCHAR(15)
, COUNTRY VARCHAR(50)
, SALESREPEMPLOYEENUMBER INTEGER
, CREDITLIMIT BIGINT
)
;
```

This DDL statement tells the database to create the table CUSTOMERS with the columns CUSTOMERNUMBER of the type INTEGER, the column CUSTOMERNAME of the type VARCHAR with length 50, and so on.

Note that INTEGER, VARCHAR, and BIGINT are HSQLDB types of data, not PDI ones. The **DML**, that is, **Data Manipulation Language** allows you to retrieve data from a database. It also lets you insert, update, or delete data from the database.

The statement you typed in the SQL editor is an example of DML:

```
SELECT
  CUSTOMERNUMBER
, CUSTOMERNAME
, CITY
, COUNTRY
  FROM CUSTOMERS
```

This statement is asking the database to retrieve all the rows for the CUSTOMERS table, showing only CUSTOMERNUMBER, CUSTOMERNAME, CITY, and COUNTRY columns. After you clicked **Execute**, PDI queried the database and showed you a window with the data you had asked for.

If you were to leave the following statement:

```
SELECT * FROM CUSTOMERS
```

the window would have showed you all columns for the CUSTOMERS table.

SELECT is the statement that allows you to retrieve data from one or more tables. It is the most commonly used DML statement and you're going to use it a lot when working with databases in PDI. You will learn more about the SELECT statement in the next section of this chapter.

Other important DML statements are:

◆ INSERT: This allows you to insert rows in a table

◆ UPDATE : This allows you to update the values in rows of a table

◆ DELETE : This statement is used to remove rows from a table

It is important to understand the meaning of these basic statements, but you are not forced to learn them as PDI offers you ways to insert, update, and delete without typing any SQL statement.

Although SQL is a standard, each database engine has its own version of the SQL language. However, all database engines support the main commands.

 When you type SQL statements in PDI, try to keep the code within the standard. Your transformations will then be reusable in case you have to change the database engine.

If you are interested in learning more about SQL, there are a lot of tutorials on the Internet. The following are a few useful links with tutorials and SQL references:

◆ http://www.sqlcourse.com/

◆ http://www.w3schools.com/SQl/

◆ http://sqlzoo.net/

Until now, you have used only HSQLDB. In the tutorials to come, you will also work with the MySQL database engine. So, you may be interested in specific documentation for MySQL, which you can find at http://dev.mysql.com/doc/. You can find even more information in books; there are plenty of books available about both SQL language and MySQL databases.

Exploring any configured database with the PDI Database explorer

The database explorer allows you to explore any configured database. When you open the database explorer, the first thing you see is a tree with the different objects of the database. As soon as you select a database table, all buttons to the right side become available for you to explore that table. The following are the functions offered by the buttons at the right side of the database explorer:

Option	Meaning
Preview first 100 rows of ...	Return the first 100 rows of the selected table, or all the rows if the table has less that 100. This option shows all columns of the table.
Preview first...rows of ...	The same as the previous option, but here you decide the number of rows to show.
Number of rows of ...	Tells you the total number of records in the table.
Show layout of ...	Shows you the metadata for the columns of the table.
Generate DDL	Shows you the DDL statement that creates the selected table.
Generate DDL for other connection	It lets you select another existent connection. Then it shows you the DDL just like the previous option. The difference is that the DDL is written with the syntax of the database engine of the selected connection.
Open SQL for ...	Lets you edit a SELECT statement to query the table. Here you decide which columns and rows to retrieve.
Truncate table	Deletes all rows from the selected table.

 In the tutorial you opened the Database explorer from the contextual menu in the Database connections tree. You can also open it by clicking the **Explore** option in the database definition window.

Have a go hero – exploring the sample data in depth

In the tutorial you just tried the **Open SQL** button. Feel free to try other buttons to explore not only the CUSTOMERS table but also the rest of the tables found in the Steel Wheels database.

Have a go hero – exploring your own databases

In the previous section, there was a Hero exercise that asked you to connect to your own databases. If you have done that, then use a database connection defined by you and explore the database. See if you can recognize the different objects of the database. Run some previews to verify that everything looks as expected.

Querying a database

So far you have just connected to a database. You haven't yet worked with the data. Now is the time to do that.

Time for action – getting data about shipped orders

Let's continue working with the sample data.

1. Create a new transformation.

2. Select the **Design** view.

3. Expand the input category of steps and drag a **Table Input** step to the canvas.

4. Double-click the step.

5. Click on the **Get SQL select statement...** button. The database explorer window appears.

6. Expand the tables list and select ORDERS.

7. Click on **OK**.

8. PDI asks if you want to include the field names in the SQL. Answer **Yes**.

9. The SQL box gets filled with a SELECT SQL statement.

```
SELECT
   ORDERNUMBER
, ORDERDATE
, REQUIREDDATE
, SHIPPEDDATE
, STATUS
, COMMENTS
, CUSTOMERNUMBER
FROM ORDERS
```

10. At the end of the SQL statement, add the following clause:

```
WHERE STATUS = 'Shipped'
```

11. Click **Preview** and then **OK**. The following window appears:

	ORDER...	ORDERDATE	REQUIREDDATE	SHIPPEDDATE	STATUS	COMMENTS	CUSTOMERNUMBER
1	10100	2003/01/06 00...	2003/01/13 00:...	2003/01/10 00...	Shipped		363
2	10101	2003/01/09 00...	2003/01/18 00:...	2003/01/11 00...	Shipped	Check on availability.	128
3	10102	2003/01/10 00...	2003/01/18 00:...	2003/01/14 00...	Shipped		181
4	10103	2003/01/29 00...	2003/02/07 00:...	2003/02/02 00...	Shipped		121
5	10104	2003/01/31 00...	2003/02/09 00:...	2003/02/01 00...	Shipped		141
6	10105	2003/02/11 00...	2003/02/21 00:...	2003/02/12 00...	Shipped		145
7	10106	2003/02/17 00...	2003/02/24 00:...	2003/02/21 00...	Shipped		278
8	10107	2003/02/24 00...	2003/03/03 00:...	2003/02/26 00...	Shipped	Difficult to negotiate with customer...	131
9	10108	2003/03/03 00...	2003/03/12 00:...	2003/03/08 00...	Shipped		385
10	10109	2003/03/10 00...	2003/03/19 00:...	2003/03/11 00...	Shipped	Customer requested that FedEx Gr...	486
11	10110	2003/03/18 00...	2003/03/24 00:...	2003/03/20 00...	Shipped		187
12	10111	2003/03/25 00...	2003/03/31 00:...	2003/03/30 00...	Shipped		129
13	10112	2003/03/24 00...	2003/04/03 00:...	2003/03/29 00...	Shipped	Customer requested that ad materi...	144

Examine preview data

Rows of step: Table input (303 rows)

Close   Show Log

12. Close the window and click **OK** to close the step configuration window.

13. After the **Table input** step add a **Calculator step**, a **Number Range** step, a **Sort** step, and a **Select values** step and link them as follows:

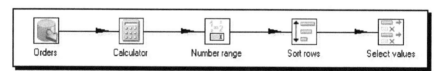

Orders   Calculator   Number range   Sort rows   Select values

14. With the **Calculator** step, add an `Integer` field to calculate the difference between the shipped date and the required date. Use the calculation **Date A – Date B (in days)** and name the field `diff_days`. Use the **Number ranges** step to classify the delays in delivery.

Number ranges

Step name: Delivery
Input field: diff_days
Output field: delivery
Default value(if no: unknown

Ranges (min <= x< n

#.	Lower Bound	Upper Bound	Value
1		0.0	Early
2	0.0	1.0	On Time
3	1.0		Late

OK   Cancel

15. Use the **Sort rows** step to sort the rows by the `diff_days` field.

16. Use the **Select values** step to select the `delivery`, ORDERNUMBER, REQUIREDDATE, and SHIPPEDDATE fields.

17. With the **Select values** step selected, do a preview. The following is how the final data will look:

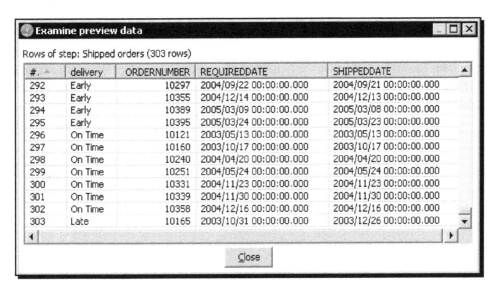

What just happened?

From the sample database, you got information about shipped orders. After you read the data from the database, you classified the orders based on the time it took to do the shipment.

Getting data from the database with the Table input step

The **Table input** step is the main step to get data from a database. In order to use it, you have to specify the connection with the database. In the tutorial you didn't explicitly specify one because there was just one connection and PDI put it as the default value.

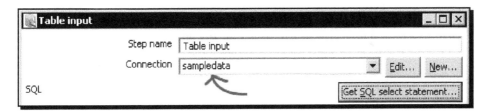

The connection was available because you shared it before. If you hadn't, you should have created here again.

The output of a **Table Input** step is a regular dataset. Each column of the SQL query leads to a new field and the rows generated by the execution of the query become the rows of the dataset.

As the data types of the databases are not exactly the same as the PDI data types, when getting data from a table, PDI implicitly converts the metadata of the new fields.

For example, consider the ORDERS table. Open the Database Explorer and look at the DDL definition for the table. Then right-click the **Table input** step and select **Show output fields** to see the metadata of the created dataset. The following table shows you how the metadata was translated:

Table columns	Database data type	PDI metadata
ORDERNUMBER, CUSTOMERNUMBER	INTEGER	Integer(9)
ORDERDATE, REQUIREDDATE, SHIPPEDDATE	TIMESTAMP	Date
STATUS	VARCHAR(15)	String(15)
COMMENTS	TEXT	String(214748364)

Once the data comes out of the **Table input** step and the metadata is adjusted, PDI forgets that it comes from a database. It treats it just as regular data, no matter if it came from a database or any other data source.

Using the SELECT statement for generating a new dataset

The SQL area of a **Table input** step is where you write the SELECT statement that will generate the new dataset. As said before, SELECT is the statement that you use to retrieve data from one or more tables in your database.

The simplest SELECT statement is as follows:

```
SELECT <values>
FROM <table name>
```

Here <table name> is the name of the table that will be queried to get the result set and <values> is the list of the desired columns of that table, separated by commas.

This is another simple SELECT statement:

```
SELECT ORDERNUMBER, ORDERDATE, STATUS
FROM ORDERS
```

If you want to select all columns, you can just put a * as here:

```
SELECT *
FROM ORDERS
```

There are some optional clauses that you can add to a SELECT statement. The most commonly used among the optional clauses are WHERE and ORDER BY. The WHERE clause limits the list of retrieved records, while ORDER BY is used to retrieve the rows sorted by one or more columns.

Another common clause is DISTINCT that can be used to return only different records.

Let's see some sample SELECT statements:

Sample statement	Output

`SELECT ORDERNUMBER, ORDERDATE`
`FROM ORDERS`
`WHERE SHIPPEDDATE IS NULL`
	Returns the number and order date for the orders that have not been shipped.

`SELECT *`
`FROM EMPLOYEES`
`WHERE JOBTITLE = 'Sales Rep'`
`ORDER BY LASTNAME, FIRSTNAME`
	Returns all columns for the employees whose job is sales representative, ordered by last name and first name.

`SELECT PRODUCTNAME`
`FROM PRODUCTS`
`WHERE PRODUCTLINE LIKE '%Cars%'`
	Returns the list of products whose product line contains cars—for example, Classic cars and Vintage cars.

`SELECT DISTINCT CUSTOMERNUMBER`
`FROM PAYMENTS`
`WHERE AMOUNT > 80000`
	Returns the list of customer numbers who have made payments with checks above USD80,000. The customers who have paid more than once with a check above USD80,000 appear more than once in the PAYMENTS table, but only once in this result set.

You can try these statements in the database explorer to check that the result sets are as explained.

When you add a **Table input** step, it comes with a default SELECT statement for you to complete.

```
SELECT <values> FROM <table name> WHERE <conditions>
```

If you need to query a single table, you can take advantage of the **Get SQL select statement...** button that generates the full statement for you. After you get the statement, you can modify it at your will by adding, say, WHERE or ORDER clauses just as you did in the tutorial. If you need to write more complex queries, you will have to do it manually.

You can write any SELECT query as long as it is a valid SQL statement for the selected type of database. Remember that every database engine has its own dialect of the language.

Whether simple or complex, you may need to pass some parameters to the query. You can do it in a couple of ways. Let's explain this with two practical examples.

Making flexible queries by using parameters

One of the ways you have to make your queries more flexible is by passing it through some parameters. In the following tutorial you will learn how to do it.

Time for action – getting orders in a range of dates by using parameters

Now you will modify your transformation so that it shows orders in a range of dates.

1. Open the transformation from the previous tutorial and save it under a new name.

2. From the **Input** category, add a **Get System Info** step.

3. Double-click it and use the step to get the **command line argument 1** and **command line argument 2** values. Name the fields as date_from and date_to respectively. Create a hop from the **Get System Info** step to the **Table input** step.

4. Double-click the **Table input** step.

5. Modify the SELECT statement as follows:

```
SELECT
    ORDERNUMBER
,   ORDERDATE
,   REQUIREDDATE
,   SHIPPEDDATE
FROM ORDERS
WHERE STATUS = 'Shipped'
AND ORDERDATE BETWEEN ? AND ?
```

6. In the drop-down list to the right side of **Insert data from step**, select the incoming step.

7. Click **OK**.

8. With the **Select values** step selected, click the **Preview** button.

9. Click on **Configure**.

10. Fill the **Arguments** grid. To the right of the argument **01**, type 2004-12-01. To the right of the argument **02**, type 2004-12-10.

11. Click **OK**. The following window appears:

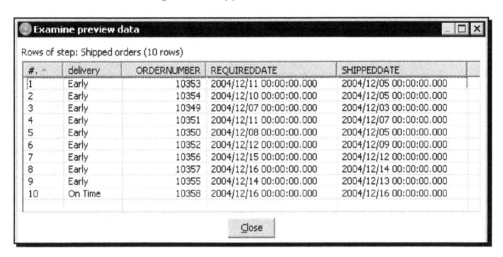

What just happened?

You modified the transformation from the previous tutorial to get orders in a range of dates coming from the command line.

Adding parameters to your queries

You can make your queries more flexible by adding parameters. Let's explain how you do it.

The first thing to do is obtain the fields that will be plugged as parameters. You can get them from any source by using any number of steps, as long as you create a hop from the last step toward the **Table input** step.

In the tutorial you just used a **Get System Info** step that read the parameters from the command line.

Once you have the parameters for the query, you have to change the **Table input** step configuration. In the **Insert data from step** option, you have to select the name of the step that the parameters will come from. In the query, you have to put a question mark (?) for each incoming parameter.

When you execute the transformation, the question marks are replaced, one by one, with the data that comes to the **Table input** step.

Let's see how it works in the tutorial. The following is the output of the **Get System Info** step:

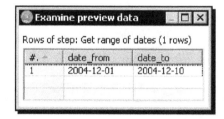

In the SQL statement, you have two question marks. The first is replaced by the value of the date_from field and the second is replaced by the value of the date_to field. Now the SQL statement becomes:

```
SELECT
   ORDERNUMBER
,  ORDERDATE
,  REQUIREDDATE
,  SHIPPEDDATE
FROM ORDERS
WHERE STATUS = 'Shipped'
AND ORDERDATE BETWEEN '2004-12-01' AND '2004-12-10'
```

Here 2004-12-01 and 2004-12-10 are the values you entered as arguments for the transformation.

The replacement of the markers respects the order of the incoming fields.

When you use question marks to parameterize a query, you can't forget the following—the number of fields coming to a **Table input** step must be exactly the same as the number of question marks found in the query.

Making flexible queries by using Kettle variables

Another way you have to make your queries flexible is by using Kettle variables. Let's explain how you do it using an example.

Time for action – getting orders in a range of dates by using variables

In this tutorial you will do the same as you did in the previous tutorial, but another method will be explained to you.

1. Open the main transformation we created in the *Time for action–getting data about shipped orders* section and save it under a new name.

2. Double-click the **Table input** step.

3. Modify the SELECT statement as follows:

```
SELECT
  ORDERNUMBER
, ORDERDATE
, REQUIREDDATE
, SHIPPEDDATE
FROM ORDERS
WHERE STATUS = 'Shipped'
AND ORDERDATE BETWEEN '${DATE_FROM}' AND '${DATE_TO}'
```

4. Tick the **Replace variables in script?** checkbox.

5. Save the transformation.

6. With the **Select values** step selected, click the **Preview** button.

7. Click on **Configure**.

8. Fill the **Variables** grid in the settings dialog window—type 2004-12-01 to the right of the **DATE_FROM** option and 2004-12-10 to the right of the **DATE_TO** option.

9. Click **OK**. This following window appears:

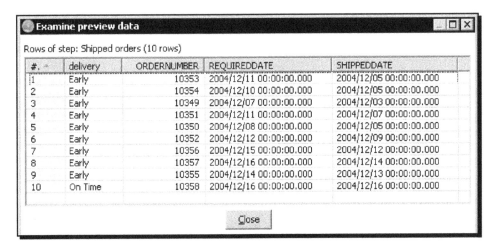

What just happened?

You modified the transformation from the previous tutorial, so the range of dates is taken from two variables—DATE_FROM and DATE_TO. The final result set was exactly the same you got in the previous version of the transformation.

Using Kettle variables in your queries

As an alternative to the use of positional parameters, you can use Kettle variables. Instead of getting the parameters from an incoming step, you check the option **Replace variables in script?** and replace the question marks by names of variables. The final result is the same.

PDI replaces the names of the variables by their values. Only after that, it sends the SQL statement to the database engine to be evaluated.

The advantage of using positional parameters over the variables is quite obvious—you don't have to define the variables in advance.

On the contrary, Kettle variables have several advantages over the use of question marks:

- ◆ You can use the same variable more than once in the same query.
- ◆ You can use variables for any portion of the query, not just the values. For example, you could have the following query:

  ```
  SELECT ORDERNUMBER FROM ${ORDER_TABLE}
  ```

  Then the result will vary upon the content of the variable ${ORDER_TABLE}. In the case of this example, the variable could be ORDERS or ORDERDETAILS.

- ◆ A query with variables is easier to understand and less error prone than a query with positional parameters. When you use positional parameters, it's quite common to get confused and make mistakes.

> Note that in order to provide parameters to a statement in a **Table input** step, it's perfectly possible to combine both methods: positional parameters and Kettle variables.

Pop quiz – database datatypes versus PDI datatypes

After you read data from the database with a **Table Input** step, what happens to the data types of that data:

a. ·They remain unchanged

b. PDI converts the database data types to internal data types

c. It depends on how you defined the database connection

Have a go hero – querying the sample data

Based on the sample data:

- ◆ Create a transformation to list the offices of Steel Wheels located in USA. Modify the transformation so that the country is entered by command line.

- ◆ Create a transformation that lists the contact information of clients whose credit limit is above USD100,000. Modify the transformation so that the threshold is 100000 by default, but can be modified when you run the transformation. (Hint: Use named parameters.)

- ◆ Create a transformation that generates two Excel files—one with a list of planes and the other with a list of ships. Include the code, name, and description of the products.

Sending data to a database

By now you know how to get data from a database. Now you will learn how to insert data into it. For the next tutorials we will use a MySQL database, so before proceeding make sure you have MySQL installed ad running.

 If you haven't yet installed MySQL, please refer to Chapter 1. It has basic instructions on installing MySQL, both on Windows and on Linux operating systems.

Time for action – loading a table with a list of manufacturers

Suppose you love jigsaw puzzles and decided to open a store for selling them. You have made all the arrangements and the only missing thing is the software. You have already acquired a software to handle your business, but you still have one hard task to do—insert data into the database, that is, load the database with the basic information about the products you are about to sell.

As this is the first of several tutorials in which you will interact with that database, the first thing you have to do is to create the database.

 For MySQL-specific tasks such as the creation of a database, we will use the MySQL Query Browser, included in the MySQL GUI Tools software. If you don't have it or don't like it, you can accomplish the same tasks by using the MySQL Command Line Client or any other GUI Tool.

1. From the Packt website, download the script file `js.sql`.

2. Launch the MySQL Query Browser.

3. A dialog window appears asking you for the connection information. Enter `localhost` as **Server Host**, and as **Username** and **Password**, enter the name and password of the user you created when you installed the software .

4. Click on **OK**.

5. From the **File** menu, select **Open Script...**.

6. Locate the downloaded file and open it.

7. Click on the **Execute** button or press *Ctrl+Enter*.

8. In the **Schemata** tab window, a new database, `js`, appears.

9. Right-click the name of the database and select **Make Default Schema**.

10. In the **Schemata** tab window, expand the `js` tree and you will see the tables of the database.

11. Close the script window.

Now that the database has been created, let's load some data into it:

1. From the Packt website, download the `manufacturers.xls` file.

2. Open Spoon and create a new transformation.

3. Create a connection to the created database. Under **Connection Type**, select **MySQL**. In the **Settings** frame, insert the same values you provided for the connection in MySQL Query Browser—enter `localhost` as **Host Name** and `js` (the database you just created) as **Database Name**, and as **User Name** and **Password**, enter the name and password of the user you created when you installed MySQL. For other settings in the window, leave the default values. Test the connection to see if it has been properly created.

 The main reason for a failed test is either erroneous data provided in the setting window or the non-functioning of the server. If the test fails, please read the error message to know exactly what the error was and act accordingly.

4. Right-click the database connection and share it.

5. Drag an **Excel Input** step to the canvas and use it to read the `manufacturers.xls` file.

6. Click on **Preview Rows** to check that you are reading the file properly. You should see the following:

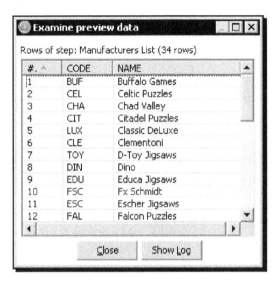

7. From the **Output** category of steps, drag a **Table Output** step to the canvas.

8. Create a hop from the **Excel Input** step to the **Table output** step.

9. Double-click the **Table output** step and fill the main settings window as follows—select `js` as **Connection**, as **Target table**, browse and select the table **manufacturers** or type it. Check the **Specify database fields** option.

> It is not mandatory but recommended in this particular exercise that you also check the **Truncate table** option. Otherwise, the output table will have duplicate records if you run the transformation more than once.

10. Select the **Database fields** tab.

11. Fill the grid as follows:

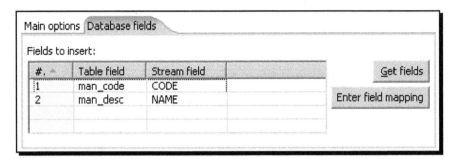

12. Click **OK**.

13. After the **Table output** step, add a **Write to log** step.

14. Right-click the **Table output** step and select **Define error handling....**

15. Fill the error handling settings window. As **Target step**, select the **Write to log** step. Check the **Enable the error handling?** option. Enter db_err_desc as **Error descriptions fieldname**, db_err_field as **Error fields fieldname**, and db_err_cod as **Error codes fieldname**.

16. Click **OK**. The following is your final transformation:

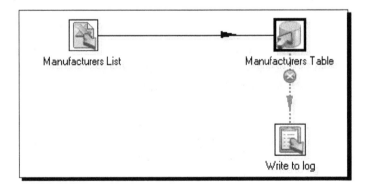

17. Save the transformation and run it.

18. Take a look at the **Steps Metrics** tab window. You will see the following:

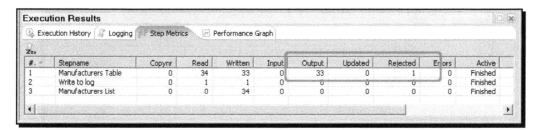

19. Now look at the **Logging** tab window. The following is what you see:

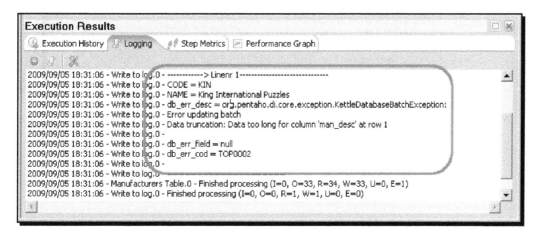

20. Switch to MySQL Query Browser.

21. In the **Schemata** window, double-click the manufacturers table.

22. The query entry box is filled with a basic SELECT statement for that table such as:

```
SELECT * FROM manufacturers m;
```

23. Click **Execute**. The following result set is shown:

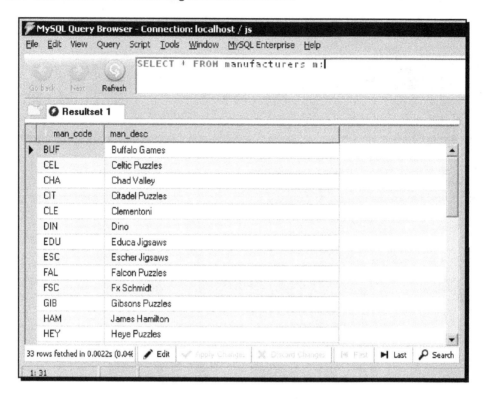

What just happened?

In the first part of the tutorial, you created the Jigsaw Puzzle database.

In Spoon, you created a connection to the new database.

Finally, you created a transformation that read an Excel file with a list of puzzle manufacturers and inserted that data into the manufacturers table. Note that not all rows were inserted. The row that couldn't be inserted was reported in the log.

In the data for the tutorial, there was a description too long to be inserted in the table. That was properly reported in the log because you implemented error handling. Doing that, you avoided the abortion of the transformation due to errors like that. As you learned in the previous chapter, when a row causes an error, it is up to you to decide what to do with that row. In this case, the row was sent to the log and wasn't inserted. Other possible options for you are:

- Fixing the problem in the Excel file and rerunning the transformation
- Validating the data and fixing it properly (for example, cutting the descriptions) before the data arrives to the **Table output** step
- Sending the full data for the erroneous rows to a file, fixing manually the data in the file, and creating a transformation that inserts only this data

Inserting new data into a database table with the Table output step

The **Table output** step is the main PDI step for inserting new data into a database table.

The use of this step is simple. You have to enter the name of the database connection and the name of the table where you want to insert data. The names for the connection and the table are mandatory, but as you can see, there are some extra settings for the **Table output** step.

The database field tab lets you specify the mapping between the dataset stream fields and the table fields.

In the tutorial the dataset had two fields—CODE and NAME. The table has two columns named man_code and man_desc.

As the names are different, you have to explicitly indicate that the CODE field is to be written in the table field named man_code, and that the NAME field is to be written in the table field named man_desc.

The following are some important tips and warnings about the use of the **Table output** step:

- If the names of the fields in the PDI stream are equal to the names of the columns in the table, you don't have to specify the mapping. In that case, you have to leave the **Specify database fields** checkbox unchecked and make sure that all the fields coming to the **Table output** step exist in the table.
- Before sending data to the **Table output** step, check your transformation against the definition of the table. All the mandatory columns that don't have a default value must have a corresponding field in the PDI stream coming to the **Table output** step.
- Check the data types for the fields you are sending to the table. It is possible that a PDI field type and the table column data type don't match. In that case, fix the problem before sending the data to the table. You can, for example, use the **Metadata** tab of a **Select values** step to change the data type of the data.

In the **Table output** step, you may have noted a button named **SQL**. This button generates the DDL to create the output table. In the tutorial, the output table, `manufacturers`, already existed. But if you want to create the table from scratch, this button allows you to do it based on the database fields you provided in the step.

Inserting or updating data by using other PDI steps

The **Table output** step provides the simplest but not the only way to insert data into a database table. In this section, you will learn some alternatives for feeding a table with PDI.

Time for action – inserting new products or updating existent ones

So far, you created the Jigsaw Puzzles database and loaded a list of puzzles manufacturers. It's time to start loading information about the products you will sell— puzzles.

Suppose, in order to show you what they are selling, the suppliers provide you with the lists of products made by the manufacturers themselves. Fortunately, they don't give you the lists in the form of papers, but they give you either plain files or spreadsheets. In this tutorial, you will take the list of products offered by the manufacturer Classic DeLuxe and load it into the puzzles table.

1. From the Packt website, download the sample lists of products.

2. Open Spoon and create a new transformation.

3. Add a **Text file input** step and configure it to read the `productlist_LUX_200908.txt` file.

Pay attention to the `each` field. It's the price of the product and must be configured as a `Number` with format $0.00.

4. Preview the file. You should see the following:

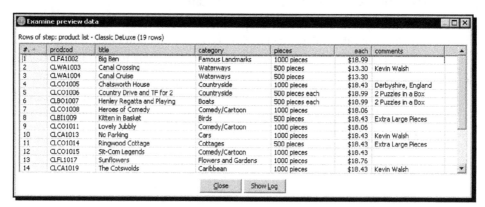

5. In the **Selected Files** grid, replace the text `productlist_LUX_200908.txt` by `${PRODUCTLISTFILE}`.

6. Click on **OK**.

7. After the **Text file input** step, add an **Add constants** step.

8. Use it to add a `String` constant named `man_code` with value `LUX`.

9. From the **Output** category of steps, drag an **Insert/Update** step to the canvas. Create a hop from the **Add constants** step to this new step.

10. Double-click the step. Select `js` as **Connection**. As **Target table**, browse and select **products**. In the upper grid of the window, add the conditions `pro_code = prodcod` and `man_code = man_code`. Click the **Edit mapping** button. The mapping dialog window shows up.

11. Under the **Source fields** list, click on `prodcod`, under the **Target fields** list click on `pro_code`, and then click the **Add** button. Again, under the **Source fields** list click on `title`, under the **Target fields** list click on `pro_name`, and then finally click **Add**. Proceed with the mapping until you get the following:

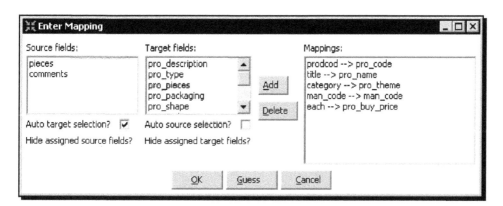

12. Click **OK**.

13. Fill the Update column for the price row with the value Y. Fill the rest of the column with the value N. The following is how the final grid looks like:

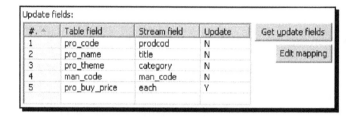

14. After the **Insert/Update** step, add a **Write to log** step.

15. Right-click the **Insert/Update** step and select **Define error handling...**.

16. Fill the error handling settings window just as you did in the previous tutorial.

17. Save the transformation and run it by pressing the *F9* key.

18. In the settings window, assign the PRODUCTLISTFILE variable with the value productlist_LUX_200908.txt.

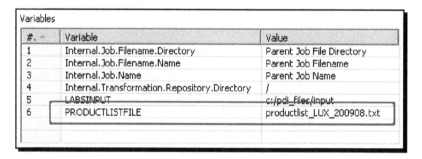

19. Click on **Launch**.

20. When the transformation ends, check the **Step Metrics**. You will see the following:

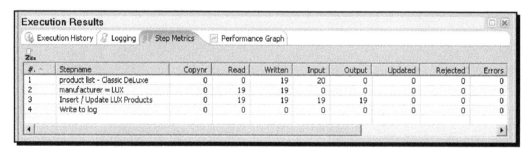

21. Switch to the SQL Query Browser application.

22. Type the following in the query entry box:

```
SELECT * FROM products p;
```

23. Click on **Execute**. The following result set is shown:

pro_code	man_code	pro_name	pro_type	pro_theme	pro_buy_price	pro_pie...
CLAI1020	LUX	Thirties Sunday and Aero Club	PUZZLE	Airplanes	18.99	NULL
CLBI1009	LUX	Kitten in Basket	PUZZLE	Birds	18.43	NULL
CLBO1007	LUX	Henley Regatta and Playing	PUZZLE	Boats	18.99	NULL
CLCA1013	LUX	No Parking	PUZZLE	Cars	18.43	NULL
CLCA1019	LUX	The Cotswolds	PUZZLE	Caribbean	18.43	NULL
CLCO1005	LUX	Chatsworth House	PUZZLE	Countryside	18.43	NULL
CLCO1006	LUX	Country Drive and TF for 2	PUZZLE	Countryside	18.99	NULL
CLCO1008	LUX	Heroes of Comedy	PUZZLE	Comedy/Cartoon	18.06	NULL
CLCO1011	LUX	Lovely Jubbly	PUZZLE	Comedy/Cartoon	18.06	NULL
CLCO1014	LUX	Ringwood Cottage	PUZZLE	Cottages	18.43	NULL
CLCO1015	LUX	Sit-Com Legends	PUZZLE	Comedy/Cartoon	18.43	NULL
CLFA1002	LUX	Big Ben	PUZZLE	Famous Landmarks	18.99	NULL
CLFA1021	LUX	Tower Bridge by Night	PUZZLE	Famous Landmarks	13.36	NULL
CLFA1023	LUX	Who's Who	PUZZLE	Fantasy	18.43	NULL
CLFL1017	LUX	Sunflowers	PUZZLE	Flowers and Gardens	18.76	NULL
CLFO1025	LUX	Ye Olde Red Horse Pub	PUZZLE	Food and Drink	18.43	NULL
CLHO1022	LUX	Whilst the Sun Shines	PUZZLE	Horses	13.30	NULL
CLWA1003	LUX	Canal Crossing	PUZZLE	Waterways	13.30	NULL
CLWA1004	LUX	Canal Cruise	PUZZLE	Waterways	13.30	NULL

What just happened?

You populated the products table with data found in text files. For inserting the data, you used the **Insert/Update** step.

As this was the first time you dealt with the products table, before you ran the transformation, the table was empty. After running the transformation, you could see how all products in the file were inserted in the table.

Time for action – testing the update of existing products

In the preceding tutorial, you used an **Insert/Update** step, but only inserted records. Let's try the transformation again to see how the update option works.

1. If you closed the transformation, please open it.

2. Press *F9* to launch the transformation again.

3. As the value for the `PRODUCTLISTFILE` variable, insert `productlist_LUX_200909.txt`.

4. Click **Launch**.

5. When the transformation ends, check the **Step Metrics** tab. You will see the following:

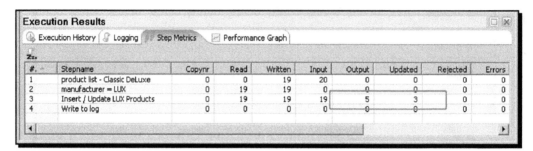

#	Stepname	Copynr	Read	Written	Input	Output	Updated	Rejected	Errors
1	product list - Classic DeLuxe	0	0	19	20	0	0	0	0
2	manufacturer = LUX	0	19	19	0	0	0	0	0
3	Insert / Update LUX Products	0	19	19	19	5	3	0	0
4	Write to log	0	0	0	0	0	0	0	0

6. Switch to the SQL Query Browser application and click **Execute** to run the query again. This time you will see this:

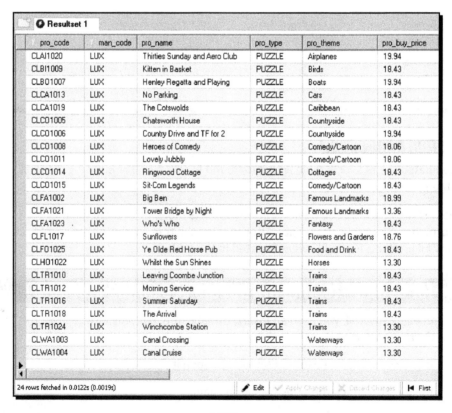

pro_code	man_code	pro_name	pro_type	pro_theme	pro_buy_price
CLAI1020	LUX	Thirties Sunday and Aero Club	PUZZLE	Airplanes	19.94
CLBI1009	LUX	Kitten in Basket	PUZZLE	Birds	18.43
CLBO1007	LUX	Henley Regatta and Playing	PUZZLE	Boats	19.94
CLCA1013	LUX	No Parking	PUZZLE	Cars	18.43
CLCA1019	LUX	The Cotswolds	PUZZLE	Caribbean	18.43
CLCO1005	LUX	Chatsworth House	PUZZLE	Countryside	18.43
CLCO1006	LUX	Country Drive and TF for 2	PUZZLE	Countryside	19.94
CLCO1008	LUX	Heroes of Comedy	PUZZLE	Comedy/Cartoon	18.06
CLCO1011	LUX	Lovely Jubbly	PUZZLE	Comedy/Cartoon	18.06
CLCO1014	LUX	Ringwood Cottage	PUZZLE	Cottages	18.43
CLCO1015	LUX	Sit-Com Legends	PUZZLE	Comedy/Cartoon	18.43
CLFA1002	LUX	Big Ben	PUZZLE	Famous Landmarks	18.99
CLFA1021	LUX	Tower Bridge by Night	PUZZLE	Famous Landmarks	13.36
CLFA1023 .	LUX	Who's Who	PUZZLE	Fantasy	18.43
CLFL1017	LUX	Sunflowers	PUZZLE	Flowers and Gardens	18.76
CLFO1025	LUX	Ye Olde Red Horse Pub	PUZZLE	Food and Drink	18.43
CLHO1022	LUX	Whilst the Sun Shines	PUZZLE	Horses	13.30
CLTR1010	LUX	Leaving Coombe Junction	PUZZLE	Trains	18.43
CLTR1012	LUX	Morning Service	PUZZLE	Trains	18.43
CLTR1016	LUX	Summer Saturday	PUZZLE	Trains	18.43
CLTR1018	LUX	The Arrival	PUZZLE	Trains	18.43
CLTR1024	LUX	Winchcombe Station	PUZZLE	Trains	13.30
CLWA1003	LUX	Canal Crossing	PUZZLE	Waterways	13.30
CLWA1004	LUX	Canal Cruise	PUZZLE	Waterways	13.30

24 rows fetched in 0.0122s (0.0019s)

What just happened?

You reran the transformation that was created in the previous tutorial, this time using a different input file. In this file there were new products and some products were removed from the list, whereas some had their descriptions, categories, and prices modified.

When you ran the transformation for the second time, the new products were added to the table. Also, the modified prices of the products were updated. In the **Step Metrics** tab window, you can see the number of inserted records (**Output** column) and the number of updated ones (**Update** column).

> Note that as the supplier may give you updated lists of products with different names of files, for the name of the file you used a variable. Doing so, you were able to reuse the transformation for reading different files each time.

Inserting or updating data with the Insert/Update step

While the **Table output** step allows you to insert brand new data, the **Insert/Update** step allows you to do both, insert and update data in a single step.

The rows coming to the **Insert/Update** step can be new data or can be data that already exists in the table. Depending on the case, the **Insert/Update** step behaves differently. Let's see each case in detail:

For each incoming row, the first thing the step does is use the lookup condition you put in the upper grid to check if the row already exists in the table.

In the tutorial you wrote two conditions: `pro_code = prodcod` and `man_code = man_code`. Doing so, you told the step to look for a row in the products table for which the table column `pro_code` is equal to the field `prodcod` of your row, and the table column `man_code` is equal to the field with the same name of your row.

If the lookup fails, that is, the row doesn't exist, the step inserts the row in the table by using the mapping you put in the lower grid.

The first time you ran the tutorial transformation, the table was empty. There were no rows against which to compare. In this case, all the lookups failed and, consequently, all rows were inserted.

This insert operation is exactly the same that you could have done with a **Table output** step. That implies that here you also have to be careful about the following:

 ◆ All the mandatory columns that don't have a default value must be present in the **Update Field** grid, including the keys you used in the upper grid

 ◆ The data types for the fields you are sending to the table must match the data type for the columns of the table

If the lookup succeeds, the step updates the table replacing the old values with the new ones. This update is made only for the fields where you put Y as the value for the **Update** column in the lower grid.

If you don't want to perform any update operation, you can check the **Don't perform any updates** option.

The second time you ran the tutorial, you had two types of products in the file—products that already existed in the database and new products. For example, consider the following row found in the second file:

```
CLTR1001|A Saint at Radley|Trains|500 pieces|$13.30|Peter Webster
```

PDI looks for a row in the table where the prod_code is equal to CLTR1001 and man_code is equal to LUX (the field added with the **Add constants** step). It doesnt find it. Then it inserts a new row with the data coming from the file.

Take another sample row:

```
CLBO1007|Henley Regatta & Playing|Boats|500 pieces each|$19.94|2
Puzzles in a Box
```

PDI looks for a row in the table where the prod_code is equal to CLBO1007 and man_code equal to LUX. It finds the following:

pro_code	man_code	pro_name	pro_type	pro_theme	pro_buy_price
CLAI1020	LUX	Thirties Sunday and Aero Club	PUZZLE	Airplanes	18.99
CLBI1009	LUX	Kitten in Basket	PUZZLE	Birds	18.43
CLBO1007	LUX	Henley Regatta and Playing	PUZZLE	Boats	18.99
CLCA1013	LUX	No Parking	PUZZLE	Cars	18.43
CLCA1019	LUX	The Cotswolds	PUZZLE	Caribbean	18.43

There are two differences between the old and the new versions of the product. Both the name and the price have changed.

As you configured the **Insert/Update** step to update only the price column, the update operation does so. The new record in the table after the execution of the transformation is this:

pro_code	man_code	pro_name	pro_type	pro_theme	pro_buy_price
CLAI1020	LUX	Thirties Sunday and Aero Club	PUZZLE	Airplanes	19.94
CLBI1009	LUX	Kitten in Basket	PUZZLE	Birds	18.43
CLBO1007	LUX	Henley Regatta and Playing	PUZZLE	Boats	19.94
CLCA1013	LUX	No Parking	PUZZLE	Cars	18.43
CLCA1019	LUX	The Cotswolds	PUZZLE	Caribbean	18.43

Have a go hero – populating a films database

From the Packt website, download the `films.sql` script file. Run the script In MySQL. A new database will be created to hold film data.

Browse the folder where you have the files for Chapter 7 and get the French films file. You will use it to populate the following tables of the `films` database: GENRES, PEOPLE, and FILMS.

Now follow these instructions:

1. Create a connection to the database.
2. In order to populate the GENRES table, you have to build a list of genres, no duplicates! For the primary key, GEN_ID, you don't have a value in the file. Create the key with an **Add sequence** step.
3. The table, PEOPLE, will have the names of both actors and directors. In order to populate that table, you will have to create a single list of people, no duplicates here either! To generate the primary key, use the same method as before.
4. Finally, populate the FILMS table with the whole list of films found in the file.

Don't forget to handle errors so that you can detect bad rows.

Have a go hero – creating the time dimension

Now you're going to finish what you started back in Chapter 6—the creation of a time dimension.

From the Packt website, download the `js_dw.sql` script file. Run the script in MySQL. A new database named `js_dw` will be created.

Now you are going to modify the `time_dimension.ktr` transformation to load the time dataset into the `lk_time` table.

The following are some tips:

◆ Create a connection to the created database

◆ Find a correspondence between each field in the dataset and each column in the
LK_TIME table

◆ Use a **Table output** step to send the dataset to the table

After running the transformation, check if all rows were inserted as expected.

> Pay attention to the main field in the time dimension—date.
>
> In the transformation the date is a field whose type is Date.
>
> However, in the table the type for the date field is CHAR(8). This column
> is meant to hold the date as a String with the format YYYYMMDD—for
> example 20090915.
>
> As explained, the data types of the data you sent to the table have to match
> the data types in the table. In this case, as the types don't match, you will
> have to use a **Select values** step and change the metadata of the date field
> from Date to String.

Have a go hero – populating the products table

This exercise has two parts. The first is intended to enrich the transformation you created
in the tutorial. The transformation processed the product list files supplied by the Classics
DeLuxe manufacturer. In the file, there was some extra information that you could put in the
table such as the number of pieces of a puzzle. However, the data didn't come ready to use.
Consider, for example, this text: 500 pieces each. In order to get the number of pieces, you
need to do some transformation. Modify the transformation so that you can enrich the data
in the products table.

The second part of the exercise has to do with populating the products table with products
from other manufacturers. Unfortunately, you can't expect that all manufacturers to share
the same structure for the list of products. Not only the structure changes, but also the
kind of information they give you can vary. On the Packt website, you have several sample
product files belonging to different manufactures. Explore them, analyze them to see if you
can identify the different data you need for the products table, and load all the products
into the database by using a different transformation for each manufacturer.

The following are some tips:

- Take as a model the transformation for the tutorial. You may reuse most of it.

- You don't have to worry about the `stock` columns or the `pro_type` column because they already have default values.

- Use the comments in the file to identify potential values for the `pro_packaging`, `pro_shape` and `pro_style` columns. Use the `pro_packaging` field for values such as `2 puzzles in a box`. Use the `pro_shape` field for values such as `Panoramic Puzzle` or `3D Puzzle`. Use the `puzzle_type` field for values such as `Glow in the Dark` or `Wooden Puzzle`.

- You can leave the `pro_description` empty or put in it whatever you feel that fits—a fix string such as `Best in market!`, or the full comment found in the file, or whatever your imagination says.

Pop quiz – Insert/Update step versus Table Output/Update steps

In the last tutorial you read a file and used an **Insert/Update** step to populate the products table. Look at the following variant of the transformation:

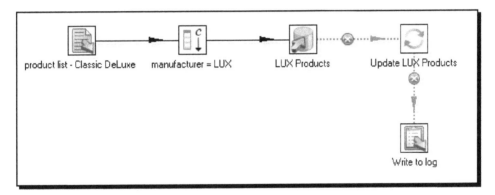

Suppose you use this transformation instead of the original. Compared to the results you got in the tutorial, after the execution of this version of the transformation, the products table will have:

a. The same number of records

b. More records

c. Less records

d. It depends on the contents of the file

Pop quiz – filtering the first 10 rows

The following SELECT statement:

```
SELECT TOP 10 * FROM CUSTOMERS
```

gives you the first ten customers in the CUSTOMERS table of the sample database.

Suppose you want to get the first ten products in the PRODUCTS table of the Jigsaw Puzzles database. Which of the following statements would do that:

    a.   SELECT TOP 10 * FROM product

    b.   SELECT * FROM product WHERE ROWNUM<11

    c.   SELECT * FROM product LIMIT 10

    d.   Any of the above statements

Eliminating data from a database

Deleting information from a database is not the most common operation with databases, but it is an important one. Now you will learn how to do it with PDI.

Time for action – deleting data about discontinued items

Suppose a manufacturer informs you about the categories of products that will no longer be available. You don't want to have in your database products something that you will not sell. Then you use PDI to delete them.

1. From the Packt website, download the LUX_discontinued.txt file.

2. Create a new transformation.

3. With a **Text file input** step, read the file.

4. Preview the file. You will see the following:

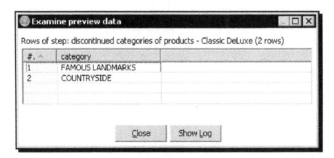

5. After the **Text file input** step, add an **Add constants** step to add a `String` constant named `man_code` with value `LUX`.

6. Expand the **Output** category of steps and drag a **Delete** step to the canvas.

7. Create a hop from the **Add constants** step to the **Delete** step.

8. Double-click the **Delete** step. Select `js` as **Connection** and, as **Target table**, browse and select **products**. In the grid add the conditions `man_code = man_code` and `pro_theme LIKE category`. After the **Delete** step, add a **Write to log** step.

9. Right-click the **Delete** step and define the error handling just like you did in each of the previous tutorials in this chapter.

10. Save the transformation.

11. Before running the transformation, open the Database Explorer.

12. Under the `js` connection, locate the `products` table and click **Open SQL for [products]**.

13. In the simple SQL editor type:

```
SELECT pro_theme, pro_name FROM js.products p
ORDER BY pro_theme, pro_name;
```

14. Click on **Execute**. You will see the following result set:

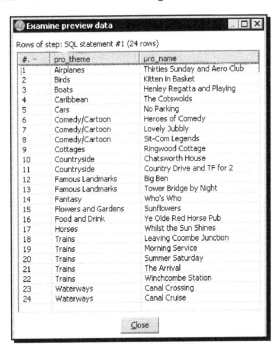

15. Close the preview data window and the results of the SQL window.

16. Minimize the database explorer window.

17. The database explorer is collapsed at the bottom of the Spoon window.

18. Run the transformation.

19. Look at the **Step Metrics**. The following is what you should see:

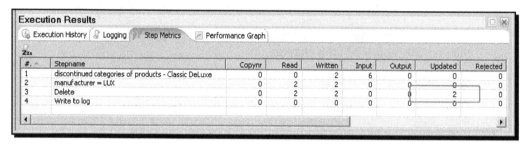

#.	Stepname	Copynr	Read	Written	Input	Output	Updated	Rejected
1	discontinued categories of products - Classic DeLuxe	0	0	2	6	0	0	0
2	manufacturer = LUX	0	2	2	0	0	0	0
3	Delete	0	2	2	0	0	2	0
4	Write to log	0	0	0	0	0	0	0

20. Maximize the database explorer window.

21. In the SQL editor window click **Execute** again. This time you will see this:

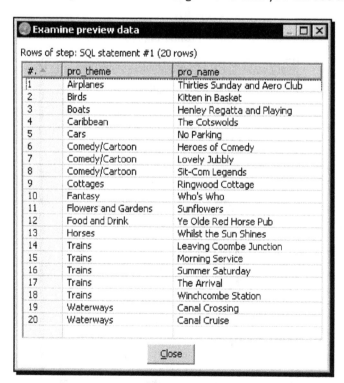

Rows of step: SQL statement #1 (20 rows)

#.	pro_theme	pro_name
1	Airplanes	Thirties Sunday and Aero Club
2	Birds	Kitten in Basket
3	Boats	Henley Regatta and Playing
4	Caribbean	The Cotswolds
5	Cars	No Parking
6	Comedy/Cartoon	Heroes of Comedy
7	Comedy/Cartoon	Lovely Jubbly
8	Comedy/Cartoon	Sit-Com Legends
9	Cottages	Ringwood Cottage
10	Fantasy	Who's Who
11	Flowers and Gardens	Sunflowers
12	Food and Drink	Ye Olde Red Horse Pub
13	Horses	Whilst the Sun Shines
14	Trains	Leaving Coombe Junction
15	Trains	Morning Service
16	Trains	Summer Saturday
17	Trains	The Arrival
18	Trains	Winchcombe Station
19	Waterways	Canal Crossing
20	Waterways	Canal Cruise

Close

What just happened?

You deleted from the `products` table all products belonging to the categories found in the `LUX_discontinued.txt` file.

Note that to query the list of products, you used the PDI Database explorer. You could have done the same by using MySQL Query Browser.

Deleting records of a database table with the Delete step

The **Delete** step allows you to delete records of a database table based on a given condition. For each row coming to the step, PDI deletes the records that match the condition set in its configuration window.

Let's see how it worked in the tutorial. The following is the dataset coming to the **Delete** step:

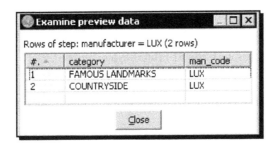

For each of these two rows PDI performs a new delete operation.

For the first row, the records deleted from the `products` table arc those where `man_code` is equal to `LUX` and `pro_theme` is like `FAMOUS LANDMARKS`.

For the second row, the records deleted from the `products` table are those where `man_code` is equal to `LUX` and `pro_theme` is like `COUNTRYSIDE`.

You can verify the performed operations by comparing the result sets you got in the database explorer before and after running the transformation.

Just for your information, you could have done the same task with the following `DELETE` statements:

```
DELETE FROM products
WHERE man_code = 'LUX' and pro_theme LIKE 'FAMOUS LANDMARKS'

DELETE FROM products
WHERE man_code = 'LUX' and pro_theme LIKE 'COUNTRYSIDE'
```

In the Step Metrics result, you may notice that the updated column for the **Delete** step has value 2. This number is the number of delete operations, not the number of deleted records, which was actually a bigger number.

Have a go hero – deleting old orders

Create a transformation that asks for a date from the command line and deletes all orders from the Steel Wheels database whose order dates are before the given date.

Summary

This chapter discussed how to use PDI to work with databases. Specifically, the chapter covered the following:

◆ Introduction to the Pentaho Sample Data Steel Wheels—the starting point for you to learn basic database theory

◆ Creating connections from PDI to different database engines

◆ Exploring databases with the PDI Database explorer

◆ Basics of SQL

◆ Performing CRUD (Create, Read, Update, and Delete) operations on databases

In the next chapter you will continue working with databases. You will learn some advanced concepts, including datawarehouse-specific operations.

9
Performing Advanced Operations with Databases

In this chapter you will learn about advanced operations with databases. The first part of the chapter includes:

- Populating the Jigsaw puzzle database so that it is prepared for the rest of the activities in the chapter
- Doing simple lookups in a database
- Doing complex lookups

The second part of the chapter is fully devoted to datawarehouse-related concepts. The list of the topics that will be covered includes:

- Introducing dimensional modeling
- Loading dimensions

Preparing the environment

In order to learn the concepts of this chapter, a database with little or no data is useless. Therefore, the first thing you'll do is populating your Jigsaw puzzle database.

Time for action – populating the Jigsaw database

To load data massively into your Jigsaw database, you must have the Jigsaw database created and the MySQL server running. You already know how to do this. If not, please refer to Chapter 1 for the installation of MySQL and Chapter 8 for the creation of the Jigsaw database.

This tutorial will overwrite all your data in the `js` database. If you don't want to overwrite the data in your `js` database, you could simply create a new database with a different name and run the `js.sql` script to create the tables in your new database.

After checking that everything is in order, follow these instructions:

1. From Packt's website download the `js_data.sql` script file.

2. Launch the MySQL query browser.

3. From the **File** menu select **Open Script....**

4. Locate the downloaded file and open it.

5. At the beginning of the script file you will see this line:

   ```
   USE js;
   ```

   If you created a new database, replace the name `js` by the name of your new database.

6. Click on the **Execute** button.

7. At the bottom of the screen, you'll see a progress message.

8. When the script execution ends, verify that the database has been populated. Execute some `SELECT` statements such as:

   ```
   SELECT * FROM cities
   ```

   All tables must have records.

Having populated the database, let's prepare the Spoon environment:

1. Edit the `kettle.properties` file located in the PDI home directory. Add the following variables: `DB_HOST`, `DB_NAME`, `DB_USER`, `DB_PASS`, and `DB_PORT`. As values put the setting for your connection to the Jigsaw database. Use the following lines as a guide:

   ```
   DB_HOST=localhost
   DB_NAME=js
   DB_USER=root
   DB_PASS=1234
   DB_PORT=3306
   ```

2. Add the following variables: DW_HOST, DW_NAME, DW_USER, DW_PASS, and DW_PORT. As values, put the setting for your connection to the js_dw database—the database you created in Chapter 8 to load the time dimension. Here are some sample lines for you to use:

```
DW_HOST=localhost
DW_NAME=js_dw
DW_USER=root
DW_PASS=1234
DW_PORT=3306
```

Save the file.

3. Included in the downloaded material is a file named shared.xml. Copy it to your PDI home directory (the same directory where the kettle.properties file is) overwriting the existing file.

 Before overwriting the file, please take a backup, as this will delete any share connections you might have created.

4. Launch Spoon. If it was running, restart it so that it recognizes the changes in the kettle.properties file.

5. Create a new transformation.

 If you don't see the shared database connections js and dw, please verify that you copied the shared.xml file to the right folder.

6. Right-click the js database connection and select **Edit**. In the **Settings** frame, instead of fixed values, you will see variables: **${DS_HOST}** for **Host Name**, **${DS_NAME}** for **Database Name**, and so on.

7. Test the connection.

8. Repeat the steps for the js_dw shared connection: Right-click the database connection and select **Edit**. In the **Settings** frame, you will see the variables you defined in the kettle.properties file—${DW_HOST}, ${DW_NAME}, and so on.

9. Test the dw_js connection.

If any of the database tests fail, please check that the connection variables you put in the `kettle.properties` file are correct. Also check that MySQL is running database.

What just happened?

In this tutorial you prepared the environment for working in the rest of the chapter.

You did two different things:

◆ First, you ran a script that emptied all the `js` database tables and loaded data into them.

◆ Then, you redefined the database connections to the databases `js` and `js_dw`.

 Note that the names for the connection don't have to match the names of the databases. This can benefit you in the following way: If you created a database with a different name for the Jigsaw database puzzle, your connection may still be named `js`, and all code you download from the Packt website should work without touching anything but the `kettle.properties` file.

You edited the `kettle.properties` file by adding variables with the database connection values such as host name, database name, and so on. Then you edited the database connections. There you saw that the database settings didn't have values but variable names—the variables you had defined in the `kettle.properties` file. For shared connections, PDI takes the database definition from the `shared.xml` file.

 Note that you didn't save the transformation you created. That was intentional. The only purpose for creating it was to be able to see the shared connections.

Exploring the Jigsaw database model

The information in this section allows you to understand the organization of the data in the Jigsaw database. In the first place, you have a DER. A **DER** or **entity relationship diagram** is a graphical representation that allows you to see how the tables in a database are related to each other. The following is the DER for the `js` database:

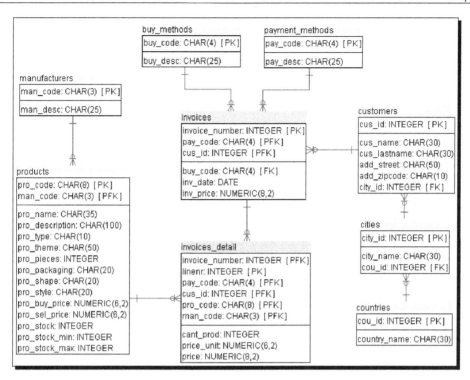

The following table contains a brief explanation of what each table is for:

Table name	Content
manufacturers	Information about manufacturers of the products.
products	It is about the products you sell such as puzzles and accessories. The table has descriptive information and data about prices and stock. The pro_type column has the type of product—puzzle, glue, and so on. Several of the columns apply only to puzzles, such as shape or pieces.
buy_methods	It contains information about the list of methods for buying—for example, in store, by telephone, and so on.
payment_methods	Information about list of methods of payment such as cash, check, credit card, and so on.
countries	The list of countries.
cities	The list of cities.
customers	A list of customers. A customer has a number, a name, and an address.
invoices	The header of invoices including date, customer number, and total amount. The invoices dates range from 2004 to 2010.

Looking up data in a database

You already know how to create, update, and delete data from a database. It's now time to learn to look up data. Lookup is the act of searching for information in a database. You can look up a column of a single table or you can do more complex lookups. Let's begin with the simplest way of looking up.

Doing simple lookups

Sometimes you need to get information from a database table based on the data you have in your main stream. Let's see how you can do it.

Time for action – using a Database lookup step to create a list of products to buy

Suppose you have an online system for your customers to order products. On a daily basis, the system creates a file with the orders information. Now you will check if you have stock for the ordered products and make a list of the products you'll have to buy.

1. Create a new transformation.

2. From the **Input** category of steps, drag a **Get data from XML** step to the canvas.

3. Use it to read the orders.xml file. In the **Content** tab, fill the **Loop XPath** option with the /orders/order string. In the **Fields** tab get the fields.

4. Do a preview. You will see the following:

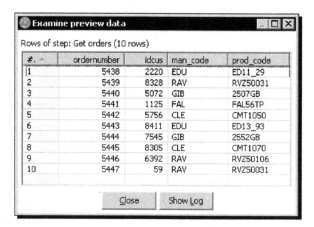

To keep this exercise simple, the file contains a single product by order.

5. Add a **Sort rows** step and use it to sort the data by `man_code, prod_code`.

6. Add a **Group by step** and double-click it.

7. Use the upper grid for grouping by `man_code` and `prod_code`.

8. Use the lower grid for adding a field with the number of orders in each group. As **Name** write `quantity`, as **Subject** `ordernumber`, and as **Type** write **Number of Values (N)**. Expand the **Lookup** category of steps.

9. Drag a **Database lookup** step to the canvas and create a hop from the **Group by** step toward this step.

10. Double-click the **Database lookup** step.

11. As **Connection**, select `js` and in **Lookup table**, browse the database and select `products` or just type its name.

12. Fill the grids as follows:

The key(s) to look up the value(s):

#.	Table field	Comparator	Field1	Field2
1	man_code	=	man_code	
2	pro_code	=	prod_code	

Values to return from the lookup table :

#.	Field	New name	Default	Type
1	pro_name			String
2	pro_stock			Integer

 If you don't see both grids, just resize the window. This is one of the few configuration steps that lack the scrollbar to the right side.

Also remember that with all grids in PDI, you always have the option to populate the grids by using the **Get Fields** and **Get lookup fields** buttons respectively.

13. Click on **OK**.

14. Add a filter step to pass only the rows where `pro_stock<quantity`.

15. Add a **Text file output** step to send the manufacturer code, the product code, the product name, and the ordered quantity to a file named `products_to_buy.txt`.

16. Run the transformation.

17. The file should have the following content:

```
man_code;prod_code;pro_name;quantity
EDU;ED13_93;Times Square;1
RAV;RVZ50031;Disney World Map;2
RAV;RVZ50106;Star Wars Clone Wars;1
```

What just happened?

You processed a file with orders. You grouped and counted the ordered products by product code. Then with the Database lookup step, you looked up the product table for the record belonging to the ordered product. You added to your stream, the name and stock for the products. After that, you kept only the rows for which the stock was lower than the units your customers ordered. With the rows that passed, you created a list of products to buy.

Looking up values in a database with the Database lookup step

The Database lookup step allows you to look up values in a database table. In the upper grid of the setting window, you specify the keys to look up. In the example you look for a record that has the same product code and manufacturer code as the codes coming in the stream.

In the lower grid you put the name of the table columns you want back. Those fields are added to the output stream. In this case, you added the name and the stock of the product.

The step returns only one row even if it doesn't find a matching record or if it finds more than one. When the step doesn't find a record with the given conditions, it returns null for all the added fields, unless you specify a default value for those new fields.

Note that this behavior is quite similar to the Stream lookup step's behavior. You search for a match and, if a record is found, the step returns you the specified fields. If not, the new fields are filled with default values. Besides the fact that the data is searched in a database, the new thing here is that you specify the comparator to be used: =, <, >, and so on. The Stream lookup step looks only for equal values. As all the products in the file existed in your database, the step found a record for every row, adding to your stream two fields: the name and the stock for the product. You can check it by doing a preview on the Database lookup step. After the Database lookup setup, you used a Filter rows step to discard the rows where the stock was lower than the required quantity of products. You can avoid adding this step by refining the lookup configuration. In the upper grid you could add the condition `pro_stock<quantity` and check the **Do not pass the row if the lookup fails** checkbox; you now get a different result. The step will look not only for the product, but also for the condition `pro_stock<quantity`. If it doesn't find a record that matches, that is, the lookup fails, the check **Do not pass the row if the lookup fails** does its work—filters the row. Doing these changes, you don't have to use the extra Filter rows step, nor add the `pro_stock` field to the stream unless you need it for another use.

As a final remark—if the lookup returns more than one row, only the first is returned. You have the option to abort the whole transformation if this happens—simply check the **Fail on multiple results?** checkbox.

Making a performance difference when looking up data in a database

Database lookups are costly and can severely impact transformation performance. However, performance can be significantly improved by using the cache feature of the Database lookup step. To enable the cache feature, just check the **Enable cache?** option.

This is how it works: Think of the cache as a buffer of high-speed memory that temporarily holds frequently requested data. By enabling the cache option, Kettle will look first in the cache and then in the database.

If the table where you look up has few records, you could preload the cache with all the data in the lookup table. You do it by checking the **Load all data from table** option. This will give you the best performance.

On the contrary, if the number of rows in the lookup table is too large to fit entirely into memory, instead of caching the whole table you can tell Kettle the maximum number of rows to hold in cache. You do it by specifying the number in the **Cache size in rows** textbox. The bigger this number, the faster the lookup process.

Be careful when setting the cache options. If you have a large table or don't have much memory, you risk running out of memory.

Have a go hero – preparing the delivery of the products

Create a new transformation and do the following. Taking as source the orders file, create a list of the customers who ordered products. Include their name, last name, and full address. Order the data by country name.

You will need two Database lookup steps—one for getting the customers' information and the other to get the name of the country.

Have a go hero – refining the transformation

Modify the original transformation. As the file may have been manipulated, it may contain invalid data. Apply the following treatment:

◆ Verify that there is a customer with the given number. If the customer doesn't exist, discard the row. Use the **Do not pass the row if the lookup fails** checkbox.

◆ In the rows that passed, verify that there is a product with the given manufacturer and product codes. If the data is valid, check the stock and proceed. If not, make a list so that the cases can be handled later by the customer care department.

Doing complex lookups

The Database lookup step is very useful and quite simple, but it lets you search only for columns of a specific table. Let's now try a step that allows you to do more complex searches.

Time for action – using a Database join step to create a list of suggested products to buy

If your customers ordered a product that is out of stock and you don't want to let them down, you will suggest them some alternative puzzles to buy.

1. Open the transformation of the previous tutorial and save it under a new name.

2. Delete the **Text file output** step.

3. Double-click the **Group by** step and add an aggregated field named `customers` with the list of customers separated by (,). Under **Subject**, select `idcus` and as **Type**, select `Concatenate strings separated by ,`.

4. Double-click the **Database lookup** step. In the **Values to return from the lookup table** grid, add `pro_theme` as value in the `String` field.

5. Add a **Select values** step. Use it to select the fields `customers`, `quantity`, `pro_theme`, and `pro_name`. Also rename `quantity` as `quantity_param` and `pro_theme` as `theme_param`. From the **Lookup** category, drag a **Database join** step to the canvas. Create a hop from the **Select values** step to this step.

6. Double-click the **Database join** step.

7. Select `js` as **Connection**.

8. In the **SQL frame** type the following statement:

```
SELECT man_code
      , pro_code
      , pro_name
FROM   products
WHERE  pro_theme like ?
AND    pro_stock>=?
```

9. In the **Number of rows to return** textbox, type 4.

10. Fill the grid as shown:

The parameters to use:		
#. ▲	Parameter fieldname	Parameter Type
1	theme_param	String
2	quantity_param	String

11. Click on **OK**. The transformation looks like this:

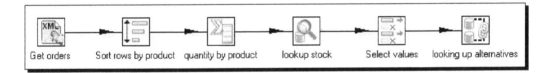

Get orders | Sort rows by product | quantity by product | lookup stock | Select values | looking up alternatives

12. With the last step selected, do a Preview.

13. You should see this:

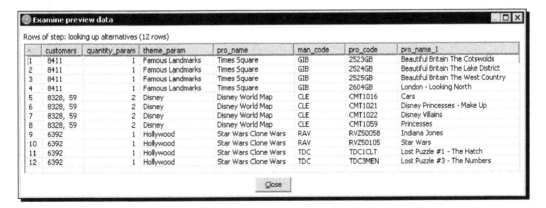

Examine preview data

Rows of step: looking up alternatives (12 rows)

	customers	quantity_param	theme_param	pro_name	man_code	pro_code	pro_name_1
1	8411	1	Famous Landmarks	Times Square	GIB	2523GB	Beautiful Britain The Cotswolds
2	8411	1	Famous Landmarks	Times Square	GIB	2524GB	Beautiful Britain The Lake District
3	8411	1	Famous Landmarks	Times Square	GIB	2525GB	Beautiful Britain The West Country
4	8411	1	Famous Landmarks	Times Square	GIB	2604GB	London - Looking North
5	8328, 59	2	Disney	Disney World Map	CLE	CMT1016	Cars
6	8328, 59	2	Disney	Disney World Map	CLE	CMT1021	Disney Princesses - Make Up
7	8328, 59	2	Disney	Disney World Map	CLE	CMT1022	Disney Villains
8	8328, 59	2	Disney	Disney World Map	CLE	CMT1059	Princesses
9	6392	1	Hollywood	Star Wars Clone Wars	RAV	RVZ50058	Indiana Jones
10	6392	1	Hollywood	Star Wars Clone Wars	RAV	RVZ50105	Star Wars
11	6392	1	Hollywood	Star Wars Clone Wars	TDC	TDC1CLT	Lost Puzzle #1 - The Hatch
12	6392	1	Hollywood	Star Wars Clone Wars	TDC	TDC3MEN	Lost Puzzle #3 - The Numbers

Close

14. In the **Step Metrics** you should see this:

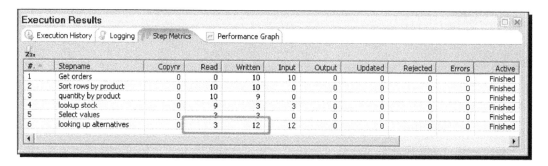

# ▲	Stepname	Copynr	Read	Written	Input	Output	Updated	Rejected	Errors	Active
1	Get orders	0	0	10	10	0	0	0	0	Finished
2	Sort rows by product	0	10	10	0	0	0	0	0	Finished
3	quantity by product	0	10	9	0	0	0	0	0	Finished
4	lookup stock	0	9	3	3	0	0	0	0	Finished
5	Select values	0	3	3	0	0	0	0	0	Finished
6	looking up alternatives	0	3	12	12	0	0	0	0	Finished

What just happened?

You took the list of orders and filtered those for which you ran out of products. For the customers that ordered those products you built a list of four alternative puzzles to buy.

The selection of the puzzles was based on the theme. To filter the suggested puzzles, you used the theme of the ordered product.

The second parameter in the Database join step, the ordered quantity, was used to offer only alternatives for products for which there is a sufficient stock.

Joining data from the database to the stream data by using a Database join step

With the Database join step, you can combine your incoming stream with data from your database, based on given conditions. The conditions are put as parameters in the query you write in the Database join step.

 Note that this is not really a database join as the name suggests; it is a join of data from the database to the stream data.

In the tutorial you used two parameters—the theme and the quantity ordered. With those parameters, you queried the list of products with the same theme:

```
where pro_theme like ?
```

and for which you have stock:

```
and pro_stock>=?
```

You set the parameters as question marks. This works like the question marks in a Table input step you learned in the last chapter—the parameters are replaced positionally. The difference is that here you define the list and the order of the parameters. You do it in the small grid at the bottom of the settings window. This means you aren't forced to use all the incoming fields as parameters, and that you also may change the order.

Just as you do in a Table input step, instead of using positional parameters, you can use Kettle variables by using the ${} notation and checking the **Replace variables** checkbox.

You don't need to add the Select values step to discard fields and rename the parameters. You did it just to have fewer fields in the final screenshot so that it was easier to understand the output of the Database join step.

The step will give you back the manufacturer code, the product code, and the product name for the matching records.

As you cannot do a preview here, you can write and try your query inside a Table input step or in MySQL Query Browser. When you are done, just copy and paste the query here.

So far, you did the same you could have done with **Database lookup** step—looking for a record with a given condition, and adding new fields to the stream. However, there is a big difference here—you put 4 as the **Number of rows to return**. This means for each incoming row, the step will give you back up to four results. The following shows you this:

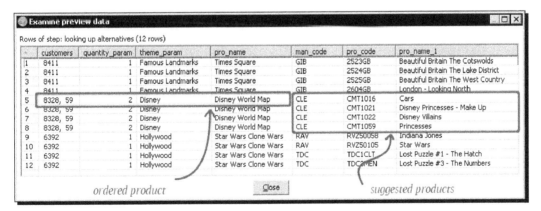

Rows of step: looking up alternatives (12 rows)

	customers	quantity_param	theme_param	pro_name	man_code	pro_code	pro_name_1
1	8411	1	Famous Landmarks	Times Square	GIB	2523GB	Beautiful Britain The Cotswolds
2	8411	1	Famous Landmarks	Times Square	GIB	2524GB	Beautiful Britain The Lake District
3	8411	1	Famous Landmarks	Times Square	GIB	2525GB	Beautiful Britain The West Country
4	8411	1	Famous Landmarks	Times Square	GIB	2604GB	London - Looking North
5	8328, 59	2	Disney	Disney World Map	CLE	CMT1016	Cars
6	8328, 59	2	Disney	Disney World Map	CLE	CMT1021	Disney Princesses - Make Up
7	8328, 59	2	Disney	Disney World Map	CLE	CMT1022	Disney Villains
8	8328, 59	2	Disney	Disney World Map	CLE	CMT1059	Princesses
9	6392	1	Hollywood	Star Wars Clone Wars	RAV	RVZ50058	Indiana Jones
10	6392	1	Hollywood	Star Wars Clone Wars	RAV	RVZ50105	Star Wars
11	6392	1	Hollywood	Star Wars Clone Wars	TDC	TDC1CLT	Lost Puzzle #1 - The Hatch
12	6392	1	Hollywood	Star Wars Clone Wars	TDC	TDC2MEN	Lost Puzzle #3 - The Numbers

ordered product   Close   *suggested products*

Note that if you had left the **Number of rows to return** empty, the step would have returned all found rows.

You may need to use a **Database join** step in several situations:

- When, as the result of the lookup, there is more than one row for each incoming row. This was the case in the tutorial.

- When you have to look in a combination of tables. Look at the following SQL statement:

```
SELECT co.country_name
FROM customers cu
    , cities    ci
    , countries co
WHERE cu.city_id = ci.city_id
AND    ci.cou_id  = co.cou_id
AND    cu.cus_id  = 1000
```

This statement returns the name of the country where the customer with id `1000` lives. If you want to look up the countries where a list of customers live, you can do it with a sentence like this by using a Database join step.

- When you want to look for an aggregate result. Look at this sample query:

```
SELECT    pro_theme
        , count(*) quant
FROM      products
GROUP BY pro_theme
ORDER BY pro_theme
```

This statement returns the number of puzzles by theme. If you have a list of themes and you want to find out how many puzzles you have for each theme, you can use a query like this also by using a Database join step.

The last option in the list can also be developed without using the Database join step. You could execute the `SELECT` statement with a Table Input step, and then look for the calculated quantity by using a Stream lookup step.

 As you can see, this is another situation where PDI offers more that one way to do the same thing. Sometimes it is a matter of taste. In general, you should test each option and choose the method which gives you the best performance.

Have a go hero – rebuilding the list of customers

Redo the Hero exercise preparing the delivery of the products, this time using a Database join step. Try to discover which one is preferable from the point of view of performance. If you don't see any difference, try with a bigger number of records in the main stream. You will have to create your own dataset for this test.

Introducing dimensional modeling

So far you have dealt with the Jigsaw puzzles database, a database used for daily operational work. In the real-world, a database like this is maintained by an **On-Line Transaction Processing (OLTP)** system. The users of an OLTP system perform operational tasks—sell products, process orders, control stock, and so on.

As a counterpart, a **datawarehouse** is a nonoperational database; it is a specialized database designed for decision support purposes. Users of a datawarehouse analyze the data, and they do it from different points of view.

The most used technique for delivering data to datawarehouse users is **dimensional modeling**. This technique makes databases simple and understandable.

The primary table in a dimensional model is the fact table. A **fact table** stores numerical measurements of the business such as quantity of products sold, amount represented by the sold products, discounts, taxes, number of invoices, number of claims, and anything that can be measured. These measurements are referred as **facts**.

A fact is useless without the dimension tables. **Dimension tables** contain the textual descriptors of the business. Typical dimensions are product, time, customers, and regions. The fact along with all the surrounding dimension tables make a star-like structure often called a **star schema**.

Datawarehouse is a very broad concept. In this book we will deal with datamarts. While a datawarehouse represents a global vision of an enterprise, a **datamart** holds the data from a single business process .

Data stored in datawarehouses and datamarts usually comes from different sources, the operational database being the main. The process that takes the information from the source, transforms it in several ways, and finally loads the data into the datamart or datawarehouse is the already mentioned **ETL** process. As said, PDI is a perfect tool for accomplishing that task. In the rest of this chapter, you will learn how to load dimension tables with PDI. This will build the basis for the final project of the book: Loading a full datamart.

Through the tutorials you will learn more about this. However, the terminology introduced here constitutes just a preamble to dimensional modeling. There is much more you can learn. If you are really interested in the subject, you should start by reading *The Data Warehouse Toolkit (Second Edition)* by Ralph Kimball and Margy Ross. The book is undoubtedly the best guide to dimensional modeling.

Loading dimensions with data

A dimension is an entity that describes your business—customers and products are examples of dimensions. A very special dimension is the time dimension that you already know. A dimension table (no surprises here) is a table that contains information about a dimension. In this section you will learn to load dimension tables, that is, fill dimension tables with data.

Time for action – loading a region dimension with a Combination lookup/update step

In this tutorial you will load a dimension that stores geographical information.

1. Launch Spoon.

2. Create a new transformation.

3. Drag a **Table input** step to the canvas and double-click it.

4. As connection select js.

5. In the SQL area type the following query:
    ```
    SELECT ci.city_id, city_name, country_name
    FROM cities ci, countries co
    WHERE ci.cou_id = co.cou_id
    ```

6. Click on **OK**.

7. Expand the **Data Warehouse** category of steps.

8. Select the **Combination lookup/update** step and drag it to the canvas.

9. Create a hop from the **Table input** step to this new step.

10. Double-click the **Combination lookup/update** step.

11. As **Connection** select dw.

12. As **Target table** browse and select `lk_regions` or simply type it.

Key fields (to look up row in table):		
#. ▲	Dimension field	Field in stream
1	id_js	city_id

13. Enter `id` as **Technical key** field and `lastupdate` as **Date of last update** field.

14. Click **OK**.

15. After the **Combination lookup/update** step, add an **Update** step.

16. Double-click the **Update** step.

17. Select `dw` as **Connection** and `lk_regions` as Target **table**.

18. Fill the upper grid adding the condition `id = id`. The `id` to the left is the table id, while the id to the right is the stream id.

19. Fill the lower grid: Add one row with the values `city` and `city_name`. Add a second row with the values `country` and `country_name`. This will update the table columns `city` and `country` with the values `city_name` and `country_name` coming in the stream.

20. Now create another stream: Add to the canvas a **Generate Rows** step, a **Table output** step, and a **Dummy** step.

21. Link the steps in the order you added them.

22. Edit the **Generate Rows** step and set **Limit** to 1.

23. Add four fields in this order: An `Integer` field named `id` with value 0, a `String` field named `city` with value `N/A`, another `String` named `country` with value `N/A`, and an `Integer` field named `id_js` with value 0. Double-click the **Table Output** step.

24. Select `dw` as **Connection** and `lk_regions` as **Target** table.

25. Click on **OK**.

26. In the **Table output** step, enable error handling and send the bad rows to the **Dummy** step.

27. The transformation looks like this:

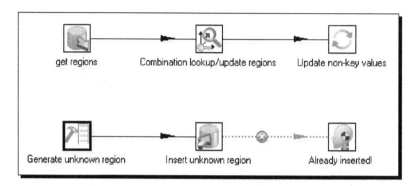

28. Save the transformation and run it.

29. The **Step metrics** looks like this:

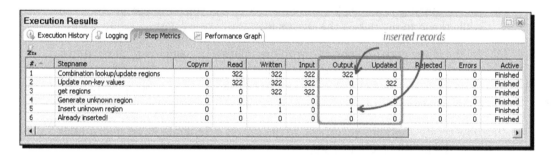

30. Explore the `js_dw` database and do a preview of the `lk_regions` table. You should see this:

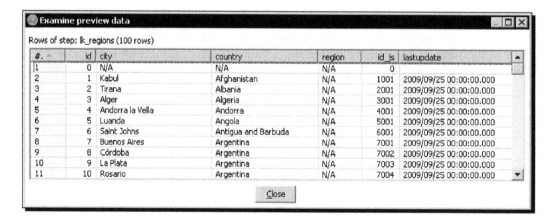

What just happened?

You loaded the region dimension with geographical information—cities and countries.

 Note that you took information from the operational database js and loaded a table in another database js_dw.

Before running the transformation, the dimension table lk_region was empty. When the transformation ran, all cities were inserted in the dimension table.

Besides the records with cities from the cities table, you also inserted a special record with values n/a for the descriptive fields. You did it in the second stream added to the transformation.

Note that the dimension table lk_regions has a column named region that you didn't update because you don't have data for that column. The column is filled with a default value set in the DDL definition of the table.

Time for action – testing the transformation that loads the region dimension

1. In the previous tutorial you loaded a dimension that stores geographical information. You ran it once, causing the insertion of one record for each city and a special record with values n/a for the descriptive fields. Let's apply some changes in the operational database, and run the transformation again to see what happens.

2. Launch MySQL Query Browser.

3. Type the following sentence to change the names of the countries to upper case:

   ```
   UPDATE countries SET country_name = UCASE(country_name)
   ```

4. Execute it.

5. If the transformation created in the last tutorial is not open, open it again.

6. Run the transformation.

7. The **Step Metrics** looks like this:

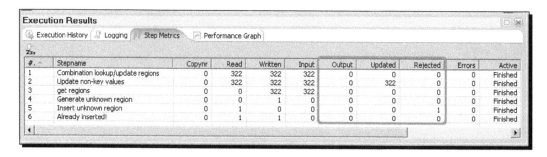

8. Explore the `js_dw` database again and do a preview of the `lk_regions` table. This time you will see the following:

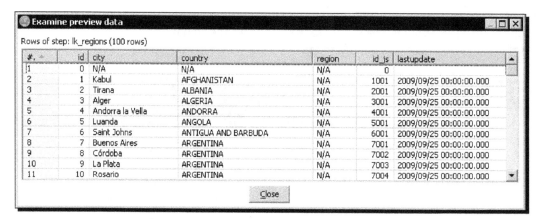

What just happened?

After changing the letter case for the names of the countries in the transactional database `js`, you again ran the transformation that updates the Regions dimension. This time the descriptions for the dimension table were updated.

As for the special record with values `n/a` for the descriptive fields, it had been created the first time the transformation ran. This time, as the record already existed, the row passed by to the **Dummy** step.

Describing data with dimensions

A **dimension** table contains descriptions about a particular entity or category of your business. Dimensions are one of the basic blocks of a datawarehouse or a datamart.

A dimension has the purpose of grouping, filtering, and describing data.

Think of a typical report you would like to have—sales grouped by region, by customer, by method of payment ordered by date. The **by** word lets you identify potential dimensions—regions, customers, method of payments, and date.

Best practices say that a dimension table must have its own technical key column different to the business key column used in the operational database. This technical key is known as a **surrogate key**. In the `lk_region` dimension table the surrogate key is the column named `id`.

While in the operational database the key may be a string such as the manufacturer code in the manufacturers table, surrogate keys are always integers. Another good practice is to have a special record for unavailable data. In the case of the regions example, this implies that besides one record for every city, you should have a record with key equal to zero, and `n/a` or `unknown` or something that represents invalid data for all the descriptive attributes.

Along with the descriptive attributes that you save in a dimension, you usually keep the business key so that you can match the data in the dimension table with the data in the source database. The following screenshot depicts typical columns in a dimension table:

Descriptive fields

id	city	country	region	id_js	lastupdate
0	N/A	N/A	N/A	0	
1	Kabul	Afghanistan	N/A	1001	2009/09/25 00:00:00.000
2	Tirana	Albania	N/A	2001	2009/09/25 00:00:00.000
3	Alger	Algeria	N/A	3001	2009/09/25 00:00:00.000
4	Andorra la Vella	Andorra	N/A	4001	2009/09/25 00:00:00.000
5	Luanda	Angola	N/A	5001	2009/09/25 00:00:00.000
6	Saint Johns	Antigua and Barbuda	N/A	6001	2009/09/25 00:00:00.000
7	Buenos Aires	Argentina	N/A	7001	2009/09/25 00:00:00.000
8	Córdoba	Argentina	N/A	7002	2009/09/25 00:00:00.000
9	La Plata	Argentina	N/A	7003	2009/09/25 00:00:00.000
10	Rosario	Argentina	N/A	7004	2009/09/25 00:00:00.000

surrogate key　　　　　　　　　　　　　　　　　　　*business key*

In the tutorial, you took information from the `cities` and `countries` tables and used that data to load the regions dimension. When there were changes in the transactional database, the changes were translated to the dimension table overwriting the old values. A dimension where changes may occur from time to time is called a **Slowly Changing Dimension** or **SCD** for short. If, when you update an SCD dimension, you don't preserve historical values but the old values, the dimension is called **Type I slowly changing dimension (Type I SCD)**.

Loading Type I SCD with a Combination lookup/update step

In the tutorial, you loaded a Type I SCD by using a Combination lookup/update step. The Combination lookup/update or Combination L/U for short, looks in the dimension table for a record that matches the key fields you put in the upper grid in the settings window. If the combination exists, the step returns the surrogate key of the found record. If it doesn't exist, the step generates a new surrogate key and inserts a row with the key fields and the generated surrogate key. In any case, the surrogate key is added to the output stream.

> Be aware that in the Combination Lookup/update step the following options do not refer to fields in the stream, but to columns in the table: **Dimension field**, **Technical key field**, and **Date of last update field**. You should read Dimension column, Technical key column, and Date of last update column.
>
> Also note that the term **Technical** refers to the surrogate key.

Let's see how the Combination lookup/update step works with an example. Look at the following screenshot:

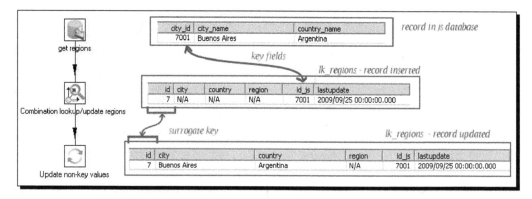

The record to the right of the Table input icon is a sample city among the cities that the Table input step gets from the `js` database.

With the Combination L/U step, PDI looks for a record in the `lk_region` table in the `dw` database, where `id_js` is equal to the field `city_id` in the incoming stream, which is 7001. The first time you run the transformation, the dimension table is empty, so the lookup fails. This causes PDI to generate a new surrogate key according to what you put in the Technical key field area of the settings window.

You told PDI that the column that holds the surrogate key is the column named `id`. You also told PDI that in order to generate the key, the value should be equal to the maximum key found in the target table plus one. In this example, it generates a key equal to 7. You may also use a sequence or an auto increment field if the database engine allows it. If that is not the case, those options are disabled.

Then PDI generates the key and inserts the record you can see to the right of the Combination L/U step in the draw. Note that the record contains only values for the key fields and the technical key field.

The Combination L/U step put the returned technical key in the output stream. Then you used that key for updating the descriptions for city and country with the use of an Update step. After that step, the record is fully generated, as shown in the record to the right of the Update icon.

As the Combination L/U only maintains the key information, if you have non-key columns in the table you must update them with an extra Update step.

Note that those values must have a default value or must allow null values. If none of these conditions is true, the insert operation will fail.

After converting to upper case, all the country names in the source database, you run the transformation again.

This time the incoming record for the same city is this:

city_id	city_name	country_name
7001	Buenos Aires	ARGENTINA

PDI looks for a record in the `lk_region` table, in the `dw` database, where `id_js` is equal to 7001. It finds it. It is the record inserted the first time you ran the transformation, as explained above.

Then, the Combination L/U simply returns the key field adding it to the output stream.

Then you use the key that the step added to update the descriptions for city and country. After the Update step, the old values for city and country name are overwritten by the new ones:

id	city	country	region	id_js	lastupdate
7	Buenos Aires	ARGENTINA	N/A	7001	2009/09/25 00:00:00.000

Have a go hero – adding regions to the Region Dimension

Modify the transformation that loads the Region dimension to fill the `region` column. Get the values from the `regions.xls` file you can find among the downloaded material for this chapter. To add the region information to your stream, use a Stream lookup step.

> While you are playing with dimensions, you may want to throw away all the inserted data and start over again. For doing that, simply explore the database and use the **Truncate table** option. You can do the same in MySQL Query Explorer. For the `lk_regions` dimension, you could execute any of the following:
>
> ```
> DELETE FROM lk_regions or TRUNCATE TABLE lk_regions
> ```

Have a go hero – loading the manufacturers dimension

Create a transformation that loads the manufacturers dimension—`lk_manufacturers`.

Here you have the table definition and some guidance for loading:

Column	Description
id	Surrogate key.
name	Name of the manufacturer.
id_js	Business key. Here you have to store the manufacturer's code (`man_code` field of the source table `manufacturers`).
lastupdate	Date of dimension update—system date.

Have a go hero – loading a mini-dimension

A **mini-dimension** is a dimension where you store the frequently analyzed or frequently changing attributes of a large dimension. Look at the products in the Jigsaw puzzles database. There are several puzzle attributes you may be interested in, for example, when you analyze the sales—number of puzzles in a single pack, number of pieces of the puzzles, material of the product, and so on. Instead of creating a big dimension with all puzzle attributes, you can create a mini-dimension that stores only a selection of attributes. There would be one row in this mini-dimension for each unique combination of the selected attributes encountered in the products table, not one row per puzzle.

In this exercise, you'll have to load a mini-dimension with puzzle attributes. Here you have the definition of the table that will hold the mini-dimension data:

Column	Description
id	Surrogate key
glowsInDark	Y/N
is3D	Y/N
wooden	Y/N
isPanoramic	Y/N
nrPuzzles	Number of puzzles in a single pack
nrPieces	Number of pieces of the puzzle

Take as a starting point the following query:

```
SELECT DISTINCT pro_type
              , pro_packaging
              , pro_shape
              , pro_style
FROM   products
WHERE  pro_type = 'PUZZLE'
```

Use the output stream for creating the fields you need for the dimension—for example, for the field is3D, you'll have to check the value of the pro_shape field.

Once you have all the fields you need, insert the records in the dimension table by using a Combination L/U step. In this mini-dimension, the key is made by all the fields of the table. As a consequence, you don't need an extra Update step.

Keeping a history of changes

The Region dimension is a typical Type I SCD dimension. If some description changes, as the country names did, it makes no sense to keep the old values. The new values simply overwrite the old ones. This is not always the best choice. Sometimes you would like to keep a history of the changes. Now you will learn to load a dimension that keeps a history.

Time for action – keeping a history of product changes with the Dimension lookup/update step

Let's load a puzzles dimension along with the history of the changes in puzzle attributes:

1. Create a new transformation.

2. Drag a **Table input** step to the work area and double-click it.

3. Select js as **Connection**.

4. Type the following query in the SQL area:

```
SELECT pro_code
     , man_code
     , pro_name
     , pro_theme
FROM   products
WHERE pro_type LIKE 'PUZZLE'
```

5. Click on **OK**.

6. Add an **Add constants** step, and create a hop from the **Table input**, step toward it.

7. Use the step to add a Date field named changedate. As **Format** type dd/MM/yyyy, and as **Value**, type 01/10/2009.

8. Expand the **Data Warehouse** category of steps.

9. Select the **Dimension lookup/update** step and drag it to the canvas.

10. Create a hop from the **Add constants** step to this new step.

11. Double-click the **Dimension lookup/update** step.

12. As **Connection** select dw.

13. As **Target table** type lk_puzzles.

14. Fill the **Key fields** as shown:

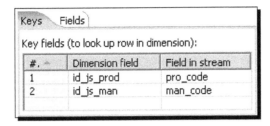

15. Select `id` as Technical key **field**.

16. In the frame **Creation of technical key**, leave the default to
Use table maximum + 1.

17. As **Version field**, select `version`.

18. As **Stream Datefield**, select `changedate`.

19. As **Date range start field**, select `start_date`.

20. As **Table daterange end**, select `end_date`.

21. Select the **Fields** tab and fill it like this:

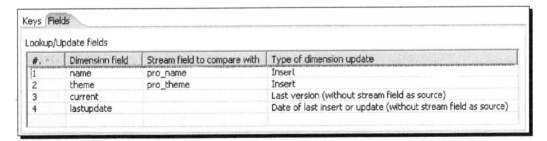

22. Close the settings window.

23. Save the transformation, and run it.

24. Explore the `js_dw` database and do a preview of the `lk_puzzles` table.

25. You should see this:

	id	name	theme	id_js_prod	id_js_man	start_date	end_date	version	current	lastupdate
1	0	N/A	N/A	0	0			1	Y	
2	1	1940s Shopping Basket	Food and Drink	2501GB	GIB	1900/01/01 ...	2199/12/31 ...	1	Y	2009/09/25 ...
3	2	1950s Shopping Basket	Food and Drink	2502GB	GIB	1900/01/01 ...	2199/12/31 ...	1	Y	2009/09/25 ...
4	3	1960s Shopping Basket	Food and Drink	2503GB	GIB	1900/01/01 ...	2199/12/31 ...	1	Y	2009/09/25 ...
5	4	1970s Shopping Basket	Food and Drink	2504GB	GIB	1900/01/01 ...	2199/12/31 ...	1	Y	2009/09/25 ...
6	5	A Jolly Good Sport	Cars	2505GB	GIB	1900/01/01 ...	2199/12/31 ...	1	Y	2009/09/25 ...
7	6	A Long Night	Christmas	2506GB	GIB	1900/01/01 ...	2199/12/31 ...	1	Y	2009/09/25 ...
8	7	A Peaceful Retreat	Artists	2507GB	GIB	1900/01/01 ...	2199/12/31 ...	1	Y	2009/09/25 ...
9	8	A Perfect View	Horses	2508GB	GIB	1900/01/01 ...	2199/12/31 ...	1	Y	2009/09/25 ...
10	9	A Summer's Evening	Caribbean	2509GB	GIB	1900/01/01 ...	2199/12/31 ...	1	Y	2009/09/25 ...
11	10	A Team Effort	Dogs	2510GB	GIB	1900/01/01 ...	2199/12/31 ...	1	Y	2009/09/25 ...

Examine preview data — Rows of step: lk_puzzles (100 rows) — Close

What just happened?

You loaded the puzzle dimension with the name and theme of the puzzles you sell. The dimension table has the usual columns for a dimension—technical id (field `id`), fields that store the key fields in the table of the operational database (`prod_code` and `man_code`), and columns for the puzzle attributes (`name` and `theme`). It also has some extra fields specially designed to keep history.

When you ran the transformation, all records were inserted in the dimension table. Also a special record was automatically inserted for unavailable data.

So far, there is nothing new except for a few extra columns with dates. In the next tutorial, you will learn more about those columns.

Time for action – testing the transformation that keeps a history of product changes

1. In the previous tutorial you loaded a dimension with products by using a Dimension lookup/update step. You ran the transformation once, causing the insertion of one record for each product and a special record with values `n/a` for the descriptive fields. Let's apply some changes in the operational database, and run the transformation again to see how the Dimension lookup/update step keeps history.

2. In MySQL Query Browser, open the script `update_jumbo_products.sql` and run it.

3. Switch to Spoon.

4. If the transformation created in the last tutorial is not open, open it again.

5. Run the transformation. Explore the `js_dw` database again. Press **Open SQL for [lk_puzzles]** and type the following sentence:

```
SELECT    *
FROM      lk_puzzles
WHERE     id_js_man = 'JUM'
ORDER BY id_js_prod
         , version
```

6. You will see this:

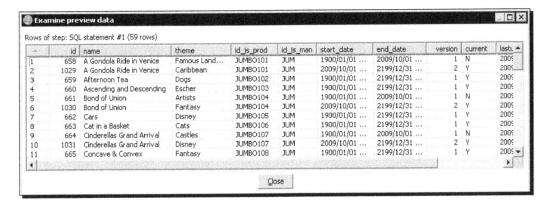

What just happened?

After making some changes in the operational database, you ran the transformation for a second time. The modifications you made caused the insertion of new records recreating the history of the puzzle attributes.

Keeping an entire history of data with a Type II slowly changing dimension

Type II SCDs differ from Type I SCDs in that a Type II keeps the whole history of the data of your dimension. Typical examples of attributes for which you would like to keep a history are sales territories that change over time, categories of products that are reclassified from time to time, and promotions that you apply to products and are valid in a given range of dates.

> There are no rules that dictate whether or not you keep/retain the history in a dimension. It's the final user who decides based on his requirements.

In the puzzle dimension, you kept information about the changes for the name and theme attributes. Let's see how the history is kept for this sample dimension.

Each puzzle is to be represented by one or more records, each with the information valid during a certain period of time, as in the following example:

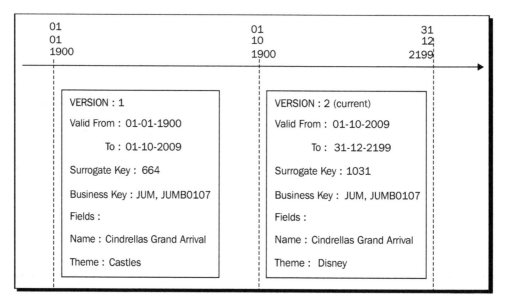

The history is kept in three extra fields in the dimension table—version, date_from, and date_to.

The version field is an automatically incremented value that maintains a revision number of the records for a particular puzzle.

The date range is used to indicate the period of applicability of the data.

In the tutorial you also had a current field, that acted as a flag to show if a record is the record valid in the present day.

The sample puzzle, Cinderellas Grand Arrival, was classified in the category Castles until October 1, 2009. After that date, the puzzle was reclassified as a Disney puzzle. This is the second version of the puzzle, as indicated by the column version. It's also the current version, as indicated by the column current.

In general, if you have to implement a Type II SCD with PDI, your dimension table must have the first three fields—`version`, `date from`, and `date to`. The current flag is optional.

Loading Type II SCDs with the Dimension lookup/update step

Type II SCDs can be loaded by using the Dimension lookup/update step. The Dimension lookup/update or Dimension L/U for short, looks in the dimension for a record that matches the information you put in the **Keys** grid of the settings window.

If the lookup fails, it inserts a new record. If a record is found, the step inserts or updates records depending on how you configured the step.

Let's explain how the Dimension L/U works with the following sample puzzle in the `js` database:

id	name	theme	id_js_prod	id_js_man	start_date	end_date	version	current	lastupdate
664	Cinderellas Grand Arrival	Castles	JUMBO107	JUM	1900/01/01 ...	2199/12/31 ...	1	Y	2009/09/25 ...

The first time you run the transformation, the step looks in the dimension for a record where `id_js_prod` is equal to JUMBO107and `id_js_man` is equal to JUM. Not only that, the period from `start_date` to `end_date` of the found record must contain the value of the `stream datefield`, which is `01/10/2009`.

Because you never loaded this table before, the table was empty and so the lookup failed.

As a result, the step inserts the following record:

pro_code	man_code	pro_name	pro_de...	pro_type	pro_theme
JUMBO107	JUM	Cinderellas Grand Arrival		PUZZLE	Castles

Note the values that the step put for the special fields:

The **version** for the new record is **1**, the current flag is set to true, and the **start_date** and **end_date** take as values the dates you put in the `Min.year` and `Max.year`: `01/01/1900` and `31/12/2199`.

After making some modifications to the operational database, you ran the transformation again. Look at the following screenshot:

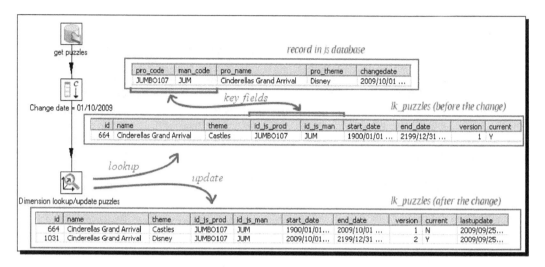

The puzzle information changed. As you see to the right of the Table input step, the puzzle is now classified as a Disney puzzle.

This time the lookup succeeds. There is a record for which the keys match and the period from `start_date` to `end_date` of the found record, `01/01/1900` to `31/12/2199`, obviously contains the value of the `stream datefield`, `01/10/2009`.

Once found, the step compares the fields you put in the **Fields** tab—`name` and `theme` in the dimension table against `pro_name` and `pro_theme` in the incoming stream.

As there is a difference in the `theme` field, the step inserts a new record, and modifies the current—it changes the validity dates and sets the current flag to false. Now this puzzle has two versions in the dimension table, as you see below the Dimension L/U icon in the drawing.

These update and insert operations are made for all records that changed.

For the records that didn't change, dimension records are found but as nothing changed, nothing is inserted or updated.

Take a note about the stream date: The field you put here is key to the loading process of the dimension, as its value is interpreted by PDI as the effective date of the change. In the tutorial, you put a fixed date—`01/10/2009`. In real situations you should use the effective or last changed date of the data if that date is available. If it is not available, leave the field blank. PDI will use the system date.

In this example, you filled the column **Type of SCD update** with the option `Insert` for every field. Doing so, you loaded a pure Type II SCD, that is, a dimension that keeps track of all changes in all fields.

In the sample puzzles dimension, you kept a history of changes both in the theme and in the name. For the sample puzzle, the theme was changed from `Castles` to `Disney`. If, after some time, you query the sales and notice that the sales for that puzzle increased after the change, then you may conclude that the customers are more interested in Disney puzzles than in castle puzzles. The possibility of creating these kinds of reports is a good reason for maintaining a Type II SCD.

On the other hand, if the name of the puzzle changes, you may not be so interested in knowing what the name was before. Fortunately, you may change the configuration and create a **Hybrid SCD**. Instead of selecting `Insert` for every field, you may select `Update` or `Punch through`:

◆ When there is a change in a field for which you chose `Update`, the new value overwrites the old value in the last dimension record version, this being the usual behavior in Type I SCDs.

◆ When there is a change in a field for which you chose `Punch through`, the new data overwrites the old value in all record versions.

Note that selecting `Punch through` for all the fields, the Dimension L/U step allows you to load a Type I SCD dimension. When you build Type I SCD you are not interested in range dates. Thus, you can leave the Stream datefield textbox empty. The current date is assumed by default.

In practice both Type I, Type II, and Hybrid SCDs are used. The choice of the type of SCD depends on the business needs.

Besides all those inserts and updates operations, the Dimension L/U automatically inserts in the dimension a record for unavailable data.

In order to insert the special record with key equal to zero, all fields must have default values or allow nulls. If none of these conditions are true, the automatic insertion will fail.

In order to load a dimension with the Dimension L/U step, your table has to have columns for the version, date from, and date to. The step automatically maintains those columns. You simply have to put their names in the right textbox in the settings window.

Besides those fields, your dimension table may have a column for the current flag, and another column for the date of last insert or update. To fill those optional columns, you have to add them in the Fields tab as you did in the tutorial.

Have a go hero – keeping a history just for the theme of a product

Modify the loading of the products dimension so that it only keeps a history of the theme. If the name of the product changes, just overwrite the old values. Modify some data in the js database and run your transformation to confirm that it works as expected.

Have a go hero – loading a Type II SCD dimension

As you saw in the Hero exercise to add regions to the Region Dimension, the countries were grouped in three: Spain, Rest of Europe, Rest of the World.

As the sales rose in several countries of the world, you decided to regroup the countries in more than three groups. However, you want to do it starting in 2008. For older sales you prefer to keep seeing the sales grouped by the original categories.

This is what you will do: Use the table named lk_regions_2 to create a Type II Region dimension. Here is a guide to follow:

Create a transformation that loads the dimension. You will take the stream date (the date you use for loading the dimension) from the command line. If the command line argument is empty, use the present day.

As the name for the sheet with the region definition, use a named parameter.

Stream date

If the command line argument is present, remember to change it to Date before using it. You do that with a Select values step.

Note that you have to define the format of the entered data in advance. Suppose that you want to enter as argument the date January 1, 2008. If you chose the format dd-mm-yyyy, you'll have to enter the argument as 01-01-2008.

In case the command line argument is absent, you can get the default with a Get System Info step. Note that the system date you add with this step is already a Date field.

Now just follow these steps:

1. Run the transformation by using the `regions.xls` file. Don't worry about the command line argument. Check that the dimension was loaded as expected. There has to be a single record for every city.

2. Run the transformation again. This time use the `regions2008.xls` file as source for the region column. As command line, enter January 1st, 2008. Remember to type the date in the expected format (check the preceding tip). Explore the dimension table. There has to be two records for each country—one valid before 2008 and one valid after that date.

3. Modify the sheet to create a new grouping for the American countries. Use your imagination for this task! Run the transformation for the third time. This time use the sheet you created and as date, type the present day (or leave the argument blank). Explore the dimension table. Now each city for the countries you regrouped has to have three versions, where the current is the version you created. The other cities should continue to have two versions each, because nothing related to those cities changed.

Pop quiz – loading slowly changing dimensions

Suppose you have DVDs with the French films in the catalog you've created so far. You rent those DVDs and keep the rental information in the database. Now you will design a dimensional model for that data.

1. You begin by designing a dimension to store the names of the films. How do you create the Films dimension:
   a. As a Type I SCD
   b. As a Type II SCD
   c. You will decide when you have rented enough films so you make the right decision.

2. In order to create that dimension, you could use:
   a. A Dimension L/U step
   b. A Combination L/U step
   c. Either of the above
   d. Neither of the above

Pop quiz – loading type III slowly changing dimensions

Type III SCD are dimensions that store the immediately preceding and current value for a descriptive field of the dimension. Each entity is stored in a single record. The field for which you want to keep the previous value has two columns assigned in the record: One for the current value and the other for the old. Sometimes, it is possible to have a third column holding the date of effective change.

Type III SCDs are appropriate when you don't want to keep all the history, but mainly when you need to support two views of the attribute simultaneously—the previous and the current. Suppose you have an Employees dimension. Among the attributes you have their position. People are promoted from time to time and you want to keep these changes in the dimension; however, you are not interested in knowing all the intermediate positions the employees have been through. In this case, you may implement a Type III SCD.

The question is, how would you load a Type III SCD with PDI:

a. With a Dimension L/U step configuring it properly

b. By using a Database lookup step to get the previous value. Then with a Dimension L/U step or a Combination L/U step to insert or update the records.

c. You can't load Type III SCDs with PDI

It's worth saying that type III SCD are used rather infrequently and not always can be automated. Sometimes they are used to represent human-applied changes and the implementation has to be made manually.

Summary

In this chapter you learned to perform some advanced operations on databases.

First, you populated the Jigsaw database in order to have data for the activities in the chapter. Then, you learned to do simple and complex searches in a database.

Then you were introduced to dimensional concepts and learned what dimensions are and how to load them with PDI. You learned about Type I, Type II, Type III SCDs and mini-dimensions. You still have to learn when and how to use those dimensions. You will do so in Chapter 12.

The steps you learned in this and the preceding chapter are far from being the full list of steps that PDI offers to work with databases. However, taking into account all you learned, you are now ready to use PDI for implementing most of your database requirements. In the next chapter, you will switch to a totally different yet core subject needed to work with PDI—jobs.

10

Creating Basic Task Flows

So far you have been working with data. You got data from a file, a sheet, or a database, transformed it somehow, and sent it back to some file or table in a database. You did it by using PDI transformations. A PDI transformation does not run in isolation. Usually, it is embedded in a bigger process. Here are some examples:

- Download a file, clean it, load the information of the file in a database, and fill an audit file with the result of the operation.
- Generate a daily report and transfer the report to a shared repository.
- Update a datawarehouse. If something goes wrong, notify the administrator by e-mail.

All these examples are typical processes of which a transformation is only a piece. These types of processes can be implemented by PDI Jobs. In this chapter, you will learn to build basic jobs. These are the topics that will be covered:

- Introduction to jobs
- Executing tasks depending upon conditions

Introducing PDI jobs

A PDI **job** is analogous to a process. As with processes in real life, there are basic jobs and there are jobs that do really complex tasks. Let's start by creating a job in the first group—a hello world job.

Time for action – creating a simple hello world job

In this tutorial, you will create a very simple job so that you get an idea of what jobs are about.

Although you will now learn how to create a job, for this tutorial you first have to create a transformation.

1. Open Spoon.

2. Create a new transformation.

3. Drag a **Generate rows** step to the canvas and double-click it.

4. Add a String value named message, with the value Hello, World!.

5. Click on **OK**.

6. Add a **Text file output** step and create a hop from the **Generate rows** step to this new step.

7. Double-click the step.

8. Type ${LABSOUTPUT}/chapter10/hello as filename.

9. In the **Fields** tab, add the only field in the stream—message.

10. Click on **OK**.

11. Inside the folder where you save your work, create a folder named transformations.

12. Save the transformation with the name hello_world_file.ktr in the folder you just created. The following is your final transformation:

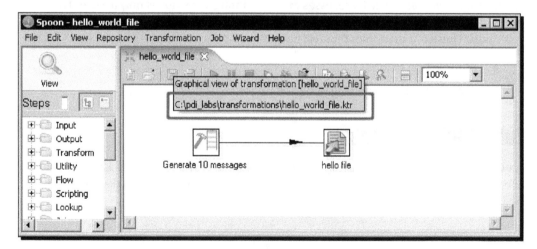

Now you are ready to create the main job.

13. Select **File | New | Job** or press *Ctrl+Alt+N*. A new job is created.

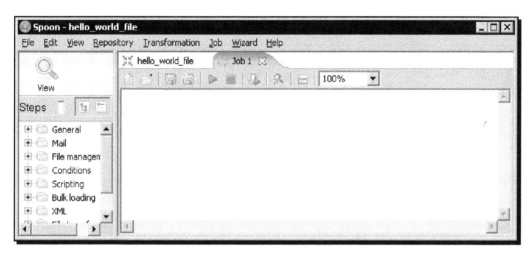

14. Press *Ctrl+J*. The Job properties window appears.

15. Give a name and description to the job.

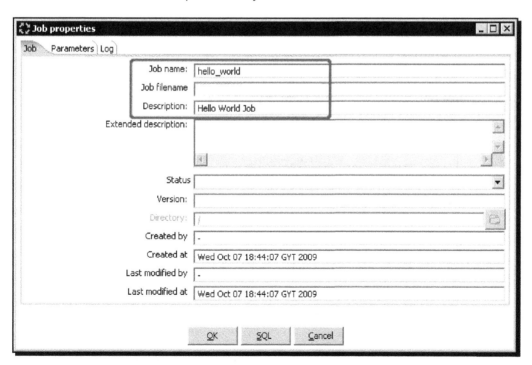

16. Save the job in the folder where you created the `transformations` folder, with the name `hello_world.kjb`.

17. To the left of the screen, there is a tree with job entries. Expand the **General** category of job entries, select the **START** entry, and drag it to the work area.

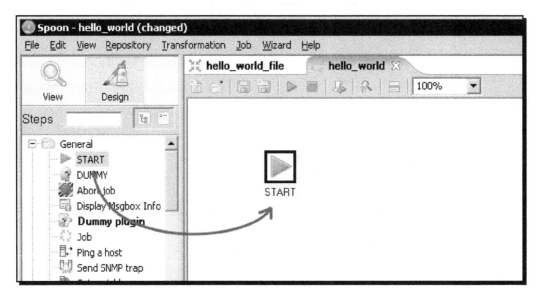

18. Expand the **File management** category, select the **Create a folder** entry, and drag it to the canvas.

19. Select both entries. With the mouse cursor over the second entry, right-click and select **New hop**. A new hop is created.

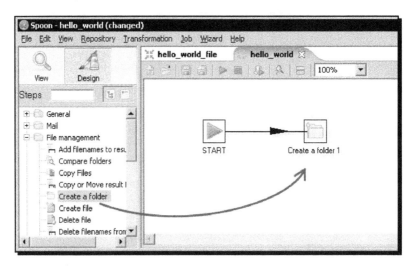

Just like in a transformation, you have several ways to create hops. For more detail, please refer to the *Time for action – creating a Hello Word transformation* section in Chapter 1 where hops were introduced or to Appendix D, *Spoon Shortcuts*.

20. Double-click the **Create a folder...** icon.

21. In the textbox next to the **Folder name** option, type `${LABSOUTPUT}/chapter10` and click on **OK**. From the **General** category, drag a transformation job entry to the canvas.

22. Create a hop from the **Create a folder** entry to the transformation entry.

23. Double-click the transformation job entry.

24. Position the cursor in the **Transformation filename** textbox, press *Ctrl+Space*, and select `${Internal.Job.Filename.Directory}`.

This variable is the counterpart to the variable `{Internal.Transformation.Filename.Directory}` you already know. `{Internal.Job.Filename.Directory}` evaluates the directory where the job resides.

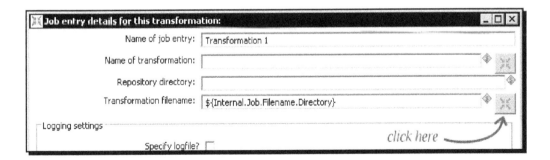

25. Click on the icon to the right of the textbox. The following dialog window shows up:

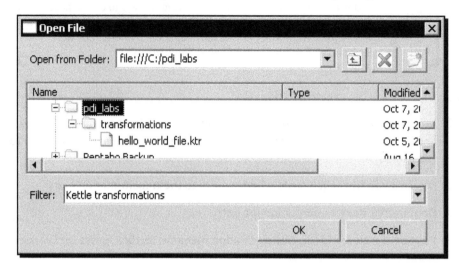

26. As you can see, the {Internal.Job.Filename.Directory} variable provides a convenient starting place for looking up the transformation file. Select the hello_world_file.ktr transformation and click **OK**.

27. Now the **Transformation filename** has the full path to the transformation. Replace the full job path back to ${Internal.Job.Filename.Directory} so that the final text for the **Transformation filename** field is as shown in the following screenshot:

28. Click on **OK**.

29. Press *Ctrl+S* to save the job.

30. Press *F9* to run the job. The following window shows up:

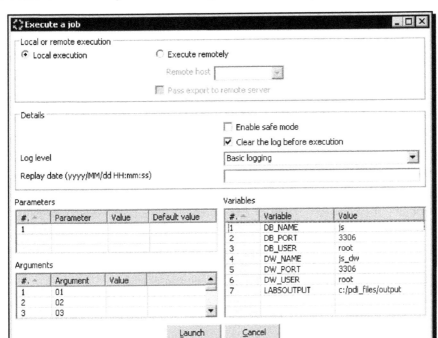

Remember that in the initial chapters, you defined the
LABSOUTPUT variable in the kettle.properties file. You
should see its value in the **Variables** grid. If you removed the
variable from that file, provide a value here.

31. Click on **Launch**.

32. At the bottom of the screen, you'll see the **Execution results**. The **Job metrics** screen
looks as follows:

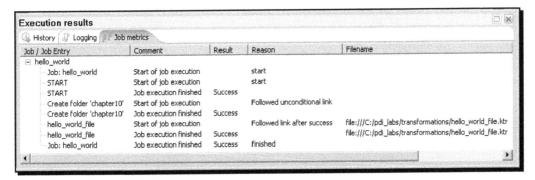

33. Select the **Logging** tab. It looks like this:

```
Execution results
History   Logging   Job metrics

2009/10/08 05:12:28 - Spoon - Starting job...
2009/10/08 05:12:28 - hello_world - Starting entry [Create folder 'chapter10']
2009/10/08 05:12:28 - hello_world - Starting entry [hello_world_file]
2009/10/08 05:12:28 - hello_world_file - Loading transformation from XML file [file:///C:/pdi_labs/transformations/hello_world_file.ktr]
2009/10/08 05:12:28 - hello_world_file - Dispatching started for transformation [hello_world_file]
2009/10/08 05:12:28 - hello_world_file - This transformation can be replayed with replay date: 2009/10/08 05:12:28
2009/10/08 05:12:28 - Generate 10 messages.0 - Finished processing (I=0, O=0, R=0, W=10, U=0, E=0)
2009/10/08 05:12:28 - hello file.0 - Finished processing (I=0, O=11, R=10, W=10, U=0, E=0)
2009/10/08 05:12:28 - hello_world - Finished job entry [hello_world_file] (result=[true])
2009/10/08 05:12:28 - hello_world - Finished job entry [Create folder 'chapter10'] (result=[true])
2009/10/08 05:12:28 - Spoon - Job has ended.
```

34. Explore the folder pointed to by your `${LABSOUTPUT}` variable—for example, `c:/pdi_files/output`. You should see a new folder named `chapter10`.

35. Inside the `chapter10` folder, you should see a file named `hello.txt`.

36. Explore the file. It should have the following content:

```
Message
Hello, World!
Hello, World!
Hello, World!
Hello, World!
```

What just happened?

First of all, you created a transformation that generated a simple file with the message `Hello, World!`. The file was configured to be created in a folder named `chapter10`.

After that, you created a PDI Job. The job was built to create a folder named `chapter10` and then to execute the `hello_world` transformation.

When you ran the job, the `chapter10` folder was created, and inside it, a file with the `Hello, World!` message was generated.

Executing processes with PDI jobs

A **Job** is a PDI entity designed for the execution of processes. In the tutorial, you ran a simple process that created a folder and then generated a file in that folder. A more complex example could be the one that truncates all the tables in a database and loads data in all the tables from a set of text files. Other examples involve sending e-mails, transferring files, and executing shell scripts.

The unit of execution inside a job is called a **job entry**. In Spoon you can see the entries grouped into categories according to the purpose of the entries. In the tutorial, you used job entries from two of those categories: **General** and **File management**.

Most of the job entries in the **File management** category have a self-explanatory name such as **Create a folder**, and their use is quite intuitive. Feel free to experiment with them!

As to the **General** category, it contains many of the most used entries. Among them is the **START** job entry that you used. A job must start with a **START** job entry.

 Don't forget to start your sequence of job entries with a **START**. A job can have any mix of job entries and hops, as long as they start with this special kind of job entry.

A **Hop** is a graphical representation that links two job entries. The direction of the hop defines the order of execution of the job entries it links. Besides, the execution of the destination job entry does not begin until the job entry that precedes it has finished. Look, for example, at the job in the tutorial. There is an entry that creates a folder, followed by an entry that executes a transformation. First of all, the job creates the folder. Once the folder has been created, the execution of the transformation begins. This allows the transformation to assume that the folder exists. So, it safely creates a file in that folder.

A hop connects only two job entries. However, a job entry may be reached by more than one hop. Also, more than one hop may leave a job entry.

A job, like a transformation, is neither a program nor an executable file. It is simply plain XML. The job contains metadata that tells the Kettle engine which processes to run and the order of execution of those processes. Therefore, it is said that a job is **flow-control oriented**.

Using Spoon to design and run jobs

As you just saw, with Spoon you not only create, preview, and run transformations, but you also create and run jobs.

You are already familiar with this graphical tool, so you don't need too much explanation about the basic work areas. So, let's do a brief review.

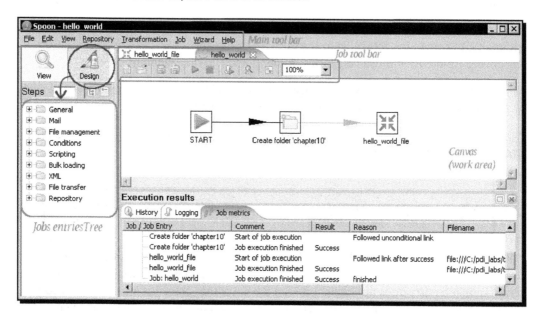

The following table describes the main differences you will notice while designing a job compared to designing a transformation:

Area	Description
Design tree	You don't see a list of steps but a list of job entries (despite on top of the list you see the word **Steps**).
Job menu	You no longer see some options that only have sense while working with datasets. One of them is the **Preview** button.
Job metrics tab (**Execution results** window)	Instead of a **Step Metrics**, you have this tab. Here you can see metrics for each job entry.

If you click the **View** icon in the upper-left corner of the screen, the tree will change to show the structure of the job currently being edited.

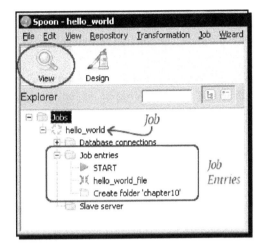

Using the transformation job entry

The transformation job entry allows you to call a transformation from a job.

There are several situations where you may need to use a transformation job entry.

In the tutorial, you had a transformation that generated a file in a given folder. You called the transformation from a job that created that folder in advance. In this case, the job and the transformation performed complementary tasks.

Sometimes the job just keeps your work organized. Consider the transformations that loaded the dimension tables for the js database. As you will usually run them together, you can embed them into a single job as shown in this figure:

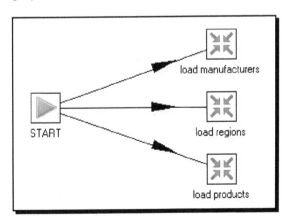

The only task done by this job is to keep the transformations together. Although the picture implies the entries are run simultaneoulsy, that is not the case.

 Job entries typically execute sequentially, this being one of the central differences between jobs and transformations.

When you link two entries with a hop, you force an order of execution. On the contrary, when you create a job as shown in this preceding figure, you needn't give an order and the entries still run in sequence, one entry after another depending on the creation sequence.

Launching job entries in parallel

As the transformations that load dimensions are not dependent on each other, as an option, you can ask the **START** entry to launch them simultaneously. For doing that, right-click the **START** entry and select **Launch next entries in parallel**. Once selected, the arrows to the next job entries will be shown in dashed lines. This option is available in any entry, not just in the **START** entry.

The jobs explained earlier are just two examples of how and when you use a transformation job entry. Note that many transformations perform their tasks by themselves. In that case you are not forced to embed them into jobs. It makes no sense to have a job with just a **START** entry, followed by a transformation job entry. You can still execute those transformations alone, as you used to do until now.

Pop quiz – defining PDI jobs

1. A job is:

    a. A big transformation that groups smaller transformations

    b. An ordered group of task definitions

    c. An unordered group of task definitions

2. For each of the following sentences select True or False. A job allows you to:

    a. Send e-mails

    b. Compare folders

    c. Run transformations

    d. Truncate database tables

    e. Transfer files with FTP

Have a go hero – loading the dimension tables

Create a job that loads the main dimension tables in the Jigsaw database—manufacturers, products, and regions. Test the job.

Receiving arguments and parameters in a job

Jobs, as well as transformations, are more flexible when receiving parameters from outside. You already learned to parameterize your transformations by using named parameters and command-line arguments. Let's extend these concepts to jobs.

Time for action – customizing the hello world file with arguments and parameters

Let's create a more flexible version of the job you did in the previous section.

1. Create a new transformation.

2. Press *Ctrl+T* to bring up the **Transformation properties** window.

3. Select the **Parameters** tab.

4. Add a named parameter HELLOFOLDER. Insert chapter10 as the default value.

5. Click on **OK**.

6. Drag a **Get System Info** step to the canvas .

7. Double-click the step.

8. Add a field named yourname. Select command line argument 1 as the **Type**.

9. Click on **OK**.

10. Now add a **Formula** step located in the **Scripting** category of steps.

11. Use the step to add a String field named message. As **Formula**, type "Hello, " & [yourname] & "!".

12. Finally, add a **Text file output** step.

13. Use the step to send the message data to a file. Enter ${LABSOUTPUT}/${HELLOFOLDER}/hello as the name of the file.

14. Save the transformation in the transformations folder you created in the previous tutorial, under the name hello_world_param.ktr.

15. Open the `hello_world.kjb` job you created in the previous tutorial and save it under a new job named `hello_world_param.kjb`.

16. Press *Ctrl+J* to open the **Job properties** window.

17. Select the **Parameters** tab.

18. Add the same named parameter you added in the transformation.

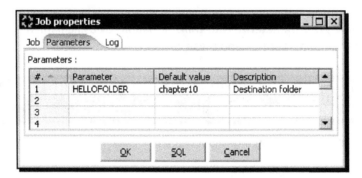

19. Click on **OK**.

20. Double-click the **Create a folder** entry.

21. Change the **Folder name** textbox content to `${LABSOUTPUT}/${HELLOFOLDER}`.

22. Double-click the **Transformation** entry.

23. Change the transformation filename textbox to point to the new transformation: `${Internal.Job.Filename.Directory}/transformations/hello_world_param.ktr`.

24. Click on **OK**.

25. Save the job and run it.

26. Fill the dialog window with a value for the named parameter and a value for the command-line argument.

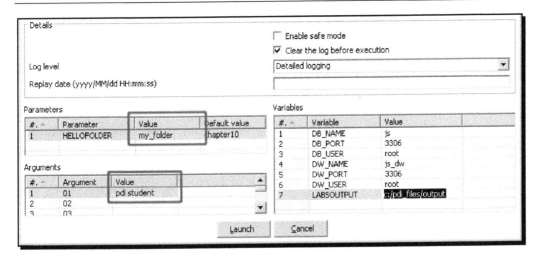

27. Click on **Launch**.

28. When the execution finishes, check the output folder. The folder named
`my_folder`, which you initially specified as a named parameter, should be created.

29. Inside that folder there should be a file named `hello.txt`. This time the content of
the file has been customized with the name you provided:

```
Hello, pdi student!
```

What just happened?

You created a transformation that generated a `hello.txt` file in a folder given as the
named parameter. The content of the file is a customized "Hello" message that gets the
name of the reader from the command line.

In the main job you also defined a named parameter, the same that you defined in the
transformation. The job needs the parameter to create the folder.

When you run the job, you provided both the command-line argument and the named
parameter in the job dialog window that shows up when you launch the execution. Then
a folder was created with the name you gave, and a file was generated with the name you
typed as argument.

Using named parameters in jobs

You can use named parameters in jobs in the same way you do in transformations. You define them in the **Job properties** window. You provide names and default values, and then you use them just as regular variables. The places where you can use variables, just as in a transformation, are identified with a dollar sign to the right of the textboxes. In the tutorial, you used a named parameter in the **Create a folder** job entry. In this particular example, you used the same named parameter both in the main job and in the transformation called by the job. So, you defined the named parameter HELLOFOLDER in two places—in the **Job settings** window and in the **Transformation properties** window.

If a named parameter is used only in the transformation, you don't need to define it in the job that calls the transformation.

Have a go hero – backing up your work

Suppose you want to back up your output files regularly, that is, the files in your ${LABSOUTPUT} directory. Build a job that creates a ZIP file with all your output files. For the name and location of the ZIP file, use two named parameters.

Use the **Zip file** job entry located in the **File management** category.

Running jobs from a terminal window

In the main tutorial of this section, both the job and the transformation called by the job used a named parameter. The transformation also required a command-line argument. When you executed the job from Spoon, you provided both the parameter and the argument in the job dialog window. You will now learn to launch the job and provide that information from a terminal window.

Time for action – executing the hello world job from a terminal window

In order to run the job from a terminal window, follow these instructions:

1. Open a terminal window.

2. Go to the directory where Kettle is installed.

    □   On Windows systems type:

        ```
        C:\pdi-ce>kitchen /file:c:/pdi_labs/hello_world_param.kjb
        Maria -param:"HELLOFOLDER=my_work" /norep
        ```

    □   On Unix, Linux, and other Unix-like systems type:

        ```
        /home/yourself/pdi-ce/kitchen.sh /file:/home/yourself/
        pdi_labs/hello_world_param.kjb Maria -param:"HELLOFOLDER=
        my_work" /norep
        ```

3. If your job is in another folder, modify the command accordingly. You may also replace the name `Maria` with your name, of course. If your name has spaces, enclose the whole argument within `" "`.

4. You will see how the job runs, following the log in the terminal:

5. Go to the output folder—the folder pointed by your `LABS_OUTPUT` variable.

6. A folder named `my_work` should have been created.

7. Check the content of the folder. A file named `hello.txt` should be there. Edit the file. You should see the following:

    ```
    Hello,Maria!
    ```

What just happened?

You ran the job with **Kitchen**, the program that executes jobs from the terminal window.

After the name of the command, `kitchen.bat` or `kitchen.sh`, depending on the platform, you provided the following:

- The full path to the job file: `/file:c:/pdi_labs/hello_world_param.kjb`
- A command-line argument: `Maria`.
- A named parameter, and a `-param`: `"HELLOFOLDER=my_work"`
- The switch `/norep` to tell Kettle not to connect to a repository

After running the job, you could see that the folder had been created and a file with a custom "Hello" message had been generated.

Here you used some of the options available when you run Kitchen. Appendix B tells you all the details about using Kitchen for running jobs.

Have a go hero – experiencing Kitchen

Run the `hello_world_param.kjb` job from Kitchen, with and without providing arguments and parameters. See what happens in each case.

Using named parameters and command-line arguments in transformations

As you know, transformations accept both arguments from the command line and named parameters. When you run a transformation from Spoon, you supply the values for arguments and named parameters in the transformation dialog window that shows up when you launch the execution. From a terminal window, you provide those values in the Pan command line.

In this chapter you learned to run a transformation embedded in a job. Here, the methods you have for supplying named parameters and arguments needed by the transformation are quite similar. From Spoon you supply the values in the job dialog window that shows up when you launch the job execution. From the terminal window you provide the values in the Kitchen command line.

> Whether you run a job from Spoon or from Kitchen, the named parameters and arguments you provide are unique and shared by the main job and all transformations called by that job. Each transformation, as well as the main job, may or may not use them according to their needs.

There is still another way in which you can pass parameters and arguments to a transformation. Let's see it by example.

Time for action – calling the hello world transformation with fixed arguments and parameters

This time you will call the parameterized transformation from a new job.

1. Open the `hello_world.kjb` job you created in the first section and save it as `hello_world_fixedvalues.kjb`.

2. Double-click the **Create a folder** job entry.

3. Replace the `chapter10` string by the string `fixedfolder`.

4. Double-click the transformation job entry.

5. Change the **Transformation filename** as `${Internal.Job.Filename.Directory}/transformations/hello_world_param.ktr`.

6. Fill the **Argument** tab as follows.

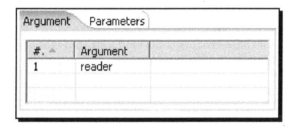

7. Click the **Parameters** tab and fill it as follows:

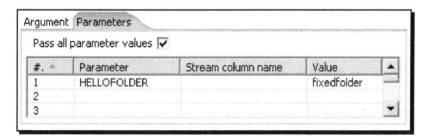

8. Click on **OK**.

9. Save the job.

10. Open a terminal window and go to the directory where Kettle is installed.

- On Windows systems type:

```
C:\pdi-ce>kitchen /file:c:/pdi_labs/
hello_world_param.kjb /norep
```

- On Unix, Linux, and other Unix-like systems type:

```
/home/yourself/pdi-ce/kitchen.sh /file:/home/yourself/
pdi_labs/hello_world_param.kjb /norep
```

11. When the execution finishes, check the output folder. A folder named `fixedfolder` has been created.

12. In that folder, you can see a `hello.txt` with the following content:

```
Hello, reader!
```

What just happened?

You reused the transformation that expects an argument and a named parameter from the command line. This time you created a job that called the transformation and set both the parameter and the argument in the transformation job entry setting window.

Then you ran the job from a terminal window, without typing any arguments or parameters. It didn't make any difference for the transformation. Whether you provide parameters and arguments from the command line or you set constant values in a transformation job entry, the transformation does its job—creating a file with a custom message in the folder with the name given by the ${HELLOFOLDER} parameter.

 Instead of running from the terminal window, you could have run the job by pressing *F9* and then clicking **Launch**, without typing anything in either the parameter or the argument grid. The final result should be exactly the same.

Have a go hero – saying hello again and again

Modify the `hello_world_param.kjb` job so that it generates three files in the default ${HELLOFOLDER}, each saying "hello" to a different person.

 After the creation of the folder, use three transformation job entries. Provide different arguments for each.

Run the job to see that it works as expected.

Have a go hero – loading the time dimension from a job

In Chapter 6, you built a transformation that created the data for a time dimension. Then in Chapter 8, you finished the transformation loading the data into a time dimension table.

The transformation had several named parameters, one of them being START_DATE. Create a job that loads a time dimension with dates starting at 01/01/2000. In technical jargon, create a job that calls your transformation and passes it a value for the START_DATE parameter.

Deciding between the use of a command-line argument and a named parameter

Both command-line arguments and named parameters are means for creating more flexible jobs and transformations. The following table summarizes the differences and the reasons for using one or the other. In the first column, the word **argument** refers to the external value you will use in your job or transformation. That argument could be implemented as a named parameter or as a command-line argument.

Situation	Solution using named parameters	Solution using arguments
It is desirable to have a default for the argument	Named parameters are perfect in this case. You provide default values at the time you define them.	Before using the command-line argument, you have to evaluate if it was provided in the command line. If not, you have to set the default value at that moment.
The argument is mandatory	You don't have means to determine if the user provided a value for the named parameter.	To know if the user provided a value for the command-line argument, you just get the command-line argument and compare it to a null value.
You need several arguments but it is probable that not all of them are present.	If you don't have a value for a named parameter, you are not forced to enter it when you run the job or transformation.	Let's suppose that you expect three command line arguments. If you have a value only for the third, you still have to provide empty values for the first and the second.
You need several arguments and it is highly probable that all of them are present.	The command line would be too long. It will help explain clearly the purpose of each parameter, but typing the command line would be tedious.	The command-line is simple as you just list the values one after the other. However, there is a risk—you may unintentionally enter the values unordered, which could lead to unexpected results.

Situation	Solution using named parameters	Solution using arguments
You want to use the argument in several places	You can do it, but you must assure that the value will not be overwritten in the middle of the execution.	You can get the command-line argument by using a **Get System Info** step as many times as you need.
You need to use the value in a place where a variable is needed	Named parameters are ready to be used as Kettle variables.	First, you need to set a variable with the command-line argument value. Usually this requires creating additional transformations to be run before any other job or transformation.

Depending on your particular situation, you would prefer one or the other solution. Note that you can mix both as you did in the previous tutorials.

Have a go hero – analysing the use of arguments and named parameters

In the *Time for action – customizing the hello world file with fixed arguments and parameters* section, you created a transformation that used an argument and a named parameter. Based on this preceding table, try to understand why the folder was defined as named parameter and the name of the person you want to say Hello to was defined as command-line argument. Would you have applied the same approach?

Running job entries under conditions

A job may contain any number of entries. Not all of them execute always. Some of them execute depending on the result of previous entries in the flow. Let's see it in practice.

Time for action – sending a sales report and warning the administrator if something is wrong

Now you will build a sales report and send it by e-mail. In order to follow the tutorial, you will need two simple prerequisites:

- As the report will be based on the Jigsaw database you created in Chapter 8, you will need the MySQL server running.

- In order to send e-mails, you will need at least one valid Gmail account. Sign up for an account. Alternatively, if you are familiar with you own SMTP configuration, you could use it instead.

Once you've checked these prerequisites, you are ready to start.

1. Create a new transformation.

2. Add a **Get System Info** step. Use it to add a field named `today`. As **Type**, select `Today 00:00:00`.

3. Now add a **Table input** step.

4. Double-click the step.

5. As **Connection**, select `js`—the name of the connection to the jigsaw puzzles database.

 Note that if the connection is not shared, you will have to define it.

6. In the SQL frame, type the following statement:

```
SELECT    pay_code
        , COUNT(*) quantity
          , SUM(inv_price) amount
FROM      invoices
WHERE     inv_date = ?
GROUP BY pay_code
```

7. In the drop-down list to the right of **Insert data from step**, select the name of the **Get System Info** step.

8. Finally, add an **Excel Output** step.

9. Double-click the step.

10. Enter type `${LABSOUTPUT}/sales_` as **Filename**.

11. Check the **Specify Date time format** option. In the **Date time format** drop-down list, select **yyyyMMdd**.

12. Make sure you don't uncheck the **Add filenames to result** option. Click on **OK**. Fill the **Fields** tab as here:

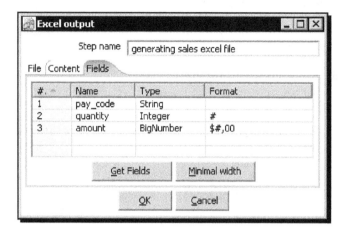

13. Save the transformation under the `transformations` folder you created in a previous tutorial, with the name `sales_report.ktr`.

14. Create a new job by pressing *Ctrl+Alt+N*.

15. Add a **START** job entry.

16. After the **START** entry, add a **Transformation** entry.

17. Double-click the **Transformation** entry.

18. Enter `${Internal.Job.Filename.Directory}/transformations/sales_report.ktr` as the transformation filename, either by hand or by browsing the folder and selecting the file.

19. Click on **OK**.

20. Expand the **Mail** category of entries and drag a **Mail** entry to the canvas.

21. Create a hop from the transformation entry to the **Mail** entry.

22. Double-click the **Mail** entry.

23. Fill the main tab **Addresses** with the destination and the sender e-mail addresses, that is, provide values for the **Destination address**, **Sender name**, and **Sender address** textboxes. If you have two accounts to play with, put one of them as destination and the other as sender. If not, use the same e-mail twice.

24. Select the **Server** tab and fill the **SMTP Server** frame as follows—enter **smtp.gmail. com** as **SMTP Server** and **465** as **Port**.

25. Fill the **Authentication** frame. Check the **Use authentication?** checkbox. Fill the **Authentication user** and **Authentication password** textboxes. For example, if your account is `pdi_account@gmail.com,` then as user enter `pdi_account` and as password provide your e-mail password.

26. Check the **Use secure authentication?** option. In **Secure connection type**, leave the default to **SSL**. Select the **Email Message** tab. In the **Message Settings** frame, check the **Only send comment in mail body?** option.

27. Fill the **Message** frame, providing a subject and a comment for the e-mail—enter **Sales report** as **Subject** and **Please check the attachment** as **Comment**. Select the **Attached Files** tab and check the **Attach file(s) to message?** option.

28. In the **Select file type** list, select the type **General**.

29. Click **OK**.

30. Drag another **Mail** job entry to the canvas.

31. Create a hop from the transformation entry to this new entry. This hop will appear in red.

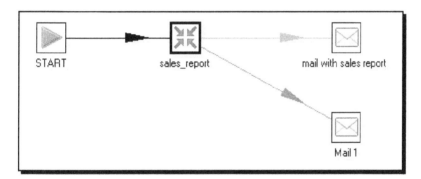

32. Double-click the new entry.

33. Fill the **Destination** and **Sender** frames with destination and sender e-mail addresses. If you have another account to use as destination, use it here. Select the **Server** tab and fill it exactly as you did in the other Mail entry.

34. Select the **Email Message** tab. In the **Subject** textbox, type `Error generating sales report.`

35. Click on **OK**.

36. Save the job and run it.

37. Once the job finished, log into your account. You should have received a mail!

38. Open the e-mail. This is what you should see:

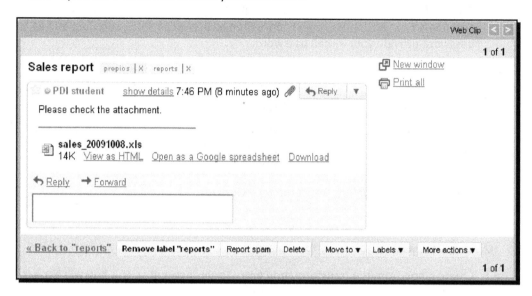

39. Click on the **Open as a Google spreadsheet** option. You will see the following:

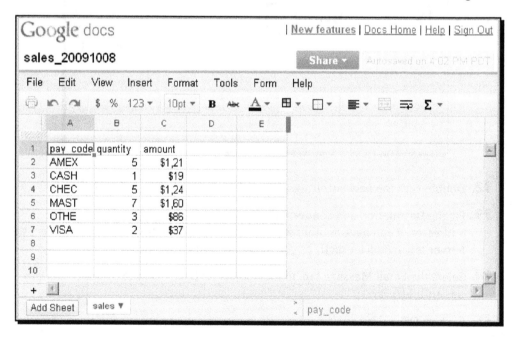

40. Simulate being an intruder and do something that makes your transformation fail. You could, for example, stop MySQL or add some strange characters in the SQL statement.

41. Run the job again.

42. Check the administrator e-mail—the mail you put as destination in the second Mail job entry.

43. The following is the e-mail you received this time:

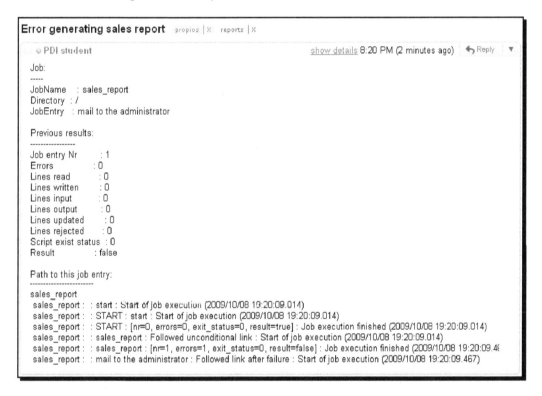

What just happened?

You generated an Excel file with a crosstab report of sales on a particular day. If the file is generated successfully, an e-mail is sent with the Excel file attached. If some error occurs, an e-mail reporting the problem is sent to the administrator.

If you skipped Chapter 8 and still know nothing about databases with PDI, don't miss this exercise. Instead of the proposed sales report, create a transformation that generates any Excel file. The contents of the sheet is not the key here. Just make sure you leave the **Add filenames to result** option checked in the Excel output configuration window. Then proceed as explained.

In this example you used Gmail accounts for sending e-mails from a PDI job. You can use any mail server as long as you have access to the information required in the **Server** tab.

Changing the flow of execution on the basis of conditions

The execution of any job entry either succeeds or fails.

In particular, the job entries under the category **Conditions** just evaluates something and success or failure depends upon the result of the evaluation.

For example, the job entry **File Exists** succeeds if the file you put in its window exists. Otherwise, it fails.

Whichever the job entry, you can use the result of its execution to decide which of the entries following it execute and which don't.

In the tutorial, you included a transformation job entry. If the transformation runs without problem, this entry succeeds. Then the execution follows the green hop to the first **Mail** job entry.

If, while running the transformation, some error occurs, the transformation entry fails. Then the execution follows the red path toward the e-mail to the administrator.

So, when you create a job, you not only arrange the entries and hops according to the expected order of execution, you also specify under which condition each job entry runs.

You can define the conditions in the hops. The following table lists the possibilities:

Color of the hop	What the color represents	The interpretation
Black	Unconditional execution	The destination entry executes no matter the result of the previous entry.
Green	Execution upon success	The destination entry executes only if the previous job entry is successful.
Red	Execution upon failure	The destination entry executes only if the previous job entry failed.

At any hop, you can define the condition under which the destination job entry will execute. By default, the first hop that leaves an entry is created green, whereas the second hop is created red. You can change the color, that is, the behavior of the hop. Just right-click on the hop, select **Evaluation**, and then the condition.

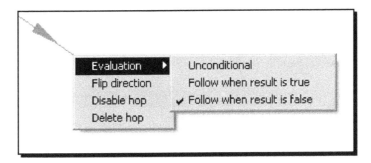

One exception is the hop or hops that leave the **START** step. You cannot edit them. The destination job entries execute unconditionally, that is, always.

Another exception is the special entry **Dummy** that does nothing, not even allowing you to decide if the job entries after it run or not. They always run.

Have a go hero – refining the sales report

Here we will modify the job that sends the e-mail containing the sales report.

1. Modify the transformation so that the file is generated in the temporary folder `${java.io.tmpdir}`. If there is no sale for today, don't generate the file. You do this by checking the **Do not create file at start** option in the Excel output step.

2. Send the e-mail only if there were sales, that is, only if the file exists.

3. After sending the e-mail with the report attached, delete the file.

Use these new job entries: **File Exists** from the **Conditions** category and **Delete file** from the **File management** category.

Creating and using a file results list

In the tutorial you configured two **Mail** job entries. In the mail that follows the green hop, you attached the Excel file generated by the transformation. However, you didn't explicitly specify the name of the file to attach. How could PDI realize that you wanted to attach that file? it could because of the **Add filenames to result** checkbox in the Excel output configuration window. By checking that option, you added the name of the Excel file to a special list named **File result**.

When PDI hits an e-mail entry where **Attach file(s) to message?** is checked, it attaches to the e-mail all files in the File result list.

Most of the transformation steps that read or write files have this checkbox, and it is checked by default. The following sample belongs to a **Text file input** step:

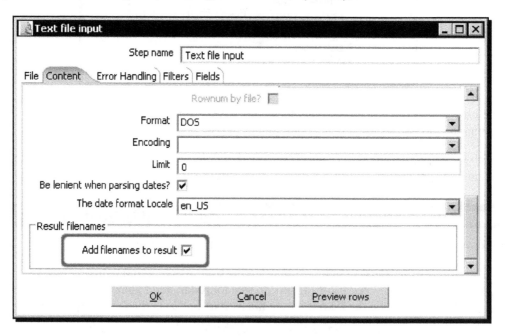

Each time you use one of these steps you are adding names of files to this list, unless you uncheck the checkbox.

There are also several job entries in the **File management** and the **File transfer** categories that add one or more files to the File result list. Consider the following **Copy Files...** entry screen:

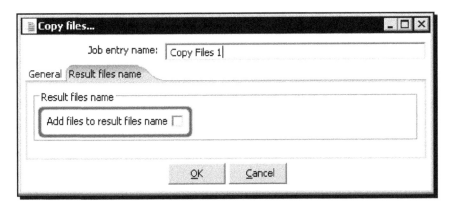

As with the Mail entry, there are some other entries that use the File result list. One example is **Copy or Move result filenames**. This entry copies or moves the files whose names are in this special list named File result.

Have a go hero – sharing your work

Suppose you want to share your PDI work with a friend. Send to him/her some of your `ktr` files by mail.

Use the **Add filenames to result** job entry located in the **File management** category to build the File result list. Then send the e-mail with the files attached.

Summary

In this chapter, you learned the basics about PDI jobs—what a job is, what you can do with a job, and how jobs are different from transformations. In particular, you learned to use a job for running one or more transformations.

You also saw how to use named parameters in jobs, and how to supply parameters and arguments to transformations when they are run from jobs.

In the next chapter, you will learn to create jobs that are a little more elaborative than the jobs you created here, which will give you more power to implement all types of processes.

11
Creating Advanced Transformations and Jobs

Iterating over a list of items (files, people, codes, and so on), implementing a process flow, and developing a reusable procedure are very common requirements in real world projects. Implementing these kind of needs in PDI is not intuitive, but it's not complicate either. It's just a matter of learning the right techniques that we will see in this chapter. Among other things, you will learn to implement process flows, nest jobs, and iterate the execution of jobs and transformations.

Enhancing your processes with the use of variables

For the tutorials in this chapter, you will take as your starting point a *Time for action* tutorial you did in Chapter 2 that involves updating a file with news about examinations. You are responsible for collecting the results of an annual examination where writing, reading, speaking, and listening skills are evaluated. The professors grade the examinations of their students in the scale 0-100 for each skill, and generate text files with the information. Then they send the files to you for integrating the results in a global list.

In the initial chapters, you were learning the basics of PDI. You were worried about how to do simple stuff such as reading a file or doing simple calculations. In this chapter, you will go beyond that and take care of the details such as making a decision if the filename expected as a command line is not provided or if it doesn't exist.

Time for action – updating a file with news about examinations by setting a variable with the name of the file

The transformation in the *Time for action* from Chapter 2 that we just talked about reads a file provided by a professor, simply by taking the name of the file from the command line, and appends the file to the global one. Let's enhance that work.

1. Copy the examination files you used in Chapter 2 to the input files and folder defined in your `kettle.properties` file. If you don't have them, download them from the Packt website.

2. Open Spoon and create a new transformation.

3. Use a **Get System Info** step to get the first command-line argument. Name the field as `filename`.

4. Add a **Filter rows** step and create a hop from the **Get System Info** step to this step.

5. From the **Flow** category drag an **Abort** step to the canvas, and from the **Job** category of steps drag a **Set Variables** step.

6. From the **Filter rows** step, create two hops—one to the **Abort** step and the other to the **Set Variables** step. Double-click the **Abort** step. As **Abort message**, put `File name is mandatory`.

7. Double-click the **Set Variables** step and click on **Get Fields**. The window will be filled as shown here:

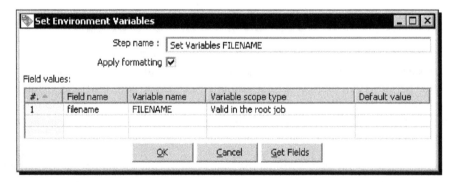

8. Click on **OK**.

9. Double-click the **Filter rows** step. Add the following filter: `filename IS NOT NULL`. In the drop-down list to the right of **Send 'true' data to step**, select the **Set Variables** step, whereas in the drop-down list to the right of **Send 'false' data to step**, select the **Abort** step.

10. The final transformation looks like this:

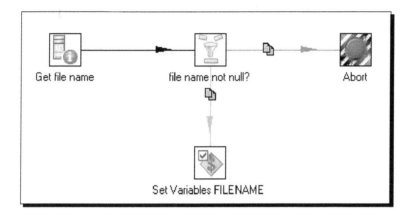

11. Save the transformation in the `transformations` folder under the name `getting_filename.ktr`.

12. Open the transformation named `examinations.ktr` that was created in Chapter 2 or download it from the Packt website. Save it in the `transformations` folder under the name `examinations_2.ktr`.

13. Delete the **Get System Info** step.

14. Double-click the **Text file input** step.

15. In the **Accept filenames from previous steps** frame, uncheck the **Accept filenames from previous step** option.

16. Under **File/Directory** in the **Selected files** grid, type `${FILENAME}`. Save the transformation.

17. Create a new job.

18. From the **General** category, drag a **START** entry and a **Transformation** entry to the canvas and link them.

19. Save the job as `examinations.kjb`.

20. Double-click the **Transformation** entry. As **Transformation filename**, put the name of the first transformation that you created: `${Internal.Job.Filename.Directory}/transformations/getting_filename.ktr`.

21. Click on **OK**.

 Remember that you can avoid typing that long variable name by clicking *Ctrl+Space* and selecting the variable from the list.

22. From the **Conditions** category, drag a **File Exists** entry to the canvas and create a hop from the **Transformation** entry to this new one.

23. Double-click the **File Exists** entry.

24. Write `${FILENAME}` in the **File name** textbox and click on **OK**.

25. Add a new **Transformation** entry and create a hop from the **File Exists** entry to this one.

26. Double-click the entry and, as **Transformation filename**, put the name of the second transformation you created:`${Internal.Job.Filename.Directory}/transformations/examinations_2.ktr`.

27. Add a **Write To Log** entry, and create a hop from the **File Exists** entry to this. The hop should be red, to indicate when execution fails. If not, right-click the hop and change the evaluation condition to `Follow when result is false`.

28. Double-click the entry and fill all the textboxes as shown:

29. Add two entries—an abort and a success. Create hops to these new entries as shown next:

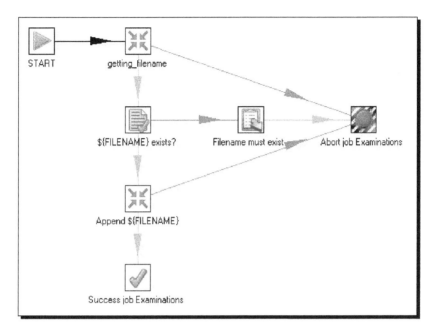

30. Save the job.

31. Press *F9* to run the job.

32. Set the logging level to **Minimal logging** and click on **Launch**.

33. The job fails. The following is what you should see in the **Logging** tab in the **Execution results** window:

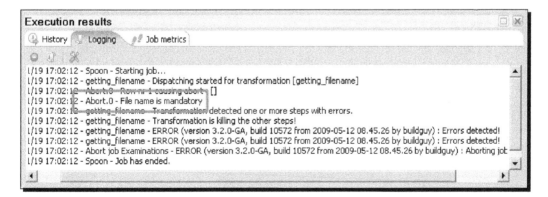

34. Press *F9* again. This time set **Basic logging** as the logging level.

35. In the arguments grid, write the name of a fictitious file—for example, `c:/pdi_files/input/nofile.txt`.

36. Click on **Launch**. This is what you see now in the **Logging** tab window:

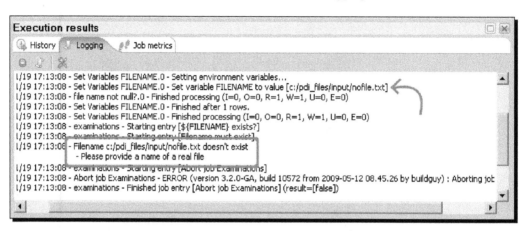

37. Press *F9* for the third time. Now provide a real examination filename such as `c:/pdi_files/input/exam1.txt`.

38. Click on **Launch**. This time you see no errors. The examination file is appended to the global file:

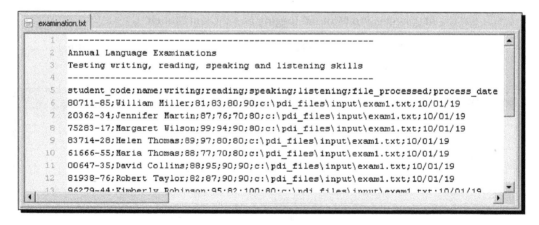

What just happened?

You enhanced the transformation you created in Chapter 3 for appending an examination file to a global examination file. This time you embedded the transformation in a job. The first transformation checks that the argument is not null. In that case, it sets a variable with the name provided. The main job verifies that the file exists. If everything is all right, then the second transformation performs the main task—it appends the given file to the global file.

Note that you changed the logging levels just according to what you needed to see—the highlighted lines in the earlier explanation.

 You may choose any logging level you want depending on the details of information you want to see.

Setting variables inside a transformation

So far, you had defined variables only in the `kettle.properties` file or inside Spoon while you were designing a transformation. In this last exercise, you learned to define your own variables at run time. You set a variable with the name of the file provided as a command-line argument. You used that variable in the main job to check if the file existed. Then you used the variable again in the main transformation. There you used it as the name of the file to read.

This example showed you the how to set a variable with the value of a command-line argument. This is not always the case. The value you set in a variable can be originated in different ways—it can be a value coming from a table in a database, a value defined with a **Generate rows** step, a value calculated with a **Formula** or a **Calculator** step, and so on.

The variables you define with a **Set variables** step can be used in the same way and the same places where you use any Kettle variable. Just take precautions to avoid using these variables in the same transformation where you have set them.

 The variables defined in a transformation are not available for using until you leave that transformation.

Have a go hero – enhancing the examination tutorial even more

Modify the job in the tutorial to avoid processing the same file twice. If the file is successfully appended to the global file, rename the original file by changing the extension to `processed`—for example, after processing the `exam1.txt` file rename it to `exam1.processed`.

After verifying if the file exists, also check whether the .processed version exists. If it exists, put a proper message in the log and abort. If someone accidently tries to process a file that is already processed, it will be ignored.

> Besides the variable with the filename, create a variable with the name for the processed file. To build this name, simply manipulate the given name with some PDI steps.

Have a go hero – enhancing the jigsaw database update process

In the *Time for action – inserting new products or updating existent ones* section in Chapter 8, you read a file with a list of products belonging to the manufacturer Classic DeLuxe. The list was expected as a named parameter. Enhance that process. Create a job that first validates the existence of the provided file. If the file doesn't exist, put the proper error message in the log. If it exists, process the list. Then move the processed file to a folder named processed.

> You don't need to create a transformation to set a variable with the name of the file. As it is expected as a named parameter, it is already available as a variable.

Have a go hero – executing the proper jigsaw database update process

In the hero exercise in Chapter 8 that involves populating the products table, you created different transformations for updating the products—one for each manufacturer. Now you will put all that work together.

Create a job that accepts two arguments—the name of the file to process and the code of the manufacturer to which the file belongs.

Create a transformation that validates that the code provided belongs to an existent manufacturer. If the code exists, set a variable named TRANSFORMATION_FILE with the name of the transformation that knows how to process the file for that manufacturer.

The transformation must also check that the name provided is not null. If it is not null, set a variable named FILENAME with the name supplied.

Then, in the job, check that the file exists. If it exists and the manufacturer code is valid, run the proper transformation. In order to do so, put ${TRANSFORMATION_FILE} as the name of the transformation in the transformation job entry dialog window. Now test your job.

Enhancing the design of your processes

When your jobs or transformations begin to grow, you may find them a little disorganized or jumbled up. It's now time to do some rework. Let's see an example of this.

Time for action – generating files with top scores

In this tutorial, you will read the examination global file and generate four files—one for each particular skill. The files will contain the top 10 scores for each skill. The scores will not be the original, but converted to a scale with values in the range 0-5.

 As you must be already quite confident with PDI, some explanations in this section will not have the full details. On the contrary, the general explanation will be focused on the structure of the jobs and transformations.

1. Create a new transformation and save it in the `transformations` folder under the name `top_scores.ktr`.

2. Use a **Text file input** step to read the global examination file generated in the previous tutorial.

3. After the **Text file input** step, add the following steps and link them in the same order:

   □ A **Select values** step to remove the unused fields—`file_processed` and `process_date`.

   □ A **Split Fields** to split the name of the students in two—`name` and `last name`.

   □ A **Formula** step to convert `name` and `last name` to uppercase.

   □ With the same **Formula** step, change the scale of the scores. Replace each skill field `writing`, `reading`, `speaking`, and `listening` with the same value divided by 20—for example, `[writing]/20`. You have already done this in Chapter 3.

4. Do a preview on completion of the final step to check that you are doing well. You should see this:

5. After the last **Formula** step, add and link in this order the following steps:

- A **Sort rows** step to order the rows in descending order by the `writing` field.

- A **JavaScript** step to filter the first 10 rows. Remember that you learned to do this in the chapter devoted to JavaScript. You do it by typing the following piece of code:

```
trans_Status = CONTINUE_TRANSFORMATION;
if (getProcessCount('r')>10) trans_Status =
SKIP_TRANSFORMATION;
```

- An **Add sequence** step to add a field named `seq_w`. Leave the defaults so that the field contains the values `1, 2, 3` ...

- A **Select values** step to rename the field `seq_w` as `position` and the field `writing` as `score`. Specify this change in the **Select & Alter** tab, and check the option **Include unspecified fields, ordered**.

- A **Text file output** step to generate a file named `writing_top10.txt` at the location specified by the `${LABSOUTPUT}` variable. In the **Fields** tab, put the following fields— `position`, `student_code`, `student_name`, `student_lastname`, and `score`.

6. Save the transformation, as you've added a lot of steps and don't want to lose your work.

7. Repeat step number 5, but this time sort by the `reading` field, rename the sequence `seq_r` as `position` and the field `reading` as `score`, and send the data to the `reading_top10.txt` file.

To save time, you can copy all those steps, paste them, and do the proper adjustments.

8. Repeat the same procedure for the `speaking` field and the `listening` field.

9. This is how the transformation looks like:

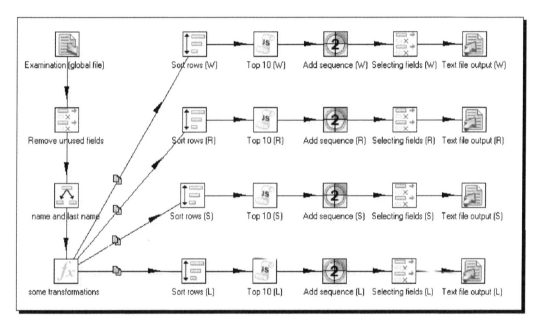

10. Save the transformation.

11. Run the transformation. Four files should have been generated. All the files should look similar. Let's check the `writing_top10.txt` file (the names and values may vary depending on the examination files that you have appended to the global file):

```
 writing_top10.txt
  1    position;student_code;student_name;student_lastname;score
  2    1;115660-70;KEVIN;JACKSON;5.00
  3    2;934087-89;MARIA;LOPEZ;5.00
  4    3;75283-17;MARGARET;WILSON;4.95
  5    4;290916-93;MARY;MARTIN;4.95
  6    5;524655-49;KEVIN;HARRIS;4.95
  7    6;7390100-17;NANCY;HALL;4.95
  8    7;3505119-73;MARY;GONZALEZ;4.95
  9    8;341336-39;GEORGE;WALKER;4.90
 10    9;004457-66;CHARLES;HARRIS;4.90
 11    10;498864-92;ELIZABETH;BROWN;4.90
 12
```

What just happened?

You read the big file with examination results and generated four files with information about the top scores—one file for each skill.

Beyond having used the **Add sequences** step for the first time, there was nothing new. However, there are several improvements you can do to this transformation. The next tutorials are meant to teach you some tricks.

Pop quiz – using the Add Sequence step

In the previous tutorial, you used different names for the sequences and then you renamed all of them to `position`. Which of the following options gives you the same results you got in the tutorial?

a. Using `position` as the name of the sequence in all **Add sequence** steps

b. Joining the four streams with a single **Add sequence** step and then splitting the stream back into four streams by using the Distribute method you learned in Chapter 4

c. Joining the four streams with a single **Add sequence** step and then splitting the stream back into four streams by using a **Switch case** step that distributes the rows properly

d. All of them

e. None of them

Reusing part of your transformations

As you noticed, the sequence of steps used to get the ranks are almost identical for the four skills. You could have avoided copying and pasting or doing the same work several times by moving those steps to a subtransformation. Let's do it.

Time for action – calculating the top scores with a subtransformation

Let's modify the transformation that calculates the top scores to avoid unnecessary duplication of steps:

1. Under the transformation folder, create a new folder named subtransformations.

2. Create a new transformation and save it in that new folder with the name scores.ktr.

3. Expand the **Mapping** category of steps. Select a **Mapping input specification** step and drag it to the work area.

4. Double-click the step and fill it like this:

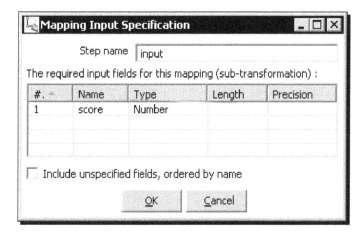

5. Add a **Sort rows** step and use it to sort the score field in descending order.

6. Add a **JavaScript** step and type the following code to filter the top 10 rows:
```
trans_Status = CONTINUE_TRANSFORMATION;
if (getProcessCount('r')>10) trans_Status = SKIP_TRANSFORMATION;
```

7. Add an **Add sequence** step to add a sequence field named seq.

8. Finally, add a **Mapping output specification** step. You will find it in the **Mapping** category of steps. Your transformation looks like this:

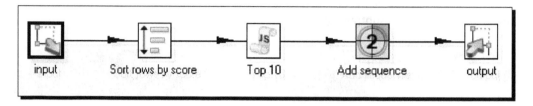

9. Save the transformation.

10. Open the transformation `top_scores.ktr` and save it as `top_scores_with_subtransformations.ktr`.

11. Modify the writing stream. Delete all steps except the **Text file output** step—the **Sort rows**, **JavaScript**, **Add sequence**, and **the Select rows** steps.

12. Drag a **Mapping (sub-transformation)** step to the canvas and put it in the place where all the deleted steps were. You should have this:

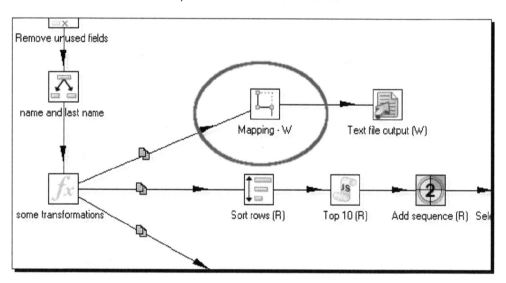

13. Double-click the **Mapping** step.

14. In the **Mapping transformation** frame, select the option named **Use a file for the mapping transformation**. In the textbox below it, type `${Internal.Transformation.Filename.Directory}/subtransformations/scores.ktr`. Select the **Input** tab, check the **Is this the main data path?** option, and fill the grid as shown:

#. ▲	Fieldname from source step	Fieldname to mapping input step
1	writing	score

15. Select the **Output** tab and fill the grid as shown:

#. ▲	Fieldname from mapping step	Fieldname to target step
1	seq	position

16. Click on **OK**.

17. Repeat the steps 11 to 16 for the other streams—reading, speaking, and listening. The only difference is what you put in the **Input** tab of the **Mapping** steps—instead of `writing`, you should put `reading`, `speaking`, and `listening`.

 Note that you added four **Mapping (subtransformation)** steps, but you only need one subtransformation file.

18. The final transformation looks as follows:

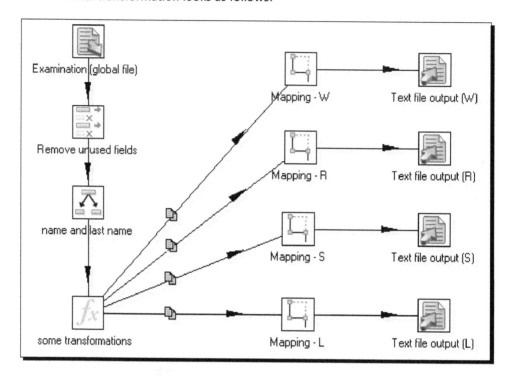

19. Save the transformation.

20. Press *F9* to run the transformation.

21. Select **Minimal logging** and click on **Launch**. The **Logging** window looks like the following:

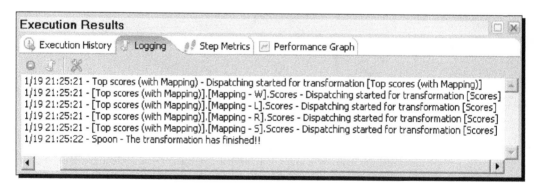

22. The output files should have been generated and should look exactly the same as before. This time let's check the `reading_top10.txt` file (the names and values may vary depending on the examination files that you appended to the global file):

```
reading_top10.txt

 1    position;student_code;student_name;student_lastname;score
 2    1;004457-66;CHARLES;HARRIS;4.95
 3    2;196629-53;RICHARD;LEE;4.90
 4    3;100344-84;CAROL;SMITH;4.90
 5    4;296271-84;ELIZABETH;HALL;4.90
 6    5;192280-03;DANIEL;SCOTT;4.90
 7    6;83714-28;HELEN;THOMAS;4.85
 8    7;601551-28;ANTHONY;HARRIS;4.85
 9    8;378127-72;SHARON;WRIGHT;4.80
10    9;099694-18;RUTH;THOMPSON;4.80
11    10;0870136-00;WILLIAM;BROWN;4.80
12
```

What just happened?

You took the bunch of steps that calculate the top scores and moved it to a subtransformation. Then, in the main transformation, you simply called the subtransformation four times, each time using a different field.

It's worth saying that the **Text file output** step could also have been moved to the subtransformation. However, instead of simplifying the work, it would have complicated it. This is because the names of the files are different in each case and, in order to build that name, it would have been necessary to add some extra logic.

Creating and using subtransformations

Subtransformations are, as the named suggests, transformations inside transformations.

> The PDI proper name for a subtransformation is **mapping**. However, as the word mapping is also used with other meanings in PDI, we will use the old, more intuitive name subtransformation.

In the tutorial, you created a subtransformation to isolate a task that you needed to apply four times. This is a common reason for creating a subtransformation—to isolate a functionality that is likely to be needed more than once. Then you called the subtransformations by using a single step.

Let's see how subtransformations work. A subtransformation is like a regular transformation, but it has input and output steps, connecting it to the transformations that use it.

The **Mapping input specification** step defines the entry point to the subtransformation. You specify here just the fields needed by the subtransformation. The **Mapping output specification** step simply defines where the flow ends.

 The presence of **Mapping input specification** and **Mapping output specification** steps is the only fact that makes a subtransformation different from a regular transformation.

In the sample subtransformation you created in the tutorial, you defined a single field named score. You sorted the rows by that field, filtered the top 10 rows, and added a sequence to identify the rank—a number from 1 to 10.

You call or execute a subtransformation by using a **Mapping (sub-transformation)** step. In order to execute the subtransformation successfully, you have to establish a relationship between your fields and the fields defined in the subtransformation.

Let's first see how to define the relationship between your data and the input specification. For the sample subtransformation, you have to define which of your fields is to be used as the input field score defined in the input specification. You can do it in an **Input** tab in the **Mapping** step dialog window. In the first **Mapping** step, you told the subtransformation to use the field writing as its score field.

If you look at the output fields coming out of the **Mapping** step, you will no longer see the writing field but a field named score. It is the same field writing that was renamed as score. If you don't want your fields to be renamed, simply check the **Ask these values to be renamed back on output?** option found in the **Input** tab. That will cause the field to be renamed back to its original name—writing in this example.

Let's now see how to define the relationship between your data and the output specification. If the subtransformation creates new fields, you may want to add them to your main dataset. To add to your dataset, a field created in the subtransformation, you use an **Output** tab of the **Mapping** step dialog window. In the tutorial, you were interested in adding the sequence. So, you configured the **Output** tab, telling the subtransformation to retrieve the field named seq in the subtransformation but renamed as position. This causes a new field named position to be added to your stream.

If you want the subtransformation to simply transform the incoming stream without adding new fields, or if you are not interested in the fields added in the subtransformation, you don't have to create an **Output** tab.

The following screenshot summarizes what was explained just now. The upper and lower grids show the datasets before and after the streams have flown through the subtransformation.

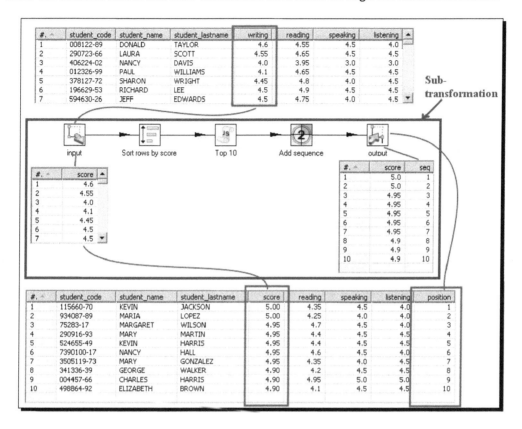

The subtransformation in the tutorial allowed you to reuse a bunch of steps that were present in several places, avoiding doing the same task several times. Another common situation where you may use subtransformations is the one where you have a transformation with too many steps. If you can identify a subset of steps that accomplish a specific purpose, you may move those steps to a subtransformation. Doing so, your transformation will become cleaner and easier to understand.

Have a go hero – refining the subtransformation

Modify the subtransformation in the following way:

Add a new field named `below_first`. The field should have the difference between the score in the current row and the maximum score. For example, if the maximum score is 5 and the current score is 4.85, the value for the field should be 0.15.

Modify the main transformation by adding the new field to all output files.

Have a go hero – counting words more precisely (second version)

Combine the following *Hero* exercises from Chapter 3:

- Counting words, discarding those that are commonly used
- Counting words more precisely

Create a subtransformation that receives a String value and cleans it. Remove extra signs that may appear as part of the string such as . ,) or ". Then convert the string to lower case.

Also create a flag that tells whether the string is a valid word. Remember that the word is valid if its length is at least 3 and if it is not in a given list of common words.

Retrieve the modified word and the flag.

Modify the main transformation by using the subtransformation. After the subtransformation step, filter the words by looking at the flag.

Creating a job as a process flow

With the implementation of a subtransformation, you simplify much of the transformation. But you still have some reworking to do. In the main transformation, you basically do two things. First you read the source data from a file and prepare it for further processing. And then, after the preparation of the data, you generate the files with the top scores. To have a clearer vision of these two tasks, you can split the transformation in two, creating a job as a process flow. Let's see how to do that.

Time for action – splitting the generation of top scores by copying and getting rows

Now you will split your transformation into two smaller transformation so that each meets a specific task. Here are the instructions.

1. Open the transformation in the previous tutorial. Select all steps related to the preparation of data, that is, all steps from the **Text file input** step upto the **Formula** step.

2. Copy the steps and paste them in a new transformation.

3. Expand the **Job** category of steps.

4. Select a **Copy rows to result** step, drag it to the canvas, and create a hop from the last step to this new one. Your transformation looks like this:

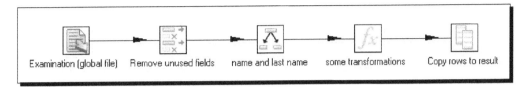

5. Save the transformation in the `transformations` folder with the name `top_scores_flow_preparing.ktr`.

6. Go back to the original transformation and select the rest of the steps, that is, the **Mapping** and the **Text file output** steps.

7. Copy the steps and paste them in a new transformation.

8. From the **Job** category of steps select a **Get rows from result** step, drag it to the canvas, and create a hop from this step to each of the **Mapping** steps. Your transformation looks like this:

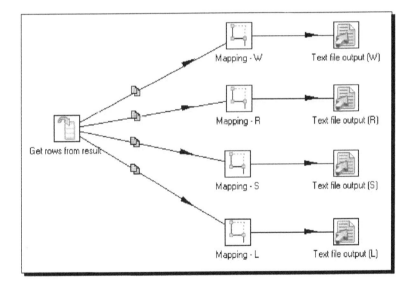

9. Save the transformation in the `transformations` folder with the name `top_scores_flow_processing.ktr`.

10. In the `top_scores_flow_preparing` transformation , right-click the step **Copy rows to result** and select **Show output fields**.

11. The grid with the output dataset shows up.

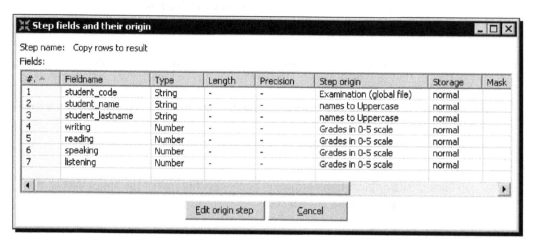

12. Select all rows. Press *Ctrl+C* to copy the rows.

13. In the `top_scores_flow_processing` transformation, double-click the step **Get rows from result**.

14. Press *Ctrl+V* to paste the values. You have the following result:

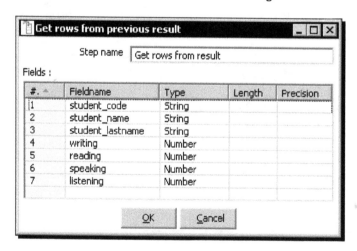

15. Save the transformation.

16. Create a new Job.

17. Add a **START** and two transformation entries to the canvas and link them one after the other.

18. Double-click the first transformation. Put `${Internal.Job.Filename.Directory}/transformations/top_scores_flow_preparing.ktr` as the name of the transformation.

19. Double-click the second transformation. Put `${Internal.Job.Filename.Directory}/transformations/top_scores_flow_processing.ktr` as the name of the transformation.

20. Your job looks like the following:

21. Save the job. Press *F9* to open the **Job properties** window and click on **Launch**. Again, the four files should have been generated, with the very same information.

What just happened?

You split the main transformation in two—one for the preparation of data and the other for the generation of the files. Then you embedded the transformations into a job that executed them one after the other. By using the **Copy rows to result** step, you sent the flow of data outside the transformation, and using **Get rows from result** step, you picked that data to continue with the flow. The final result was the same as before the change.

 Notice that you split the last version of the transformation—the one with the subtransformations inside. You could have split the original. The result would have been exactly the same.

Transferring data between transformations by using the copy /get rows mechanism

The copy/get rows mechanism allows you to transfer data between two transformations, creating a **process flow**. The following drawing shows you how it works:

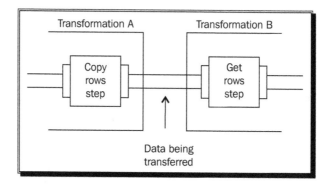

The **Copy rows to result** step transfers your rows of data to the outside of the transformation. You can then pick that data by using a **Get rows from result** step. In the preceding image, Transformation A copies the rows and, Transformation B, which executes right after Transformation A, gets the rows. If you create a single transformation with all steps from Transformation A followed by all steps from Transformation B, you would get the same result.

The copy of the dataset is made in memory. It's useful when you have small datasets. For bigger datasets, you should prefer saving the data in a temporary file or database table in the first transformation, and then create the dataset from the file or table in the second transformation.

The **Serialize to file /De-serialize from file** steps are very useful for this, as the data and the metadata are saved together.

There is no limit to the number of transformations that can be chained using this mechanism. Look at the following image:

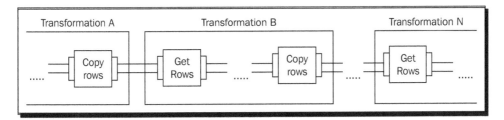

As you can see, you may have a transformation that copies the rows, followed by another that gets the rows and copies again, followed by a third transformation that gets the rows, and so on.

Have a go hero – modifying the flow

Modify the last exercise in the following way:

♦ Include just the students who had an average score above 70.

 Note that you have to modify just the transformation that prepares the information, without caring about what the second process does with that data.

♦ Generate just the top five scores for every skill.

 Note that you have to modify just the transformation (or the subtransformation) that processes the information, without caring about how the list of students was built.

♦ Create each file in a different transformation. The transformations execute one after the other.

This exercise requires that you modify the flow. Each transformation gets the rows from the previous transformation, then generates a file, and copies the rows to the result to be used for the next transformation.

Nesting jobs

Suppose that every time you append a file with examination results, you want to generate updated files with the top 10 scores. You can do it manually, running one job after the other, or you can nest jobs.

Time for action – generating the files with top scores by nesting jobs

Let's modify the job that updates the global examination file, so at the end it generates updated top scores files:

1. Open the `examinations` job you created in the first tutorial of this chapter.

2. After the last transformation job entry, add a job entry as **Job**. You will find it under the **General** category of entries.

3. Double-click the **Job** job entry.

4. Type `${Internal.Job.Filename.Directory}/top_scores_flow.kjb` as **Job filename**.

5. Click on **OK**.

6. Save the job.

7. Pick an examination that you have not yet appended to the global file—for example, `exam5.txt`.

8. Press *F9*.

9. In the **Arguments** grid, type the full path of the chosen file: `c:/pdi_files/input/exam5.txt`.

10. Click on **Launch**.

11. In the **Job metrics** tab of the **Execution results** window, you will see the following:

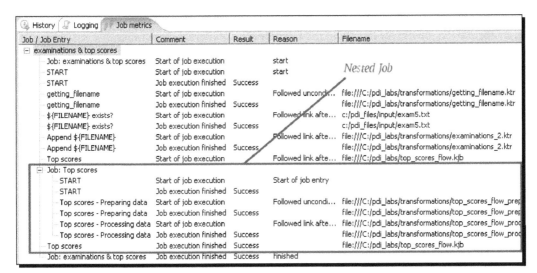

12. Also the chosen file should have been added to the global file, and updated files with top scores should have been generated.

What just happened?

You modified the job that updates the global examination file by including the generation of the files with top scores as part of the process. You did it by using a **Job** job entry whose task is to run a job inside a job.

In the **Job metrics**, you could see a hierarchy showing the details of the nested job as a sub-tree of that hierarchy.

Running a job inside another job with a job entry

The job entry, **Job**, allows you to run a job inside a job. Just like any job entry, this entry may end successfully or fail. Upon that result, the main job decides which of the entries that follows it will execute. None of the entries following the job entry starts until the nested job ends its execution. There is no limit to the levels of nesting. You may call a job, which calls a job, which again calls a job, and so on. Usually you will not need more than two or three levels.

As with a transformation job entry, you must specify the location and name of the job file. If the job (or any transformation inside the nested job) uses arguments or has defined named parameters, you have the possibility of providing fixed values just as you do in a **Transformation** job entry—by filling the **Arguments** and **Parameters** tabs.

Understanding the scope of variables

By nesting jobs, you implicitly create a relationship between the jobs. Look at the following diagram:

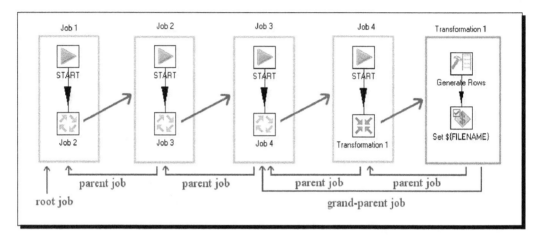

Here you can see how a job, and even a transformation, may have parents and grandparents. The main job is called **root job**. This hierarchy is useful to understand the scope of variables. When you define a variable, you have the option to set the scope, that is, define the places where the variable is visible.

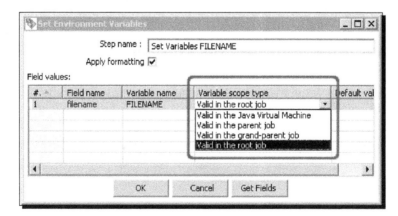

The following table explains which jobs and transformations can access the variable depending on the variable's scope.

Variable scope type	Visibility of the variable
Valid in the parent job	Can be seen by the job that called the transformation and any transformation called by this job.
Valid in the grand-parent job	Can be seen by the job that called the transformation, the job that called that job, and any transformation called by any of these jobs.
Valid in the root job	Can be seen by all jobs in the chain starting with the main job, and any transformation called by any of these jobs.
Valid in the Java Virtual Machine	Seen by all the jobs and transformations run from the same Java Virtual Machine. For example, suppose that you define a variable with scope in the Java Virtual Machine. If you run the transformation from Spoon, then the variable will be available in all jobs and transformations you run from Spoon as long as you don't exit Spoon.

Pop quiz – deciding the scope of variables

In the first tutorial you created a transformation that set a variable with the name of a file. For the scope, you left the default value: Valid in the root job. Which of the following scope types could you have chosen getting the same results (you may select more than one):

a. Valid in the parent job

b. Valid in the grand-parent job

c. Valid in the Java Virtual Machine

 In general, if you have doubts about which scope type to use, you can use **Valid in the root job** and you will be good. Simply ensure that you are not using the same name of variable for different purposes.

Iterating jobs and transformations

It may happen that you develop a job or a transformation to be executed several times, once for each different row of your data. Consider that you have to send a custom e-mail to a list of customers. You would build a job that, for a given customer, get the relevant data such as name or e-mail account and send the e-mail. You would then run the job manually several times, once for each customer. Instead of doing that, PDI allows you to execute the job automatically once for each customer in your list.

The same applies to transformations. If you have to execute the same transformation several times, once for each row of a set of data, you can do it by iterating the execution. The next *Time for action* tutorial shows you how to do this.

Time for action – generating custom files by executing a transformation for every input row

Suppose that 60 is the threshold below which a student must retake the examination. Let's find out the list of students with a score below 60, that is, those who didn't succeed in the writing examination. Then, let's create one file per student telling him/her about this.

First of all, let's create a transformation that generates the list of students who will take the examination:

1. Create a new transformation.

2. Drag a **Text file input**, a **Filter rows**, and a **Select values** step to the canvas and link them in that order.

3. Use the **Text file input** step to read the global examination file.

4. Use the **Filter rows** step to keep only those students with a writing score below 60.

5. With the **Select values** step, keep just the student_code and name values.

6. After this last step, add a **Copy rows to result** step.

7. Do a preview on this last step. You will see the following (the exact names and values depend on the number of files you have appended to the global file):

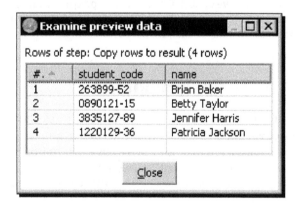

8. Save the transformation in the transformations folder with the name students_list.ktr.

Now let's create a transformation that generates a single file. This transformation will be executed for each student in the list shown in the preceding screenshot:

1. Create a new transformation.

2. Drag a **Get rows from result** step to the canvas.

3. Double-click the **Get rows from result** step and use it to define two String fields—a field named student_code and another field named name.

4. Add a **Formula** step and create a hop from the **Get rows from result** step to this new step.

5. Use the **Formula** step to create a new String field named text. As value, type: **"You'll have to take the examination again, " & [name] & "."**.

6. After the **Formula** step, add a **Delay row** step. You will find it under the **Utility** category of steps.

7. Finally, add a **Text file output** step, and double-click the step to configure it.

8. As filename type ${LABSOUTPUT}/hello. Check the option **Include time in filename?**.

9. In the content tab, uncheck **Header**. As Field, select the field text.

10. This is how your final transformation looks:

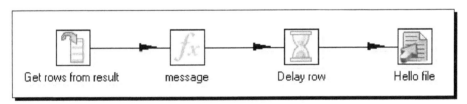

Get rows from result   message   Delay row   Hello file

11. Save the transformation in the transformations folder under the name hello_each.ktr.

> You can't test this transformation alone. If you want to test it, just replace temporarily the **Copy rows from result** step with a **Generate rows** step, generate a single row with fixed values for the fields, and run the transformation.

Let's create a job that puts everything together:

1. Create a job.

2. Drag a **START**, a **Delete files**, and two transformation entries to the canvas, and link them one after the other as shown:

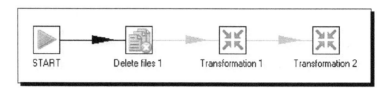

3. Save the job.

4. Double-click the **Delete files** step. Fill the **Files/Folders:** grid with a single row—under **File/Folder** type ${LABSOUTPUT} and under **Wilcard (RegExp)** type hello.*\.txt. This regular expression includes all .txt files whose name start with the string "hello" in the ${LABSOUTPUT} folder.

5. Double-click the first transformation entry. As **Transformation filename**, put ${Internal.Job.Filename.Directory}/transformations/student_list.ktr and click on **OK**.

6. Double-click the second transformation entry. As **Transformation filename**, put ${Internal.Job.Filename.Directory}/transformations/hello_each.ktr.

7. Check the option **Execute for every input row?** and click on **OK**.

8. Save the job and press *F9* to run it.

9. When the execution finishes, explore the folder pointed by your ${LABSOUTPUT} variable. You should see one file for each student in the list. The files are named hello_<hhmmddss>.txt where <hhmmddss> is the time in your system at the moment that the file was generated. The generated files look like the following:

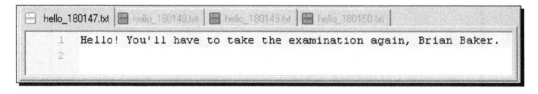

What just happened?

You built a list of students who had to retake the writing examination and, for each student, you generated a file with a custom message.

First, you created a transformation that built the list of the students and copied the rows outside the transformation by using the **Copy rows to result** step.

Then you created another transformation that gets a row from the result and generates a file with a custom hello message.

Finally, you created the main job. First of all, the job deletes all files just in case you run the job more than once. Then it calls the first transformation and then executes the transformation that generates the file once for every copied row, that is, once for every student. Each time the transformation gets the rows from the result, it gets a single row with information about a single student and generates a file with the message for that student.

Before proceeding with the details about executing each row mechanism, let's briefly explain the new step used here—the **Delay row** step that is used to deliberately slow down a transformation. For each incoming row, the step waits for the amount of time indicated in its setting window which, by default, is **1** second. After that time, the row is given to the next step.

In this tutorial, the **Delay row** step is used to ensure that each time the transformation executes, the name of the file is different. As part of the name for the file, you put the time of your system including hours, minutes, and seconds. By waiting for a second, you can be sure that in every execution of the transformation the name of the file will be different from the name of the previous file.

Executing for each row

The **execute for every input row?** option you have in the transformation entry setting window allows you to run the transformation once for every row copied in a previous transformation by using the **Copy rows to result** step. PDI executes the transformation as many times as the number of copied rows, one after the other. Each time the transformation executes and gets the rows from the result, it actually gets a different row.

 Note that in the transformation you don't limit the number of incoming rows. You simply assume that you are receiving a single row. If you forget to set the **execute for every input row?** option in the job, the transformation will run but you will get unexpected results.

This drawing shows you the mechanism for a dataset with three rows:

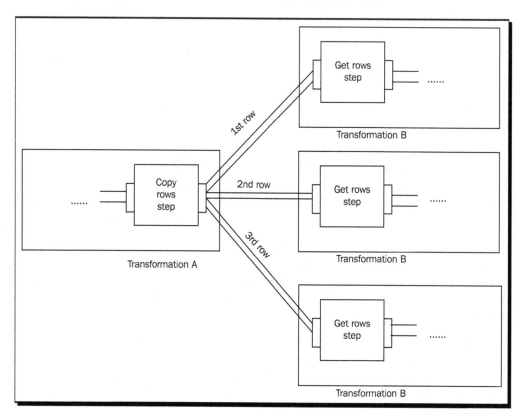

The transformation A in the example copies three rows. Then the transformation B is executed three times—first for the first copied row, then for the second, and finally for the third row.

If you look at the log in the tutorial, you can see it working:

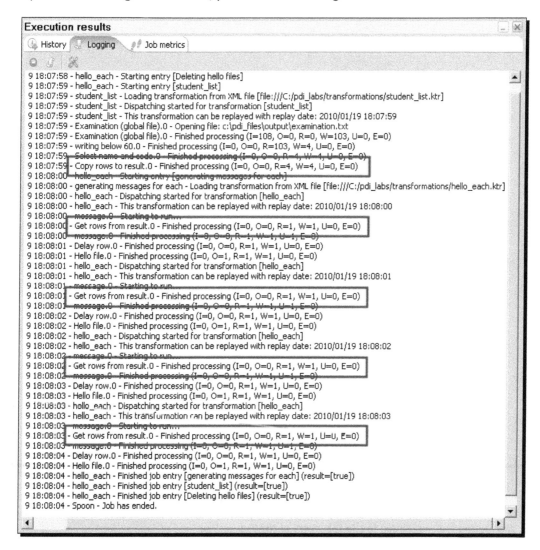

The transformation that builds the list of students copies four rows to the results. Then the main job executes the second transformation four times—once for each of those students.

The following sketch shows it clearly:

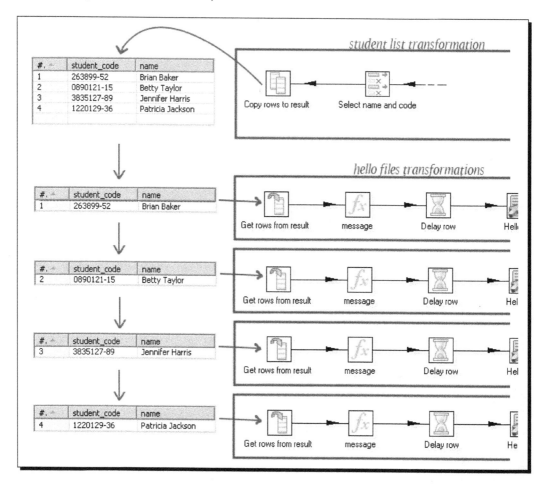

This mechanism of executing for every input row applies also to jobs. To execute a single job several times, once for every copied row, you have to check the **execute for every input row?** option that you have in the job entry settings window.

Have a go hero – processing several files at once

Modify the first tutorial about *Updating a file with news about examinations*. But this time accept a folder as parameter. Then process all the text files in that folder, ordered by date of the file. For each processed file, put a line in the log telling the name of the processed file.

You can use the following hint. Create a first transformation that, instead of validating the parameter as a file, validates it as a folder. In order to do that, use the **File exists** step inside the **Lookup** category of steps.

If the folder exists, use a **Get File Names** step. That step allows you to retrieve the list of filenames in a given folder, including the attributes for those files. To define which files to get, use the options in the box **Filenames from field**. Sort the list by file date and copy the names to the results.

In the second transformation, executed for every input row, get a row from the result, then use a **Text file input** step accepting the name from the previous step, and proceed as usual.

> As you may find it difficult to use steps you never used before, you may download a working version for the first transformation. You'll find it among the material for this chapter.

Have a go hero – building lists of products to buy

This exercise is related to the JS database.

Create a transformation to find out the manufacturers for the products that have been sold best in the current month. Take the first three manufacturers in the list.

Create another transformation that, for every manufacturer in that list, builds a file with a list of products out of stock.

Hint

The first transformation must copy the rows to the result. The second transformation must execute for every input row. Start the transformation with a **Get rows from result** step, then a **Table Input** step that receives as parameter a manufacturer's code. The SQL to use could be something like:

```
SELECT *
FROM products
WHERE code_man LIKE '?' AND pro_stock<pro_stock_min
```

Have a go hero – e-mail students to let them know how they did

Suppose some students have asked you to send them an e-mail to tell them how they did in the examination. Get the list of students from a file you'll find inside the **resources**, find out their scores, and send them an e-mail with that information.

Hint

Create a transformation that builds the list of students that have asked you to send them the examination results, along with their e-mail and scores, and copies the rows to the result.

Create a job that does the following: Call a transformation that gets a row from a result with the name, e-mail, and scores for a single student. Use that information to create variables needed to send an e-mail, for example **Subject**. After calling that transformation, use a **Mail** entry to send the e-mail by using the defined variables.

Create a main job. Execute the transformation that builds the list followed by the job described above, executing it for every input row.

To test the job that sends e-mails, you may temporarily replace the **Get rows from result** step with a **Generate rows with fixed values** step.

To test the main job, replace the e-mail accounts in the file with accounts you have access to.

Summary

In this chapter you learned techniques to combine jobs and transformations in different ways.

First, you learned to define your own variables at run time. You defined variables in one transformation and then used them in other jobs and/or transformations. You also learned to define different scopes for those variables.

After that, you learned to isolate part of a transformation as a subtransformation. You also learned to implement process flows by copying and getting rows, and how to nest jobs. By using all these PDI capabilities, your work will look cleaner and will be more organized.

Finally, you learned to iterate the execution of jobs and transformations.

Let's say that this was a really productive chapter. By now, you should be equipped with enough knowledge to use PDI for developing most of your requirements.

You're now ready for the next chapter, where you will develop the final project that will allow you to review a little of everything you've learned throughout the book.

12

Developing and Implementing a Simple Datamart

In this chapter you will develop a simple but complete process of loading a datamart while reviewing all concepts you learned throughout the book.

The chapter will cover the following:

- Introduction to a sales datamart based on the Jigsaw puzzles database
- Loading the dimensions of the sales datamart
- Loading the fact table for the sales datamart
- Automating what has been done

Exploring the sales datamart

In Chapter 9, you were introduced to star schemas. In short, a star schema consists of a central table known as the fact table, surrounded by dimension tables. While the fact has indicators of your business such as sales in dollars, the dimensions have descriptive information for the attributes of your business such as time, customers, and products.

A star that addresses a specific department's needs or that is built for use by a particular group of users is called a **datamart**. You can have datamarts focused on customer relationship management, inventory, human resources management, budget, and more. In this chapter, you will load a datamart focused on sales.

Sometimes the term datamart is confused with **datawarehouse**. However, datamarts and datawarehouses are not the same.

The main difference between datamarts and datawarehouses is that datawarehouses address the needs of the whole organization, whereas a datamarts addresses the needs of a particular department.

Datawarehouses contain information from multiple subject areas, allowing you to have a global vision of your business. Therefore, they are oriented to the company's staff such as executives or managers.

The following star represents your sales datamart—a central fact named **SALES**, surrounded by six dimensions:

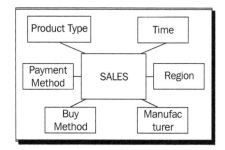

The following is a brief description for the dimensions in your SALES star:

Dimension	Description
Time	The date on which the sales occurred
Regions	The geographical area where the products were sold
Manufacturers	The name of the manufacturers that build the products sold
Payment method	Cash, Check, and so on
Buy method	Internet, by telephone, and so on
Product type	Puzzle, glue, frame, and so on

 In real models you may find two types of dimensions related with time—a dimension holding calendar day attributes and a separate dimension with attributes such as hours, minutes, and seconds.

Let's now look at the DER for the database that represents this model. The fact table is represented by a table named `ft_sales`.

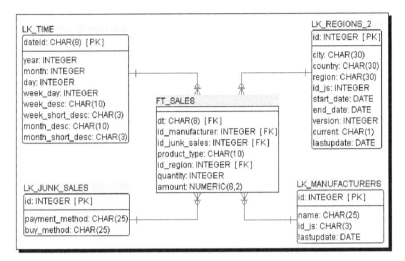

The following table shows you the correspondence between the dimensions in the model and the tables in the database:

Dimension	Table
Manufacturers	`lk_manufacturer`
Time	`lk_time`
Regions	`lk_regions_2`
Payment method	`lk_junk_sales`
Buy method	`lk_junk_sales`
Product type	none

As you can see, there is no one-to-one relationship between the dimensions in the model and the tables in the database.

> A one-to-one relationship between a dimension and a database table is not required, but may coincidentally exist.

The first three dimensions have their corresponding tables.

The payment and buy method dimensions share a junk dimension. A **junk dimension** is an abstract dimension that groups unrelated low-cardinality flags, indicators, and attributes. Each of those items could technically be a dimension on its own, but grouping them into a junk dimension has the advantage of keeping your database model simple and it also saves space.

The last dimension, product type, doesn't have a separate table. It is so simple that it isn't worth creating a dimension table. Instead, its values are stored in a dedicated field in the fact table. This kind of dimension is called **degenerate dimension**.

Deciding the level of granularity

The level of detail in your star model is called **grain**. The granularity is directly related to the types of questions you expect your model to answer. Let's see some examples.

The product-related information your model has is the manufacturer and the kind of product (puzzle, glue, and so on). Thus, it allows you to ask questions such as:

◆ Beyond puzzles, what type of product is the best sold?

◆ Do you sell more products manufactured by Ravensburger than products manufactured by Educa Jigsaws?

What if you want to know the names of the top ten products sold? You simply can't, as that level of detail is not stored in the model. For answering this type of question, you need a lower level of granularity. You could have that by adding a product dimension where each record represents a particular product.

Now let's see the time dimension. Each record in that dimension represents a particular calendar day. This allows you to answer questions such as: how many products did you sell every day in the last four months?

If you were not interested in daily, but in monthly information, you could have designed a model with a higher level of granularity by creating a time dimension with just one record per month.

Understanding the level of granularity of your model is a key to the process of loading the fact table, as you will see when you load the sales fact table.

Loading the dimensions

As you saw, the sales star model consists of a fact surrounded by the dimension tables. In order to load the star, first you have to load the dimensions. You already learned how to load dimension tables. Here you will load the dimensions for the sales star.

Time for action – loading dimensions for the sales datamart

In this tutorial, you will load each dimension for the sales datamart and enclose them into a single job. Before starting, check the following things:

◆ Check that the database engine is up and that both the `js` and the `js_dw` databases are accessible from PDI.

◆ If your time dimension table, `lk_time`, has data, truncate the table. You may do it by using the **Truncate table [lk_time]** option in the database explorer.

> You may reuse the `js_dw` database in which you have been loading data in previous chapters. There is no problem with that. However, creating a whole new database is preferred so that you can see how the entire process works.

The explanation will be focused on the general process. For details of creating a transformation that loads a particular type of dimension, please refer to *Chapter 9*. You can also download the full material for this chapter where the transformations and jobs are ready to browse and try.

1. Create a new transformation and use it to load the manufacturer dimension. This is a Type I SCD dimension. The data for the dimension comes from the `manufacturers` table in the `js` database. The dimension table in `js_dw` is `lk_manufacturer`. Use the following screenshot as a guide:

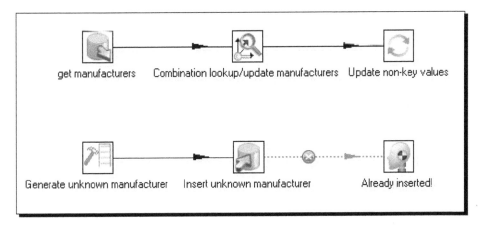

2. Save the transformation the `lk_transformations`.

3. Create a new transformation and use it to load the regions dimension.

> You already loaded this dimension in the *Time for action – loading a region dimension with a Combination lookup/ update step* section in Chapter 9. The load of the region field was part of a Hero exercise in that chapter. If you did it, you may skip this step.

4. The region dimension is a Type II SCD dimension. The data for the dimension comes from the `city` and `country` tables. The information about regions is in Excel files that you can download from the Packt web site. The dimension table in `js_dw` is `lk_regions_2`. Use the following screenshot as a guide:

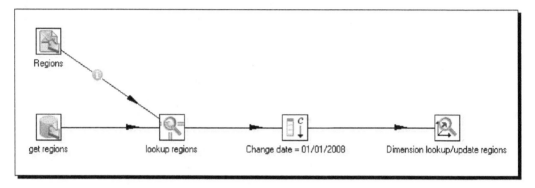

5. Save the transformation in the `lk_transformations` folder.

6. Create a new transformation and use it to load the time dimension.

> You already created the dataset for the time dimension in the *Time for action –creating the time dimension dataset* section in Chapter 6. Then in Chapter 8 the loading of the data into a table was part of a Hero exercise. If you have done it, you may skip this step.

The dimension table in `js_dw` is `lk_time`.

7. Save the transformation in the `lk_transformations` folder.

Now you will create a job to put it all together:

8. Create a new job and save it in the same folder where you created the `lk_transformations` folder.

9. Drag a **START** entry and two **Transformation** job entries to the canvas.

10. Create a hop from the **START** entry to each of the transformation entries. You have the following:

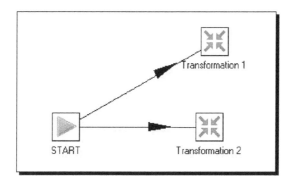

11. Use one of the transformation entries to execute the transformation that loads the manufacturer dimension.

12. Use the other transformation entry to execute the transformation that loads the region dimension.

13. Add an **Evaluate rows number in a table** entry to the canvas. You'll find it under the **Conditions** category.

14. Create a hop from the **START** entry towards this new entry.

15. Double-click the new entry and fill it like shown:

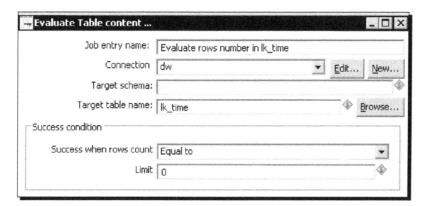

16. After this entry, add another transformation entry and use it to execute the transformation that loads the time dimension.

17. Finally, from the **General** category add a **Success** entry.

18. Create a hop from the **Evaluate...** step to this entry. The hop should be red, meaning that this step executes when the evaluation fails.

19. Your final job looks like this:

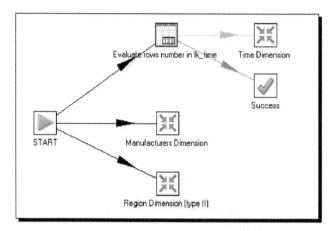

20. Save the job.

21. Run the job. The manufacturer and regions dimensions should be loaded. You can verify it by exploring the tables from the PDI explorer or in MySQL query browser.

22. In the logging window, you'll see that the evaluation succeeded and so the time dimension is also loaded:

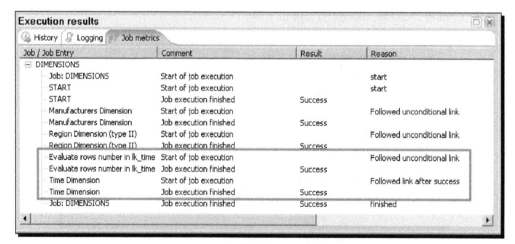

23. You can check it by exploring the table.

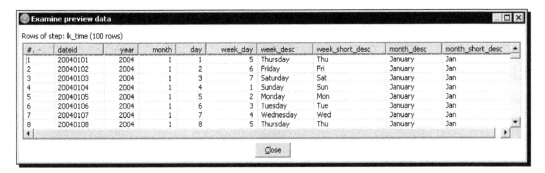

24. Run the transformation again. This time the evaluation fails and the transformation that loads the time dimension is not executed this time.

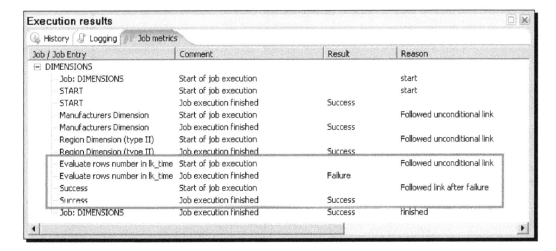

What just happened?

You created the transformations to load the dimensions you need for your sales star.

As already explained in Chapter 10, the job entries connected to the **START** entry run one after the other, not in parallel as the arrangement in the work area might suggest.

As for the time dimension, once it is loaded, you don't need to load it again. Therefore, you put an evaluation entry to check if the table had already been loaded. The first time you run the job, there were no records, so the time dimension was loaded. The second time, the time dimension had already been loaded. This time the evaluation failed, avoiding the execution of the transformation that loaded the time dimension.

Note that you put in a **Success** entry to avoid the job failing after the failed evaluation.

Extending the sales datamart model

You may, and you usually, have more than one fact table sharing some of the dimensions. Look at the following diagram:

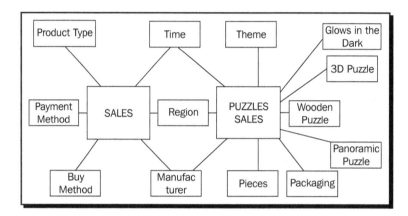

It shows two stars sharing three dimensions: **Regions**, **Manufacturers**, and **Time**. The star model to the left is the sales star model you already know. The star model to the right doesn't have data for accessories, but does have more detail for puzzles such as the number of pieces they have or the category or theme they belong to. When you have more than one fact table sharing dimensions as here, you have what is called a **constellation**.

The following table summarizes the dimensions added to the datamart:

Dimension	Description
Pieces	Number of pieces of the puzzle, grouped in the following ranges: 0-25, 26-100, and so on
Theme	Classification of the puzzle in any of the following categories: Fantasy, Castles, Landscapes, and so on
Glows in the dark	Yes/No
3D puzzle	Yes/No
Wooden puzzle	Yes/No
Panoramic puzzle	Yes/No
Packaging	Number of puzzles packed together: 1, 2, 3, 4

The following is the updated ERD for the database that represents the model:

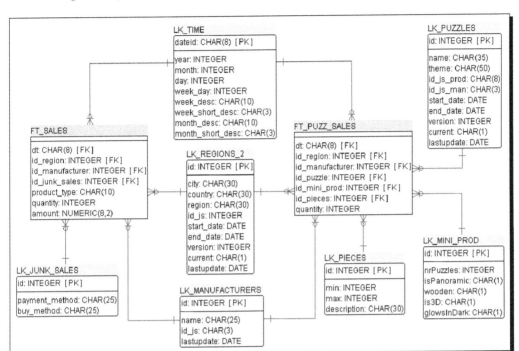

The new fact table is represented by a table named `ft_puzz_sales`.

The following table shows you the correspondence between the dimensions added to the model and the tables in the database.

Dimension	Table
Pieces	`lk_pieces`
Theme	`lk_puzzles`
Glows in the dark	`lk_mini_prod`
3D puzzle	`lk_mini_prod`
Wooden puzzle	`lk_mini_prod`
Panoramic	`lk_mini_prod`
Packaging	`lk_mini_prod`

The following Hero exercise allows you to practice what you learned in the tutorial, but this time applied to the puzzle star model.

Have a go hero – loading the dimensions for the puzzles star model

In this exercise you will load some of the dimensions that were added to the model.

♦ Create a transformation that loads the `lk_pieces` dimension. You may create any range you like. The following table may help you in the creation:

min	max	description
0	25	Under 25
26	100	26-100
101	1000	101-1000
1001	2000	1001-2000
2000	99999	>2000

♦ Create another transformation that loads the `lk_puzzles` dimensions. This is a Type II SCD, and you have already loaded it in Chapter 9. If you have the transformation that does it, half of your work is done.

♦ Finally, modify the job in the tutorial by adding the execution of these new transformations. Note that the `lk_pieces` dimension has to be loaded just once.

Loading a fact table with aggregated data

Now that you have data in your dimensions, you are ready to load the sales fact table. In this section, you will learn how to do it.

Time for action – loading the sales fact table by looking up dimensions

Let's load the sales fact table, `ft_sales`, with sales information for a given range of dates. Before doing this exercise, be sure that you have already loaded the dimensions. You did it in the previous tutorial.

Also check that the database engine is up and that both the `js` and the `js_dw` databases are accessible from PDI. If everything is in order, you are ready to start:

1. Create a new transformation.

2. Drag a **Table input** step to the canvas.

3. Double-click the step. Select **js** as **Connection**—the connection to the operational database.

4. In the **SQL** frame type the following query:

```
SELECT i.inv_date
       ,d.man_code
       ,cu.city_id
       ,pr.pro_type        product_type
       ,b.buy_desc
       ,p.pay_desc
       ,sum(d.cant_prod) quantity
       ,sum(d.price)     amount
FROM    invoices          i
       ,invoices_detail   d
       ,customers         cu
       ,buy_methods       b
       ,payment_methods   p
       ,products          pr
WHERE i.invoice_number = d.invoice_number
  AND        i.cus_id   = cu.cus_id
  AND        i.buy_code = b.buy_code
  AND        i.pay_code = p.pay_code
  AND        d.pro_code = pr.pro_code
  AND        d.man_code = pr.man_code
  AND i.inv_date BETWEEN cast('${DATE_FROM}' as date)
                     AND cast('${DATE_TO}'   as date)
GROUP BY i.inv_date
       ,d.man_code
          ,cu.city_id
          ,pr.pro_type
          ,b.buy_desc
          ,p.pay_desc
```

5. Check the **Replace variables in script?** option and click **OK**.

Let's retrieve the surrogate key for the manufacturer:

6. From the **Lookup** category, drag a **Database lookup** step to the canvas.

7. Create a hop from the **Table input step** to this new step.

8. Double-click the **Database lookup** step.

9. Select dw as **Connection**—the connection to the datamart database.

10. Click on **Browse...**and select the lk_manufacturers table.

11. Fill the upper grid with the following condition: id_js = man_code.

12. Fill the lower grid—under **Field** type id, as **New name** type id_manufacturer, as **Default** type 0, and as **Type** select **Integer**.

13. Click on **OK**.

Now you will get the surrogate key for the region:

14. From the **Data Warehouse** category drag a **Dimension lookup/update** step to the canvas.

15. Create a hop from the **Database lookup** step to this new step.

16. Double-click the **Dimension lookup/update** step.

17. As **Connection** select dw.

18. Browse and select the lk_regions_2 table.

19. Fill the **Keys** grid as shown next:

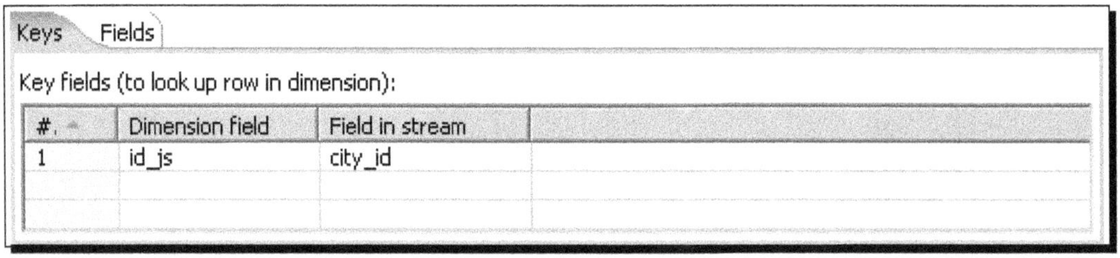

Keys	Fields		
Key fields (to look up row in dimension):			
#. ▲	Dimension field	Field in stream	
1	id_js	city_id	

20. Select **id** as **Technical key field**. In the **new name** textbox, type id_region.

21. As **Stream Datefield** select inv_date.

22. As **Date range star field** and **Table daterange end** select start_date and end_date respectively.

23. Select the **Fields** tab and fill it like here:

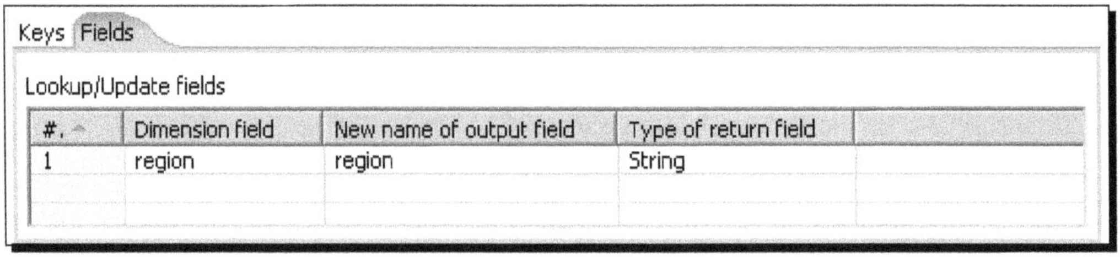

Keys	Fields		
Lookup/Update fields			
#. ▲	Dimension field	New name of output field	Type of return field
1	region	region	String

Now it's time to generate the surrogate key for the junk dimension:

24. From the **Data Warehouse** category drag a **Combination lookup/update** step to the canvas.

25. Create a hop from the **Dimension lookup/update** step to this new step.

26. Double-click the **Combination lookup/update** step.

27. Select dw as **Connection**.

28. Browse and select the lk_junk_sales table.

29. Fill the grid as shown:

Key fields (to look up row in table):

#, ▲	Dimension field	Field in stream	
1	buy_method	buy_desc	
2	payment_method	pay_desc	

30. As **Technical key field** type id. In the **Creation of technical key** frame, leave the default value **Use table maximum + 1**.

31. Click **OK**.

32. Add a **Select values** step and use it to rename the field id to id_junk_sales.

Finally, let's do some adjustments and send the data to the fact table:

33. Add another **Select values** step to change the metadata of the inv_date field as shown:

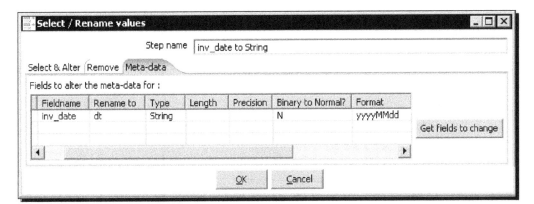

34. Add a **Table output** step and double-click it.

35. Select dw as **Connection**.

36. Browse and select the ft_sales table.

37. Check the **Specify database fields** option, select the **Database fields** grid, and fill it as shown:

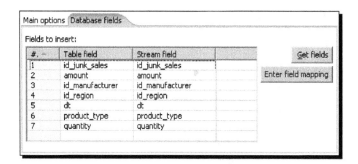

> Remember that you can avoid typing by using the **Get fields** button.

38. Click on **OK**. The following is your final transformation. Press *Ctrl+S* to save it.

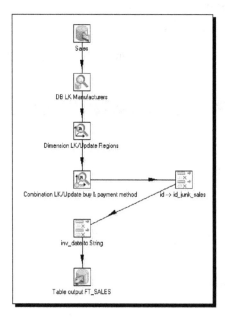

39. Press *F9* to run it.

40. In the settings window, provide some values for the date range.

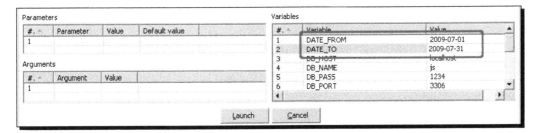

41. Click on **Launch**.

42. The fact table should have been loaded. To check it, open the database explorer and run the following query:

```
SELECT * FROM ft_sales
```

You will get the following:

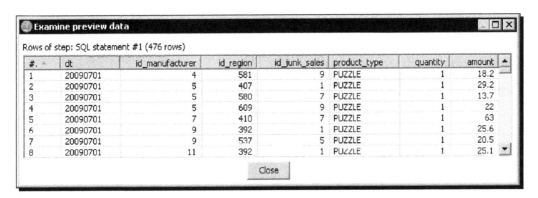

43. To verify that only the sales between the provided dates were processed, run the following query:

```
SELECT MIN(dt), MAX(dt) FROM ft_sales
```

44. You will get the following:

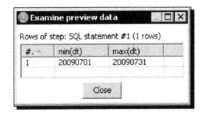

What just happened?

You loaded the sales fact table with the sales in a given range of dates.

First of all you got the information from the source database. You did it by typing an SQL query in a **Table input** step. You already know how a **Table input** step works.

As said, a fact table has foreign keys to the primary key of the dimension tables. The query you wrote gave you business keys. So, after getting the data from the source, you translated the business keys into surrogate keys. You did it in different ways depending on the kind of each related dimension.

Finally, you inserted the obtained data into the fact table ft_sales.

Getting the information from the source with SQL queries

You already know how to use a **Table input** step to get information from any database. However, the query in the tutorial may have looked strange or long compared with the queries you wrote in previous chapters. There is nothing mysterious in that query: It's simply a matter of knowing what to put in it. Let's explain it in detail.

The first thing you have to do in order to load the fact table is to look at the grain.

As mentioned at the beginning of the chapter, the grain, or level of detail, of the fact is implicitly expressed in terms of the dimension.

Looking at the model, you can see the following dimensions, along with their level of detail:

Dimension	Level of detail (most atomic data)
Manufacturers	manufacturer
Regions	city
Time	day
Product Type	product type
Payment method	payment method
Buy method	buy method

Does this have anything to do with loading the fact? Well, the answer is *yes*. This is because the numbers you have to put as measures in the numeric fields must be aggregated accordingly to the dimensions. These are the measurements—quantity representing the number of products sold and Sales representing the amounts.

So, in order to feed the table, what you need to take from the source is the sum of quantity and the sum of sales for every combination of manufacturer, day, city, product type, payment method, and buy method.

In SQL terms you do it with a query such as the one you wrote in the **Table input** step. The query is not as complicated as it may seem at first. Let's dissect the query, beginning with the FROM clause.

```
FROM    invoices            i
        ,invoices_detail    d
        ,customers          cu
        ,buy_methods        b
        ,payment_methods    p
        ,products           pr
```

These are the tables to take the information from. The word following the name of the table is an alias for the table—for example, pr for the table products. The **alias** is used to distinguish fields that have the same name but are in different tables.

The database engine takes all the records for all the listed tables, side by side, and creates all the possible combination of records where each new record has all the fields for all the tables.

```
WHERE  i.invoice_number = d.invoice_number
   AND         i.cus_id   = cu.cus_id
   AND         i.buy_code = b.buy_code
   AND         i.pay_code = p.pay_code
   AND         d.pro_code = pr.pro_code
   AND         d.man_code = pr.man_code
```

These conditions represent the join between tables. A **join** limits the number of records you have when combining tables as explained above. For example, consider the following condition:

```
i.cus_id = cu.cus_id
```

This condition implies that out of all the records, the engine keeps only those where the customer ID in the table invoices is the same as that of the customer ID in the table customers.

```
AND i.inv_date BETWEEN cast('${DATE_FROM}' as date)
                   AND cast('${DATE_TO}'   as date)
```

This query simply filters the sales in the given range. The cast function converts a string to a date.

Different engines have different ways to cast or convert fields from one data type to another. If you are using an engine different from MySQL, you may have to check your database documentation and fix this part of the query.

```
GROUP BY i.inv_date
        ,d.man_code
        ,cu.city_id
        ,pr.pro_type
        ,b.buy_desc
        ,p.pay_desc
```

By using the GROUP BY clause, you ask the SQL engine that for each different combination of the listed fields, it should return just one record.

Finally, look at the fields following the SELECT clause:

```
SELECT i.inv_date
       ,d.man_code
       ,cu.city_id
       ,pr.pro_type      product_type
       ,b.buy_desc
       ,p.pay_desc
       ,sum(d.cant_prod)  quantity
       ,sum(d.price)      amount
```

These fields are the business keys you need—date of sale, manufacturer, city, and so on—one for each dimension in the sales model. Note the word product_type after the pro_type field. This is an alias for the field. Using an alia,s the field is renamed in the output.

As you can see, with the exception of the highlighted fields, the fields you put after the SELECT clause are exactly the same as you put in the GROUP BY clause. When you have a GROUP BY clause in your sentence, after the SELECT clause you can put only those fields that are listed in the GROUP BY clause or aggregated functions such as the following:

```
       ,sum(d.cant_prod)  quantity
       ,sum(d.price)      amount
```

sum() is an aggregate function that gives you the sum of the column you put into brackets. Therefore, these last two fields are the sum of the cant_prod field and the sum of the price field for all the grouped records. These two fields give you the measures for your fact table.

To confirm that the GROUP BY works as explained, let's explore one example. Remove from the query, the sum() functions, leaving just the fields, along with the GROUP BY clause. Do a preview setting 2009-07-07 both as start_date and end_date. You will see the following:

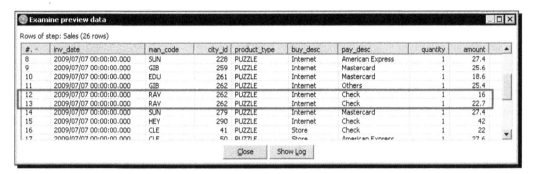

As you can see, in the same day, in the same city, you sold two products of the same type, made for the same manufacturer, by using the same payment and buy method. In the fact table you will not save two records, but will save a single record. Restore the original query and do a preview. You will see the following:

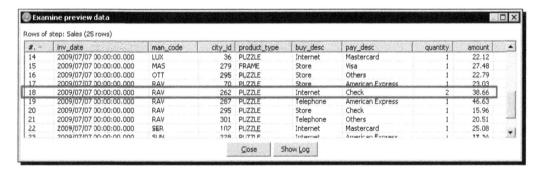

Here you can see that the GROUP BY clause has grouped those two records into a single one. For quantity and amount it summed the individual values.

Note that the GROUP BY clause, along with the aggregate functions, does the same as you could have done by using a **Sort rows** step to sort by the listed fields, followed by a **Group by** step to get the sum of the numeric fields.

Wherever the database can do the operations, for performance reasons it's recommended that you allow the database engine do it.

Translating the business keys into surrogate keys

You already have the transactional data for the fact table. But that data contains business keys. Look at the fields definition for your fact table:

```
dt CHAR(8) NOT NULL,
id_manufacturer INT(10) NOT NULL,
id_region INT(4) NOT NULL,
id_junk_sales INT(10) NOT NULL,
product_type CHAR(10) NOT NULL,
quantity INT(6) DEFAULT 0 NOT NULL,
amount NUMERIC(8,2) DEFAULT 0 NOT NULL
```

id_manufacturer, id_region, and id_junk_sales are foreign keys to surrogate keys. So, before inserting the data into the fact, for each business key you have to find the proper surrogate key. Depending on the kind of dimensions referenced by the IDs in the fact table, you get those IDs in a different way. Let's see in the following section, how you do it in each case.

Obtaining the surrogate key for a Type I SCD

For getting the surrogate key in the case of a Type I SCD such as the Manufacturer one, you used a Database lookup step. You are already familiar with this step, so understanding how to use it is easy.

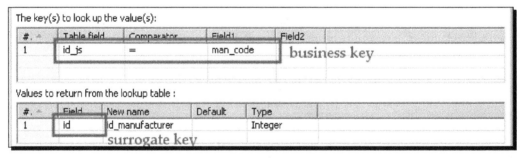

In the first grid you provided the business keys. The key to look up in the incoming stream is man_code, whereas the key to look up in the dimension table is stored in the field id_js.

With the **Database lookup** step you returned the field named id, which is the field that stores the surrogate key. You renamed it to id_manufacturer, as this is the name you need for the fact table.

If the key is not found, you use 0 as default, that is, the record in the dimension reserved for unknown values.

The following screenshot shows you how it works:

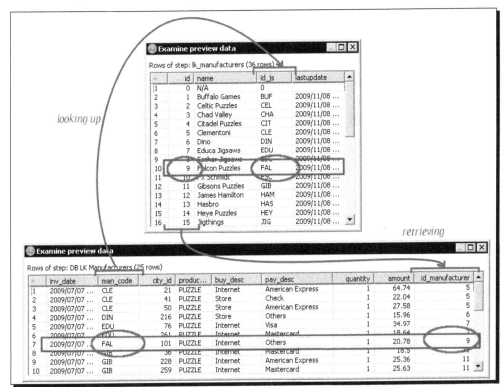

Obtaining the surrogate key for a Type II SCD

In the case of a Type II SCD such as the Region dimension, you used the same step that was used to load the table dimension—a **Dimension L/U** step. The difference is that here you unchecked the **Update the dimension?** option. By doing that, the step behaves just as a database lookup—you provide the keys to lookup and the step returns the fields you put both in the **Fields** tab and in the **Technical key field** option. The difference with this step is that here you have to provide time information. By using that time information, PDI finds and returns, from the Type II SCD, the proper record in time:

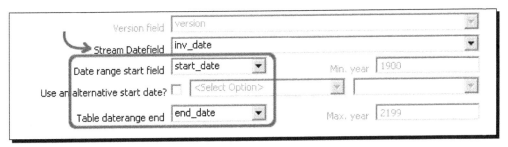

Here you give PDI the names for the columns that store the data ranges—`start_date` and `end_date`. You also give it the name of the field stream to use in order to compare the dates—in this case `inv_date`, that is, the date of the sale.

Look at the following screenshot to understand how the lookup works:

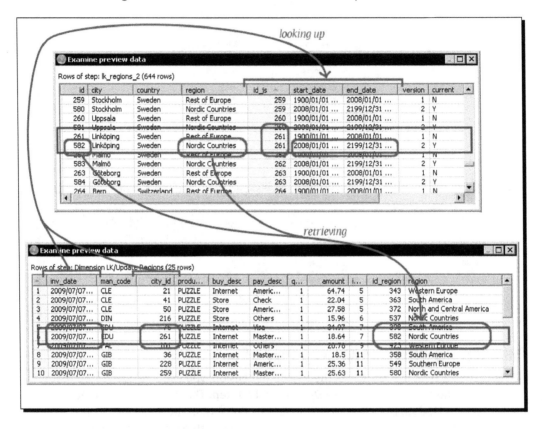

The step has to get the surrogate key for the city with ID `261`. There are two records for that city. The key is in finding the proper record, the record valid on `07/07/2009`. So, PDI compares the date provided against the `start_date` and `end_date` fields and returns the surrogate key `582`, for which the city is classified as belonging to the `Nordic Countries` region.

If no record is found for the given keys on the given date, the step retrieves the ID `0`, which is used for the unknown data.

Obtaining the surrogate key for the Junk dimension

The payment and buy methods are stored in a junk dimension. A junk dimension can be loaded by using a **Combination L/U** step. You learned how to use this step in the *Time for action* named *Loading a region dimension with a Combination lookup/update step* in *Chapter 9*. As all the fields in a junk dimension are part of the primary key, you don't need an extra **Update** step to load it.

In the tutorial, you loaded the dimension at the same time you loaded the fact. You know from Chapter 9 that when you use a **Combination L/U** step, the step returns you the generated key. So, the use of the step here for loading and getting the key at the same time fits perfectly.

 If the dimension had been loaded previously, instead of a **Combination L/U** step you could have used a **Database lookup** step by putting the key fields in the upper grid and the key in the lower grid of the Database lookup configuration window.

Obtaining the surrogate key for the Time dimension

You already obtained the surrogate keys for Type I and Type II SCDs and for the Junk dimension. Finally, there is a Time dimension. As for the key, you use the date in string format; the method for getting the surrogate key is simply changing the metadata from date to string by using the proper format. Once again, if you had used a regular surrogate key instead of the date, for getting the surrogate key you would have to use a **Database lookup** step.

The following table summarizes the different possibilities:

Dimension type	Method for getting the surrogate key	Sample dimension
Type I SCD	**Database lookup** step.	Manufacturer
Type II SCD	**Dimension L/U** step.	Regions
Junk and Mini	**Combination L/U** step if you load the dimension at the same time as you load the fact (as in the tutorial).	Sales Junk dimension
	Database lookup step if the dimension is already loaded.	
Degenerate	As you don't have a table nor key to translate, you just store the data as a field in the fact. You don't have to worry about getting surrogate keys.	Product Type
Time	Change the metadata to the proper format if you use date as the key (as in the tutorial).	Time
	Dimension L/U step if you use a normal surrogate key.	

Pop quiz – modifying a star model and loading the star with PDI

Suppose you want to do some modifications to your star model. What are the changes you'll have to make in each case:

1. Instead of using a region dimension that keeps history of the changes (Type II SCD), you want to use a classic region dimension (Type I).

    a. As table for the region dimension:

       i. You reuse the table `lk_regions_2`.

       ii. You use a different table.

       iii. Any of the above.

    b. As field with the foreign key in the fact table:

       i. You reuse the `id_region` field.

       ii. You create a new field.

    c. For getting the surrogate key:

       i. You keep using the **Dimension lookup/update** step.

       ii. You replace the **Dimension lookup/update** step by another step.

       iii. It depends on the how your dimension table looks.

2. You want to change the grain for the Time dimension; you are interested in monthly information.

    a. As table for the time dimension:

       i. You reuse the table `lk_time`.

       ii. You use a different table.

       iii. Any of the above.

    b. As field with the foreign key in the fact table:

       i. You reuse the `dt` field.

       ii. You create a new field.

    c. For getting the surrogate key:

       i. You keep using the **Select values** step and changing the metadata.

       ii. You use another method.

3. You decided to create a new table for the product type dimension. The table will have the following columns: `id`, `product_type_description`, and `product_type`. As data you would have, for example: `1`, `puzzle`, `puzzle` for the product type puzzle, or `2`, `glue`, `accessory` for the product type glue.

   a. As field with the foreign key in the fact table:

      i. You reuse the `product_type` field.

      ii. You create a new field.

   b. For getting the surrogate key:

      i. You use a **Combination lookup/update** step

      ii. You use a **Dimension lookup/update** step

      iii. You use a **Database lookup/update** step

Have a go hero – loading a puzzles fact table

In the previous Hero exercise you were asked to load the dimensions for the puzzle star model. Now you will load the fact table.

To load the fact table you'll need to build a query taking data from the source. Try to figure out what the query looks like. Then you may try writing the query by yourself, or you may cheat; this query will serve you as a starting point:

```
SELECT
      i.inv_date
     ,d.man_code
     ,cu.city_id
     ,pr.pro_theme
     ,pr.pro_pieces
     ,pr.pro_packaging
     ,pr.pro_shape
     ,pr.pro_style
     ,SUM(d.cant_prod) quantity
FROM   invoices         i
     ,invoices_detail d
     ,customers         cu
     ,products          pr
WHERE i.invoice_number = d.invoice_number
  AND        i.cus_id   = cu.cus_id
  AND        d.pro_code = pr.pro_code
  AND        d.man_code = pr.man_code
  AND pr.pro_type like 'PUZZLE'
  AND i.inv_date BETWEEN cast('${DATE_FROM}' as date)
                 AND cast('${DATE_TO}' as date)
```

```
GROUP BY i.inv_date
        ,d.man_code
        ,cu.city_id
        ,pr.pro_theme
        ,pr.pro_pieces
        ,pr.pro_packaging
        ,pr.pro_shape
        ,pr.pro_style
```

After that, look for the surrogate keys for dimensions of Type I and II.

Here you have a mini-dimension. You may load it at the same time you load the fact as you did in the tutorial with the Junk dimension. Also, make sure that you properly modify the metadata for the time field.

Insert the data into the fact, and check whether the data was loaded as expected.

Getting facts and dimensions together

Loading the star involves both loading the dimensions and loading the fact. You already loaded the dimensions and the fact separately. In the following two tutorials, you will put it all together:

Time for action – loading the fact table using a range of dates obtained from the command line

Now you will get the range of dates from the command line and load the fact table using that range:

1. Create a new transformation.

2. With a **Get system info** step, get the first two arguments from the command line and name them date_from and date_to.

3. By using a couple of steps, check that the arguments are not null, have the proper format (yyyy-mm-dd), and are valid dates.

4. If something is wrong with the arguments, abort.

5. If the arguments are valid, use a **Set variables** step to set two variables named DATE_FROM and DATE_TO.

6. Save the transformation in the same folder you saved the transformation that loads the fact table.

7. Test the transformation by providing valid and invalid arguments to see that it works as expected.

8. Create a job and save it in the same folder you saved the job that loads the dimensions.

9. Drag to the canvas a **START** and two transformation job entries, and link them one after the other.

10. Use the first transformation entry to execute the transformation you just created.

11. Use the second transformation entry to execute the transformation that loads the fact table.

12. This is how your job should look like:

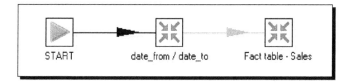

13. Save the job.

14. Press *F9* to run the job.

15. Fill the job settings window as follows:

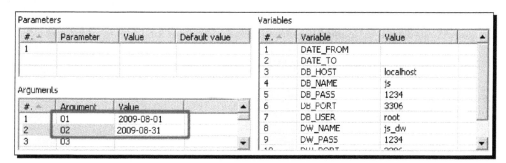

16. Click on **Launch**.

17. When the execution finishes, explore the database to check that the data for the given dates was loaded in the fact table. You will see this:

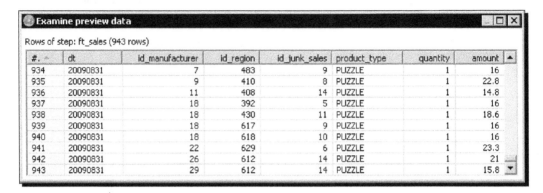

What just happened?

You built a main job that loads the sales fact table. First, it reads from the command line the range of dates to be used for loading the fact and validates it. If they are not valid, the process aborts. If they are valid, the fact table is loaded for the dates in that range.

Time for action – loading the sales star

You already created a job for loading the dimensions and another job for loading the fact.

In this tutorial, you will put them together in a single main job:

1. Create a new job in the same folder in which you saved those jobs. Name this job `load_dm_sales.kjb`.

2. Drag to the canvas a **START** and two job entries, and link them one after the other.

3. Use the first job entry to execute the job that loads the dimensions.

4. Use the second Job entry to execute the job you just created for loading the fact table.

5. Save the job. This is how it looks:

6. Press *F9* to run the job.

7. As arguments, provide a new range of dates: `2009-09-01`, `2009-09-30`. Then press **Launch**.

8. The dimensions will be loaded first, followed by the loading of the fact table.

9. The **Job metrics** tab in the **Execution results** window shows you the whole process running:

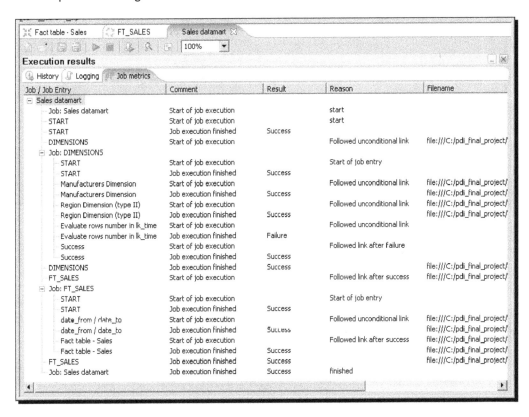

10. Exploring the database, you'll see once again the data updated:

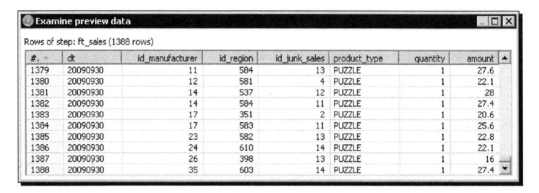

# ▲	dt	id_manufacturer	id_region	id_junk_sales	product_type	quantity	amount ▲
1379	20090930	11	584	13	PUZZLE	1	27.6
1380	20090930	12	581	4	PUZZLE	1	22.1
1381	20090930	14	537	12	PUZZLE	1	28
1382	20090930	14	584	11	PUZZLE	1	27.4
1383	20090930	17	351	2	PUZZLE	1	20.6
1384	20090930	17	583	11	PUZZLE	1	25.6
1385	20090930	23	582	13	PUZZLE	1	22.8
1386	20090930	24	610	14	PUZZLE	1	22.1
1387	20090930	26	398	13	PUZZLE	1	16
1388	20090930	35	603	14	PUZZLE	1	27.4

What just happened?

You built a main job that loads the sales datamart. First, it loads the dimensions. After that, it loads the fact table by filtering sales in a range of dates coming from the command line.

Have a go hero – enhancing the loading process of the sales fact table

Facts tables are rarely updated. Usually you just insert new data. However, after loading a fact, you may detect that there were errors in the source. Or it could also happen that some data arrives late to the system. In order to take into account those situations, you should have the possibility to reprocess data already processed. To avoid duplicates in the fact table, do the following modification to the loading process:

After getting the start and end date and before loading the fact table, delete the records that may have been inserted in a previous execution for the given range of dates.

Have a go hero – loading the puzzles sales star

Modify the main job so that it also loads the puzzle fact table.

Make sure that the job that loads the dimensions includes all the dimensions needed for both fact tables. Also, pay attention that you don't read and validate the arguments twice.

Have a go hero – loading the facts once a month

Modify the whole solution so the loading of the fact tables is made once a month. Don't modify the model! You still want to have daily information in the fact tables; what you want to do is simply replace the daily updating process with a monthly process. Ask for a single parameter as yyyymm and validate it. Replace the old parameters START_DATE and END_DATE with this new one, wherever you use them.

Getting rid of administrative tasks

The solution you built during the chapter loads both dimensions and fact in a star model for a given range of dates. Now suppose that you want to keep your datamart always updated. Would you sit every day in front of your computer, and run the same job over and over again? You probably would, but you know that it wouldn't be a good idea. There are better ways to do this. Let's see how you can get rid of that task.

Time for action – automating the loading of the sales datamart

Suppose that every day you want to update your sales datamart by adding the information about the sales for the day before. Let's do some modifications to the jobs and transformations you did so that the job can run automatically.

In order to test the changes, you'll have to change the date for your system. Set the current date as 2009-10-02.

1. Create a new transformation.

2. Drag to the canvas a **Get system data** step and fill it like here:

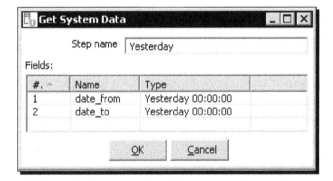

3. With a **Select values** step, change the metadata of both fields: As type put String and as format, yyyy-MM-dd.

4. Add a **Set variables** step and use the two fields to create two variables named START_DATE and END_DATE.

5. Save the transformation in the same folder you saved the transformation that loads the fact.

6. Modify the job that loads the fact so that instead of executing, the transformation that takes the range of dates from the command line executes this one. The job looks like this:

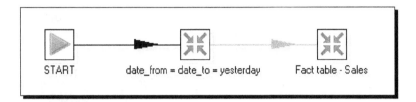

7. Save it.

Now let's create the scripts for executing the job from the command line:

1. Create a folder named `log` in the folder of your choice.

2. Open a terminal window.

3. Create a new file with your favorite text editor.

4. If your system is not Windows, go to step 7.

5. Under Windows systems, type the following:

```
for /f "tokens=1-3 delims=/- " %%a in ('date /t') do set
XDate=%%c%%b%%a
for /f "tokens=1-2 delims=: " %%a in ('time /t') do set
XTime=%%a.%%b

set path_etl=C:\pdi_labs
set path_log=C:\logs

c:\
cd ..
cd pdi-ce
kitchen.bat /file:%path_etl%\load_dm_sales.kjb /level:Detailed >>
%path_log%\sales_"%Xdate% %XTime%".log
```

6. Save the file as `dm_sales.bat` in a folder of your choice. Skip the following two steps.

7. Under Linux, Unix, and similar systems, type the following:

```
UNXETL=/pdi_labs
UNXLOG=/logs

cd /pdi-ce
kitchen.sh /file:$UNXETL/load_dm_sales.kjb /level:Detailed >>
$UNXLOG/sales_'date +%y%m%d-%H%M'.log
```

8. Save the file as dm_sales.sh in a folder of your choice.

 Irrespective of your system, please replace the names of the folders in the highlighted lines with the names of your own folders, that is path_etl (the folder where your main job is), path_log (the folder you just created), and pdi-ce (the folder where PDI is installed).

Now let's test what you've done:

1. Execute the batch you created:

Under windows, type: dm_sales.bat

Under Unix-like systems, type: sh dm_sales.sh

2. When the prompt in the command window is available, it means that the batch ended. Check the log folder. You'll find a new file with the extension log, named sales followed by the date and hour, for example:sales_0210Fri 06.46.log.

3. Edit the log. You'll see the full log for the execution of the job. Within the lines, you'll see these:

```
INFO   02-10 17:46:39,015 - Set Variables DATE_FROM and DATE_TO.0
- Set variable DATE_FROM to value [2009-10-01]
INFO   02-10 17:46:39,015 - Set Variables DATE_FROM and DATE_TO.0
- Set variable DATE_TO to value [2009-10-01]
```

4. Also check the fact table. The fact should have data for the sales made yesterday:

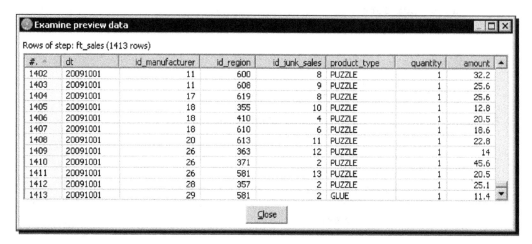

#.	dt	id_manufacturer	id_region	id_junk_sales	product_type	quantity	amount
1402	20091001	11	600	8	PUZZLE	1	32.2
1403	20091001	11	608	9	PUZZLE	1	25.6
1404	20091001	17	619	8	PUZZLE	1	25.6
1405	20091001	18	355	10	PUZZLE	1	12.8
1406	20091001	18	410	4	PUZZLE	1	20.5
1407	20091001	18	610	6	PUZZLE	1	18.6
1408	20091001	20	613	11	PUZZLE	1	22.8
1409	20091001	26	363	12	PUZZLE	1	14
1410	20091001	26	371	2	PUZZLE	1	45.6
1411	20091001	26	581	13	PUZZLE	1	20.5
1412	20091001	28	357	2	PUZZLE	1	25.1
1413	20091001	29	581	2	GLUE	1	11.4

 Don't forget to restore the date in your system!

What just happened?

You modified the job that loads the sales datamart so that it always loads the sales from a day before. You also created a script that embedded the execution of the Kitchen command and sent the result to a log. The name of the log is different for every day; this allows you keep a history of logs.

To understand exactly the full Kitchen command line you put into the scripts, please refer to Appendix B, *Pan and Kitchen: Launching Transformations and Jobs from the Command Line.*

Doing all this, you don't have to worry about providing dates for the process, nor running Spoon, nor remembering the syntax of the Kitchen command. Not only that, if you use a system utility such as a cron in Unix or the scheduler in Windows to schedule this script to run every day after midnight, you are done. You got rid of all the administrative tasks!

Have a go hero – Creating a back up of your work automatically

Choose a folder where you use to save your work (it could be for example the `pdi_labs` folder) Create a job that zips your work under the name `backup_yyyymmdd.zip` where `yyyymmdd` represents the system date. Test the job.

Then create a `.bat` or `.sh` file that executes your job sending the log to a file. Test the script.

Finally, schedule the script to be executed weekly.

Have a go hero – enhancing the automate process by sending an e-mail if an error occurs

Modify the main job so if something goes wrong, it sends you an e-mail reporting the problem. Doing so, you don't have to worry about checking the daily log to see if everything went fine. Unless there is a problem with the e-mail server, you'll be notified whenever some error occurs.

Summary

In this chapter you created a set of jobs and transformations that loads a sales datamart. Specifically, you learned how to load a fact table and to embed that process into a bigger one—the process that loads a full datamart.

You also learned to automate PDI processes, which is useful to get rid of tedious and repetitive manual tasks. In particular, you automated the loading of your sales datamart.

Beyond that, you must have found this chapter useful for reviewing all you learned since the first chapter. If you can't wait for more, read the next chapter. There you will find useful information for going further.

13
Taking it Further

The lessons learned in previous chapters gave you the basis of PDI. If you liked working with PDI and intend to use it in your own projects, there is much more ranging from applying best practices to using PDI integrated with the Pentaho BI Suite.

This chapter points you the right direction for taking it further. The chapter begins by giving you some advice to take into account in your daily work with PDI. After that it introduces you some advanced PDI concepts for you to know to what extent you can use the tool beyond the basics.

PDI best practices

If you intend to work seriously with PDI, knowing how to accomplish different tasks is not enough. Here are some guidelines that will help you go in the right direction.

- **Outline your ideas on paper before creating a transformation or a job:**

  Don't drop steps randomly on the canvas trying to get things working. You could end up with a transformation or job that is difficult to understand and even useless.

- **Document your work**:

  Write at least a simple description in the transformations and jobs setting windows. Replace the default names of steps and job entries with meaningful ones. Use notes to clarify the purpose of the transformations and jobs. Doing this, your work will be quite self documented.

♦ **Make your jobs and transformations clear to understand**:

Arrange the elements in the canvas so that it doesn't look like a puzzle to solve. Memorize the shortcuts for arrangement and alignment, and use them regularly. You'll find a full list in Appendix D, *Spoon shortcuts*.

♦ **Organize PDI elements in folders**:

Don't save all the transformations and jobs in the same folder. Organize them according to their purpose.

♦ **Make your work flexible and reusable**:

Make use of arguments, variables, and named parameters. If you identify tasks that are going to be used in several situations, create subtransformations.

♦ **Make your work portable (ready for deployment)**:

This involves making sure even if you move your work to another machine or another folder, or the paths to source or destination files change, or the connection properties to the databases change, everything should work either with minimal changes or without changes. In order to make ensure that, don't use fixed names but variables. If you know the values for the variables beforehand, define the variables in the `kettle.properties` file. For the name of the transformations and jobs, use relative paths—use the `${Internal.Job.Filename.Directory}` and `${Internal.Transformation.Filename.Directory}` variables.

♦ **Avoid overloading your transformations**:

A transformation should do a precise task. If it doesn't, think of splitting it in two or more, or create subtransformations. Doing this will make your transformation clearer and also reusable in the case of subtransformations.

♦ **Handle errors**:

Try to figure out the kind of errors that may happen and trap them by validating and handling errors, and taking appropriate actions such as fixing data, taking alternative paths, sending friendly message to the log files, and so on.

♦ **Do everything you can to optimize the PDI performance**:

You can find a full checklist at `http://wiki.pentaho.com/display/COM/PDI+Performance+tuning+check-list`. As of version 3.1.0, PDI introduced a tool for tracking the performance of individual steps in a transformation. You can find more information at `http://wiki.pentaho.com/display/EAI/Step+performance+monitoring`.

◆ **Keep track of jobs and transformations history**:

You can use a versioning system such as subversion. Doing so, you could recover older versions of your jobs and transformations or examine the history of how they changed. For more on subversion, visit `http://subversion.tigris.org/`.

Bookmark the forum page and visit it frequently. The PDI forum is available at `http://forums.pentaho.org/forumdisplay.php?f=135`.

The following is the main PDI forum page:

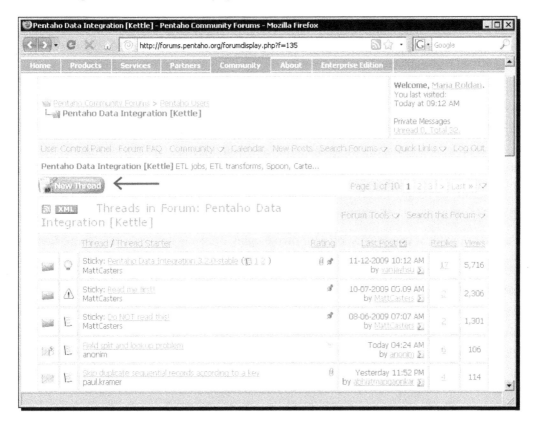

If you get stuck with something, search for a solution in the forum. If you don't find what you're looking for, create a new thread, expose your doubts or scenario clearly, and you'll get a prompt answer, as the Pentaho community, and particularly the PDI one, is quite active.

Getting the most out of PDI

Throughout the book you learned, step by step, how to use PDI for accomplishing several kinds of tasks— reading from different kinds of sources, writing back to them, transforming data in several ways, loading data into databases, and even loading a full data mart. You already have the knowledge and the experience to do anything you want or you need with PDI from now on. However, PDI offers you some more features that may be useful for you as well. The following sections will introduce them and will guide you so that you know where to look for in case they want to put them into practice.

Extending Kettle with plugins

As you could see while learning Kettle, there is a large set of steps and job entries to choose from when designing jobs and transformations. The number rises above 200 between steps and entries! If you still feel like you need more, there are more options—plugins.

Kettle plugins are basically steps or job entries that you install separately. The available plugins are listed at `http://wiki.pentaho.org/display/EAI/List+of+Available+Pentaho+Data+Integration+Plugins`.

Most of the listed plugins can be downloaded and used for free. Some are so popular or useful that they end up becoming standard steps of PDI—for example, the **Formula** step that you used several times throughout the book.

There are other plugins that come as a trial version and you have to pay to use them.

It's also possible for you to develop your own plugins. The only prerequisite is knowing how to develop code in Java. If you are interested in the subject, you can get more information at `http://wiki.pentaho.com/display/EAI/Writing+your+own+Pentaho+Data+Integration+Plug-In`.

It's no coincidence that the author of those pages is Jens Bleuel. Jens used the plugin architecture back in 2004, in order to connect Kettle with SAP, when he was working at Proratio. The plugin support was incorporated in Kettle 2.0 and the PRORATIO - SAP Connector, today available as a commercial plugin, was one of the first developed Kettle plugins.

 You should know that 3.x plugins no longer work on Kettle 4.0.

Have a go hero – listing the top 10 students by using the Head plugin step

Browse the plugin page and look for a plugin named Head. As described in the page, this plugin is a step that keeps the first x rows of the stream. Download the plugin and install it. The installation process is really straightforward. You have to copy a couple of `*.jar` files to the `libext` directory inside the PDI installation folder, add the environment variable for the PDI to find the libraries, and restart Spoon. The downloaded file includes a documentation with full instructions. Once installed, the **Head** will appear as a new step within the **Transformation** category of steps as shown here:

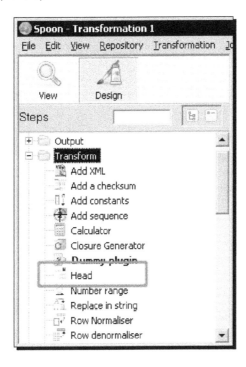

Create a transformation that reads the examination file that was used in the *Time for Action – reviewing examination by using the Calculator step* section in Chapter 3 and some other chapters as well. Generate an output file with the top 10 students by average score in descending order. In order to keep the top 10, use the Head plugin.

Before knowing of the existence of this plugin, you used to do this kind of filtering by using the **JavaScript** step. Another way to do it is by using an **Add sequence** step followed by a **Filter rows** step. Note that none of these methods use an ad hoc step.

Overcoming real world risks with some remote execution

In order to learn to use Kettle, you used very simple and small sets of data. It's worth saying that all you learned can be also applied for processing huge files and databases with millions of records. However, that's not for free! When you deal with such datasets, there are many risks—your transformations slow down, you may run out of memory, and so on.

The first step in trying to overcome those problems is to do some remote execution. Suppose you have to process a huge file located at a remote machine and that the only thing you have to do with that file is to get some statistics such as the maximum, minimum, and average value for a particular piece of data in the file. If you do it in the classic way, the data in the file would travel along the network for being processed by Kettle in your machine, loading the network unnecessarily.

PDI offers you the possibility to execute the tasks remotely. The remote execution capability allows you to run the transformation in the machine where the data resides. Doing so, the only data that would travel through the network will be the calculated data.

This kind of remote execution is done by **Carte**, a simple server that you can install in a remote machine and that does nothing but run jobs and transformations on demand. Therefore, it is called a **slave server**. You can start, monitor, and stop the execution of jobs and transformations remotely as depicted here:

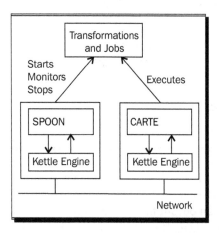

You don't need to download additional software because Carte is distributed as part of the Kettle software. For documentation on carte, follow this link: `http://wiki.pentaho.com/display/EAI/Carte+User+Documentation`.

Scaling out to overcome bigger risks

As mentioned above, PDI can handle huge volumes of data. However, the bigger the volume or complexity of your tasks, the bigger the risks. The solution not only lies in executing remotely, but in order to enhance your performance and avoid undesirable situations, you'd better increase your power. You basically have two options—you can either scale up or scale out. **Scaling up** involves buying a better processor, more memory, or disks with more capacity. **Scaling out** means to provide more processing power by distributing the work over multiple machines.

With PDI you can scale out by executing jobs and transformations in a cluster. A **cluster** is a group of Carte instances or slave servers that collectively execute a job or a transformation. One of those servers is designed as the **master** and takes care of controlling the execution across the cluster. Each server executes only a portion of the whole task.

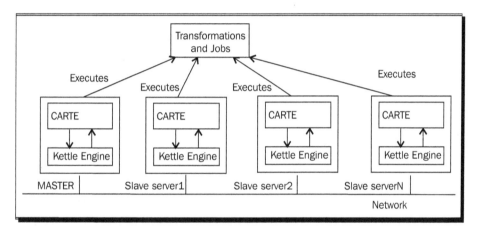

The list of servers that would make up a cluster may be known in advance, or you can have **dynamic clusters**—clusters where the slave servers are known only at run time. This feature allows you to hire resources—for example, server machines provided as a service over the Internet, and run your jobs and transformations processes over those servers in a dynamic cluster. This kind of Internet service is quite new and is known as **cloud-computing**, Amazon EC2 being one of the most popular.

If you are interested in the subject, there is an interesting paper named *Pentaho Data Integration: Scaling Out Large Data Volume Processing in the Cloud or on Premise*, presented by the Pentaho partner Bayon Technologies. You can download it from `http://www.bayontechnologies.com`.

Pop quiz – remote execution and clustering

For each of the following, decide if the sentence is true or false:

a. Carte is a graphical tool for designing jobs and transformations that are going to be run remotely.

b. In order to run a transformation remotely you have to define a cluster.

c. When you have very complex transformations or huge datasets you have to execute in a cluster because PDI doesn't support that load in a single machine.

d. To run a transformation in a cluster you have to know the list of servers in advance.

e. If you want to run jobs or transformations remotely or in a cluster you need the PDI Enterprise Edition.

Integrating PDI and the Pentaho BI suite

In this book you learned to use PDI standalone, but as mentioned in the first chapter, it is possible to use it integrated with the rest of the suite. There are a couple of options for doing so.

PDI as a process action

In Chapter 1 you were introduced to the Pentaho platform. Everything in the Pentaho platform is made by action sequences. An **action sequence** is, as its name suggests, a sequence of atomic actions that together accomplish small business processes.

Look at the following sample with regard to the Puzzle business:

Consider that you regularly receive updated price lists (one for each manufacturer) and you drop the files in a given folder. When you decide to hike the prices, you process one of those files and get a web-based report with the updated prices. You can implement that process with an action sequence.

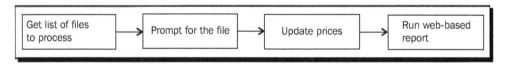

There are four atomic actions in this sequence. You already know how to do the first and third actions (building the list of available price lists and updating the prices) with PDI. You can create transformations or jobs that perform these tasks and then use them as actions in an action sequence. The following is a sample screenshot of **Design Studio**, the action sequence editor:

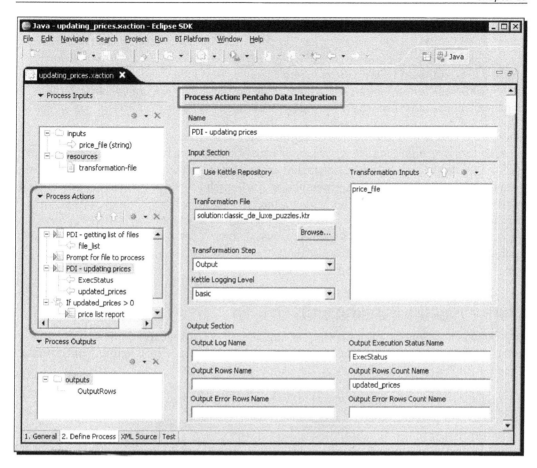

The screenshot shows how the action sequence editor looks like while editing the explained action sequence. In the tree at the left side, you can see the list of actions, while the right section allows you to configure each action. The action being edited in the screenshot is the PDI transformation that updates the prices.

PDI as a datasource

You already created several transformations that, after doing some data manipulation, generated plain files or Excel sheets. What if, instead of these types of output files, you wanted the same data displayed as a more attractive, colorful, and interactive web-based report? You can't do it with PDI alone. With the newest Pentaho report engine you can take the data that came out of a transformation and use it as the data source for your report. Having the data, the reporting tool allows you to generate any kind of output.

If you want to learn more about Pentaho reporting, you can start by visiting the wiki at `http://wiki.pentaho.com/display/Reporting/Pentaho+Reporting+Community+Documentation`. Or you can buy the book *Pentaho Reporting 3.5 for Java Developers* (ISBN: 3193), authored by Will Gorman, published by Packt Publishing. Despite its name, it is not just a book for developers; it's a great book for those who are unfamiliar with the tool and who want to learn how to create reports with it.

Data coming out of a transformation can also be used as a source data for a CDF dashboard. A **dashboard** is an application that shows you visual indicators such as charts, traffic lights, or dials. A CDF dashboard is a dashboard created with a toolkit, known as **Community Dashboard Framework**, which is developed by members of the Pentaho community. The CDF dashboards, recently incorporated as part of the Pentaho suite, accept many types of data sources, PDI transformations being one of them. The only restriction (at least for now) is that they only accept transformations stored in a repository (see Chapter 1 and Appendix A for details). For more about CDF here is a link to the wiki page: `http://wiki.pentaho.com/display/COM/Community+Dashboard+Framework`.

More about the Pentaho suite

The options mentioned earlier for using PDI integrated with other components of the suite are a good starting point to begin working with the Pentaho BI suite. By putting into practice those examples, you can gradually get familiarized with the suite.

There is much more to learn once you get started. Look at the following sample screen:

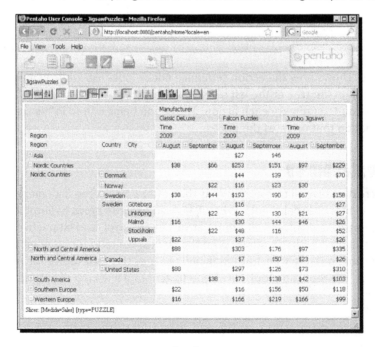

This represents a multidimensional view of your sales data mart. Here you can see cross-tab information for puzzle sales in August and September for three specific manufacturers across different regions, countries, and cities. It looks really useful for exploring your sales numbers, doesn't it? Well, this is just an example of what you can do with Pentaho beyond using PDI reporting and dashboard tools mentioned earlier.

For more about the suite, you can visit the wiki page http://wiki.pentaho.com/ or the Pentaho site (www.pentaho.com). If, instead of browsing here and there, you prefer to read it all in a single place, there is also a new book that brings you a good introduction to the whole suite. The book is titled *Pentaho Solutions* (Wiley publishing), authored by Roland Bouman and Jos van Dongen—two seasoned Pentaho community members.

PDI Enterprise Edition and Kettle Developer Support

Pentaho offers an Enterprise Edition of the Pentaho BI Suite and also for PDI. The **PDI Enterprise Edition** adds an **Enterprise Console** for performance monitoring, remote administration, and alerting. There are also a growing number of extra plugins for enterprise customers. In addition to the PDI extensions, customers get services and support, indemnification, software maintenance (fix versions, e.g. 3.2.2), and a knowledge base with additional technical resources.

Since the end of 2009, Pentaho also offers **Kettle Developer Support** for the **Community Edition**. With this, you can get direct assistance from the product experts for the design, development, and testing phases of the ETL lifecycle. This option is perfect for getting started, removing roadblocks, and troubleshooting ETL processes.

For further information, check the Pentaho site (www.pentaho.com).

Summary

This chapter provided you with a list of best practices to apply while working with PDI. If you follow the given advice, your work will not only be useful, but also flexible, reusable, documented, and neatly presented.

You were introduced to PDI plugins, a mechanism that allows you to customize the tool.

A quick review about remote execution and clustering was given for those interested in developing PDI in large environments.

Finally, an introduction was given showing you how PDI can be used not only as a standalone tool but can also be integrated with the Pentaho BI suite.

Some links and references were provided for those of you who, after reading the book and particularly this chapter, are anxious to learn more.

I hope you enjoyed reading the book and learning PDI, and will start using PDI to solve all your data requirements.

Working with Repositories

Spoon allows you to store your transformations and jobs under two different configurations—file based and repository based. In contrast to the file-based configuration that keeps the transformations and jobs in XML format such as `*.ktr` *and* `*.kjb` *files in the local file system, the repository-based configuration keeps the same information in tables in a relational database.*

While working with the file-based system is simple and practical, the repository-based system can be convenient in some situations. The following is a list of some of the distinctive repository features:

- Repositories implement security. In order to work with a repository, you need credentials. You can create users and profiles with different permissions on the repository; however, keep in mind that the kind of permissions you may apply is limited.

- Repositories are prepared for basic team development. The elements you create (transformations, jobs, database connections, and so on) are shared by all repository users as soon as you create them.

- If you want to use PDI as the input source in dashboards made with the CDF (refer to Chapter 13 for details), the only way you have is by working with repositories.

- PDI 4, in its Enterprise version, will include a lot of new repository features such as version control.

Before you decide on working with a repository, you have to be aware of the file-based system benefits that you may lose out on. Here are some examples:

◆ When working with the repository-based system, you need access to the repository database. If, for some reason, you cannot access the database (due to a network problem or any other issue), you will not be able to work. You don't have this restriction when working with files—you need only the software and the `.ktr`/`.kjb` files.

◆ When working with repositories, it is difficult to keep track of the changes. On the other hand, when you work with the file system, it's easier to know which jobs or transformations are modified. If you use **Subversion**, you even have version control.

◆ Suppose you want to search and replace some text in all jobs and transformations. If you are working with repositories, you would have to do it for each table in the repository database. When working with the file-based system, this task is quite simple—you could create an **Eclipse** project, load the root directory of your jobs and transformations, and do the task by using the Eclipse utilities.

This appendix explains how to create a repository and how to work with it. You can give repositories a try and decide for yourself which method, repository-based or file-based, suits you best.

Creating a repository

If you want to work with the repository-based configuration, you have to create a repository in advance.

Time for action – creating a PDI repository

To create a repository, follow these steps:

1. Open MySQL Command Line Client.

2. In the command window, type the following:

```
CREATE DATABASE PDI_REPO;
```

3. Open Spoon.

4. If the repository dialog appears, skip to step 6.

5. Open the repository dialog from the **Repository | Connect to repository** menu.

6. Click on **New** to create a new repository. The repository information dialog shows up. Click on **New** to create a new database connection.

7. The database connection window appears. Define a connection to the database you have just created and give a name to the connection— PDI_REPO_CONN in this case.

 If you want to refer to the steps on creating the database connection, check out *Time for action – creating a connection to the Steel Wheels database* section in Chapter 8.

8. Test the connection to see that it is properly configured.

9. Click **OK** to close the database connection window. The **Select database connection** box will show the created connection.

10. Give the name MY_REPO to the repository. As description, type **My first repository**.

11. Click on **Create or Upgrade**.

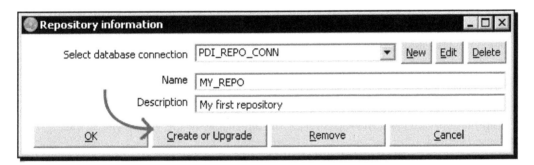

12. PDI will ask you if you are sure you want to create the repository on the specified database connection. Answer **Yes** if you are sure of the settings you entered.

13. A dialog appears asking if you want to do a dry run to evaluate the generated SQL before execution.

14. Answer **No** unless you want to preview the SQL that will create the reposProgress progress window appears showing you the progress while the repository is being created.

15. Finally, you see a window with the message **Kettle created the repository on the specified connection**. Close the dialog window.

16. Click on **OK** to close the repository information window. You will be back in the repository dialog, this time with a new repository available in the repository drop-down list.

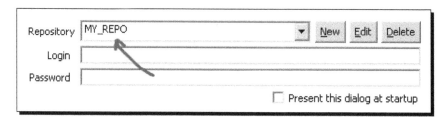

17. If you want to start working with the created repository, please refer to the *Working with the repository storage system* section. If not, click on **No Repository**. This will close the window.

What just happened?

In MySQL you created a new database named PDI_REPO. Then you used that database to create a PDI repository.

Creating repositories to store your transformations and jobs

A Kettle **repository** is a database that provides you with a storage system for your transformations and jobs. The repository is the alternative to the *.ktr and *.kjb file-based system.

In order to create a new repository, a database must have been created previously. In the tutorial, the repository was created in a MySQL RDBMS. However, you can create your repositories in any relational database.

 The PDI repository database should be used exclusively for its purpose!

Note that if the repository has already been created from another machine or by another user, that is, another profile in the operating system, you don't have to create the repository again. In that case, just define the connection to the repository but don't create it again. In other words, follow all the instructions but don't click the **Create or Upgrade** button.

Once you have created a repository, its name, description, and connection information are stored in a file named repositories.xml, which is located in the PDI home directory. The repository database is populated with a bunch of tables with familiar names such as transformation, job, steps, and steps_type.

Note that you may have more than one repository—different repositories for different projects, different repositories for different versions of a project, a repository just for testing new PDI features, and another for serious development, and so on. Therefore, it is important that you give the repositories meaningful names and descriptions so that you don't get confused if you have more than one.

Working with the repository storage system

In order to work with a repository, you must have created at least one. If you haven't, please refer to the section *Creating a repository*.

If you already have a repository and you want to work with it, the first thing you have to do is to log into it. The next tutorial helps you do this.

Time for action – logging into a repository

To log into an existent repository, follow these instructions:

1. Launch Spoon.

2. If the repository dialog window doesn't show up, select **Repository** | **Connect to repository** from the main menu. The repository dialog window appears.

3. In the drop-down list, select the repository you want to log into.

4. Type your username and password. If you have never created any users, use the default username and password—admin and admin. Click on **OK**.

5. You will now be logged into the repository. You will see the name of the repository in the upper-left corner of Spoon:

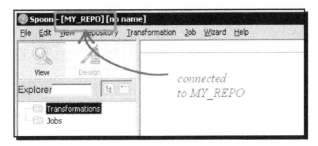

What just happened?

You opened Spoon and logged into a repository. In order to do that, you provided the name of the repository and proper credentials. Once you did it, you were ready to start working with the repository.

Logging into a repository by using credentials

If you want to work with the repository storage system, you have to log into the repository before you begin your work. In order to do that, you have to choose the repository and provide a repository username and password.

The repository dialog that allows you to log into the repository can be opened from the main Spoon menu. If you intend to log into the repository often, you'd better select **Edit | Options...** and check the general option **Show repository dialog at startup?**. This will cause the repository dialog to always show up when you launch Spoon.

It is possible to log into the repository automatically. Let's assume you have a repository named MY_REPO and you use the default user. Add the following lines to the kettle.properties file:

```
KETTLE_REPOSITORY=MY_REPO
KETTLE_USER=admin
KETTLE_PASSWORD=admin
```

The next time you launch Spoon, you will be logged into the repository automatically.

 For details about the kettle.properties file, refer to the section on Kettle variables in Chapter 2.

 Because the log information is exposed, auto login is not recommended.

Defining repository user accounts

To log into a repository, you need a user account. Every repository user has a profile that dictates the permissions that the user has on the repository. There are three predefined profiles:

Profile	Permissions
Read-only	Cannot create nor modify any element in the repository
User	Can create, modify, and delete any object in the repository excepting users and profiles
Administrator	Has full permissions, including creating new users and profiles

There are also two predefined users:

- ◆ admin: A user with Administrator profile. This is the user you used to log into the repository for the first time. It has full permissions on the repository.

- ◆ guest: A user with Read-only profile.

If you have Administrator profile, you can create, modify, rename, or delete users and profiles from the Repository explorer. For details, please refer to the section *Examining and modifying the contents of a repository with the Repository explorer*, later in this chapter. Any user may change his/her own user information both from the Repository explorer and from the **Repository | Edit current user** menu option.

Creating transformations and jobs in repository folders

In a repository, the jobs and transformations are organized in folders. A folder in a repository fulfills the same purpose as a folder in your drive—it allows you to keep your work organized. Once you create a folder, you can save both transformations and jobs in it.

While connected to a repository you design, preview, and run jobs and transformations just as you do with files. However, there are some differences when it comes to opening, creating, or saving your work. So, let's summarize how you do those tasks when logged into a repository:

Task	Procedure
Open a transformation / job	Select **File	Open**. The Repository explorer shows up. Navigate the repository until you find the transformation or job you want to open. Double-click it.
Create a folder	Select **Repository	Explore repository**, expand the transformation or job tree, locate the parent folder, right-click and create the folder. Alternatively, double-click the parent folder.
Create a transformation	Select **File	New	Transformation** or press *Ctrl+N*.
Create a Job	Select **File	New	Job** or press *Ctrl+Alt+N*.
Save a transformation	Press *Ctrl+T*. Give a name to the transformation. In the **Directory** textbox, select the folder where the transformation is going to be saved. Press *Ctrl+S*. The transformation will now be saved in the selected directory under the given name.
Save a job	Press *Ctrl+J*. Give a name to the job. In the **Directory** textbox, select the folder where the job is going to be saved. Press **Ctrl+S**. The job will be saved in the selected directory under the given name.

Creating database connections, partitions, servers, and clusters

Besides users, profiles, jobs, and transformations, there are some additional PDI elements that you can define:

Element	Description
Database connections	Connection definitions to relational databases. These are covered in Chapter 8.
Partition schemas	Partitioning is a mechanism by which you send individual rows to different copies of the same step—for example, based on a field value.
	This is an advanced topic not covered in this book.
Slave servers	Slave servers are installed in remote machines to execute jobs and transformations remotely. They are introduced in Chapter 13.
Clusters	Clusters are groups of slave servers that collectively execute a job or a transformation. They are also introduced in Chapter 13.

All these elements can also be created, modified, and deleted from the Repository explorer.

Once you create any of these elements, it is automatically shared by all repository users.

Backing up and restoring a repository

A PDI repository is a database. As such, you may regularly backup it with the utilities provided by the RDBMS. However, PDI offers you a method for creating a backup in an XML file.

You create a backup from the Repository explorer. Right-click the name of the repository and select **Export all objects to an XML file**. You will be asked for the name and location of the XML file that will contain the backup data. In order to back up a single folder, instead of right-clicking the repository name, right-click the name of the folder.

You can restore a backup made in an XML file also from the Repository explorer. Right-click the name of the repository and select **Import all objects from an XML file**. You will be asked for the name and location of the XML file that contains the backup.

Examining and modifying the contents of a repository with the Repository explorer

The **Repository explorer** shows you a tree view of the repository to which you are connected. From the main Spoon menu, select **Repository | Explore Repository** and you get to the explorer window. The following screenshot shows you a sample **Repository explorer** screen:

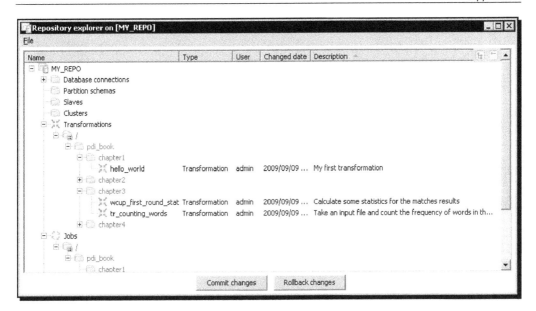

In the tree you can see: **Database connections**, **Partition schemas**, **Slave servers** (slaves in the tree), **Clusters**, **Transformations**, **Jobs**, **Users**, and **Profiles**.

You can sort the different elements by name, user, changed data, or description by just clicking on the appropriate column header: **Name**, **User**, **Changed date**, or **Description**. The sort is made within each folder.

The Repository explorer not only shows you these elements, but also allows you to create, modify, rename, and delete them. The following table summarizes the available actions:

Action	Procedure	Example
Create a new element (any but transformations and jobs)	Double-click the name of the element at the top of the list. Alternatively, right-click any element in its category and select the **New** option.	In order to create a new user, double-click the word **Users** at the top of the users list, or right-click any user and select **New User**.
Open an element for editing	Right-click it and select the **Open** option. Alternatively, double-click it.	In order to edit a job, double-click it, or right-click and select **Open job**.
Delete an element	Right-click it and select the **Delete** option.	In order to delete a user, right-click it and select **Delete user**.

When you explore the repository, you don't see jobs and transformations mixed. Consequently, the whole folder tree appears twice—once under **Transformations** and then under **Jobs**.

In order to confirm your work, click on **Commit changes**. If you make a mistake, click on **Rollback changes**.

Migrating from a file-based system to a repository-based system and vice-versa

No matter which storage system you are using, file based or repository based, you may want to move your work to the other system. The following tables summarize the procedure for doing that:

Migrating from file-based configuration to repository-based configuration:

PDI element	Procedure for migrating from file to repository
Transformations or jobs	From **File	Import from an XML file**, browse to locate the .ktr/.kjb file to import and open it. Once the file has been imported, you can save it into the repository as usual.
Database connections, partition schemas, slaves, and clusters	When importing from XML, a job or transformation that uses the database connection, the connection is imported as well. The same applies to partitions, slave servers, and clusters.

Migrating from file-based configuration to repository-based configuration:

PDI element	Procedure for migrating from repository to file
Single transformation or job	Open the job or transformation, select **File	Export to an XML file**, browse to the folder where you want to save the job or transformation, and save it. Once it has been exported, it will be available to work with under the file storage method or to import from another repository.
All transformations saved in a folder	In the Repository explorer, right-click the name of the folder and select **Export transformations**. You will be asked to select the directory where the folder along with all its subfolders and transformations will be exported to. If you right-click the name of the repository or the root folder in the transformation tree, you may export all the transformations.

PDI element	Procedure for migrating from repository to file
All jobs saved in a folder	In the Repository explorer, right-click the name of the folder and select **Export Jobs**. You will be asked to select the directory where the folder along with all its subfolders and jobs will be exported to. If you right-click the name of the repository or the root folder in the job tree, you may export all the jobs.
Database connections, partition schemas, slaves and clusters	When exporting to XML a job or transformation that uses the database connection, the connection is exported as well (it's saved as part of the KTR/KJB file). The same applies to partitions, slave servers, and clusters.

 You have to be logged into the repository in order to perform any of the explained operations.

If you share a database connection, a partition schema, a slave server, or a cluster, it will be available for using both from a file and from any repository, as the shared elements are always saved in the `shared.xml` file in the Kettle home directory.

Summary

This appendix covered the basics concepts for working with repositories. Besides the topics covered here, working with repositories is pretty much the same as working with files.

Although the tutorials in this book were explained assuming that you work with files, all of them can be implemented under a repository-based configuration with minimal changes. For example, instead of saving a transformation in `c:\pdi_labs\hello.ktr`, you could save it in a folder named `pdi_labs` with the name `hello`. Besides these tiny details, you shouldn't have any trouble in developing and testing the exercises.

B

Pan and Kitchen: Launching Transformations and Jobs from the Command Line

All the transformations and jobs you design in Spoon end up being used as part of batch processes—for example, processes that run every night in a scheduled fashion. When it comes to running them in that way, you need Pan and Kitchen.

◆ **Pan** is a command line program that lets you launch the transformations designed in Spoon, both from `.ktr` files and from a repository.

◆ The counterpart to Pan is **Kitchen** that allows you to run jobs both from `.kjb` files and from a repository.

This appendix shows you different options you have to run these commands.

Running transformations and jobs stored in files

In order to run a transformation or job stored as a `.ktr` / `.kjb` file, follow these steps:

1. Open a terminal window.
2. Go to the Kettle installation directory.
3. Run the proper command according to the following table:

Running a ...	Windows	Unix-like system
transformation	`pan.bat /file:<ktr file name>`	`pan.sh /file:<ktr file name>`
job	`kitchen.bat /file:<kjb file name>`	`kitchen.sh /file:<kjb file name>`

When specifying the .ktr/.kjb filename, you must include the full path. If the name contains spaces, surround it with double quotes.

Here are some examples:

◆ Suppose that you work with Windows and that your Kettle installation directory is c:\pdi-ce. In order to execute a transformation stored in the file c:\pdi_labs\hello.ktr, you have to type the following commands:

C:

cd \pdi-ce

pan.bat /file:"c:\pdi_labs\hello.ktr"

◆ Suppose that you work with a Unix-like system and that your Kettle installation directory is /home/yourself/pdi-ce. In order to execute a job stored in the file /home/pdi_labs/hellojob.kjb, you have to type the following commands:

cd /home/yourself/pdi-ce

kitchen.sh /file:"/home/yourself/pdi-ce/hellojob.kjb"

 If you have a repository with auto login (refer Appendix A), as part of the command, add /norep. This will avoid that PDI login to the repository.

Running transformations and jobs from a repository

In order to run a transformation or job stored in a repository follow these steps:

1. Open a terminal window.
2. Go to the Kettle installation directory.
3. Run the proper command according to the following table:

Running a ...	Windows	Unix-like system
transformation	pan.bat /rep:<value> /user:<user> /pass:<value> /trans:<value> /dir:<value>	pan.sh /rep:<value> /user:<user> /pass:<value> /trans:<value> /dir:<value>
job	kitchen.bat /rep:<value> /user:<user> /pass:<value> /job:<value> /dir:<value>	kitchen.sh /rep:<value> /user:<user> /pass:<value> /job:<value> /dir:<value>

In this preceding table:

- `rep` is the name of the repository to log into
- `user` and `pass` are the credentials to log into the repository
- `trans` and `job` are the names of the transformation or job to run
- `dir` is the name of the directory where the transformation or job is located

The parameters are shown on different lines for you to clearly identify all the options.

 When you type the command, you have to write all the parameters on the same line.

Suppose that you work on Windows, you have a repository named `MY_REPO`, and you log into the repository with user `PDI_USER` and password `1234`. To run a transformation named `Hello` located in a directory named `MY_WORK` in that repository, type the following:

```
pan.bat /rep:"MY_REPO" /user:"PDI_USER" /pass:"1234" /trans:"Hello" /
dir:"/MY_WORK/"
```

 If you defined auto-login, you don't need to provide the repository information— the rep, user, and pass command line parameters— as part of the command.

Specifying command line options

In the examples provided in this appendix, all options are specified by using the `/option:value` syntax—for example, `/trans:"Hello"`.

Instead of /, you can also use -. Between the name of the option and the value, you can also use =. This means the options `/trans:"Hello"` and `-trans="Hello"` are equivalents.

You may use any combination of /,-, :, and =.

 In Windows, the use of - and = may cause problems; it's recommended that you use the `/option:value` syntax.

If there are spaces in the values, you can use quotes (' ') or double quotes (" ") to keep the values together. If there are no spaces, the quotes are optional.

Checking the exit code

Both Pan and Kitchen return an error code based on how the execution went. To check the exit code of Pan or Kitchen under Windows, type the following command:

```
echo %ERRORLEVEL%
```

To check the exit code of Pan or Kitchen under Unix-like systems, type the following command:

```
echo $?
```

If you get a zero, it means that there are no errors, whereas a value greater than zero implies failure. To understand the meaning of the error, please refer to the Pan / Kitchen documentation; URL references are provided at the end of the appendix.

Providing options when running Pan and Kitchen

When you execute a transformation or a job with Spoon, you have the option to provide additional information such as named parameters. The following Spoon dialog window shows you an example of that:

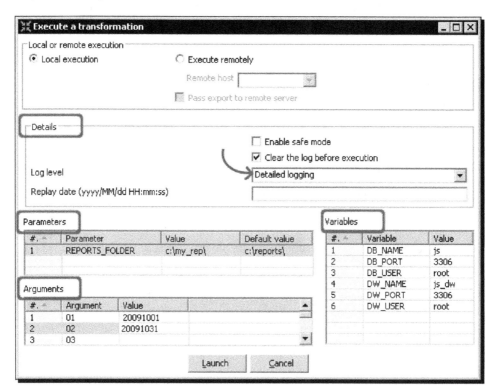

When you execute the transformation or job with Pan or Kitchen respectively, you provide this same information as options in the command line. This is how you do it compared side-by-side with Spoon:

Log details

Spoon	Pan/Kitchen option	Example

You specify the log level in the drop-down list inside the **Details** box.
 	
When the transformation or job runs, the log is shown in the **Execution Results** window.
	`/level:<logging level>`
	
	where the logging level can be one of the following:
	
	`Error, Nothing, Minimal, Basic, Detailed, Debug,` or `Rowlevel.`
		`/level:Detailed`
		
		The log appears in the terminal window, but you can use the command language of your operating system to redirect it to a file.

Named parameters

Spoon	Pan/Kitchen option	Example

You specify the named parameters in the **Parameters** box. The window shows you the name of the defined named parameters for you to fill the values or keep the default values.	`/param:`
	
	`<parameter name>=`
	
	`<parameter value>`
		`/param:`
		
		`"REPORTS_FOLDER=`
		
		`c:\my_rep\"`

Arguments

Spoon	PAN/Kitchen option	Example
You specify the command line arguments in the **Arguments** grid. Each line corresponds to a different argument.	You type them in order as part of the command.	`20091001 20091031`

Variables

Spoon	Pan/Kitchen
The grid named **Variables** shows the variables used in the transformation/job as well as their current values. At the time of the execution, you can type different values.	You cannot set variables either in the Pan or in the Kitchen command. The variables have to exist. You may define them in the `kettle.properties` file. To get the details of this file, refer to the *Kettle Variables* section in Chapter 2.

Suppose that the sample transformation shown in the screenshot is located at `c:\pdi_labs\sales_report.ktr`. Then the following Pan command

```
pan.bat /file:"c:\pdi_labs\sales_report.ktr" 20091001 20091031 /level:De-
tailed > c:\pdi_labs\logs\sales_report.log
```

executes the transformation with the same options shown in the screenshot. The command redirects the log to the file `c:\pdi_labs\logs\sales_report.log`.

Besides these, both Pan and Kitchen have additional options. For a full list and more examples, visit the Pan and Kitchen documentation at `http://wiki.pentaho.com/display/EAI/Pan+User+Documentation` and `http://wiki.pentaho.com/display/EAI/Kitchen+User+Documentation`.

C
Quick Reference: Steps and Job Entries

This appendix summarizes the purpose of the steps and job entries used in the tutorials throughout the book. For each of them, you can see the name of the *Time for action* section where it was introduced and also a reference to the chapters where you can find more examples that use it.

How to use this reference

Suppose you are inside Spoon, editing a Transformation. If the transformation uses a step that you don't know and you want to understand what it does or how to use it, double-click the step and take note of the title of the settings window; that title is the name of the step. Then search for that name in the transformation steps reference table. The steps are listed in alphabetical order so that you can find them quickly. The last column will take you to the place in the book where the step is explained.

The same applies to jobs. If you see in a job an unknown entry, double-click the entry and take note of the title of the settings window; that title is the name of the entry. Then search for that name in the job entries reference table. The job entries are also listed in alphabetical order.

Transformation steps

The following table includes all the transformation steps used in the book. For a full list of steps and their descriptions, select **Help | Show step plug-in information** in Spoon's main menu.

You can also visit `http://wiki.pentaho.com/display/EAI/Pentaho+Data+Integration+v3.2.+Steps` for a full step reference along with some examples.

Icon	Name	Purpose	Time for action
	Abort	Aborts a transformation	Aborting when there are too many errors (Chapter 7); also in Chapters 11 and 12
	Add constants	Adds one or more constant fields to the stream	Gathering progress and merging all together (Chapter 4); also in Chapters 7, 8, and 9
	Add sequence	Gets the next value from a sequence	Assigning tasks by Distributing (Chapter 4); also in Chapters 6 and 11
	Append streams	Appends two streams in an ordered way	Giving priority to Bouchard by using Append Stream (Chapter 4)
	Calculator	Creates new fields by performing simple calculations	Reviewing examination by using the Calculator step (Chapter 3); also in Chapters 6 and 8
	Combination lookup/update	Updates a junk dimension. Alternatively, it can be used to update Type I SCD.	Loading a region dimension with a Combination lookup/update step (Chapter 9); also in Chapter 12
	Copy rows to result	Write rows to the executing job. The information will then be passed to the next entry in the job.	Splitting the generation of top scores by copying and getting rows (Chapter 11)
	Data Validator	Validates fields based on a set of rules	Checking films file with the Data Validator (Chapter 7)
	Database join	Executes a database query using stream values as parameters	Using a Database join step to create a list of suggested products to buy (Chapter 9)
	Database lookup	Looks up values in a database table	Using a Database lookup step to create a list of products to buy (Chapter 9), also in Chapter 12

Icon	Name	Purpose	Time for action
	Delay row	For each incoming row, waits a given time before giving the row to the next step	Generating custom files by executing a transformation for every input row (Chapter 11)
	Delete	Delete data in a database table	Deleting data about discontinued items (Chapter 8)
	Dimension lookup/update	Updates or looks up a Type II SCD. Alternatively, it can be used to update Type I SCD or hybrid dimensions.	Keeping a history of product changes with the Dimension lookup/update step (Chapter 9), also in Chapter 12
	Dummy (do nothing)	This step type doesn't do anything! However it is used often.	Creating a hello world transformation (Chapter 1), also in Chapters 2, 3, 7, and 9
	Excel Input	Reads data from a Microsoft Excel (.xls) file	Browsing PDI new features by copying a dataset (Chapter 4); also in Chapter 8
	Excel Output	Writes data to a Microsoft Excel (.xls) file	Getting data from an XML file with information about countries (Chapter 2); also in Chapters 4 and10
	Filter rows	Splits the stream in two upon a given condition. Alternatively, it is used to let pass just the rows that meet the condition.	Counting frequent words by filtering (Chapter 3); also in Chapters 4, 6, 7, 9, 11, and 12
	Fixed file input	Reads data from a fixed width file	Calculating Scores with JavaScript (Chapter 5)
	Formula	Creates new fields by using formulas. It uses Pentaho's libformula.	Reviewing examination by using the Formula step (Chapter 3); also in Chapters 10 and 11
	Generate Rows	Generates a number of equal rows	Creating a hello world transformation (Chapter 1); also in Chapters 6, 9, and 10
	Get data from XML	Gets data from XML files	Getting data from an XML file with information about countries(Chapter 2); also in chapters 3 and 9

Icon	Name	Purpose	Time for action
	Get rows from result	Reads rows from a previous entry in a job	Splitting the generation of top scores by copying and getting rows (Chapter 11)
	Get System Info	Gets information from the system like system date, arguments, etc.	Updating a file with news about examination (Chapter 2) also in Chapters 7, 8, 10, 11, and12
	Get Variables	Takes the values of environment or Kettle variables and adds them as fields in the stream	Creating the time dimension dataset(Chapter 6)
	Group by	Builds aggregates in a group by fashion. This works only on a sorted input. If the input is not sorted, only double consecutive rows are handled correctly	Calculating World Cup statistics by grouping data (Chapter 3); also in Chapters 4, 7, and 9
	If field value is null	If a field is null, it changes its value to a constant. It can be applied to all fields of a same data type, or to particular fields	Enhancing a films file by converting rows to columns (Chapter 6)
	Insert / Update	Updates or inserts rows in a database table	Inserting new products or updating existent ones (Chapter 8)
	Mapping (sub-transformation)	Runs a subtransformation	Calculating the top scores with a subtransformation (Chapter 11)
	Mapping input specification	Specifies the input interface of a sub-transformation	Calculating the top scores with a subtransformation (Chapter 11)
	Mapping output specification	Specifies the output interface of a sub-transformation	Calculating the top scores with a subtransformation (Chapter 11)
	Modified Java Script Value	Allows you to code Javascript to modify or create new fields. It's also possible to code Java	Calculating Scores with JavaScript(Chapter 5); also in Chapters 6, 7, and 11
	Number range	Creates ranges based on a numeric field	Capturing errors while calculating the age of a film (Chapter 7); also in Chapter 8

Icon	Name	Purpose	Time for action
	Regex Evaluation	Evaluates a field with a regular expression	Validating Genres with a Regex Evaluation step (Chapter 7); also in Chapter 12
	Row denormaliser	Denormalises rows by looking up key-value pairs	Enhancing a films file by converting rows to columns (Chapter 6)
	Row Normaliser	Normalises data de-normalised	Enhancing the matches file by normalizing the dataset (Chapter 6)
	Select values	Selects, reorders, or removes fields. Also allows you to change the metadata of fields	Reading all your files at a time using a single Text file input step (Chapter 2); also in Chapters 3, 4, 6, 7, 8, 9, 11, and 12
	Set Variables	Sets Kettle variables based on a single input row	Updating a file with news about examinations by setting a variable with the name of the file (Chapter 11); also in Chapter 12
	Sort rows	Sorts rows based upon field values, ascending or descending	Reviewing examinations by using the Calculator step (Chapter 3); also in Chapters 4, 6, 7, 8, 9, and 11
	Split field to rows	Splits a single string field and creates a new row for each split term	Counting frequent words by filtering (Chapter 3)
	Split Fields	Splits a single field into more than one	Calculating World Cup statistics by grouping data (Chapter 3); also in Chapters 6 and 11
	Stream lookup	Looks up values coming from another stream in the transformation	Finding out which language people speak (Chapter 3); also in Chapter 6
	Switch / Case	Switches a row to a certain target step based on the value of a field	Assigning tasks by filtering priorities with the Switch/ Case step (Chapter 4)
	Table input	Reads data from a database table	Getting data about shipped orders (Chapter 8); also in Chapters 9, 10, and 12
	Table output	Writes data to a database table	Loading a table with a list of manufacturers (Chapter 8), also in Chapters 9 and 12

Icon	Name	Purpose	Time for action
	Text file input	Reads data from a text file	Reading all your files at a time using a single Text file input step (Chapter 2); also in Chapters 3, 5, 6, 7, 8, and 11
	Text file output	Writes data to a text file	Sending the results of matches to a plain file (Chapter 2); also in Chapters 3, 7, 9, 10, and 11
	Update	Updates data in a database table	Loading a region dimension with a Combination lookup/ update step (Chapter 9)
	Value Mapper	Maps values of a certain field from one value to another	Browsing PDI new features by copying a dataset (Chapter 4)

Job entries

The following table includes all the job entries used in the book. For a full list of job entries and their descriptions, select **Help | Show job entries plug-in information** in Spoon's main menu.

You can also visit `http://wiki.pentaho.com/display/EAI/Pentaho+Data+Integra tion+v3.2.+Job+Entries` for more information.

There you'll find a full job entries reference and some examples as well.

Icon	Name	Purpose	Time for action
	Abort job	Aborts the job	Updating a file with news about examinations by setting a variable with the name of the file (Chapter 11)
	Create a folder	Creates a folder	Creating a simple Hello world job (Chapter 10)
	Delete file	Deletes a file	Generating custom files by executing a transformation for every input row (Chapter 11)
	Evaluate rows number in a table	Evaluates the content of a table	Loading the dimensions for the sales datamart (Chapter 12)

Icon	Name	Purpose	Time for action
	File Exists	Checks if a file exists	Updating a file with news about examinations by setting a variable with the name of the file (Chapter 11)
	Job	Executes a job	Generating the files with top scores by nesting jobs (Chapter 11); also in Chapter 12
	Mail	Sends an e-mail	Sending a sales report and warning the administrator if something were wrong (Chapter 10)
	Special entries	Start job entry; mandatory at the beginning of a job	Creating a simple Hello world job (Chapter 10); also in Chapters 11 and 12
	Success	Forces the success of a job execution	Updating a file with news about examinations by setting a variable with the name of the file (Chapter 11); also in Chapter 12
	Transformation	Executes a transformation	Creating a simple Hello world job (Chapter 10); also in Chapters 11 and 12

> Note that this appendix is just a quick reference. It's not meant at all for learning to use PDI. In order to learn from scratch, you should read the book starting from the first chapter.

D
Spoon Shortcuts

The following tables summarize the main Spoon shortcuts. Have this appendix handy; it will save a lot of time while working with Spoon.

 If you are a Mac user, please be aware that a mixture of Windows and Mac keys is used. Thus, the shortcut keys are not always what you expect. For example, in some cases you copy with *Ctrl+C*, while in others you do it with *Command+C*.

General shortcuts

The following table lists general Spoon shortcuts:

Action	Shortcut
New job	*Ctrl+Alt+N*
New transformation	*Ctrl+N*
Open a job/transformation	*Ctrl+O*
Save a job/transformation	*Ctrl+S*
Close a job/transformation	*Ctrl+F4*
Run a job/transformation	*F9*
Preview a transformation	*F10*
Debug a transformation	*Shift+F10*
Verify a transformation	*F11*
Job settings	*Ctrl+J*
Transformation settings	*Ctrl+T*
Search metadata	*Ctrl+F*
Set environment variables	*Ctrl+Alt+J*
Show environment variables	*Ctrl+L*
Show arguments	*Ctrl+Alt+U*

Designing transformations and jobs

The following are the shortcuts that help the design of transformations and jobs:

Action	Shortcut
New step/job entry	Drag the step/job entry icon to the work area and drop it there
Edit step/job entry	Double-click
Edit step description	Double-click *the middle mouse button*
New hop	Click a step and drag toward the second step while *holding down the middle mouse button* or while pressing *Shift* and *holding down the left mouse button*
Edit a hop	Double-click in transformations, *right-click* in jobs
Split a hop	Drag a step over the hop until it gets wider
Select some steps/job entries	*Ctrl+click*
Select all steps	*Ctrl+A*
Clear selection	*Esc*
Copy selected steps/job entries to clipboard	*Ctrl+C*
Paste from clipboard to work area	*Ctrl+V*
Delete selected steps/job entries	*Del*
Align selected steps/job entries to top	*Ctrl+Up*
Align selected steps/job entries to bottom	*Ctrl+Down*
Align selected steps/job entries to left	*Ctrl+Left*
Align selected steps/job entries to right	*Ctrl+Right*
Distribute selected steps/job entries horizontally	*Alt+Right*
Distribute selected steps/job entries vertically	*Alt+Up*
Zoom in	*Page up*
Zoom out	*Page down*
Zoom 100%	*Home*
Snap to grid	*Alt+Home*
Undo	*Ctrl+Z*
Redo	*Ctrl+Y*
Show output stream (only available in transformations)	Position the mouse cursor over the step; then press Space bar

Grids

Action	Shortcut
Move a row up	*Ctrl+Up*
Move a row down	*Ctrl+Down*
Resize all columns to see the full values (header included)	*F3*
Resize all columns to see the full values (header excluded)	*F4*
Select all rows	*Ctrl+A*
Clear selection	*Esc*
Copy selected lines to clipboard	*Ctrl+C*
Paste from clipboard to grid	*Ctrl+V*
Cut selected lines	*Ctrl+X*
Delete selected lines	*Del*
Keep only selected lines	*Ctrl+K*
Undo	*Ctrl+Z*
Redo	*Ctrl+Y*

Repositories

Action	Shortcut
Connect to repository	*Ctrl+R*
Disconnect repository	*Ctr+D*
Explore repository	*Ctrl+E*
Edit current user	*Ctrl+U*

Introducing PDI 4 Features

While writing this book, version 4.0 of PDI was still under development. Kettle 4.0 was mainly created to provide a new **API** for the future—the API that is cleaned up, flexible, more pluggable, and so on. Beside those architectural changes, Kettle 4.0 also includes some new functional features. This appendix will quickly introduce you to those features.

Agile BI

Pentaho Agile Business Intelligence (**Agile BI**) is a new, iterative design approach to BI development. Agile BI provides an integrated solution that enables you, as an ETL designer, to work iteratively, modeling the data, visualizing it, and finally providing the data to users for self-service reporting and analysis. Agile BI is delivered as a plugin to Pentaho Data Integration. You can learn more about Agile BI at `http://wiki.pentaho.com/display/AGILEBI/Documentation`.

Visual improvements for designing transformations and jobs

The new version of the product includes mainly Enterprise or advanced features. There are, however, a couple of novelties in the Community Edition that will catch your attention as soon as you start using the new version of the software. In this section you will learn about those novelties.

Experiencing the mouse-over assistance

The **mouse-over assistance** is the first new feature you will notice. It assists you while editing jobs and transformations. Let's see it working.

Time for action – creating a hop with the mouse-over assistance

You already know several ways to create a hop between two job entries or two steps. Now you will learn a new way:

1. Create a job and drag two job entries to the canvas. Name the entries A and B.

2. Position the mouse cursor over the entry named A and wait until a tiny toolbar shows up below the entry icon as shown:

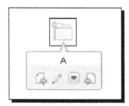

3. Click on the output connector (the last icon in the toolbar), and drag toward the entry named B. A grayed hop is displayed.

4. When the mouse cursor is over the B entry, release the mouse button. A hop is created from the A entry to the B entry.

What just happened?

You created a hop between two job entries by using the mouse-over assistance—a feature incorporated in PDI 4.

Using the mouse-over assistance toolbar

When you position the mouse cursor over a step in a transformation or a job entry in a job, a tiny toolbar shows up to assist you. The following diagram depicts its options:

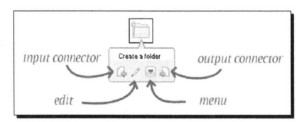

The following table explains each button in this toolbar:

Button	Description
Edit	Equivalent to double-clicking the job entry/step to edit it.
Menu	Equivalent to right-clicking the job entry/step to bring up the contextual menu.
Input connector	Assistant for creating hops leaving from this job entry/step. If the job entry/step doesn't accept any input (that is, **START** entry job or **Generate Rows** step), the input connector is disabled.
Output connector	Assistant for creating hops directed toward this job entry/step. It's used as shown in the tutorial, but the direction of the created hop is the opposite.

In the tutorial, you created a simple hop between two job entries. You can create hops between steps in the same way. In this case, depending on the kind of source step, you might be prompted for the kind of hop to create. For example, when leaving a **Filter rows** step, you will be asked if the destination step is where you'll send the "true" data, or where you will send the "false" data, or if this is the main output of the step.

Experiencing the sniff-testing feature

The **sniff-testing** feature allows you to see the rows that are coming into or out of a step in real time. While a transformation is running, right-click a step, select **Sniff test during execution | Sniff test output rows**. A window appears showing you the output data as it is being processed. In the same way, you can select **Sniff test during execution | Sniff test input rows** to see the incoming rows.

 Note that the sniff-testing feature slows down the transformation and its use is recommended just for debugging purposes.

Experiencing the job drill-down feature

In Chapters 10 and 11, you learned how to nest jobs and transformations. You even learned how to create subtransformations. Whichever the case, when you ran the main job or transformation, there was a single log tab showing the log for the main and all nested jobs and transformations.

In PDI 4.0, when a job entry is running, you can drill-down into that. **Drilling down** means opening that entry and seeing what's going on inside that job or transformation. In a separate window, you'll see both the step metrics and the log. If there are more nested transformations or jobs, you can continue drilling down. You can go even further into a running subtransformation. In any of these jobs or transformations, you may sniff test as well, as described above.

Drilling down is useful, for example, to understand why your jobs or transformations don't behave as expected or to find out where a performance problem is.

You can see the job drill-down and sniff-testing in action in two videos made by Matt Casters, Kettle chief leader and author of these features at: `http://www.ibridge.be/?p=179`.

Experiencing even more visual changes

Besides the features that we have just seen, there are some other UI improvements worth mentioning:

- **Enhanced notes editor**: Now you can apply different fonts and colors to the notes you create in Spoon.
- **Color-coded logs**: Now it is easier to read a log, as different colors allow you to quickly identify different kinds of log messages.
- **Revamped Repository explorer**: The Repository explorer has been completely redesigned, making this a major UI improvement in Kettle 4.0.

Enterprise features

As said, most of the functional features included in Kettle 4.0 apply only to the Enterprise version of the product. Among those features, the following are the most remarkable:

- Job and transformation versioning and locking
- Robust security and administration capabilities
- Ability to schedule jobs and transformations from Spoon
- Enhanced logging architecture for real-time monitoring and debugging of transformations

Summary

This appendix introduced you to the main features included in Kettle 4.0. All the explanations and exercises in this book have been developed, explained, and tested in the latest stable version 3.2. However, as the new version of the product includes mainly Enterprise or advanced features, working with Kettle 4.0 Community Edition is not so different from working with Kettle 3.2. You can try all the examples and exercises in the book in Kettle 4.0 if you want to. You shouldn't have any difficulties.

F
Pop Quiz Answers

Chapter 1

PDI data sources

1	5

PDI prerequisites

1	1 and 3

PDI basics

1	False (Spoon is the only graphical tool)
2	True
3	False (Spoon doesn't generate code, but interprets Transformation and Jobs)
4	False (The grid size is intended to line up steps in the screen)
5	False (As an example the transformation in this chapter created the rows of data from scratch; it didn't use external data)

Chapter 2

formatting data

1	(a) and (b). The field is already a Number, so you may define the output field as a Number, taking care of the format you apply. If you define the output field as a String and you don't set a format, Kettle will send the field to the output as 1.0, 2.0, 3.0, etc., which clearly is not the same as your code. Just to confirm this, create a single file and a transformation to see the results for yourself.

Chapter 3

concatenating strings

1	(a) and (c). The calculator allows you to use the + operator both for adding numbers and for concatenating text. The Formula step makes a difference: To add numbers you use +; to concatenate text you have to use & instead.

Chapter 4

data movement (copying and distributing)

1	(b). In the second transformation the rows are copied, so all the unassigned rows reach the dummy step. In the first transformation the rows are distributed, so to the filter step arrives half of the rows. When you do the preview, you see only the unassigned tasks for this half; you don't see the unassigned tasks that went to the other stream.

splitting a stream

1	(c). Both (a) and (b) solve the situation.

Chapter 5

finding the seven errors

1	1. The type of log `a` doesn't exist. Look at the sample provided for the function to see the valid options.
	2. The variable `uSkill` is not defined. Its definition is required if you want to add it to the list of new fields.
	3. `setValue()` cause an error without compatibility mode. To change the value of the `Country` field, a new variable should be used instead.
	4. A variable named `average` is calculated but `wAverage` is used as the new field.
	5. It is not `trans_status`; it is `trans_Status`.
	6. No data type was specified for the `totalScore` field.
	7. The sentence `writeToLog('Ready to calculate averages...')` will be written for every row. To write it at the beginning, you have to put it in a `Start script`, not in the main.

Chapter 6

using Kettle variables inside transformations

1	(a). You don't need a **Get Variables** step in this case. As name of the file you simply type `hello_${user.name}` or `hello_%%user.name%%`.
	In (b) and (c) you need to add the variables `${user.name}` and `${user.language}` respectively as fields of your dataset. You do it with a **Get Variables** step.

Chapter 7

PDI error handling

1	(c). With PDI you cannot avoid unexpected errors; you can capture them avoiding the crash of the transformation. After that, discarding or treating the bad rows is up to you.

Chapter 8

defining database connections

1	(c)

database datatypes versus PDI datatypes

1	(b)

Insert/Update step versus Table Output/Update steps

1	(a) If an incoming row belongs to a product that doesn't exist in the products table, both the **Insert/Update** step and the **Table output** step will insert the record.
	If an incoming row belongs to a product that already exist in the products table, the **Insert/Update** step updates it. In this alternative version, the **Table output** will fail (there cannot be two products with the same value for the primary key) but the failing row goes to the Update step that updates the record.
	If an incoming row contains invalid data (for example, a price with a non numeric value), neither of the **Insert/Update** step, the **Table output** step, and the **Update** step would insert or update the table with this product.

filtering the first 10 rows

1	(c). To limit the number of rows in MySQL you use the clause LIMIT. (a) and (b) are dialects: (a) is valid in HSQLDB. (b) is valid in Oracle. If you put any of this options in a Table Input for querying the js database, the transformation would fail

Chapter 9

loading slowly changing dimensions

1	(a). The decision for the kind of dimension is not related to data you have. You just have to know your business, so the last option is out. You don't need to keep history for the name of the film. If the name changes it is because it was misspelled, or because you want to change the name to upper case, or something like that. It doesn't have sense to keep the old value. So you create a Type I SCD.
2	(c). You can use any of these steps for loading a Type I SCD. In the tutorial for loading a type I SCD you used a Combination L/U, but you could have used the other too, as explained above.

loading type III slowly changing dimensions

1	(b). With a Database lookup to get the current value stored in the dimension. If there is no data in the dimension table, the lookup fails and returns null; that is not a problem. After that, you compare the found data with the new one and set the proper values for the dimension columns. Then you load the dimension either with a Combination L/U or with a Dimension lookup, just as you do for a regular Type I SCD.

Chapter 10

defining PDI jobs

1	(b)
2	All the given options are True. Simply explore the Job entries tree and you'll find the answers.

Chapter 11

using the Add sequence step

1	(e) None of the proposed solution gives you the same results you obtained in the tutorial. The Add sequence step gives you the next value in a sequence which can be a database sequence or transformation counter. In the tutorial you used a transformation counter. In the options (b) and (c), instead of four sequences from 1 to 10, a single sequence from 1 to 40 would have been generated. No matter which method you use for generating the sequence, if you use the same name of sequence in more than one Add sequence step, the sequence is the same and is shared by all those steps. Therefore, the option (a) also would have generated a single sequence from 1 to 40 shared by the four streams.
	Besides these details about the generation of sequences, the (b) option introduces an extra inconvenience. By distributing rows, you cannot be sure that the rows will go to the proper stream. PDI would have distributed them in its own fashion.

deciding the scope of variables

1	All the options are valid. In the tutorial you had just a transformation and its parent job, that is also the root job. So (a) is valid. The grand-parent job scope includes the parent job so option (b) is valid too. Option (c) includes all the other options, so it is a valid option too.

Chapter 12

modifying a star model and loading the star with PDI

1	a	iii	As mentioned in Chapter 9, despite being designed for building Type II SCDs, the Dimension L/U step can be used for building Type I SCDs as well. So, you have two options: Reuse the table (modifying the transformation that loads it) and get the surrogate key with a Dimension L/U step, or use another table without all fields specific to Type II dimensions and, for getting the surrogate key, use a DB Lookup step.
	b	i	
	c	iii	
			In any case, you may reuse the `id_region` field, as it is a integer and serves in any situation.
2	a	ii	The dimension table has to have one record by month. Therefore a different table is needed. For the key you could use a string with the format `yyyymm`. If you don't want to change the fact table, you may reuse the `dt` field leaving blank the last two characters, but it would be more appropriate to have a string field with just 6 positions. For getting the surrogate key you use a **Select values** step changing the metadata but this time you put as format the new mask `yyyymm`.
	b	ii	
	c	i	
3	a	ii	The `product_type` field is a string; it's not the proper field for referencing a surrogate key from a fact table, so you have to define a new field for that purpose. For getting the right key you use a **Database lookup** step.
	b	iii	

Chapter 13

remote execution and clustering

| 1 | None of the sentences are true. |

Index

Thank you for buying
Pentaho 3.2 Data Integration: Beginner's Guide

Packt Open Source Project Royalties

When we sell a book written on an Open Source project, we pay a royalty directly to that project. Therefore by purchasing Pentaho 3.2 Data Integration: Beginner's Guide, Packt will have given some of the money received to the Pentaho Data Integration project.

In the long term, we see ourselves and you—customers and readers of our books—as part of the Open Source ecosystem, providing sustainable revenue for the projects we publish on. Our aim at Packt is to establish publishing royalties as an essential part of the service and support a business model that sustains Open Source.

If you're working with an Open Source project that you would like us to publish on, and subsequently pay royalties to, please get in touch with us.

Writing for Packt

We welcome all inquiries from people who are interested in authoring. Book proposals should be sent to author@packtpub.com. If your book idea is still at an early stage and you would like to discuss it first before writing a formal book proposal, contact us; one of our commissioning editors will get in touch with you.

We're not just looking for published authors; if you have strong technical skills but no writing experience, our experienced editors can help you develop a writing career, or simply get some additional reward for your expertise.

About Packt Publishing

Packt, pronounced 'packed', published its first book "Mastering phpMyAdmin for Effective MySQL Management" in April 2004 and subsequently continued to specialize in publishing highly focused books on specific technologies and solutions.

Our books and publications share the experiences of your fellow IT professionals in adapting and customizing today's systems, applications, and frameworks. Our solution-based books give you the knowledge and power to customize the software and technologies you're using to get the job done. Packt books are more specific and less general than the IT books you have seen in the past. Our unique business model allows us to bring you more focused information, giving you more of what you need to know, and less of what you don't.

Packt is a modern, yet unique publishing company, which focuses on producing quality, cutting-edge books for communities of developers, administrators, and newbies alike. For more information, please visit our website: www.PacktPub.com.

PUBLISHING

Pentaho Reporting 3.5
for Java Developers

Create advanced reports, including cross tabs, sub-reports, and
charts that connect to practically any data source using open
source Pentaho Reporting

Foreword by Thomas Morgner, Chief Architect, Pentaho Reporting

Will Gorman

PACKT

Pentaho Reporting 3.5 for Java Developers

ISBN: 978-1-847193-19-3 Paperback: 384 pages

Create advanced reports, including cross tabs, sub-reports, and charts that connect to practically any data source using open source Pentaho Reporting

1. # Create great-looking enterprise reports in PDF, Excel, and HTML with Pentaho's Open Source Reporting Suite, and integrate report generation into your existing Java application with minimal hassle

2. Use data source options to develop advanced graphs, graphics, cross tabs, and sub-reports

3. Dive deeply into the Pentaho Reporting Engine's XML and Java APIs to create dynamic reports

Practical Data Analysis and Reporting with
BIRT

Use the open-source Eclipse-based Business Intelligence and
Reporting Tools system to design and create reports as quickly
as possible

John Ward

PACKT

Practical Data Analysis and Reporting with BIRT

ISBN: 978-1-847191-09-0 Paperback: 312 pages

Use the open-source Eclipse-based Business Intelligence and Reporting Tools system to design and create reports quickly

1. Get started with BIRT Report Designer

2. Develop the skills to get the most from it

3. Transform raw data into visual and interactive content

4. Design, manage, format, and deploy high-quality reports

Please check **www.PacktPub.com** for information on our titles

Oracle Warehouse Builder 11g: Getting Started

ISBN: 978-1-847195-74-6   Paperback: 368 pages

Extract, Transform, and Load data to build a dynamic, operational data warehouse

1. Build a working data warehouse from scratch with Oracle Warehouse Builder

2. Cover techniques in Extracting, Transforming, and Loading data into your data warehouse

3. Learn about the design of a data warehouse by using a multi-dimensional design with an underlying relational star schema.

Creating your MySQL Database: Practical Design Tips and Techniques

ISBN: 978-1-904811-30-5   Paperback: 108 pages

A short guide for everyone on how to structure your data and set-up your MySQL database tables efficiently and easily

1. How best to collect, name, group, and structure your data

2. Design your data with future growth in mind

3. Practical examples from initial ideas to final designs

4. The quickest way to learn how to design good data structures for MySQL

Please check **www.PacktPub.com** for information on our titles

www.ingramcontent.com/pod-product-compliance
Lightning Source LLC
Chambersburg PA
CBHW081455050326
40690CB00015B/2803